Teaching and Learning at a Distance

Foundations of Distance Education

FIFTH EDITION

Michael Simonson
Nova Southeastern University

Sharon Smaldino
Northern Illinois University

Michael Albright

Susan Zvacek
University of Kansas

PEARSON

Boston   Columbus   Indianapolis   New York   San Francisco   Upper Saddle River
Amsterdam   Cape Town   Dubai   London   Madrid   Milan   Munich   Paris   Montreal   Toronto
Delhi   Mexico City   Sao Paulo   Sydney   Hong Kong   Seoul   Singapore   Taipei   Tokyo

Senior Editor: Kelly Villella Canton
Editorial Assistant: Annalea Manalili
Senior Marketing Manager: Darcy Betts
Production Editor: Renata Butera
Editorial Production Service: George Jacob
Electronic Composition: Integra Software Services, Pvt. Ltd.
Photo Research: Annie Pickert
Cover Designer: Bruce Kenselaar
Creative Art Director: Jayne Conte
Cover Image: Shutterstock

Credits and acknowledgments borrowed from other sources and reproduced, with permission, in this textbook appear on appropriate page within text.

Library of Congress Cataloging-in-Publication Data
Teaching and learning at a distance : foundations of distance education/Michael
    Simonson . . . [et al.].—5th ed.
    p. cm.
ISBN-13: 978-0-13-248731-3 (alk. paper)
ISBN-10: 0-13-248731-4 (alk. paper)
1. Distance education.   I. Simonson, Michael R.
LC5800.T43 2012
371.35--dc22

                                                                2010041781

Chapter Opener Photo Credits: Property of AT&T Archives and History Center, p2, VTEL Products Corporation pp. 32, 63, 193, 218, 242, 294; Polycom, pp. 89, 150, 262, 317, 347

10 9 8 7 6 5 4 3 2 1 15 14 13 12 11

www.pearsonhighered.com

ISBN-10:   0-13-248731-4
ISBN-13: 978-0-13-248731-3

ABOUT THE AUTHORS

Michael Simonson is a program professor at Nova Southeastern University in the Instructional Technology and Distance Education program. He earned his Ph.D. from the University of Iowa in Instructional Systems. He works with schools, organizations, and corporations to assist them to integrate instructional technology and distance education into teaching and training, and on the development of virtual schools. Simonson has authored four major textbooks dealing with distance education, instructional technology, instructional computing, and instructional media. Mike has over 150 scholarly publications, and in excess of 200 professional presentations dealing with distance education and instructional technology. Simonson has considerable experience working with domestic and international businesses and industries, especially on projects related to instructional technology, virtual schools, and distance education. Technology planning, distance education/virtual school policy development and effective design of online instruction are current projects. He is editor of the *Quarterly Review of Distance Education*, *Distance Learning Journal*, and *Proceedings of Selected Research and Development Papers* presented at the Annual Conventions of the Association for Educational Communications and Technology. He has won the award for most outstanding research in the field of distance education presented by the United States Distance Learning Association. Most recently he has been an external evaluator South Dakota's *Connecting the Schools* and *Digital Dakota Network* projects, and is a consultant for the U.S. Army Research Institute. Simonson was honorably discharged as a Captain from the United States Marine Corps (R).

Sharon E. Smaldino holds the L. D. and Ruth Morgridge Endowed Chair for Teacher Education in the College of Education at Northern Illinois University (NIU). She was a professor of Educational Technology at the University of Northern Iowa for many years prior to moving to NIU. Sharon received her Ph.D. from Southern Illinois University, Carbondale. Prior to that she received an M.A. in Elementary Education and served for more than a dozen years as teacher, speech therapist, and special educator in school districts from Florida to Minnesota. Dr. Smaldino teaches graduate courses in Instructional Development, Distance Education, and Professional Standards and Ethical Practice. She has received several awards for her outstanding teaching. In her current role, she is focused on working with faculty and P–12 teachers to integrate technology into the learning process. Presenting at state, national, and international conferences, Sharon has become an important voice on applications of technology in the classroom and in distance education. In addition to her teaching and consulting, Dr. Smaldino has served as president of AECT, has served on the board of directors of International Visual Literacy Association, and has written articles for state and national journals on her primary research interests—effective technology integration and distance education for learning. She worked on a Preparing Tomorrow's Teachers to use Technology (PT3) grant using the Web to deliver information and case studies of teachers using technology in schools. She has also worked on a Teacher Quality Enhancement grant that identified technology as an important aspect of ensuring quality learning environments. She has served as the editor of TechTrends, an AECT publication.

Dr. Michael J. Albright has been active in the fields of instructional technology and distance education since 1973. He made his first conference presentation on distance learing technologies in 1984, wrote his dissertation on a model for delivering university courses by satellite in the mid-1980s, and published an article on course management systems in 1997, before most people knew what they were, and when WebCT and Blackboard (then CourseInfo) were still in beta-testing. He retired in 2008 as director of online learning at Dakota Wesleyan University. Dr. Albright has extensive experience in course design and development for online learning, faculty support and training in online pedagogies, establishment of an effective institutional infrastructure to support and promote online learning, and quality control of online programs. As an adjunct for Nova Southeastern University, he taught a doctoral-level course in management and evaluation of instructional technology and distance education, the last 10 sections of which were totally online, and he has taught numerous other graduate courses either online or in a hybrid format. Dr. Albright received his Ph.D. in instructional technology from Iowa State University.

Susan M. Zvacek, Director of Instructional Development and Support at the University of Kansas, has been involved with distance learning and educational technology for over twenty years and has worked in community college, university, and corporate environments. Her teaching experience includes faculty/adjunct faculty positions at the University of Northern Colorado, Old Dominion University, and Nova Southeastern University. Her consulting, speaking, and research have included activities in the Czech Republic, Cyprus, Portugal, Slovakia, and throughout the United States.

BRIEF CONTENTS

CONTENTS

PART II ■ TEACHING AND LEARNING AT A DISTANCE 149

PART III ■ MANAGING AND EVALUATING DISTANCE EDUCATION   293

PREFACE

Distance education has become an important way to learn, and teaching online is a basic skill of the teacher and trainer. Recent reports have revealed that over 20% of college students are enrolled in at least one course delivered at a distance, and the U.S. Department of Education has released a meta-analysis that claims that those who study at a distance learn just as well as do traditional learners. Teaching and training the distance student are critical to education in the twenty-first century.

Teaching and Learning at a Distance is written to meet the needs of teachers and trainers who are learning about distance education. The text is to be used in courses for preservice or in-service teachers, for corporate trainers, and for staff development programs that address teaching distant learners or managing distance education systems. The teacher or trainer who uses this book will be able to select appropriate strategies for teaching the distant learner. It provides readers with a comprehensive coverage of information about distance education. The field of distance education has changed dramatically in the last few years, and so has this book. Over 30% of the content of this edition is new.

This text has five themes. These themes have been included in previous editions of this book, but for this edition the themes have been emphasized and are a significant improvement in this edition.

The first theme is *the definition of distance education.* Before the authors started writing the first edition of *Teaching and Learning at a Distance* they carefully reviewed the literature to determine the definition that would be at the foundation of writing. The definition presented in this book is based on the work of Desmond Keegan, but it is unique to this text. A significant improvement for this edition of the book is the validation of the definition of *distance education.* In 2009, the text's definition was included in, and adopted by, the *Encyclopaedia Britannica.* Additionally, our definition of distance education has been adopted by the Association for Educational Communications and Technology.

A second theme of the book is *the importance of research to the development of the content of the book.* The best practices presented in *Teaching and Learning at a Distance* are in most cases supported by scientific evidence. Certainly there are "rules of thumb," but every attempt has been made to include only those recommendations that can be supported by research. Throughout the book, recent research results are included, and in Chapter 3, the chapter that deals with research in distance education, a number of new and important research reports and research analyses are summarized. Thus, the reader of this text can be confident that the information included is current and based on the best research-based evidence.

The third theme of *Teaching and Learning at a Distance* is derived from Richard Clark's famous quote published in the *Review of Educational Research* that states that *media are mere vehicles that do not directly influence achievement*. Clark's controversial work is discussed in these pages and is fundamental to the book's advocacy for distance education—in other words, the authors did not make the claim that education delivered at a distance was inherently better than other ways people learn. Distance-delivered instruction is not a "magical" approach that makes learners achieve more. Rather, it is a viable and increasingly important alternative for teaching and learning. Additional information about the Clark controversy is included, such as references to podcasts and newly written comments about the "mere vehicles" position.

The fourth theme emphasized in this book is *equivalency theory*. This theory proposes the concept that learners should receive instruction that is equivalent rather than identical to what might be delivered in a traditional environment. Equivalency theory helps the instructional designer approach the development of instruction for each learner without attempting to duplicate what happens in a face-to-face classroom. Recently, equivalency theory has been carefully studied. The results of these studies are included.

The final theme for *Teaching and Learning at a Distance* is the idea that *the book should be comprehensive*—which means it should cover as much as possible of the various ways instruction is made available to distant learners. The book is a single source of information about the field. Distance education has expanded tremendously since the 4th edition of *Teaching and Learning at a Distance* was published. The field has moved from the periphery of education to the mainstream, as evidenced by the many Sloan-C reports. Strategies for teaching and learning at a distance have evolved dramatically, also. Newer course management systems have been developed, online teaching has moved to the Web in most cases, and virtual K–12 schools have become commonplace. These events are discussed throughout the book.

Organization of the Text

Teaching and Learning at a Distance has three types of chapters: foundation chapters, teaching and learning chapters, and managing and evaluating chapters. Chapters 1 through 4 provide a conceptual, theoretical, and research-based foundation for the rest of the text. Chapters 5 through 9 provide educators with the practical skills and information they need to function in a distance learning environment. Chapters 10 through 12 discuss managerial and administrative concerns in distance education environments.

Chapter 1 discusses the status of distance education and also explains what distance education is as compared to traditional education, and it presents the field's impact on education and training. This chapter concludes with a vision for schools made possible because of distance education. Approximately 30% of the content of this chapter has been revised.

Chapter 2 reviews definitions of distance education that have been, and still are, used. Because distance education is a field with a long history, that background is discussed. This chapter covers the field, beginning with correspondence study. Finally, theories related to the practice of distance education are presented, including a proposed

American theory of distance education—equivalency theory. There have been a number of research reports and literature analyses published since the 4th edition of this text was published. These reports are summarized and analyzed.

Chapter 3 reviews the extensive research on distance education, including specific areas of practice as well as more general and comprehensive summaries of what is presented in the research. *Teaching and Learning at a Distance* is a research-based textbook grounded on a thorough study of the empirical information about distance education. This research-based approach is found in all chapters but is emphasized in Chapter 3. Research in distance education has become sophisticated in recent years, moving from anecdotal reports to rigorous scientific studies.

Chapter 4 presents comprehensive information about the technologies used in distance education systems. Technology, generally, and instructional or communications technology, specifically, are broadly defined, and this chapter includes discussions, explanations, and many visuals to provide the reader with practical knowledge about how information is communicated and how synchronous and asynchronous distance education systems operate. The use of the Internet and the Web for distance education is also discussed extensively. This information has been modified significantly from previous editions. The Internet has become the basic method for delivery of most instruction offered at a distance. Information about the Internet and World Wide Web are now widely understood; therefore, this chapter of *Teaching and Learning at a Distance* has been significantly updated to reflect changes in the backgrounds of teachers and trainers.

Chapter 5 discusses instructional design, which is the systematic process for using instructional technology for teaching and training. This chapter presents the procedures to be followed when courses, or components of courses, are designed for distance delivery. In this edition, the Unit–Module–Topic (U–M–T) approach for organizing instruction is emphasized. The U–M–T approach has become a main design approach of the field. This is a significant change from previous editions.

Chapters 6 and 7 explain the unique responsibilities of the instructor and the learner involved in distance education. It is clear from the research and from practical experience that learning and teaching at a distance are not significantly different from traditional education. However, there are some special responsibilities and expectations for students and instructors involved in distance education. The roles of teachers and students have evolved as distance education has become more widely practiced.

Chapter 8 is one of the most important chapters of the book. Handouts, study guides, and visuals are important tools and techniques of the effective educator, generally, and the distance educator, specifically. The interactive study guide with its word pictures, visual analogies, and visualization is a significant tool used in distance education systems. Certainly, visualization is an important component of any effective instruction. This chapter includes new information to support the need for literate visuals.

Chapter 9 presents thoroughly revised techniques for assessing learning, assigning grades, and determining academic progress of students in a distance learning environment. Many educators question the rigor and fidelity of assessment at a distance. This chapter provides research-based approaches for the valid assessment of learning. Recent legislation has mandated that distance education institutions verify the identity of distance learners. This legislation has impacted strategies for assessment.

Thus, Chapter 9 has been modified to reflect the requirements of legislation and of the need for rigorous assessment.

Chapter 10 deals with the rules, regulations, and procedures of copyright—regulations that the distance educator should understand. This edition reflects major updates in the interpretation of copyright case law, providing a more comprehensive and applied perspective. Distance educators transmit information, much of which may be copyrighted. Copyright interpretations have evolved in the last few years and this has clarified copyright requirements for the distance educator.

Chapter 11 illustrates how distance education has become an enterprise, even a business, and discusses the techniques for managing and leading an organization dedicated to the delivery of distance instruction. Education and training leaders are expected to plan and develop online programs. This chapter looks at recently developed academic technology planning, distance education policies, and managerial requirements for distance education programs.

Practitioners in the field of distance education have always recognized the critical importance of evaluation, and Chapter 12 discusses the strategies for the evaluation of distance teaching and distance education systems, and gives specific examples of procedures to follow. New examples and approaches are included in this chapter. Assessment and evaluation are closely related, but evaluation is of special importance to the distance educator.

Features New to This Edition

- Chapter **goals and objectives** provide an organizational plan for the student and structure the information. Approximately 30% of the objectives have been revised for this edition.
- **A Look at Best Practice Issues,** a feature found throughout the text, presents critical issues in the field of distance education. This feature is designed to be the starting point for discussions about how distance education is changing teaching and learning. Dozens of best practices are included in this edition.
- Dozens of new **visuals** have been added to clarify ideas and explain procedures, and references and resources have been updated in each section and every chapter to make this book as current and relevant as possible. Over 30% percent of the visuals, references, and resources are new in this edition.
- All new chapter **discussion questions** are provided to review key ideas, and are included to replace self-test questions. Discussion questions are included because the field has evolved from solitary learners testing themselves to groups of learners, studying in different places, interacting as a learning community and discussing important issues. The discussion questions at the end of each chapter are designed for the instructor to post as a start for threaded discussions.
- Stronger emphasis in this edition is placed on **how to design, deliver, and evaluate** online instruction. This has become critical information as distance education has matured and the importance of online, Web-based instruction has grown. Best practices are now supported by research; thus, the design, delivery, and evaluation recommendations of previous editions have been replaced by best practices that are supported by research.

- Distance education has grown as a mainstream teaching and learning approach. Many new strategies are included in this edition to help the learner, teacher, and manager understand the impact of new ideas, such as open source course management systems.
- This edition has been streamlined so that it now contains 12 chapters.
- Finally, each chapter has a comprehensive list of **references.** In some instances, nonprint resources, especially relevant websites, are provided. Over 30% of the resources included in this edition of *Teaching and Learning at a Distance* are new.

Additional Resources   Three categories of additional resources are available to support the user of *Teaching and Learning at a Distance*. About 30% of these additional resources are new or have been revised since the 4th edition was published.

1. Videos
2. Interactive Study Guides and PowerPoint Presentations
3. Columns and Podcasts

Videos.   The following 11 videos, developed to support courses such as this, are available for use during class and outside of the class. These are available from the Association for Educational Communications and Technology, 1800 N. Stonelake Dr., Suite 2, Bloomington, IN 47404 (877-677-2328).

Introductory Video Title: *A Room with a View*
Description: Distance education offers significant new opportunities to learners of all ages. With construction of the Iowa Communications Network, linking more than 100 educational sites, Iowa has demonstrated its commitment to a high-quality, innovative educational system. This video discusses the opportunities offered by this new technology and presents vignettes from actual distance education classrooms. (15 min.)

Foundations and Applications of Distance Education

Foundations

Definitions and Background	The historical development of distance education and the definition of distance education. (12 min.)
Research and Theory	The implications of research for distance education practice. (13 min.)
Technologies and Terminology	An explanation of telecommunications technologies. (14 min.)
The Classroom	The hardware of a typical two-way interactive distance education classroom. (14 min.)
Distance Education Costs	The costs involved in constructing a distance education system, including distance education classrooms. (12 min.)

Applications

The Teacher	The skills needed for successful distance teaching. (18 min.)
The Student	The skills needed for successful distance education. (7 min.)
The Curriculum	How distance education can support and enrich the curriculum. (11 min.)
ICN	The purpose, structure, and capabilities of Iowa's 3,000-mile fiber-optic network. (12 min.)
Three Statewide Approaches	How distance education is practiced in three states: Kentucky, Mississippi, and Iowa. (18 min.)

Interactive Study Guides and PowerPoint Presentations. PowerPoint presentations and interactive study guides are designed to be used during classroom presentations. The masters for the PowerPoint presentations and interactive study guides are available at **www.nova.edu/~simsmich**. Click on "Presentations" on the left side of the screen. The titles include:

1. Copyright
2. Definition and Terminology
3. Distance Education and the World Wide Web
4. World Wide Web—Design
5. Preparing Faculty for Distance Education
6. Telelaw
7. Telepharmacy
8. Managing the Mandate—Distance Education and Teacher Education
9. Equivalency and Distance Education
10. Assessment of the Distant Learner
11. Systems
12. Handouts and Study Guides
13. Instructional Design
14. Interaction and Distance Education
15. Internet
16. Teaching Techniques

Columns and Podcasts. Podcasts are audio files that discuss critical ideas related to distance education. The following podcasts are available at **www.nova. edu/~simsmich**. Click on "Distance Education Resources" on the left side of the screen.

Simonson on Equivalency Theory—Distance Learning Journal:

1.1 *Coal Slurry Ponds—Quality Indicators*
1.3 *Distance Learning Leaders*
1.4 *Class Size, Where Is the Research?*

Quarterly Review of Distance Education:

ACKNOWLEDGMENTS

Many individuals participated in the development of the ideas presented in this text. In particular, we thank Dan Hanson, Nancy Maushak, Charles Schlosser, and Mary Anderson of the Technology Research and Evaluation Group at Iowa State University, who contributed a great deal to the development of *Teaching and Learning at a Distance*.

We would also like to thank the reviewers of this edition for the valuable feedback they provided during the writing process: Abigail Garthwait, University of Maine; Allan Jeong, Florida State University; and Carmen L. Lamboy, Laureate Education.

Foundations

CHAPTER 1

Foundations of Distance Education

CHAPTER GOAL

The purpose of this chapter is to discuss the importance of distance education and the impact that distance education has on the improvement of education.

CHAPTER OBJECTIVES

After reading and reviewing this chapter, you should be able to

1. Explain why students demand to learn at a distance even though they may prefer to learn in the classroom with the teacher and their classmates.
2. Define *distance education.*
3. Explain Coldeway's quadrants.
4. Discuss Richard Clark's "mere vehicles" quote as it relates to distance education.
5. Explain how Jim Finn might compare stirrups to distance education.
6. Give examples of how distance education is being used in several locations of the world and in the United States.
7. Discuss telemedicine and relate the topic to distance education. Explain a vision for education and schooling in the future.
8. Define disruptive technology and relate distance education to this concept.

CHEMISTRY AT A DISTANCE? A TRUE STORY

Chemistry is a hands-on, laboratory-based course that many consider one of the most rigorous in the average high school curriculum. Many students dread taking chemistry, and in many small communities there is only one chemistry teacher in the school.

Recently, four high school chemistry teachers decided that they could improve their basic chemistry course if they collaborated and team-taught. The only problem was that their schools were about 60 miles from each other.

This did not stop them, however, because their schools were connected with a fiber-optic network that permitted full-motion video signals to be sent between the four schools. The network also carried a high-speed Internet connection that allowed easy access to the Web.

Not only did the four teachers want to collaborate but, more importantly, they wanted their students to collaborate. To accomplish this, they decided on some basic objectives and then planned the curriculum.

The teachers decided that they would teach concepts cooperatively, act as laboratory supervisors for each other's students, and serve as partners with student collaborators. They also decided on another important goal: to have their students cooperate across schools. Finally, they agreed that the chemistry projects should be authentic and deal with local, real-world issues.

Next, the four teachers met to plan their curriculum.

Increasingly, courses such as chemistry are being taught to distant and local learners synchronously and asynchronously.

They identified eight modules that could be shared among the four schools. These modules were taught by one or two of the four chemistry teachers, and required collaboration by the students from the four schools. The modules included live television instruction presented by one of the teachers, collaborative work by students who communicated with each other by television and the Internet, and class assignments that dealt with various aspects of a specific chemistry concept, such as the local ecology. Students investigated their portion of the problem and then shared results with their distant classmates. Each module ended with a live, interactive discussion, presentation, and sharing of information over the fiber-optic television network.

For all practical purposes, the students in the four schools became one large class, with subgroups of students who worked with classmates from their own school and with distant friends. The teachers served as presenters some of the time, but most often as tutors who worked with subgroups of students. The Internet and e-mail were used to keep everyone communicating outside of class, and even outside of school.

By any measure, the course was a huge success. Students learned chemistry, as evidenced by their test scores. They also discovered how to collaborate as real scientists with colleagues at distant locations, and they discovered the power of distance education to open up their school to resources available elsewhere.

Telecommunications technology made this possible. Their chemistry classroom became a "room with a view," connected to other chemistry classrooms and to the resources of the world available through the Internet. The course became more like real chemistry—chemistry practiced to solve actual problems outside the school, involving experts from a number of areas brought together because of their expertise, without regard for geography or time.

Distance education is one of the most dramatic of the recent technology-based innovations influencing education. The scenario just described is only one of thousands of examples of how distance education is changing learning and teaching.

DISTANCE EDUCATION TODAY AND TOMORROW

In the last few years, distance education has become a major topic in education. In a recent year, over 60 conferences dealt with some aspect of distance education, and almost every professional organization's publications and conferences have shown a huge increase in the number of presentations and articles related to distance education. Many educators are making grand claims about how distance education is likely to change education and training. Certainly, the concept is exciting, and recent hardware and software innovations are making telecommunications distance education systems more available, easier to use, and less costly. Distance education has begun to enter the mainstream.

Whether distance education is a mainstream form of education has been examined for several years by the Sloan Consortium. *Learning on Demand* (Allen & Seaman, 2010) is the seventh annual report by the Sloan Consortium; it presents the latest data about the growth and spread of online education in higher education in the United States. The first report, *Sizing the Opportunity* (Allen & Seaman, 2003), indicated that online and/or distance education was growing rapidly and was perceived positively by faculty and administrators. The authors of this report defined *online learning* to be courses where most or all of the content is delivered online. Typically, these courses have no face-to-face meetings.

One indication that online courses are a regular activity of institutions of higher education is the role of core faculty in online instruction. There has been a long-held belief that online courses are taught by adjunct professors rather than full-time staff. *Growing by Degrees* (Allen & Seaman, 2005) refutes this perception. It reports that about two-thirds of online courses are taught by regular faculty, a percentage that is often higher than that of regular courses taught by core faculty.

Another indicator of the growth of online education is the importance of this instructional approach to the long-term strategy of the institution. In 2009, approximately 60% of institutions indicated that online instruction was critical to their long-term plans, up from 49% in 2003. The only institutions that did not see online instruction as part of their long-term strategies were the smallest nonprofit colleges. In 2008, enrollment in online courses increased to about 4.6 million from 2 million in 2003. Growth has been continuous, often exceeding the expectations of organizational planners.

Another interesting report dealing with distance education in the Midwest was released by the Sloan Consortium (Allen & Seaman, 2007). This report indicated that:

■ The 11 midwestern states represent about 15% of online enrollment, with over 460,000 students taking at least one online course in fall 2005.
■ The proportion of midwestern institutions with fully online programs rises steadily as institutional size increases, and about two-thirds of the very largest

institutions have fully online programs, compared to only about one-sixth of the smallest institutions.

■ Midwestern doctoral/research institutions have the greatest penetration of offering online programs as well as the highest overall rate (more than 90%) of having some form of online offering (either courses or full programs).

■ The proportion of people who believe that online learning outcomes are superior to those for face-to-face learning is still relatively small but has grown by 34% since 2003, from 10.2% to 13.7%.

The Sloan Consortium reports (Allen & Seaman, 2010; Picciano & Seaman, 2007) also provide excellent criteria for distinguishing among online courses, blended/hybrid courses, and Web-facilitated courses. An *online course* is one where most of the content is delivered online, which means at least 80% of the course content. A *blended* or *hybrid course* combines online and face-to-face delivery; thus, 30% to 79% of the course's content is delivered online. A *Web-facilitated course* uses Web-based technology, but less than 29% of the content is delivered online.

In spite of the phenomenal growth of distance education, two conflicting pressures confront distance educators (Figure 1–1). First, *students say their first choice is not to learn at a distance.* When asked, they say they prefer meeting with the learning group and the instructor in the classroom, the lecture hall, the seminar room, or the laboratory. Students report that they value the presence of a learning group, and that the informal interactions that occur before and after, and sometimes during, a formal class are valuable components of the total learning experience. Second, and conversely, evidence suggests that *students are increasingly demanding to be allowed to learn at a distance.* They want to be able to supplement,

FIGURE 1–1   There are conflicting pressures on distance educators—students prefer to learn in a classroom, but demand to be permitted to learn at a distance.

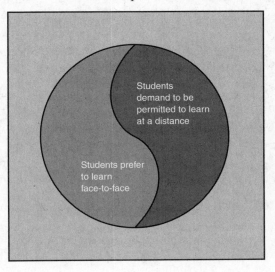

and even replace, conventional learning experiences with distance education experiences. Learners say this is because many other considerations besides personal preferences motivate them, especially considerations about where and when they learn (Picciano & Seaman, 2007).

These opposing preferences pose a dilemma for the educational community. Should resources be dedicated to improving the traditional educational infrastructure of buildings, classrooms, laboratories, and offices? Should students be transported to these facilities? Or should money be used to develop modern and sophisticated telecommunications systems? The trend seems to be toward telecommunications. Because of advances in technology, effective educational experiences can be provided for learners, no matter where they are located. In other words, technologies are now available to develop cost-effective distance learning systems.

Virtual schools are becoming important in many locations (Berge & Clark, 2009). The Florida Virtual School, established in the late 1990s, offers a wide selection of courses (Johnson, 2007). The Arkansas Virtual School is another successful example of a state-adopted distance education program (Falduto & Ihde, 2007).

Compressed video systems use telelphone lines and Internet connection to permit live, two-way, interactive televised instruction.

Universities are also sponsoring virtual schools. Indiana University High School and the University of Missouri's Columbia High School are examples of university-sponsored virtual schools. The North Central Association of Colleges and Schools has accredited both schools. The Indiana and Missouri schools are financially independent of their universities. High school students pay tuition for courses that are developed and taught by certified teachers. A large number of other states are following the lead of Florida, Arkansas, Indiana, and Missouri. Concepts such as the virtual school have caused the practice of distance education to dramatically change in the last decade. Traditional approaches to distance education based on the delivery of print and broadcast media technologies are no longer as relevant to the field as they once were.

As a matter of fact, a redefinition of distance education has occurred. *Distance education* is now often defined as:

> institution-based, formal education where the learning group is separated, and where interactive telecommunications systems are used to connect learners, resources, and instructors. (Schlosser & Simonson, 2009, p. 1)

This definition was recently adopted by the Encyclopedia Britannica.

THE EFFECTIVENESS OF DISTANCE EDUCATION—IN CASE YOU WONDER

Many who begin studying distance education wonder about the effectiveness of this approach to teaching and learning, and although Chapter 3 discusses distance education research in depth, this section summarizes that research and briefly describes what we know about the effectiveness of distance teaching and distance learning.

> According to the 248 studies that were compiled by Russell (1999), there is no significant difference between distance learning and traditional classroom learning. In other words, distance learning (can be) considered as effective as face-to-face learning, and our results support this conclusion. (Dean, Stah, Swlwester, & Pear, 2001, p. 252)

Russell (1999) and Dean and colleagues (2001) reported results that are indicative of the research on the field of distance education. Most who are deeply involved in the field of distance education are unsurprised by these summaries of the research. As a matter of fact, it is very clear that instruction delivered to distant learners is effective and that learning outcomes can be successfully attained when offered to students at a distance (Anglin & Morrison, 2000; Cavanaugh, Gillan, Kromey, Hess, & Blomeyer, 2004; Hanson, Maushak, Schlosser, Anderson, & Sorenson, 1997; Simonson, 2002).

In 1983, Clark clearly stated that the media used to deliver instruction had no significant impact on learning:

> The best current evidence is that media are mere vehicles that deliver instruction but do not influence student achievement any more than the truck that delivers our groceries causes changes in nutrition . . . only the content of the vehicle can influence achievement. (p. 445)

After more than a decade of criticism and attempts to refute his review of over 50 years of instructional technology research, Clark (1994) once again reviewed the research on technology used to deliver instruction and noted:

> It is likely that when different media treatments of the same informational content to the same students yield similar learning results the cause of the results can be found in a method which the two treatments share in common . . . give up your enthusiasm for the belief that media attributes cause learning. (p. 28)

Since the publication of Clark's widely distributed comments, a number of researchers have attempted to find fault with his premise. They have not been successful. It is currently the consensus that "media are mere vehicles" and that we should "give up [our] enthusiasm" that the delivery media for instructional content significantly influences learning.

Unfortunately, some have misinterpreted the "no significant differences" phenomenon and assumed that instructional technology and distance education do not promote learning. This is incorrect. Actually, the evidence is quite clear that students of all ages can learn from instruction delivered using technology, and that distance education works.

In the first years of widespread growth of distance education in the United States, Hanson and colleagues (1997) summarized the research on distance education in a publication of the Association for Educational Communications and Technology. This widely distributed review concluded that

> comparative research studies on achievement tend to show no significant difference between different delivery systems and between distance education and traditional education. . . . Several recent studies indicate a significant higher achievement level in those learning at a distance. . . . The accepted position is that the delivery system affects no inherent difference on achievement. (p. 22)

In other words, it is not the fact that instruction is delivered in a traditional, face-to-face environment or at a distance that predicts learning (Anglin & Morrison, 2000; Berge & Mrozowski, 2001; Darwazeh, 2000; Simonson, 2002).

It is clear from the research literature that distance education works (e.g., Hanson et al., 1997; Simonson, 2002). Why it works and how it works are important concepts to understand, however. The following conclusions about instruction delivered to distant learners are directly related to effectiveness:

- Training in effective instructional strategies is critical for teachers of distant learners.
- Distance education courses should be carefully designed and developed before instruction begins.
- Visualization of ideas and concepts is critical when designing instruction to be delivered to distant learners.
- Adequate support systems must be in place to provide the distant learner with access to resources and services.
- Interaction between the instructor and students and among students must be possible and encouraged.
- Assessment should be designed to relate to the specific learning outcomes of the instructional experiences.

© 2007 Polycom, Inc.

Distance education efforts are increasingly being concentrated on K-12 education.

In summary, distance education can be as effective as any other category of instruction. Learning occurs and knowledge is retained. Students report that they have learned and that they feel their distance learning experiences are as successful as more traditional education. The keys to successful distance education are in the design, development, and delivery of instruction, and are not related to geography or time.

WHAT IS DISTANCE EDUCATION?

It is the nature of questions that they are easier to ask than to answer. This is true of the question "What is distance education?" for several reasons. First, *distance* has multiple meanings, although this book advocates the definition presented earlier and in Chapter 2. *Distance* can mean geographical distance, time distance, and possibly even intellectual distance.

Second, the term *distance education* has been applied to a tremendous variety of programs serving numerous audiences via a wide variety of media. Some use print, some use telecommunications, and many use both. Finally, rapid changes in technology challenge the traditional ways in which distance education is defined.

Dan Coldeway, of South Dakota's Dakota State University, provided a framework useful in helping to define four ways in which education can be practiced. This framework, which considers the two variables of time and place, gives insight into different approaches to the practice of education and distance education. Combinations of time and place result in four approaches to education: same-time, same-place education (ST-SP); different-time, same-place education (DT-SP); same-time, different-place education (ST-DP); and different-time, different-place education (DT-DP).

Traditional education takes place at the same time in the same place. This is typically the regular self-contained classroom that most often is teacher centered. Different-time, same-place education means that individual learning occurs in a learning center, or that multiple sections of the same classes are offered so students can attend the class in the same place at a time they choose. This is education that is available at different times to students but in the same place, such as the media center or computer laboratory.

The last two categories focus on education occurring in different places. Instruction can take place in different places at the same time when telecommunications systems are used. Often, television is used to connect the local classroom with the teacher and students to learners at a distance. Satellite, compressed video, and fiber-optic systems are increasingly used for same-time, different-place education. This approach is also called *distance learning*. Students can also learn at different times and in different places. Simonson (2003) has said that the purest form of distance education occurs at different times and in different places. In other words, learners choose when and where to learn and when and where to access instructional materials. Recently, Web-based courses have been offered to learners anywhere they have access and whenever they choose. This approach is called *asynchronous distance learning*.

FACTS ABOUT DISTANCE EDUCATION

Here are a few little-known facts about the field of distance education.

- Eminent historian Frederick Jackson Turner ran the correspondence program of the University of Wisconsin in the late 1800s.
- The state of Iowa has a state-owned, 3,000-mile fiber-optic network, called the Iowa Communications Network, with nearly 1,000 high-tech classrooms for the purpose of offering distance instruction throughout the state.
- *Telemedicine* refers to medicine at a distance, and *telelaw* refers to law at a distance.
- Research on the effectiveness of distance education clearly shows that students who learn at a distance do not learn any worse, or any better, than traditional students.
- The United States Distance Learning Association is a professional organization of those involved in distance education.
- Universities such as the University of Chicago, the University of Wisconsin, and the University of Iowa championed correspondence education in the later years of the nineteenth century and early in the twentieth century.
- Satellites used for distance education orbit approximately 23,000 miles about the equator at an orbiting speed that matches the rotation of the Earth. This geosynchronous orbit makes these satellites appear to be stationary on the surface of the Earth. The location where the satellites orbit is called the Clarke Belt, after science fiction writer Arthur C. Clarke, who wrote about communication satellites in geosynchronous orbit in a story published in the 1940s.
- The foundations of the Internet were begun by the U.S. Department of Defense and by a number of research universities as a way to share scientific and technical information between scientists.
- *IP* stands for *Internet Protocol*, the rules used to send information over the Internet.

- The Internet is a packet-switched network, meaning that messages are divided into packets that are disassembled and then sent to the distant site where the packets are reassembled into the complete message.
- Star Schools is the name of a program of the U.S. Department of Education that funds the implementation of distance education in schools and colleges in the United States. The term was coined by Senator Ted Kennedy, who was opposed to the use of satellites for "star wars," so he advocated the use of satellites for education and proposed the Star Schools program.

Distance Education as a Disruptive Technology:

A disruptive technology or disruptive innovation is a technological innovation, product, or service that eventually overturns the existing dominant technology or product in the market. Disruptive innovations can be broadly classified into lower-end and new-market disruptive innovations. A new-market disruptive innovation is often aimed at non-consumption, whereas a lower-end disruptive innovation is aimed at mainstream customers who were ignored by established companies. Sometimes, a disruptive technology comes to dominate an existing market by either filling a role in a new market that the older technology could not fill or by successively moving up-market through performance improvements until finally displacing the market incumbents. (Simonson, 2010, p. 74)

By contrast, "sustaining technology or innovation" improves product performance of established products. Sustaining technologies are often incremental." Sustaining technologies maintain a rate of improvement, give users something more or better that they value (Teets, 2002).

Thus, technological innovations might be categorized along a continuum from *sustaining* to *disruptive*. In education, a sustaining technology might be a SmartBoard, which in most applications is a way to present information dynamically and efficiently—a sustaining upgrade to the chalkboard and overhead projector.

As a matter of fact, most attempts to integrate instructional technology into the traditional classroom are examples of sustaining technologies—computer data projectors, DVD players, e-books—all of which "improve product performance of *established* products." Most integrated technologies sustain, and do not disrupt.

On the other hand, distance education is certainly not a sustaining technology. Rather, distance education, virtual schooling, and e-learning are disruptive.

For example, distance education is aimed at students (older, working, remotely located learners) who are "ignored by established companies" (traditional schools). Distance education presents a different package of performance attributes that are not valued by existing customers. Distance education has come to "dominate . . . by filling a role . . . that the older technology could not fill"(Teets, 2002, p. 7).

Clayton Christensen (2003) and Christensen, Anthony and Roth (2004) have written extensively about the concept of disruptive technologies. Christensen's work has been widely embraced in business. His work helps explain why some established industries fail, and others spring up, seemingly from nowhere. There is no better example than the personal computer. Not a single mini-computer manufacturer has been a successful manufacturer of personal computers—they did not see the power of the new technology until others had captured market share.

Similarly, most educators have ignored the potential of looking at the ideas behind Christensen's theory, and how disruptive technologies might transform education and training.

In Florida, there is a mandate that every public school district must establish a virtual K–8 and 9–12 school (Simonson, 2009). Many have wondered why Florida legislators would pass such a sweeping law—perhaps the answer is disruptive technology. Whatever the reason for Florida to establish virtual schools, it is clear that distance education and virtual schooling are disrupting traditional education, and this may be a good thing. It might be a good idea for educators to become more cognizant of Clayton Christensen's work, and the power of disruptive technologies to change education.

MEDIA IN EDUCATION: EARLIER DEBATES

The discussion about distance education is somewhat reminiscent of a recent debate in the educational technology field referred to previously that began when Richard Clark (1983), a researcher and theorist, published a classic article containing his now famous "mere vehicles" analogy.

Clark (1983) summarized over six decades of educational media research. It was obvious to him that many researchers were reporting about flawed studies involving media. Clark believed that many educators did not understand the last 60 years of research about media and learning.

Even more alarming was that many practitioners were making unrealistic claims about the impact of technology on learning. According to Clark, a large segment of the educational community felt that media-based instruction was inherently better than teaching when media were not used.

In 1983, Clark wrote in the *Review of Educational Research* that:

> the best current evidence is that media are *mere vehicles* that deliver instruction but do not influence student achievement any more than the truck that delivers our groceries causes changes in nutrition . . . only the content of the vehicle can influence achievement. (p. 445)

Clark's (1983) article went on to claim convincingly that instructional media were excellent for storing educational messages and for delivering them almost anywhere. However, media were not responsible for a learning effect. Learning was not enhanced because instruction was media based. Rather, the content of the instruction, the method used to promote learning, and the involvement of the learner in the instructional experience were what, in part, influenced learning. Although many did not, and still do not, agree with Clark, his article caused a reassessment of how educators looked at the impact of media. Clark 1994 continued to implore the education community to "give up your enthusiasm for media effects on learning," which was the theme of an additional publication on this topic. "Give up your enthusiasm" has become the new rallying cry for those who do not believe there is a media effect.

Certainly, some distance educators claim that distance education is the best way to learn because it allows students to acquire knowledge when it is most relevant to them.

However, most who have studied distance learning make few claims about the approach being better. Rather, they say it is a viable and important approach to learning and teaching that should be one option of many available.

A second analogy by another great technology pioneer also has relevance to distance education. In the 1960s, Jim Finn from the University of Southern California talked about the stirrup as a technological innovation that changed society. He often told a story that went like this:

> The Anglo-Saxons, a dominating enemy of Charles Martel's Franks, had the stirrup but did not truly understand its implications for warfare. The stirrup made possible the emergence of a warrior called the knight who understood that the stirrup enabled the rider not only to keep his seat, but also to deliver a blow with a lance having the combined weight of the rider and charging horse. This simple concept permitted the Franks to conquer the Anglo-Saxons and change the face of western civilization. Martel had a vision to seize the idea and to use it. He did not invent the stirrup, but knew how to use it purposefully. (Finn, 1964, p. 24)

Finn (1964) summarized the implications of this story as follows:

> The acceptance or rejection of an invention, or the extent to which its implications are realized if it is accepted, depends quite as much upon the condition of society, and upon the imagination of its leadership, as upon the nature of the technological item itself. . . . The Anglo-Saxons used the stirrup, but did not comprehend it; and for this they paid a fearful price. . . . It was the Franks alone—presumably led by Charles Martel's genius— who fully grasped the possibilities inherent in the stirrup and created in terms of it a new type of warfare supported by a novel structure of a society that we call feudalism. . . . For a thousand years feudal institutions bore the marks of their birth from the new military technologies of the eighth century. (p. 24)

What Clark strongly proposed with his "mere vehicles" and "give up your enthusiasm" arguments was that media and technology did not directly affect learning. He forcefully argued that educators should not claim that technology-based learning, such as modern distance education systems, had any inherent advantage (or disadvantage for that matter) over other methods of learning. Like Finn, Clark proposed that technologies might provide ways of accomplishing tasks that are new and not readily obvious. Finn advocated that practitioners should attempt to identify unique approaches for change by using new technologies in new ways. Finn's story explained that the stirrup not only made getting on and off a horse easier but it also made possible a new, previously unheard-of consequence—the emergence of the knight—and it was the knight who caused significant and long-lasting changes in society. Perhaps the correct application of distance education will significantly change and restructure learning and teaching on par with the societal change—called feudalism— needed to support the knight.

The implication of the arguments of these two educators is that when new technologies emerge, they often allow users to be more efficient. However, it is not technologies themselves that cause changes; rather, changes occur because of new ways of doing things that are enabled by technologies. The stirrup made riding horses easier and more efficient, but it was the knight who changed medieval society.

STATUS OF DISTANCE EDUCATION

Worldwide Examples

Distance education has a major and varied impact worldwide. Whereas politics and economics influence how distance education is employed, a strong demand exists in the world for distance education opportunities. The five examples that follow illustrate some of the factors that influence distance education and show the demand for distance learning opportunities.

1. Anadolu University in Turkey reaches over 500,000 distance education students, which makes it the largest university on Earth, according to the World Bank (Demiray, 2005; Macwilliams, 2000). The university was created in 1981 during a sweeping reorganization of Turkey's higher education system. Its mission is to provide distance instruction to the citizens of Turkey. In 1983, it had almost 30,000 students in business administration and economics, making the university an immediate success. As of 2010, approximately 34% of the students who enrolled in the two-year degree programs graduated in two years, and about 23% of those enrolled in four-year programs graduated in four years. The vast majority of the students enrolled at Anadolu University were working adults with full- or part-time jobs. Distance education offered by Anadolu University has made postsecondary education a possibility for many in Turkey who would not have access to higher education. Professors at Anadolu publish an online journal that can be accessed at http://tojde.anadolu.edu.tr.

2. The Open University of Hong Kong opened in 1989 to serve residents of that huge metropolitan area. The university has begun to market itself to learners in China, and it has thousands of students from the mainland (Zhang, 2006). Unlike Hong Kong's eight conventional universities, the Open University accepts all applicants. It has had over 100,000 students, of which approximately 10% have graduated. Administrators from the Open University of Hong Kong plan to offer distance education throughout China and Southeast Asia (Zhang, 2005; Zhang, Perris, & Yeung, 2005).

3. In sub-Saharan Africa, political instability and economic depression have caused a decline in educational standards in some countries. As the population increased in these countries, a tremendous classroom shortage emerged, and both the number of qualified teachers and the availability of instructional materials became inadequate. Distance education is seen as having the potential to contribute to national reconstruction by providing economically feasible educational opportunities to many people. Collaboration with a variety of international distance education organizations has provided expertise and support for the field. As a result, distance education at a basic level, as it is practiced in many regions of Africa, has expanded quite sharply. However, although growth in distance education in sub-Saharan African countries is evident, it does not yet have a wide impact. Lack of funding prevents distance education institutions from reaching many potential students (Day, 2005; Visser, Visser, & Buendia, 2005; Visser & West, 2005). According to Nsomwe-a-nfunkwa (2009), the enrollment in the French Digital Campus of Kinshasa (Congo) more than doubled from 2004 to 2008.

4. China developed a national higher distance education program in the late 1970s and early 1980s in response to a growth in population and a high cost per capita for the craftlike approach to regular higher education in the country. Because China could not afford to meet the higher education needs of the expanding population, a national radio and TV university system was developed. By 1985, China had over 30,000 TV classes throughout the country and employed almost 25,000 academics. One in five students studying in higher education was enrolled in a radio and TV university. This national system incorporated a centralized approach to course development, delivery, and examinations. However, despite an increase in offerings, student numbers have significantly decreased. Recently, only 1 in every 13 students in higher education was enrolled in a radio and TV university and this prompted a move from TV broadcasting to e-learning (Gao & Zhang, 2009).

Socioeconomic factors have caused changes in the mass market for higher education in China. The centralized approach to course development and delivery no longer meets the diverse needs of learners and does not adapt itself quickly to the new conditions. In response, China's radio and TV universities have changed from a central system of course development and delivery to a regionally responsive system that provides a wide variety of both diploma and nondiploma courses (Ding, 1994, 1995; Hurd & Xiao, 2006; Yang, Wang, Shen, & Han, 2007; Yan & Linder, 2007).

5. Distance education has had a long history in European countries. The continuation of this tradition is evident in the vast array of programs offered by European Union countries. In some countries, open distance teaching universities offer the majority of the country's online education programming. Spain's Universidad Nacional de Educación a Distancia is Europe's largest distance teaching university, with a current enrollment of about 130,000 students. In other countries, traditional universities deliver the majority of the courses. France, for example, has no national distance teaching university, but offers higher distance education through 22 offices within traditional universities. Recently, 34,000 students were enrolled in these programs. In some cases, governments provide substantial distance education training opportunities that do not lead to a university degree. France is a leader in this area, providing over 350,000 students a year with opportunities at a range of levels: elementary school, high school, technical and professional qualifications, teacher training, and university-level and postgraduate courses. Distance instruction in the European Union uses a wide variety of media to deliver courses. These range from traditional correspondence delivery, to computer conferencing, to two-way audio and video virtual classrooms (Holmberg, 1995; Keegan, 1995). Using these technologies, the established distance education and training organizations of Europe will continue to play a significant role in education in and beyond the European Union (Vrasidas, 2008).

United States

Distance educators are often asked about the quality and extent of online education in the United States. Many individuals, especially new students, want to know if instruction delivered at a distance is of high quality, and if distance education is a passing fad or a viable approach to teaching and learning. The Sloan Consortium has attempted to answer these questions. The Sloan Consortium is a collection of institutions and organizations committed to quality online education. Their reports (Allen & Seaman, 2010) provide a wealth of information about the field of distance education in general, and about online instruction more specifically.

The Sloan reports used surveys to obtain information related to four fundamental questions:

1. Will students embrace online education as a delivery method?
2. Will institutions embrace online education as a delivery method?
3. Will faculty embrace online education as a delivery method?
4. Will the quality of online education match that of face-to-face instruction?

Almost 1,000 surveys set by the Sloan Consortium (about 33% of those sent) were returned from chief academic officers from accredited degree-granting institutions of higher education in the United States. The Sloan report is interesting reading, and the results are important, if not surprising, to those in the field:

■ The majority of chief academic officers believe that the learning out comes in online courses will equal or exceed that of face-to-face courses within 3 years.
■ The overall growth rate for enrollment in online courses is expected to be 20%.
■ Profit institutions expect a growth rate that is faster than that of other institutions (40%).
■ Private, nonprofit institutions expect to use online education less than other institutions.
■ Given an option, students will enroll in online courses.
■ Overall, attitudes of faculty remain conservative about the quality of online education.

Other interesting results from the Sloan Consortium Survey (2010) show that over 90% of public universities offer online courses, and about half offer degree programs online. About 85% of public universities consider online education critical to their long-term academic strategies, as compared with about 50% for private institutions. Faculty at public universities are more accepting of the value of online education than their colleagues at private universities, and public universities enrolled over 2 million students in online courses.

The Sloan Consortium reports authenticate the amazing growth of distance education, yet they also identify the very important issues that still confront the field if distance education is to continue to grow in importance.

At the university level, it is reported that distance education enrollment is in the high six figures nationally. This includes enrollment in courses offered by traditional universities and those offered by distance learning universities. The U.S. military is heavily involved in distance education technology because it is viewed as a cost-efficient way to deliver technical training to a large number of soldiers. The development of new weapons systems and other technologies increases the demand for this type of training. The army's Interactive Teletraining Network, the navy's Video

Teletraining Network, the air force's Teleteach Expanded Delivery System, and NASA's Digital Learning Network (Tally, 2009) all provide distance training opportunities for personnel across the United States and around the world.

A focus on education in primary and secondary schools separates American distance education from traditional European distance education. This emphasis on kindergarten through grade 12 (K–12) students is demonstrated by the growth of virtual schools (Berge & Clark, 2005) and in the federally funded Star Schools projects. The U.S. Department of Education began the Star Schools program "to encourage improved instruction in mathematics, science, foreign languages, literacy skills, and vocational education for underserved populations through the use of telecommunications networks" (Simonson, 1995, pp. 3–4). Although these projects are not limited to K–12 programming, their primary emphasis is on K–12 students and teachers. A variety of network technologies including satellite, cable, telephone networks, fiber optics, microcomputer-based laboratories, multimedia, and electronic networking technologies have been used to deliver instructional programming to over 6,000 schools nationwide through the Star Schools project (U.S. Department of Education, 1995).

Typically, the Star Schools project has funded programs that provide satellite delivery of instruction to a large number of students in many states. One of the largest is the Star Schools Project of the Los Angeles County Office of Education, which is a consortium of education and public television agencies in over 10 states. The consortium provides math, science, social science, language arts, and technology programming to over 1,300 school sites and 125,000 students in grades 4 through 7. In addition, the project provides professional development opportunities for over 4,000 teachers. The Star Schools project funds a number of similar satellite-based projects.

The Star Schools project has sponsored several special statewide projects that fund the development of statewide infrastructures, allowing for synchronous interaction between students and instructors. The most comprehensive is in Iowa. Currently, Iowa's 3,000-mile statewide fiber-optic network connects more than 700 educational sites, with over 300 more sites to be added in the next few years. Hundreds of thousands of hours of K–12 programming are provided each year, in addition to teacher professional development and higher education course opportunities. Kentucky and Mississippi have joined Iowa in developing statewide systems that promote personalized interactive instruction and learning.

South Dakota is another state that has significantly committed to distance education for K–12 students. The Digital Dakota Network links every school building to a compressed video network. Over 300 sites are located throughout the state (Figure 1–2). Teachers have been trained in special month-long distance teaching and learning academies, and teachers and university faculties have designed curriculum materials, including entire courses. South Dakota educators have also conducted major research and evaluation activities to document the impact of distance education in the state (Bauck, 2001; Simonson, 2005). As the examples show, distance education has a major impact worldwide. In addition to economics and politics, the growth and impact of distance education is directly

FIGURE 1–2   South Dakota has the Digital Dakota Network that links hundreds of sites in the state for interactive instruction.

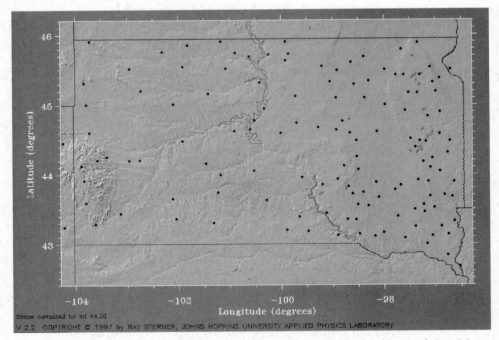

Source: Ray Sterner of the Johns Hopkins Applied Physics Laboratory, licensed by North Star Science and Technology, LLC. [Online.] Available at: www.landforms.biz. Reprinted with permission.

linked to the availability of new technologies. "As technology links distant sites in an electronic web of information and new communication channels, people around the globe are pulled together" (Thach & Murphy, 1994, p. 5). This type of communication has contributed to globalization. Globalization implies that people are connected more or less contemporaneously with distant events. The new computer-mediated communications and telecommunications technologies contribute to globalization.

Other significant distance education initiatives are Network Nebraska (Decker, 2008), Western Governors University (Eastmond, 2007), Capella University (Thornton, 2007), and Walden University (Shepard, 2008). Distance educators will be challenged both by globalization and by the emerging technologies. How they take advantage of these opportunities will give new meaning to the practice of distance education.

Accreditation.   Many people in traditional education worry about the quality of distance education programs. Some have called distance education institutions diploma mills, especially those programs that generate profits. A *diploma mill* has the following characteristics: no classrooms, untrained or nonexistent faculties, and unqualified administrators with profit as their primary motivation (Simonson, 2004).

Legitimate institutions have expended considerable effort to demonstrate the quality of their distance education programs. One of the most important activities involves *accreditation*. Probably the most important form of accreditation, which involves in-depth scrutiny of a school or college's entire program by outside evaluators, comes from regional accrediting agencies, such as the North Central Association (NCA) and the Southern Association of Colleges and Schools (SACS). The NCA and SACS are examples of regional agencies that accredit institutions in their geographic areas. Generally, the same standards are applied to traditional and distance education programs. National accreditation agencies also accredit colleges.

TELEMEDICINE

Tele- means "at a distance," so in its simplest form, *telemedicine* is defined as medicine at a distance. The Institute of Medicine defines *telemedicine* as the use of electronic information and communications technologies to provide and support health care when distance separates the participants (Grigsby & Sanders, 1998). Grigsby and Sanders (1998) define *telemedicine* as the use of telecommunications and information technology to provide health care services to persons at a distance from the provider. Actually, there exist in the literature dozens of definitions of telemedicine, but all contain these components:

1. Separation or distance between individuals and/or resources
2. Use of telecommunications technologies
3. Interaction between individuals and/or resources
4. Medical or health care

Also, it is implied in most definitions that telemedicine refers to health care offered by recognized, formally accredited medical organizations. Organizational affiliation differentiates telemedicine from self-diagnosis, unsanctioned medical treatment, and quackery.

Background

The term *telemedicine* has become common in medical literature during the last decade. However, most give credit for originating the term to Kenneth Byrd, who, along with several other physicians, formed a video microwave network in 1968 from Massachusetts General Hospital to Boston's Logan Airport. There were a number of other projects at about the same time, but this effort is considered the modern launching of the concept of telemedicine.

Telemedicine is a growing field within the profession of medicine. It has journals, such as the *Journal of Telemedicine, Telemedicine Today,* and *Telemedicine and e-Health,* has a professional association (the American Telemedicine Association, http://www.atmeda.org/), and holds an annual professional meeting.

Articles dealing with various aspects of telemedicine can be found in the journals of the various subdisciplines of medicine, and scientific research is being conducted and reported with increasing frequency in prestigious journals of the profession. Finally, federal and state governments and private organizations are funding telemedicine projects totaling tens to hundreds of millions of dollars. The communications revolution is having an impact on medicine just as it is on education, training, government, business, and law (Tulu, Chatterjee, & Maheshwari, 2007).

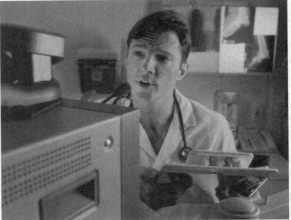

Physicians can consult with specialists using desktop video conferencing systems.

Applications

Kvedar, Menn, and Loughlin (1998) list four major applications for telemedicine: remote consultation, remote monitoring, remote education, and telementoring.

Remote consultation is the most common telemedicine application and what most refer to when they use the term *telemedicine.* This application implies one health care provider seeking the advice of a professional colleague or subspecialist to resolve a patient's problem.

Interactive telecommunications technologies expand the specialized information available to doctors.

Mobile videoconferencing systems increase access to medical information anywhere it is needed.

Remote monitoring is a long-standing application where the most common use is to access a patient's vital signs at a distance using telecommunications technologies.

Remote education is increasingly important as the geographically concentrated expertise of a medical unit is redistributed to isolated practicing professionals and professionals in training.

Telementoring involves the development of techniques to share the output of surgical tools such as endoscopes and laparoscopes with distant locations.

The Institute of Medicine (Grigsby & Sanders, 1998) organizes applications of telemedicine differently and identifies five areas of emphasis: patient care, professional education, patient education, research, and health care administration.

Impediments to Telemedicine

The Institute of Medicine identifies five concerns that prevent and slow the growth of telemedicine: professional licensure; malpractice liability; privacy, confidentiality, and security; payment policies; and regulation of medical devices.

Professional licensure issues stem from the traditional view of professional practice as involving a face-to-face encounter between clinician and patient. Telemedicine breaks the physical link and may complicate where a telemedicine practitioner should be licensed if the professional and the patient are in different states. Currently, multiple state licenses are required.

Malpractice liability is usually described as a deviation from the accepted medical standard of care. For telemedicine practitioners, the subject of malpractice presents potentially complicated legal issues, since state law generally governs liability.

Privacy, confidentiality, and security issues relate to serious questions that have been raised about current legal protections for medical privacy and confidentiality. The Hippocratic oath requires that physicians keep silent about what they learn from patients, "counting such things to be as sacred secrets." Information and telecommunications links present new opportunities for privacy infringements.

Payment policies for telemedicine are a major barrier to the growth of telemedicine. Until 1999, telemedicine did not meet the requirements of the Health Care Financing Administration (now known as the Centers for Medicare and Medicaid Services) for in-person, face-to-face contact between providers and patients. Although most medical consultations using telemedicine have been ineligible for payment in the past, guidelines for reimbursement are still evolving. Currently, Medicare covers interactive video systems (Grigsby & Sanders, 1998), and for this reason most health care organizations are using two-way videoconferencing for their initial telemedicine initiatives.

Regulation of medical devices is of concern because the federal Food and Drug Administration (FDA), through its center, regulates some of the devices used in telemedicine.

In summary, the issues that have slowed the growth of telemedicine are important and should be addressed. However, they are not necessarily unique within the medical profession. Rather, they are issues that are resolved continuously as the health care field adopts new technologies, both medical and informational.

Limited research is reported on the medical effectiveness and cost effectiveness of telemedicine. Current research seems to support the conclusion that telemedicine is effective when practiced correctly but additional evaluation and assessment activities need to be conducted (Grigsby & Sanders, 1998).

Telemedicine will continue to be a dynamic influence within the profession of medicine. The benefits of this innovation will be in two primary areas: medical benefits and cost benefits. First, telemedicine is a logical extension of the growth of the technical and technological aspects of health care. The medical benefits of an active telemedicine program are related to how professionals use the technology. A modification of a famous analogy used in educational research when applied to telemedicine summarizes the medical impact of telemedicine. Telemedicine and information technologies are *mere vehicles* that permit the delivery of health services, but they have no greater impact on health care than, as Clark said, the truck that delivers our groceries has on nutrition. It is the content of the vehicle that permits effective health care, not the vehicle itself (Clark, 1983). Second, cost effectiveness is likely to be the most significant outcome of telemedicine. The significant costs of medical care and the increased requirements for services that are projected for the next several decades forecast a cost advantage for the organizations that understand and utilize technologies effectively. Certainly, telemedicine is only one category of technology, but it may soon be the "ears and eyes" of the health care organization.

In summary, *telemedicine* is a recognized subcategory of the health services profession. As a technique and tool in the modern medical center it has the potential to expand and accelerate the services offered and the impact made. Other professions, such as law, are moving cautiously to adopt distance education concepts. Nova Southeastern University's law school was recently recognized as the "nation's most wired law school." Telecommunications technologies will have increasing impact on most fields of endeavor, not just education, as they improve and become more widely available.

Businesses, including health organizations, are using video-conferencing to replace travel.

CHARACTERISTICS OF DISTANCE EDUCATION: TWO VISIONS

Recently, a number of advances have been made in the study of learning and teaching that are providing educators with strategies for improving the educational experience. Often, these advances are considered to be in opposition to the common practices of distance education because of the misconception that teachers lecture to distant learners. This is changing dramatically, however, as distance education systems attempt to provide a learning site that is a "room with a view."

The First Scenario: Distance Education in Schools

This emerging approach relies strongly on distance education and suggests a scenario for the school and classroom of the future similar to the following scenario, which implies that classrooms of the future will be rich in technology and will continue to have teachers who are responsible for the learning events that occur:

> In every community and neighborhood there are schools surrounded by playgrounds and sports fields with trees and grass. The schools themselves look modern but very familiar. The schools are open 24 hours a day, every day, all year. Each is a part of a locally controlled and supported district that is one of several hundred that make up a technology-rich statewide educational system. Classrooms are considered rooms with a view. Every learner and teacher possess a high-powered multimedia computer that is connected to a worldwide network containing virtually unlimited educational resources. The network connects the learner to multisensory multimedia resources that are accessible from school, home, and business. Education is learner and learning centered and technology supported. Schools are small, with about 600 to 800 students, and classes never exceed 25. In the evenings the classrooms are converted to learning laboratories that are used by the entire community. Each classroom has full-motion video links to state and national networks that permit true interactive learning. Students also have desktop video access through their computers. The educational philosophy of this school is to promote authentic, student-centered learning activities that are cognitively situated whenever possible in real-world events. The school and its classrooms are a community resource. Outside of school, students continue to learn, even when on vacation. A robust network connects students to their teachers and to the resources needed for learning. Schools provide computers when students need them, and the high-speed network is a free wireless canopy that covers the community.

This scenario could be considered a dream rather than a vision. However, it is based on the following widely available and generally accepted techniques and technologies. First, instruction is learner centered. The networked computer permits the learner to access events of instruction that can be tailored to meet individual needs. Second, multimedia instruction is routine, especially when networked computer and video systems are used. Interactive instruction is possible because telecommunications technologies permit the learner to contact databases, information sources, instructional experts, and other students in real-time and interactive ways. For example, individual students can use their computers to contact other students or individuals who have information they need. Also, the entire class can participate in interactive video sessions with teachers from remote sites or with groups of students from other

Training of staff is cost effective when videoconferencing is used.

schools. Instruction is authentic because it is not teacher centered; rather it is content and learner centered.

The teacher orchestrates the individual learning activities of students who collaborate with classmates, distant learners, the teacher, and multimedia technology available locally or from the Web. Finally, the learning environment of the future encourages collaboration without the limitations inherent in the self-contained classroom.

The Second Scenario: Distance Education in the Corporation

The corporation headquarters looks like an inviting place to work. When employees report to work they find that every office has a large flat-panel display connected to a small, nearly invisible powerful computer that is connected to a high-speed local and wide area network. Also connected to the computer is a small, high-quality video camera with microphone and speakers. The office looks modern but familiar. It is one in a cluster that constitutes the on-site work sites of a team of seven professionals. At any one time only a few of the office cubicles have someone in them, but in all cases they are easily seen on the displays in the home offices of physically missing employees. The work group is continuously connected for the sharing of video, audio, and information.

The computer network is connected to online resources that permit "just-in-time" access to information and data. Members of the team effortlessly work with colleagues in

Students can easily interact with students and teachers from remote sites using videoconferencing.

VTEL Products Corporation

the work group without regard for their physical location, and other teams can be contacted with the click of a mouse button. Employees are provided with high-speed, wireless hand-held devices that keep them connected to each other and to the resources needed to conduct business.

Office cubicles are located near a conference room that contains an interactive telecommunications system that can be connected to other systems using a variety of networking protocols. This room is used for training when group interaction is important. Large, flat-panel television displays permit easy viewing and simple yet powerful cameras and microphones facilitate group interaction at a distance. The classroom is connected to a bridge that can connect dozens of sites, including the locations of those working at home or employees who are in the field.

At home, members of the team have similar configurations of technology, although the settings are much less formal and more varied. Working at home is encouraged.

The office of tomorrow will have readily accessible videoconferencing systems.

© 2007 Polycom, Inc.

Industries bring distance education technologies right to the worker on the plant floor.

Of critical importance to the work group is access to training, which is a continuous need. Learning about new products, new ideas, and new approaches is a regular requirement of the job. Training is conducted synchronously and asynchronously by trainers who are part of the corporate training team, and by outside experts who are brought in electronically when their specific skills are needed. Learning objects are used by corporate trainers to design instructional packages that are offered over the network to employees of the corporation. Training events are archived for later review.

Training is technologically based, highly visual, and available on demand. The employees of the corporation have access to trainers whenever training is needed. Trainers work in teams, and have access to a wealth of resources, including subject-matter experts from inside and outside the company. Trainers are a corporation resource who provide training at a distance to the members of the corporate community. Information and training are as important to the corporation as are products and sales.

The criminal justice system is using videoconferencing to reduce the need to travel.

Businesses will increasingly have access to seminar rooms that use videoconferencing.

Why scenarios? Much of this is possible because of the concept of distance education, which is the bringing of learners and the content of instruction together no matter where each is located. Interactive, real-time, on-demand, learner-centered, authentic, and learner-constructed events will characterize the educational environment of the future. Ultimately, the concept of distance will disappear as insignificant, and the idea of interaction will replace it.

The home office will use video-conferencing to keep employees and their colleagues connected.

SUMMARY

Separation of the student and the teacher is a fundamental characteristic of distance education. More often, educators are using technology to increase the access of the distant learner to the local classroom, to improve access of all learners to resources, and to make the experience of the remote student comparable with the experience of the local learner.

Distance education is a dramatic idea. It may change, even restructure, education, but only if it is possible to make the experience of the distant learner as complete, satisfying, and acceptable as the experience of the local learner. If distance education is to be a successful and mainstream approach, then it is imperative that distance education systems be designed to permit equivalent learning experiences for distant and local students. Distance education using telecommunications technologies is an exciting emerging field. However, practitioners should not promote this type of education as the next great technological solution to education's problems, nor make grand claims about the impact of telecommunications systems. Rather, distance education specialists should strive to understand technology and technological approaches that make the experiences of distant and local learners positive and equivalent, at least until someone's genius identifies an approach to learning using telecommunications systems to change education, just as Charles Martel's use of the stirrup changed society.

DISCUSSION QUESTIONS

1. What are Coldeway's quadrants, and which quadrant did Coldeway consider the purest form of distance education? What are the pros and cons of dividing educational events into one of Coldeway's four categories?
2. What is the fundamental characteristic of distance education? Discuss what this means. What are the various kinds of distance?
3. Learners prefer not to learn at a distance. Explain.
4. Richard Clark says media are "mere vehicles that deliver instruction but do not influence student achievement." Discuss Clark's analogy and decide if it is accurate. Are media vehicles? What does the word *mere* imply?
5. What do stirrups and distance education have in common? Discuss the concept of innovations and how they are used or not used. Has the computer changed teaching and learning?
6. Write a vision for a school 10 years from today.

REFERENCES

Allen, I., & Seaman, J. (2003). *Sizing the opportunity: The quality and extent of online education in the United States, 2002 and 2003.* Wellesley, MA: Sloan Consortium.

Allen, I., & Seaman, J. (2005). *Growing by degrees: Online education in the United States, 2005.* Wellesley, MA: Sloan Consortium.

Allen, I., & Seaman, J. (2007). *Making the grade: Online education in the United States, 2006: Midwestern edition.* Wellesley, MA: Sloan Consortium.

Allen, I., & Seaman, J. (2010). *Learning on Demand: Online education in the United States, 2009.* Wellesley, MA: Sloan Consortium.

Anglin, G., & Morrison, G. (2000). An analysis of distance education research: Implications for the field. *Quarterly Review of Distance Education, 1*(3), 189–194.

Bauck, T. (2001). Distance education in South Dakota. *Tech Trends, 23*(2), 22–25.

Berge, Z., & Clark, T. (2005). *Virtual schools: Planning for success.* New York: Teachers College Press.

Berge, Z., & Clark, T. (2009). Virtual schools: What every superintendent needs to know. *Distance Learning: For educators, trainers, and leaders, 6*(2), 1–9.

Berge, Z., & Mrozowski, S. (2001). Review of research in distance education. *The American Journal of Distance Education, 15*(3), 5–19.

Cavanaugh, C., Gillian, K., Kromey, J., Hess, J., & Blomeyer, R. (2004). *The effects of distance education on K–12 student outcomes: A meta-analysis.* Naperville, IL: Learning Point Associates.

Christensen, C. (2003). *The innovator's dilemma: The revolutionary book that will change the way you do business.* New York: HarperCollins.

Christensen, C., Anthony, S., & Roth, E. (2004). *Seeing what's next.* Cambridge, MA: Harvard Business School Press.

Clark, R. (1983). Reconsidering research on learning from media. *Review of Educational Research, 53*(4), 445–459.

Clark, R. (1994). Media will never influence learning. *Educational Technology Research and Development, 42*(2), 21–29.

Darwazeh, A. N. (2000). Variables affecting university academic achievement in a distance versus conventional education setting. *Quarterly Review of Distance Education, 1*(2), 157–167.

Day, B. (2005). Open and distance learning enhanced through ICTs: A toy for Africa's elite or an essential tool for sustainable development. In Y. Visser, L. Visser, M. Simonson, & R. Amirault (Eds.), *Trends and issues in distance education: International perspectives* (pp. 171–182). Charlotte, NC: Information Age Publishing.

Dean, P., Stah, M., Swlwester, D., & Pear, J. (2001). Effectiveness of combined delivery modalities for distance learning and resident learning. *Quarterly Review of Distance Education, 2*(3), 247–254.

Decker, B. (2008). Constructing the 39th statewide network: The story of network Nebraska. *Distance Learning: For educators, trainers, and leaders, 5*(3), 1–10.

Demiray, U. (2005). Distance education in Turkey: Experiences and issues. In Y. Visser, L. Visser, M. Simonson, & R. Amirault (Eds.), *Trends and issues in distance education: International perspectives* (pp. 163–170). Charlotte, NC: Information Age Publishing.

Ding, X. (1994). China's higher distance education—Its four systems and their structural characteristics at three levels. *Distance Education, 15*(2), 327–346.

Ding, X. (1995). From Fordism to new-Fordism: Industrialisation theory and distance education—A Chinese perspective. *Distance Education, 16*(2), 217–240.

Eastmond, D. (2007). Education without borders: The Western Governors University story. *Distance Learning: For educators, trainers, and leaders, 4*(2), 1–14.

Falduto, V., & Ihde, R. (2007). The Arkansas Virtual high school: A learning environment approach. *Distance Learning, 4*(2), 71–79.

Finn, J. (1964). The Franks had the right idea. *NEA Journal, 53*(4), 24–27.

Gao, P. E., & Zhang, R. (2009). Moving from TV broadcasting to e-learning. *Campus-wide Information Systems, 26*(2), 98–107.

Grigsby, J., & Sanders, J. (1998). Telemedicine: Where it is and where it is going. *Annals of Internal Medicine, 129*(2), 123–127.

Hanson, D., Maushak, N., Schlosser, C., Anderson, M., & Sorensen, M. (1997). *Distance education: Review of the literature* (2nd ed.). Washington, DC: Association for Educational Communications and Technology.

Holmberg, B. (1995). The evolution of the character and practice of distance education. *Open Learning, 10*(2), 47–53.

Hurd, S., & Xiao, J. (2006). Open and distance language learning at the Shantou Radio and TV University, China, and the Open University, United Kingdom: A cross-cultural perspective. *Open Learning, 21*(3), 205–219.

Johnson, K. (2007). Florida Virtual School: Growing and managing a virtual giant. *Distance Learning, 4*(1), 1–6.

Keegan, D. (1995). *Distance education technology for the new millennium: Compressed video teaching.* (ERIC Document Reproduction Service No. ED 389931).

Kvedar, J., Menn, E., & Loughlin, K. (1998). Telemedicine: Present applications and future prospects. *Urologic Clinics of North America, 25*(1), 137–149.

Macwilliams, B. (2000, September 22). Turkey's old-fashioned distance education draws the largest student body on earth. *Chronicle of Higher Education,* pp. A41–42.

Nsomwe-a-nfunkwa. (2009). Increasing the need for distance learning in the Democratic Republic of the Congo. *Distance Learning: For educators, trainers, and leaders, 6*(1), 1–6.

Picciano, A., & Seaman, J. (2007). *K–12 online learning: A survey of U.S. school district administrators.* Needham, MA: Sloan Consortium.

Russell, T. (1999). *No significant difference phenomenon.* Raleigh: North Carolina State University.

Schlosser, L., & Simonson, M. (2009). *Distance education: Definition and glossary of terms* (3rd ed.). Charlotte, NC: Information Age Publishing.

Shepard, M. (2008). A walk around Walden Pond: Reflections on the educational technology PHD specialization, Walden University. *Distance Learning: For educators, trainers, and leaders, 5*(4), 1–6.

Simonson, M. (1995). Overview of the Teacher Education Alliance, Iowa Distance Education Alliance research plan. In C. Sorensen, C. Schlosser, M. Anderson, & M. Simonson (Eds.), *Encyclopedia of distance education research in Iowa* (pp. 3–6). Ames, IA: Teacher Education Alliance.

Simonson, M. (2002). In case you are asked: Effectiveness of distance education. *Quarterly Review of Distance Education, 3*(4), vii–ix.

Simonson, M. (2003). Dan Coldeway. *Quarterly Review of Distance Education, 4*(2), vii–viii.

Simonson, M. (2004). Diploma mills and distance education. *Quarterly Review of Distance Education. 5*(3), vii–viii.

Simonson, M. (2005). South Dakota's statewide distance education project: Diffusion of an innovation. In Z. Berge & T. Clark (Eds.), *Virtual schools: Planning for success.* New York: Teachers College Press.

Simonson, M. (2009). Distance learning: Education beyond buildings. *Encyclopaedia Britannica 2009 Book of the Year,* p. 231.

Simonson, M. (2010). Distance education as a disruptive technology. *Distance Learning, 7*(1), 74–73.

Tally, D. (2009). Reaching beyond the conventional classroom: NASA's digital learning network. *Distance Learning: For educators, trainers, and leaders, 6*(4), 1–8.

Teets, J. (2002). www.**distechs**.com; http://www.distechs.com/index.php?page=disruptive-technology-defined.

Thach, L., & Murphy, L. (1994). Collaboration in distance education: From local to international perspectives. *The American Journal of Distance Education, 8*(3), 5–21.

Thornton, N. (2007). Capella University. *Distance Learning: For educators, trainers, and leaders, 4*(3), 1–8.

Tulu, B., Chatterjee, S., & Maheshwari, M. (2007). Telemedicine taxonomy. *Telemedicine and e-Health, 13*(3), 349–358.

U.S. Department of Education. (1995). *The Star Schools program.* (Available from Star Schools, U.S. Department of Education, 555 New Jersey Avenue NW, Washington, DC 20208-5644).

Visser, L., & West, P. (2005). The promise of M-learning for distance education in South Africa and other developing nations. In Y. Visser, L. Visser, M. Simonson, & R. Amirault (Eds.), *Trends and issues in distance education: International perspectives* (pp. 131–136). Charlotte, NC: Information Age Publishing.

Visser, M., Visser, J., & Buendia, M. (2005). Thank you for (not) forgetting us: A reflection on the trials, tribulations, and take-off of distance education in Mozambique. In Y. Visser, L. Visser, M. Simonson, & R. Amirault (Eds.), *Trends and issues in distance education: International perspectives* (pp. 217–244). Charlotte, NC: Information Age Publishing.

Vrasidas, C. (2008). Perspectives on e-learning: Case studies from cyprus. *Distance Learning: For Educators, Trainers and Leaders, 5*(2), 1–8.

Yan, L., & Linder, J. (2007). Faculty adoption behaviour about Web-based distance education: A case study from China Agricultural University. *British Journal of Educational Technology, 38*(1), 83–94.

Yang, F., Wang, M., Shen, R., & Han, P. (2007). Community-organizing agent: An artificial intelligent system for building learning communities among large numbers of learners. *Computers & Education, 49*(2), 131–147.

Zhang, W., Perris, K., & Yeung, L. (2005). Online tutorial support in open and distance learning: Students' perceptions. *British Journal of Educational Technology, 36*(5), 789–804.

Zhang, J. (2006). Instructors' self-perceived pedagogical principle implementation in an online environment. *The Quarterly Review of Distance Education, 7(4),* 413–426.

SUGGESTED READINGS

Hanna, D. (1995). *Mainstreaming distance education.* Conference of the National Association of State University and Land Grant Colleges, Madison, WI.

Jurasek, K. (1993). Distance education via compressed video. Unpublished master's thesis, Iowa State University, Ames.

Kozma, R. (1994). Will media influence learning: Reframing the debate. *Educational Technology Research and Development, 42*(2), 7–19.

Schlosser, C., & Anderson, M. (1994). *Distance education: Review of the literature.* Washington, DC: Association for Educational Communications and Technology.

Simonson, M. (1996). Reinventing distance education. Paper presented at the 1996 Annual Convention of the U.S. Distance Learning Association, Washington, DC.

Simonson, M. (2008). Virtual schools mandated. *Distance Learning, 5*(4), 84–83.

Simonson, M., & Schlosser, C. (1995). More than fiber: Distance education in Iowa. *Tech Trends, 40*(3), 13–15.

CHAPTER 2

Definitions, History, and Theories of Distance Education

CHAPTER GOAL

The purpose of this chapter is to review the definitions, history, and theories of distance education.

CHAPTER OBJECTIVES

After reading and reviewing this chapter, you should be able to

1. Discuss the reason for different definitions of distance education.
2. Describe the various definitions of distance education that have been offered.
3. List and explain the five main elements of the various definitions of distance education given by Keegan.
4. Give the emerging definition of distance education that is appropriate for the United States.
5. Outline the general history of distance education, explaining how it began with correspondence study and evolved into the use of electronic communications media.
6. Discuss the emergence of distance teaching universities.
7. Explain the various theoretical approaches to distance education, including theories of independence, industrialization, and interaction and communication.
8. Synthesize the various theories of distance education.
9. Describe the emerging theory of distance education that relates to equivalence of learning experiences.
10. Explain Fordism, neo-Fordism, and post-Fordism.

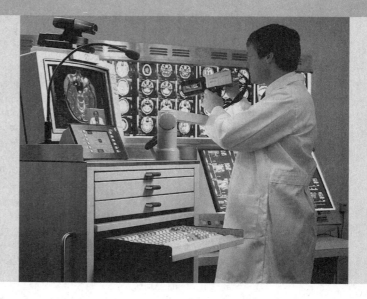

DEFINING DISTANCE EDUCATION

Distance education was defined in Chapter 1 as institution-based, formal education where the learning group is separated, and where interactive telecommunications systems are used to connect learners, resources, and instructors . This definition has gained wide acceptance. The Association for Educational Communications and Technology has published a monograph that explains this definition (Schlosser & Simonson, 2009), and in the *2009 Encyclopaedia Britannica Book of the Year*, distance education/learning is explained and defined on page 231.

> Four characteristics distinguished distance education. First, distance education was by definition carried out through institutions; it was not self-study or a nonacademic learning

environment. The institutions might or might not offer traditional classroom-based instruction as well, but they were eligible for accreditation by the same agencies as those employing traditional methods.

Second, geographic separation was inherent in distance learning, and time might also separate students and teachers. Accessibility and convenience were important advantages of this mode of education. Well-designed programs could also bridge intellectual, cultural, and social differences between students.

Third, interactive telecommunications connected the learning group with each other and with the teacher. Most often, electronic communications, such as e-mail, were used, but traditional forms of communication, such as the postal system, might also play a role. Whatever the medium, interaction was essential to distance education, as it was to any education. The connections of learners, teachers, and instructional resources became less dependent on physical proximity as communications systems became more sophisticated and widely available; consequently, the Internet, cell phones, and e-mail had contributed to the rapid growth in distance education.

Finally, distance education, like any education, established a learning group, sometimes called a learning community, which was composed of students, a teacher, and instructional resources—i.e., the books, sound, video, and graphic displays that allowed the student to access the content of instruction.

Four main components comprise this definition (Figure 2–1). First is the concept that distance education is *institutionally based.* This is what differentiates distance education from self-study. Whereas the institution referred to in this definition could be a traditional educational school or college, nontraditional institutions that offer education to students at a distance are increasingly emerging. Businesses, companies, and corporations are offering instruction at a distance. Many educators and trainers are advocating the accreditation of institutions that offer distance education to add credibility, improve quality, and eliminate diploma mills.

FIGURE 2–1   There are four components to the definition of distance education.

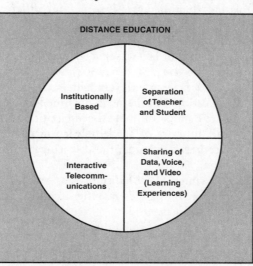

The second component of the definition of distance education is the concept of *separation of the teacher and student.* Most often, separation is thought of in geographic terms—teachers are in one location and students are in another. Also implied by the definition is the separation of teachers and students in time. *Asynchronous distance education* means that instruction is offered and students access it at separate times, or anytime it is convenient to them. Finally, intellectual separation of teachers and learners is important. Obviously, teachers have an understanding of the concepts presented in a course that students do not possess. In this case, the reduction of separation is a goal of the distance education system.

Interactive telecommunications is the third component of the definition of distance education. Interaction can be synchronous or asynchronous—at the same time, or at different times. Interaction is critical, but not at the expense of content. In other words, it is important that learners be able to interact with each other, with resources of instruction, and with their teacher. However, interaction should not be the primary characteristic of instruction but should be available, commonplace, and relevant.

The phrase *telecommunications systems* implies electronic media, such as television, telephone, and the Internet, but this term need not be limited to only electronic media. *Telecommunications* is defined as communicating at a distance. This definition includes communication with the postal system, as in correspondence study, and other nonelectronic methods for communication. Obviously, as electronic telecommunications systems improve and become more pervasive, they likely will be the mainstay of modern distance education systems. However, older, less sophisticated systems of telecommunication will continue to be important.

Finally, we examine the concept of *connecting learners, resources, and instructors.* This means that there are instructors who interact with learners and that resources are available that permit learning to occur. Resources should be subjected to instructional design procedures that organize them into learning experiences that promote learning, including resources that can be observed, felt, heard, or completed.

The definition of distance education includes these four components. If one or more are missing, then the event is something different, if only slightly, than distance education.

This definition is not the only one and certainly is not the first offered for distance education. As a matter of fact, distance education has been defined from a number of perspectives over the years. Moore (2007) writes that distance education originated in Germany and the University of Tubingen and Rudolf Manfred Delling (1985) stated that distance education, in general, is a planned and systematic activity that comprises the choice, didactic preparation, and presentation of teaching materials as well as the supervision and support of student learning, which is achieved by bridging the physical distance between student and teacher by means of at least one appropriate technical medium.

For Hilary Perraton (1988), distance education is an educational process in which a significant proportion of the teaching is conducted by someone removed in space and/or time from the learner.

The U.S. Department of Education's Office of Educational Research and Improvement defines distance education as "the application of telecommunications and electronic devices which enable students and learners to receive instruction that originates from some distant location" (2006). Typically, the learner may interact with the instructor or program directly, and may meet with the instructor on a periodic basis.

Grenville Rumble (1989) also offered a definition of distance education. He noted that, in any distance education process, there must be a teacher; one or more students; a course or curriculum that the teacher is capable of teaching and the student is trying to learn; and a contract, implicit or explicit, between the student and the teacher or the institution employing the teacher that acknowledges their respective teaching/learning roles.

- Distance education is a method of education in which the learner is physically separate from the teacher. It may be used on its own, or in conjunction with other forms of education, including face-to-face. In distance education, learners are physically separated from the institution that sponsors the instruction.
- The teaching/learning contract requires that the student be taught, assessed, given guidance, and, where appropriate, prepared for examinations that may or may not be conducted by the institution. This must be accomplished by two-way communication. Learning may be undertaken individually or in groups; in either case, it is accomplished in the physical absence of the teacher.

For Desmond Keegan (1996), the following four definitions were central to an attempt to identify the elements of a single, unifying definition of distance education:

- The French government, as part of a law passed in 1971, defined distance education as education that either does not imply the physical presence of the teacher appointed to dispense it in the place where it is received or in which the teacher is present only on occasion or for selected tasks.
- According to Börje Holmberg (1985), distance education covers the various forms of study at all levels that are not under the continuous, immediate supervision of tutors present with their students in lecture rooms or on the same premises but which, nevertheless, benefit from the planning, guidance, and teaching of a supporting organization.
- Otto Peters (1988) emphasized the role of technology, saying that distance teaching/education (*Fernunterricht*) is a method of imparting knowledge, skills, and attitudes. It is rationalized by the application of division of labor and organizational principles as well as by the extensive use of technical media, especially for the purpose of reproducing high-quality teaching material, which makes it possible to instruct great numbers of students at the same time wherever they live. It is an industrialized form of teaching and learning.
- For Michael Moore (2007), the related concept of distance teaching was defined as the family of instructional methods in which the teaching behaviors are executed apart from the learning behaviors, including those that in a contiguous situation would be performed in the learner's presence, so that communication between the teacher and the learner must be facilitated by print, electronic, mechanical, or other devices.

Keegan identified five main elements of these definitions and used them to compose a comprehensive definition of distance education.

1. The quasi-permanent separation of teacher and learner throughout the length of the learning process (this distinguishes it from conventional, face-to-face education).
2. The influence of an educational organization both in the planning and preparation of learning materials and in the provision of student support services (this distinguishes it from private study and teach-yourself programs).
3. The use of technical media—print, audio, video, or computer—to unite teacher and learner and carry the content of the course.
4. The provision of two-way communication so that the student may benefit from or even initiate dialogue (this distinguishes it from other uses of technology in education).
5. The quasi-permanent absence of the learning group throughout the length of the learning process so that people are usually taught as individuals and not in groups, with the possibility of occasional meetings for both didactic and socialization purposes.

Garrison and Shale (1987) argued that, in light of advances in distance education delivery technologies, Keegan's definition was too narrow and did not correspond to the existing reality and future possibilities. Although declining to offer a definition of distance education, Garrison and Shale offered the following three criteria they regarded as essential for characterizing the distance education process:

1. Distance education implies that the majority of educational communication between (among) teacher and student(s) occurs noncontiguously.
2. Distance education must involve two-way communication between (among) teacher and student(s) for the purpose of facilitating and supporting the educational process.
3. Distance education uses technology to mediate the necessary two-way communication.

Keegan's definition and the definitions preceding it define the traditional view of distance education. Rapid changes in society and technology are challenging these traditional definitions.

EMERGING DEFINITIONS

The contemporary period is often characterized as one of unpredictable change. Globalization, brought on by supersonic air travel, satellite television, computer communications, and societal changes, has inspired new ways of looking at distance education. Edwards (1995) uses the term *open learning* to describe a new way of looking at education in a quickly changing and diverse world. He indicates that distance education and open learning are two distinct approaches to education. Although he does not define the two, he states that distance education provides distance learning opportunities using mass-produced courseware to a mass market. In contrast, open learning places greater emphasis on the current specific needs and/or markets available by recognizing local requirements and differences instead of delivering an established curriculum. Open learning shifts from mass production and mass consumption to a focus on local and individual needs and requirements. Edwards states that this can occur outside of the traditional organization of education. This is a major difference between his description of open learning and the previous definitions of distance education.

More recently, the idea of the "virtual school" has become popular and is often used when referring to distance education in schools. *Virtual* is defined as something quasi, or pseudo. Virtual is often a potential state that at some time might become "actual." And, just to add to the confusion, *actual* is generally considered to be the opposite of *virtual*. So, it must be that a virtual school would be a potential sschool as compared to an actual school.

Increasingly, the popular press and the educational literature talk about distance education—teaching and learning at a distance—as virtual education that happens in a virtual school. Most definitions of distance education do not imply anything virtual or potential, or pseudo. Rather, distance education is about as real and actual as education can be. Some are advocating for the field of distance education to find better words than *virtual* to describe the process of educating using technology without the need for the instructor and the learner to be in the same location, or for them to be communicating at the same time. The Florida Virtual School has the phrase "Any time, any place, any path, any pace" to indicate its approach to teaching and learning. It is a real school—an institution where learning occurs because of the efforts of teachers. The phrase *virtual school* tends to be used most often in K–12 education (Simonson, 2007b).

A BRIEF HISTORY OF DISTANCE EDUCATION

Distance education seems to be a new idea to most educators of today. However, the concepts that form the basis of this type of education are more than a century old. Certainly, distance education has experienced growth and change recently, but the long traditions of the field continue to give it direction for the future. This section offers a brief history of distance education, from correspondence study, to electronic communications, to distance teaching universities.

Correspondence Study

The roots of distance education are at least 160 years old. An advertisement in a Swedish newspaper in 1833 touted the opportunity to study "composition through the medium of the post." In 1840, England's newly established penny post allowed Isaac Pitman to offer shorthand instruction via correspondence. Three years later, instruction was formalized with the founding of the Phonographic Correspondence Society, precursor of Sir Isaac Pitman's Correspondence Colleges. Distance education, in the form of correspondence study, was established in Germany by Charles Toussaint and Gustav Langenscheidt, who taught language in Berlin. Correspondence study crossed the Atlantic in 1873 when Anna Eliot Ticknor founded a Boston-based society to encourage study at home. The Society to Encourage Studies at Home attracted more than 10,000 students in 24 years. Students of the classical curriculum (mostly women) corresponded monthly with teachers, who offered guided readings and frequent tests.

From 1883 to 1891, academic degrees were authorized by the state of New York through the Chautauqua College of Liberal Arts to students who completed the required summer institutes and correspondence courses. William Rainey Harper, the Yale professor who headed the program, was effusive in his support of correspondence study, and confident in the future viability of the new educational form: The student who has prepared a certain number of lessons in the correspondence school knows more of the subject treated in those lessons, and knows it better, than the student who has covered the same ground in the classroom.

The day is coming when the work done by correspondence will be greater in amount than that done in the classrooms of our academies and colleges; when the students who shall recite by correspondence will far outnumber those who make oral recitations.

In 1891, Thomas J. Foster, editor of the *Mining Herald,* a daily newspaper in eastern Pennsylvania, began offering a correspondence course in mining and the prevention of mine accidents. His business developed into the International Correspondence Schools, a commercial school whose enrollment exploded in the first two decades of the twentieth century, from 225,000 in 1900 to more than 2 million in 1920. In 1886, H. S. Hermod of Sweden, began teaching English by correspondence. In 1898, he founded Hermod's, which would become one of the world's largest and most influential distance teaching organizations.

Correspondence study continued to develop in Britain with the founding of a number of correspondence institutions, such as Skerry's College in Edinburgh in 1878 and University Correspondence College in London in 1887. At the same time, the university extension movement in the United States and England promoted the correspondence method. Among the pioneers in the field were Illinois Wesleyan in 1877 and the University Extension Department of the University of Chicago in 1892. Illinois Wesleyan offered bachelor's, master's, and doctoral degrees as part of a program modeled on the Oxford, Cambridge, and London model. Between 1881 and 1890, 750 students were enrolled; and in 1900, nearly 500 students were seeking degrees. However, concerns about the quality of the program prompted a recommendation that it be terminated by 1906.

Correspondence study was integral to the University of Chicago. The school, founded in 1890, created a university extension as one of its five divisions, the first such division in an American university. The extension division was divided into five departments: lecture study, class study, correspondence teaching, library, and training.

The correspondence study department of the University of Chicago was successful, at least in terms of numbers. Each year, 125 instructors taught 3,000 students enrolled in 350 courses. Nevertheless, enthusiasm within the university for the program waned, partly for financial reasons.

At the University of Wisconsin, the development of the "short course" and farmers' institutes in 1885 formed the foundation for university extension. Six years later, the university announced a program of correspondence study led by eminent historian Frederick Jackson Turner. However, as at the University of Chicago, faculty interest waned. Further, public response was minimal, and the correspondence study program was discontinued in 1899. Correspondence study would have to wait another seven years to be reborn under a new, stronger correspondence study department within the school's university extension division.

Moody Bible Institute, founded in 1886, formed a correspondence department in 1901 that continues today, with a record of over 1 million enrollments from all over the world. Correspondence study/distance education has had a significant impact on religious education that emphasizes the social context within which a student lives.

Distance education began to enrich the secondary school curriculum in the 1920s. Students in Benton Harbor, Michigan, were offered vocational courses in 1923, and six years later, the University of Nebraska began experimenting with correspondence courses in high schools.

In France, the Ministry of Education set up a government correspondence college in response to the impending World War II. Although the Centre National d'Enseignement par Correspondences was established for the education of children, it has since become a huge distance teaching organization for adult education.

The original target groups of distance education efforts were adults with occupational, social, and family commitments. This remains the primary target group today. Distance education provides the opportunity to widen intellectual horizons, as well as the chance to improve and update professional knowledge. Further, it stresses individuality of learning and flexibility in both the time and place of study.

Two philosophies of distance education became identifiable. The full liberalism of programs offered by Hermod's, in Sweden, emphasized the free pacing of progress through the program by the student. Other programs, such as those offered by the University of Chicago, offered a more rigid schedule of weekly lessons.

Electronic Communications

Europe experienced a steady expansion of distance education, without radical changes in structure, but with gradually more sophisticated methods and media employed. Audio recordings were used in instruction for the blind and in language teaching for all students. Laboratory kits were used in such subjects as electronics and radio engineering. Virtually all large-scale distance teaching organizations were private correspondence schools.

In the United States, advances in electronic communications technology helped determine the dominant medium of distance education. In the 1920s, at least 176 radio stations were constructed at educational institutions, although most were gone by the end of the decade. The surviving stations were mostly at land-grant colleges.

In the early 1930s, experimental television teaching programs were produced at the University of Iowa, Purdue University, and Kansas State College. However, it was not until the 1950s that college credit courses were offered via broadcast television: Western Reserve University was the first to offer a continuous series of such courses, beginning in 1951. Sunrise Semester was a well-known televised series of college courses offered by New York University on CBS from 1957 to 1982.

Satellite technology, developed in the 1960s and made cost effective in the 1980s, enabled the rapid spread of instructional television. Federally funded experiments in the United States and Canada, such as the Appalachian Education Satellite Project

(1974–1975), demonstrated the feasibility of satellite-delivered instruction. However, these early experiments were loudly criticized for being poorly planned. More recent attempts at satellite-delivered distance education have been more successful. The first state educational satellite system, Learn/Alaska, was created in 1980. It offered six hours of instructional television daily to 100 villages, some of them accessible only by air. The privately operated TI-IN Network, of San Antonio, Texas, has delivered a wide variety of courses via satellite to high schools across the United States since 1985.

In the late 1980s and early 1990s, the development of fiber-optic communication systems allowed for the expansion of live, two-way, high-quality audio and video systems in education. Whereas the initial cost of fiber-optic systems may be high, the long-term savings and benefits of the technology outweigh the initial costs. Many now consider fiber-optic delivery systems as the least expensive option for the high-quality, two-way audio and video required for live two-way interactive distance education. Iowa has the largest statewide fiber-optic system. Currently the Iowa Communications Network (ICN) provides full-motion, two-way interactive video, data (Internet), and voice services to over 600 Iowa classrooms. In the near future, all school districts, area education agencies, and public libraries in Iowa will have classrooms connected to the fiber-optics of the ICN. The ICN also serves as the backbone for computer telecommunications, and asynchronous, Internet-based programs are being offered to distant learners. Over 100,000 hours of formal educational opportunities were offered during the first 18 months of the network's service. Recently, 100,000 hours were being offered every month.

Distance education opportunities are quickly growing through the use of computer-mediated communications and the Internet. Both credit and noncredit courses have been offered over the Internet since the mid-1980s. In most cases, a teacher organizes the course materials, readings, and assignments. The students read the material, complete assignments, and participate in online discussions with other classmates. The advent of computer conferencing capabilities has had an impact on the traditional approach to the design of distance education instruction. Computer conferencing increases the potential for interaction and collaborative work among the students. This type of collaboration among students was difficult with previous forms of distance education.

In addition, computer networks are a convenient way to distribute course materials to students around the world. Many faculty members now use the convenient user interface of the Web to make course materials available to their students. The British Open University, Fern Universität in Germany, and the University of Twente in the Netherlands are some of the leading providers of online courses in Europe. In the United States, the American Open University, Nova Southeastern University, and the University of Phoenix have been traditional leaders in providing distance education. They, along with many other universities, now offer hundreds of courses online.

Distance Teaching Universities

The 1962 decision that the University of South Africa would become a distance teaching university brought about a fundamental change in the way distance education was practiced in much of the world. Another landmark was the founding, in 1971, of the

Open University of the United Kingdom, a degree-giving distance teaching university offering full degree programs, sophisticated courses, and the innovative use of media (Holmberg, 1986). The Open University brought heightened prestige to distance education and spurred the establishment of similar institutions in industrial nations such as West Germany, Japan, and Canada, as well as in such lesser-developed nations as Sri Lanka and Pakistan.

Although the distance teaching universities shared numerous similarities, they were not identical in their mission or practice. Two of the largest and most influential, the Open University of the United Kingdom and the German Fern Universität, differ widely. The British school favors employed, part-time students of above-normal study age, and allows them to enroll without formal entrance qualifications.

The German Fern Universität, founded in 1975, offers a more rigorous program than its British counterpart. Despite strict, formal entrance requirements, it had 28,000 students in 1985. However, the dropout rate is very high, and in its first decade, only 500 students completed the full curricula for a university degree.

Holmberg (1986) offers numerous political, economic, and educational reasons for the founding of distance teaching universities, including:

- The need felt in many countries to increase the offerings of university education generally
- A realization that adults with jobs, family responsibilities, and social commitments form a large group of prospective part-time university students
- A wish to serve both individuals and society by offering study opportunities to adults, among them disadvantaged groups
- The need found in many professions for further training at an advanced level
- A wish to support educational innovation
- A belief in the feasibility of an economical use of educational resources by mediated teaching

THEORY AND DISTANCE EDUCATION

Most students, and many teachers, cringe at the thought of a discussion of theory. This need not be the case. This section is designed not to intimidate or to bore, but to inform. Theory is important to the study of distance education because it directly impacts the practice of the field.

Traditionally, theories of distance education have come from sources external to North America. Recently, the field in the United States has matured to the point where indigenous definitions and theories have begun to emerge.

The Need for Theory

Although forms of distance education have existed since the 1840s and attempts at theoretical explanations of distance education had been undertaken by leading scholars in the field, the need for a theory base of distance education was still largely unfulfilled in the 1970s. Holmberg (1985) stated that further theoretical considerations would contribute results that would give distance educators a firmly based theory, a touchstone against which decisions could be made with confidence. In 1986, Holmberg continued to recognize the need for theoretical considerations:

> One consequence of such understanding and explanation will be that hypotheses can be developed and submitted to falsification attempts. This will lead to insights telling us what in distance education is to be expected under what conditions and circumstances, thus paving the way for corroborated practical methodological application. (p. 3)

Moore (1994) was concerned that the progress of distance education would be hindered by the lack of attention to what he called the "macro factors." He indicated that in this area of education there was a need to describe and define the field, to discriminate between the various components of the field, and to identify the critical elements of the various forms of learning and teaching.

Keegan (1988) implied the continued need for a theory of distance education when he lamented the lack of it:

> Lack of accepted theory has weakened distance education: there has been a lack of identity, a sense of belonging to the periphery and the lack of a touchstone against which decisions on methods, on media, on financing, on student support, when they have to be made, can be made with confidence. (p. 63)

Keegan (1988) stated his ideas about what the theory should encompass. According to Keegan, a firmly based theory of distance education will be one that can provide the touchstone against which decisions—political, financial, educational, social—when they have to be made can be made with confidence. This would replace the ad hoc response to a set of conditions that arises in some "crisis" situation of problem solving, which normally characterizes this field of education.

In a general sense, *theory* is taken to mean a set of hypotheses logically related to one another in explaining and predicting occurrences. Holmberg (1985) stated the following:

> . . . the aim of the theoretician is to find explanatory theories; that is to say, the theories that describe certain structural properties of the world, and which permit us to deduce, with the help of initial conditions, the effects to be explained. . . . Theoretical, to bring explanation, on the other hand practical, to provide for application or technology. (p. 5)

Keegan (1995) added:

> A theory is something that eventually can be reduced to a phrase, a sentence or a paragraph and which, while subsuming all the practical research, gives the foundation on which the structures of need, purpose and administration can be erected. (p. 20)

In 1995 Holmberg gave a more specific definition of the concept of theory. He stated that a theory means:

> a systematic ordering of ideas about the phenomenon of our field of inquiry and an overarching logical structure of reasoned suppositions which can generate intersubjectively testable hypotheses. (p. 4)

Holmberg (1995) further suggested that distance education has been characterized by a trial-and-error approach with little consideration being given to a theoretical basis for decision making. He suggested that the theoretical underpinnings of distance education are fragile. Most efforts in this field have been practical or mechanical and have concentrated on the logistics of the enterprise.

To some, distance education represents a deviation from conventional education. Holmberg claimed it was a distinct form of education. Keegan (1996) also concluded that distance education is a distinct field of education, parallel to and a complement of conventional education. Shale (1988) countered that all of what constitutes the process of education when teacher and student are able to meet face-to-face also constitutes the process of education when the teacher and student are physically separated.

Cropley and Kahl (1983) compared and contrasted distance education and face-to-face education in terms of psychological dimensions, and claimed neither set of principles emerged in a pure form. Peters (1988) strongly stated:

> Anyone professionally involved in education is compelled to presume the existence of two forms of instruction which are strictly separable: traditional face-to-face teaching based on interpersonal communication and industrialized teaching, which is based on objectivized, rationalized technologically-produced interaction. (p. 20)

In his landmark work *The Foundations of Distance Education*, Keegan (1996) classified theories of distance education into three groups:

■ Theories of independence and autonomy
■ Theories of industrialization of teaching
■ Theories of interaction and communication

A fourth category seeks to explain distance education in a synthesis of existing theories of communication and diffusion, as well as philosophies of education.

Theory of Independent Study — Charles Wedemeyer

For Wedemeyer (1981), the essence of distance education was the independence of the student. This was reflected in his preference for the term *independent study* for distance education at the college or university level. Wedemeyer was critical of contemporary patterns of higher education. He believed that outdated concepts of learning and teaching were being employed, and that they failed to utilize modern technologies in ways that could alter the institution.

Wedemeyer set forth a system with 10 characteristics emphasizing learner independence and adoption of technology as a way to implement that independence. According to Wedemeyer (1981), the system should do the following:

1. Be capable of operation anyplace where there are students—or even only one student—whether or not there are teachers at the same place at the same time
2. Place greater responsibility for learning on the student
3. Free faculty members from custodial-type duties so that more time can be given to truly educational tasks
4. Offer students and adults wider choices (more opportunities) in courses, formats, and methodologies

5. Use, as appropriate, all the teaching media and methods that have been proven effective
6. Mix media and methods so that each subject or unit within a subject is taught in the best way known
7. Cause the redesign and development of courses to fit into an "articulated media program"
8. Preserve and enhance opportunities for adaptation to individual differences
9. Evaluate student achievement simply, not by raising barriers concerned with the place, rate, method, or sequence of student study
10. Permit students to start, stop, and learn at their own pace

Wedemeyer proposed separating teaching from learning as a way of breaking education's "space-time barriers." He suggested six characteristics of independent study systems:

1. The student and teacher are separated.
2. The normal processes of teaching and learning are carried out in writing or through some other medium.
3. Teaching is individualized.
4. Learning takes place through the student's activity.
5. Learning is made convenient for the student in his or her own environment.
6. The learner takes responsibility for the pace of his or her own progress, with freedom to start and stop at any time.

Wedemeyer noted four elements of every teaching/learning situation: a teacher, a learner or learners, a communications system or mode, and something to be taught or learned. He proposed a reorganization of these elements that would accommodate physical space and allow greater learner freedom. Key to the success of distance education, Wedemeyer believed, was the development of the relationship between student and teacher.

Theory of Independent Study and Theory of Transactional Distance—Michael Moore

Formulated in the early 1970s, Moore's theory of distance education, which he calls *independent study,* is a classification method for distance education programs. Shaped in part by Moore's adult education and university extension experience, it examines two variables in educational programs: the amount of learner autonomy and the distance between teacher and learner. *Transactional distance* "connote[s] the interplay among the environment, the individuals and the patterns of behaviors in a situation" (Moore, 2007, p. 91). Moore states that the theory of transactional distance is a "typology of all education programs having this distinguishing characteristic of separation of teacher and learner" (p. 91). He also believes that transactional distance is relative rather than absolute, and describes the fullest range of all possible degrees of structure, dialogue, and autonomy in environments that have the special characteristic of teacher and student being spatially separate from one another (Moore, 2007).

For Moore, distance education is composed of two elements, each of which can be measured. First is the provision for two-way communication (dialog). Some systems or programs offer greater amounts of two-way communication than others. Second is the extent to which a program is responsive to the needs of the individual learner (structure). Some programs are very structured, while others are very responsive to the needs and goals of the individual student.

In the second part of Moore's (2007) theory of transactional distance, he addresses learner autonomy. He notes that in traditional school settings, learners are very dependent on teachers for guidance, and that in most programs, conventional and distance, the teacher is active whereas the student is passive. In distance education, there is a gap between teacher and student, so the student must accept a high degree of responsibility for the conduct of the learning program. The autonomous learner needs little help from the teacher, who may be more of a respondent than a director. Some adult learners, however, require help in formulating their learning objectives, identifying sources of information, and measuring objectives.

Moore (2007) classifies distance education programs as *autonomous* (learner determined) or *nonautonomous* (teacher determined), and gauges the degree of autonomy accorded the learner by answers to the following three questions:

1. Is the selection of learning objectives in the program the responsibility of the learner or of the teacher? (autonomy in setting of objectives)
2. Is the selection and use of resource persons, of bodies and other media, the decision of the teacher or the learner? (autonomy in methods of study)
3. Are the decisions about the method of evaluation and criteria to be used made by the learner or the teacher? (autonomy in evaluation)

Theory of Industrialization of Teaching—Otto Peters

In a major treatise on education, Otto Peters of Germany developed a view of distance education as an industrialized form of teaching and learning. He examined a research base that included an extensive analysis of the distance teaching organizations of the 1960s. This led him to propose that distance education could be analyzed by comparing it with the industrial production of goods. He stated that from many points of view, conventional, oral, group-based education was a preindustrial form of education. His statement implied that distance teaching could not have existed before the industrial era. Using economic and industrial theory, Peters (1988) proposed the following new categories (terminology) for the analysis of distance education:

■ **Rationalization.** The use of methodical measures to reduce the required amount of input of power, time, and money. In distance education, ways of thinking, attitudes, and procedures can be found that only established themselves in the wake of an increased rationalization in the industrialization of production processes.
■ **Division of labor.** The division of a task into simpler components or subtasks. In distance education, the tasks of conveying information, counseling, assessment, and recording performance are performed by separate individuals.

To Peters, the division of labor is the main prerequisite for the advantages of distance education to become effective.

- **Mechanization.**   The use of machines in a work process. Distance education, Peters noted, would be impossible without machines. Duplicating machines and transport systems are prerequisites, and later forms of distance teaching have the additional facilities of modern means of communication and electronic data processing installations.
- **Assembly line.**   Commonly, a method of work in which workers remain stationary, while objects they are working on move past them. In traditional distance education programs, materials for both teacher and student are not the product of an individual. Rather, instructional materials are designed, printed, stored, distributed, and graded by specialists.
- **Mass production.**   The production of goods in large quantities. Peters noted that because demand outstrips supply at colleges and universities, there has been a trend toward large-scale operations not entirely consistent with traditional forms of academic teaching. Mass production of distance education courses, however, can enhance quality. Peters believed that the large number of courses produced forced distance teaching organizations to analyze the requirements of potential distance learners far more carefully than in conventional teaching and to improve the quality of the courses.
- **Preparatory work.**   Determining how workers, machines, and materials can usefully relate to each other during each phase of the production process. Peters believed that the success of distance education depended decisively on a preparatory phase. The preparatory phase concerns the development of the distance study course involving experts in the various specialist fields whose qualifications are often higher than those of other teachers involved in distance study.
- **Planning.**   The system of decisions that determines an operation prior to it being carried out. Peters noted that planning was important in the development phase of distance education, as the contents of correspondence units, from the first to the last, must be determined in detail, adjusted in relation to each other, and represented in a predetermined number of correspondence units. The importance of planning is even greater when residential study is a component of a distance education program.
- **Organization.**   Creating general or permanent arrangements for purpose-oriented activity. Peters noted the relationship between rational organization and effectiveness of the teaching method. Organization makes it possible for students to receive exactly predetermined documents at appointed times, for an appropriate university teacher to be immediately available for each assignment sent in, and for consultations to take place at fixed locations at fixed times. Organization, Peters pointed out, was optimized in large distance education programs.
- **Scientific control methods.**   The methods by which work processes are analyzed systematically, particularly by time studies, and in accordance with the results obtained from measurements and empirical data. The work processes are tested and controlled in their elementary details in a planned way, in order to increase productivity, all the time making the best possible use of working time

and the staff available. In distance education, some institutions hire experts to apply techniques of scientific analysis to the evaluation of courses.

■ **Formalization.**   The predetermination of the phases of the manufacturing process. In distance education, all the points in the cycle, from student, to distance teaching establishment, to the academics allocated, must be determined exactly.

■ **Standardization.**   The limitations of manufacture to a restricted number of types of one product, in order to make them more suitable for their purpose, cheaper to produce, and easier to replace. In distance education, not only is the format of correspondence units standardized, so are the stationery for written communication between student and lecturer, the organizational support, and the academic content.

■ **Change of function.**   The change of the role or job of the worker in the production process. In distance education, change of function is evident in the role of the lecturer. The original role of provider of knowledge in the form of the lecturer is split into that of study unit author and that of marker; the role of counselor is allocated to a particular person or position. Frequently, the original role of lecturer is reduced to that of consultant whose involvement in distance teaching manifests itself in periodically recurrent contributions.

■ **Objectification.**   The loss, in the production process, of the subjective element that was used to determine work to a considerable degree. In distance education, most teaching functions are objectified as they are determined by the distance study course as well as technical means. Only in written communication with the distance learner, or possibly in a consultation or the brief additional face-to-face events on campus, does the teacher have some individual scope left for subjectively determined variants in teaching method.

■ **Concentration and centralization.**   Economies of scale and better returns on investment are possible when distance education is centralized and little competition is allowed. Because of the large amounts of capital required for mass production and the division of labor, there has been a trend toward large industrial concerns with a concentration of capital, a centralized administration, and a market that is monopolized. Peters noted the trend toward distance education institutions serving very large numbers of students. The Open University of the United Kingdom, for instance, recently had an enrollment of more than 70,000 students. It is more economical to establish a small number of such institutions serving a national population, rather than a larger number of institutions serving regional populations.

Peters (1988) concluded that for distance teaching to become effective, the principle of the division of labor is a constituent element of distance teaching. The teaching process in his theory of industrialization is gradually restructured through increasing mechanization and automation. He noted that:

■ The development of distance study courses is just as important as the preparatory work—taking place prior to the production process.
■ The effectiveness of the teaching process particularly depends on planning and organization.
■ Courses must be formalized and expectations of students must be standardized.

- The teaching process is largely objectified.
- The function of academics teaching at a distance has changed considerably vis-à-vis university teachers in conventional teaching.
- Distance study can only be economical with a concentration of the available resources and a centralized administration.

According to Peters (1988), within the complex overall distance teaching activity, one area has been exposed to investigation that had been regularly omitted from traditional analysis. New concepts were used to describe new facts that merit attention. He did not deny that a theory of the industrialization of teaching had disadvantages, but in any exploration of teaching, the industrial structures characteristic of distance teaching need to be taken into account in decision making.

Theory of Interaction and Communication— Börje Holmberg

Holmberg's theory of distance education, what he calls *guided didactic conversation*, falls into the general category of communication theory. Holmberg (1985) noted that his theory had explanatory value in relating teaching effectiveness to the impact of feelings of belonging and cooperation as well as to the actual exchange of questions, answers, and arguments in mediated communication. Holmberg offers seven background assumptions for his theory:

1. The core of teaching is interaction between the teaching and learning parties; it is assumed that simulated interaction through subject-matter presentation in preproduced courses can take over part of the interaction by causing students to consider different views, approaches, and solutions and generally interact with a course.
2. Emotional involvement in the study and feelings of personal relation between the teaching and learning parties are likely to contribute to learning pleasure.
3. Learning pleasure supports student motivation.
4. Participation in decision making concerning the study is favorable to student motivation.
5. Strong student motivation facilitates learning.
6. A friendly, personal tone and easy access to the subject matter contribute to learning pleasure, support student motivation, and thus facilitate learning from the presentations of preproduced courses (i.e., from teaching in the form of one-way traffic simulating interaction, as well as from didactic communication in the form of two-way traffic between the teaching and learning parties).
7. The effectiveness of teaching is demonstrated by students' learning of what has been taught.

These assumptions, Holmberg (1986) believes, are the basis of the essential teaching principles of distance education. From these assumptions he formed his theory that distance teaching will support student motivation, promote learning pleasure, and make the study relevant to the individual learner and his or her needs, by creating feelings of rapport between the learner and the distance education institution (its tutors, counselors, etc.); facilitating access to course content; engaging the learner in activities, discussions, and decisions; and generally catering to helpful real and simulated communication to and from the learner.

Holmberg notes that this is admittedly a leaky theory. However, he adds, it is not devoid of explanatory power—it does, in fact, indicate essential characteristics of effective distance education.

In 1995, Holmberg significantly broadened his theory of distance education. His new comprehensive theory of distance education is divided into eight parts. This expanded theory encompasses the theory just stated previously, plus these additions:

1. Distance education serves individual learners who cannot or do not want to make use of face-to-face teaching. These learners are very heterogeneous.
2. Distance education means learners no longer have to be bound by decisions made by others about place of study, division of the year into study terms and vacations, timetables, and entry requirements. Distance education thus promotes students' freedom of choice and independence.
3. Society benefits from distance education, on the one hand, from the liberal study opportunities it affords individual learners, and, on the other hand, from the professional/occupational training it provides.
4. Distance education is an instrument for recurrent and lifelong learning and for free access to learning opportunities and equity.
5. All learning concerned with the acquisition of cognitive knowledge and cognitive skills as well as affective learning and some psychomotor learning are effectively provided for by distance education. Distance education may inspire meta-cognitive approaches.
6. Distance education is based on deep learning as an individual activity. Learning is guided and supported by noncontiguous means. Teaching and learning rely on mediated communication, usually based on preproduced courses.
7. Distance education is open to behaviorist, cognitive, constructivist, and other modes of learning. It has an element of industrialization with division of labor, use of mechanical devices, electronic data processing, and mass communication, usually based on preproduced courses.
8. Personal relations, study pleasure, and empathy between students and those supporting them (tutors, counselors, etc.) are central to learning in distance education. Feelings of empathy and belonging promote students' motivation to learn and influence the learning favorably. Such feelings are conveyed by students being engaged in decision making; by lucid, problem-oriented, conversation-like presentations of learning matter that may be anchored in existing knowledge; by friendly, noncontiguous interaction between students and tutors, counselors, and others supporting them; and by liberal organizational/administrative structures and processes.

Although it is an effective mode of training, distance education runs the risk of leading to mere fact learning and reproduction of accepted "truths." However, it can be organized and carried out in such a way that students are encouraged to search, criticize, and identify positions of their own. It thus serves conceptual learning, problem learning, and genuinely academic ends.

In sum, the previous list represents, on the one hand, a description of distance education and, on the other hand, a theory from which hypotheses are generated and that has explanatory power in that it identifies a general approach favorable to learning and to the teaching efforts conducive to learning.

Andragogy—Malcolm Knowles

Most now consider Knowles's work to be a theory of distance education; it is relevant because most often adults are involved in distance education, and andragogy deals with frameworks for programs designed for the adult learner. At its core is the idea that "the attainment of adulthood is concomitant on adults' coming to perceive themselves as self-directing individuals" (Brookfield, 1986).

Knowles spent a career formulating a theory of adult learning based on research and experience related to the characteristics of the adult learner (Knowles, 1990). The andragogical process consists of seven elements:

1. The establishment of a climate conducive to adult learning, which includes a physical environment that is conducive to the physical well-being of the adult learner, and a psychological environment that provides for a feeling of mutual respect, collaborativeness, trust, openness, and authenticity
2. The creation of an organizational structure for participatory learning that includes planning groups where learners provide input about what is to be learned and options regarding learning activities
3. The diagnosis of needs for learning that includes differentiating between felt needs and ascribed needs
4. The formulation of directions for learning that includes objectives with terminal behaviors to be achieved and directions for improvement of abilities
5. The development of a design for activities that clarifies resources and strategies to accomplish objectives
6. The development of a plan that provides evidence when objectives are accomplished
7. The use of quantitative and qualitative evaluation that provides a rediagnosis of needs for learning

Knowles's andragogy suggests a number of characteristics needed in distance education systems designed for adults. For example:

- The physical environment of a television classroom used by adults should be designed so that participants are able to see what is occurring, not just hear it.
- The environment should be one that promotes respect and dignity for the adult learner.
- Adult learners must feel supported, and when criticism is a part of discussions or presentations made by adults, it is important that clear ground rules be

established so comments are not directed toward a person, but instead concentrate on content and ideas.

■ A starting point for a course, or module of a course, should be the needs and interests of the adult learner.

■ Course plans should include clear course descriptions, learning objectives, resources, and timelines for events.

■ General-to-specific patterns of content presentation work best for adult learners.

■ Active participation should be encouraged, such as by the use of work groups or study teams.

A Synthesis of Existing Theories—Hilary Perraton

Perraton's (1988) theory of distance education is composed of elements from existing theories of communication and diffusion, as well as philosophies of education. It is expressed in the form of 14 statements, or hypotheses. The first five of these statements concern the way distance teaching can be used to maximize education:

■ You can use any medium to teach anything.

■ Distance teaching can break the integuments of fixed staffing ratios that limited the expansion of education when the teacher and the student had to be in the same place at the same time.

■ There are circumstances under which distance teaching can be cheaper than orthodox education, whether measured in terms of audience reached or of learning.

■ The economies achievable by distance education are functions of the level of education, size of audience, choice of media, and sophistication of production.

[handwritten margin note: Cheaper the production]

■ Distance teaching can reach audiences who would not be reached by ordinary means.

The following four statements address the need to increase dialog:

■ It is possible to organize distance teaching in such a way that there is dialog.

■ Where a tutor meets distance students face-to-face, the tutor's role is changed from that of a communicator of information to that of a facilitator of learning.

■ Group discussion is an effective method of learning when distance teaching is used to bring relevant information to the group.

■ In most communities, resources are available that can be used to support distance learning to its educational and economic advantage.

The final five statements deal with method:

■ A multimedia program is likely to be more effective than one that relies on a single medium.

■ A systems approach is helpful in planning distance education.

■ Feedback is a necessary part of a distance learning system.

■ To be effective, distance teaching materials should ensure that students undertake frequent and regular activities over and above reading, watching, or listening.

■ In choosing among media, the key decision on which the rest depend concerns the use of face-to-face learning.

Equivalency Theory: An American Theory of Distance Education

The impact of new technologies on distance education is far-ranging. Desmond Keegan (1995) suggests that electronically linking instructor and students at various locations creates a virtual classroom. Keegan goes on to state:

> The theoretical analyses of virtual education, however, have not yet been addressed by the literature: Is it a subset of distance education or to be regarded as a separate field of educational endeavor? What are its didactic structures? What is the relationship of its cost effectiveness and of its educational effectiveness to distance education and to conventional education? (p. 21)

It is in this environment of virtual education that the equivalency theory of distance education has emerged. Some advocates of distance education have mistakenly tried to provide identical instructional situations for all students, no matter when or where they learn. Since it is more difficult to control the situations of distant learners, some have decided that all learners should participate as distant learners. This is based on the belief that learners should have identical opportunities to learn. This is a mistake. Schlosser and Simonson (2009) theorize that for distance education to be successful in the United States, its appropriate application should be based on the approach

> that the more equivalent the learning experiences of distant students are to that of local students, the more equivalent will be the outcomes of the learning experience. (p. 25)

In other words, equivalent, rather than identical, learning experiences should be provided to each learner whether local or distant, and the expectation should be that equivalent outcomes, rather than identical, should be expected of each learner. Thus, each learner might access different, unequal, yet equivalent instructional strategies, varying instructional resources, or individually prescribed activities that are different from what is prescribed to other students. If the distance education course is effectively designed and equivalent experiences are available, then potential learners will reach the course's instructional objectives (Simonson & Schlosser, 1999).

This theory is based on the definition of distance education as formal, institutionally based education where the learning group is separated, and where interactive telecommunications systems are used to connect learners, resources, and instructors.

Simonson and Schlosser (1995) in elaborating on this theory say:

> It should not be necessary for any group of learners to compensate for different, possibly lesser, instructional experiences. Thus, those developing distance educational systems should strive to make equivalent the learning experiences of all students no matter how they are linked to the resources or instruction they require. (pp. 71–72)

One key to this theoretical approach is the concept of equivalency. Local and distant learners have fundamentally different environments in which they learn. It is the responsibility of the distance educator to design, even overdesign, learning events that provide experiences with equivalent value for learners. Just as a triangle and a square may have the same *area* and be considered equivalent even though they are quite different geometrical shapes, the experiences of the local learner and the distant learner should have *equivalent value* even though these experiences might be quite different. In 2006, the U.S. Department of Education's Office of Postsecondary Education released an interesting report titled "Evidence of Quality in Distance Education Programs Drawn from Interviews with the Accreditation Community." In this report it was noted that a "red flag" or warning sign of ineffective distance education programs was issued when faculty attempted or were encouraged to directly convert regular courses into distance-delivered courses (Simonson, 2007a). Identical traditional and distance-delivered courses are not likely to be effective, rather, a variety of equivalent instructional approaches should be provided for students—local and distant—to learn from.

Another key to this approach is the concept of the learning experience. A *learning experience* is anything that promotes learning, including what is observed, felt, heard, or done. It is likely that different students in various locations, learning at different times, may require a different mix of learning experiences. Some will need a greater amount of observing, and others a larger dosage of doing. The goal of instructional planning is to make the sum of learning experiences for each learner equivalent. Instructional design procedures should attempt to anticipate and provide the collection of experiences that will be most suitable for each student or group of students (Schlosser & Simonson, 2009).

A Theoretical Framework for Distance Education—Desmond Keegan

Keegan (1996) suggested that the theoretician had to answer three questions before developing a theory of distance education:

1. *Is distance education an educational activity?* Keegan's answer was that although distance education institutions possess some of the characteristics of businesses, rather than of traditional schools, their educational activities are dominant. Distance education is a more industrialized form of education. The theoretical bases for distance education, Keegan pointed out, are within general education theory.

2. *Is distance education a form of conventional education?* Keegan believed that because distance education is not based on interpersonal communication and is characterized by a privatization of institutionalized learning (as is conventional education), it is a distinct form of education. Therefore, although the theoretical basis for distance education could be found within general education theory, it could not be found within the theoretical structures of oral, group-based education.

    However, Keegan considered virtual systems based on teaching face-to-face at a distance to be a new cognate field of study to distance education. He believed that a theoretical analysis of virtual education still needed to be addressed.

3. *Is distance education possible, or is it a contradiction in terms?* Keegan pointed out that if education requires *intersubjectivity*—a shared experience in which teacher and learner are united by a common zeal—then distance education is a contradiction in terms. Distance instruction is possible, but distance education is not. Again, the advent of virtual systems used in distance education challenges the traditional answer to this question.

Central to Keegan's concept of distance education is the separation of the teaching acts in time and place from the learning acts. Successful distance education, he believes, requires the reintegration of the two acts:

■ The intersubjectivity of teacher and learner, in which learning from teaching occurs, has to be artificially re-created. Over space and time, a distance system seeks to reconstruct the moment in which the teaching/learning interaction occurs. The linking of learning materials to learning is central to this process (Keegan, 1996, pp. 43–45).

■ Reintegration of the act of teaching at a distance is attempted in two ways. First, learning materials, both print and nonprint, are designed to achieve as many of the characteristics of interpersonal communication as possible. Second, when courses are presented, reintegration of the teaching act is attempted by a variety of techniques, including communication by correspondence, telephone tutorial, online computer communication, comments on assignments by tutors or computers, and teleconferences.

The process of reintegrating the act of teaching in distance education, Keegan suggests, results in at least five changes to the normal structure of oral, group-based education:

1. The industrialization of teaching
2. The privatization of institutional learning
3. Change of administrative structure
4. Different plants and buildings
5. Change of costing structures

Keegan offers three hypotheses drawn from his theoretical framework:

1. Distance students have a tendency to drop out of those institutions in which structures for the reintegration of the teaching acts are not satisfactorily achieved.
2. Distance students have difficulty achieving quality of learning in those institutions in which structures for the reintegration of the teaching acts are not satisfactorily achieved.
3. The status of learning at a distance may be questioned in those institutions in which the reintegration of the teaching acts is not satisfactorily achieved.

Fordism, Neo-Fordism, Post-Fordism: A Theoretical Debate

Peters's (1988) view of distance education has received considerable attention. His theory of industrialized education is a point of departure and is extended and revised based on contemporary industrial transformation in a debate on the future of distance education. *Fordism* and *post-Fordism* are the terms borrowed from industrial sociology to classify the opposing views of the debate. This debate deals with changes in the practice of distance education and represents wider debates about the nature of change in the contemporary period (Edwards, 1995). Although not all would agree that the Fordist framework applies to distance education (Rumble, 1995a, 1995b, 1995c), it has become the mainstream theory of distance education in international literature and provides a useful analogy in debating the practice of distance education.

The term *Fordism* is derived from Henry Ford's approach to the mass production for mass consumption of automobiles early in the twentieth century. *Fordism, neo-Fordism,* and *post-Fordism* are terms that represent three ways to conceptualize the production of distance education. Each of these ideal-type models suggests very different social, political, and educational outcomes. Badham and Mathews (1989) provide a clear model for understanding the three categories of distance education production.

They proposed that a firm's production process and its production strategy can be defined in terms of the three variables of product variety, process innovation, and labor responsibility, and they suggested that a production paradigm represents an exemplary model of efficient production, which guides organizational strategy.

In looking at these three variables, Fordism would be described as having low product innovation, low process variability, and low labor responsibility. Neo-Fordism would have high product innovation and high process variability, but would maintain the low labor responsibility of the Fordism definition. High product innovation, high process variability, and high labor responsibility would typify the post-Fordism model. Campion (1995) illustrated how these three different production processes relate to distance education:

■ The *Fordist strategy* for distance education suggests a fully centralized, single-mode, national distance education provider, gaining greater economies of scale by offering courses to a mass market, thereby justifying a greater investment in more expensive course materials. Rationalization of this kind allows for increased administrative control and a more extreme division of labor as the production process is fragmented into an increasing number of component tasks.

■ The *neo-Fordist strategy* extends the Fordist system by allowing much higher levels of flexibility and diversity, and by combining low volumes with high levels of product and process innovation. However, neo-Fordist production retains a highly centralized Fordist approach to labor organization and control. A neo-Fordist expression of distance education might well be represented by a centrally controlled, perhaps multinational yet locally administered, model of distance education. By also using self-instructional course materials for teaching on-campus students, it has the potential to massively reduce costs across the whole student population. However, and most importantly, a neo-Fordist manifestation of distance education bears a strong relationship to that of the Fordist route inasmuch as it has an overall despoiling effect on academic staff.

■ *High levels of all three variables characterize the post-Fordist strategy:* product innovation, process variability, and labor responsibility. It is opposed to neo-Fordism and to Fordism, dispensing with a division of labor and rigid managerial control and deliberately fostering a skilled and responsible workforce. A post-Fordist model of distance education would be decentralized and retain integration between the study modes. Academic staff would, however, retain autonomous control of their administered courses, and in so doing, would be able rapidly to adjust course curriculum and delivery to the changing needs of students.

In general, Fordist distance education involves mass production for mass consumption. It encompasses centralized control, a division of work tasks associated with distance education, and the creation of management for the division of the work tasks. Courses are developed by a small core of skilled workers and delivered centrally, with a de-skilling effect on the teacher. In a neo-Fordist system, course development, delivery, and administration are mixed between a centralized office and regional or local offices. This allows for more flexibility in course development and delivery. In the neo-Fordist model, the teacher is still given little responsibility beyond delivering the developed materials.

The post-Fordist approach to distance education would focus on the consumer rather than the product. Administration would be decentralized, democratic, and participatory, and the division of labor would be informal and flexible. Teachers would have a high responsibility to develop curriculum and respond to the learning needs of their students. Much of education as it developed over the past century fits the Fordist paradigm. Renner (1995) states that education became a formalized system of production that could be monitored, maintained, and controlled in the same way as the factory. The practice of distance education has also been greatly influenced by the Fordist paradigm. It has been argued that Fordism is still the dominant international paradigm in distance education.

Distance education has been influenced by the Fordist paradigm because it is the model that has been most successful in business throughout this century. Evans (1995) maintains that distance education can be seen as both a product and a process of modernity. Its administrative systems, distribution networks, and print production processes are characteristic of modern societies with developed mass production, consumption, and management. The Fordist approach to distance education provides cost efficiencies and quality production of materials unachievable outside of the Fordist model. In addition, global competition in distance education will favor the marketing power of large educational providers. The Fordist approach to the practice of distance education provides obvious advantages.

However, major concerns about the continuation of the Fordist paradigm in distance education have been expressed. These concerns revolve around the following themes:

- Mass markets for delivered instruction have changed, reducing the demand for centrally produced instruction for mass delivery.
- The Fordism model is unable to adapt to the needs of a fast-changing society.
- The focus on instructional production and the systematic use of preprogrammed curricula are incompatible with higher levels of educational quality.

With heightened competition, diversification of demand, and rapid developments in communication and information technology, the Fordist rationale, which presumes a uniform mass market to support mass production, is inappropriate. As a result, the cost effectiveness and cost efficiency of centrally developed and delivered instruction has declined.

The Fordist structure is not well suited to adapt easily to the changing needs in society. If we combine an increasingly differentiated consumer market with the power and speed of contemporary interactive computer communications technologies and add to this a more highly educated workforce, then the bureaucratic practices of the past would seem far from sustainable. This new environment requires a flexible structure in which ideas are readily tried and shared. In China, Ding (1995) found that the Fordist structure could not adapt itself to the new conditions of the market immediately and quickly. He stated that the Fordist structure could not adapt curricula to the regional needs of the country or alter the structure and content of the course to the needs of the students. The answer, according to Renner (1995), is to place an emphasis on labor flexibility that would allow individual academics to produce and deliver quality curriculum more readily customized to student needs. It is felt that post-Fordist systems of distance education would be able to rapidly respond to the needs of society.

Renner's statement that the systematic use of preprogrammed curricula is incompatible with higher levels of educational quality suggests a controversy that goes beyond the debate on Fordism. Preprogrammed curricula used in the Fordist approach to distance education are products of instructional design based on behaviorism.

Post-Fordism is directly linked to constructivism. Renner (1995) sees the relationship between constructivism and post-Fordism as intimate. The constructivist believes that the individual gives meaning to the world through experience. Ideally, it is a process of personal and cooperative experimentation, questioning, and problem solving through which meaning can be constructed. This approach to learning is viewed as incompatible with mass production of instructional curricula developed with instructional design methods based in behaviorism that assume a more passive approach to learning. For constructivist learning to occur, teaching must remain flexible and sensitive to learner needs, from intellectual, cognitive, and psychological perspectives. Centrally devised educational courseware that dictates teaching sequences to students and de-skilled staff discourage the customization and construction of knowledge.

For the advocates of post-Fordism, neo-Fordism is no more acceptable than Fordism. Although there is higher product innovation and process variability, labor responsibility is still low. This view of the role of labor divides the neo-Fordist approach from the post-Fordist approach. The neo-Fordism division of labor leaves the teacher and the academic staff divorced from research, curriculum development, and scholarly inquiry. They simply deliver the curriculum prepared for them. Proponents of the post-Fordist paradigm have two disagreements with this approach. First, this approach again assumes a behavioral-based instructional design method for curricula development. The preceding paragraph outlined the post-Fordist's concerns about this method. Second, post-Fordists would see this approach as exploiting the worker. High product innovation and high process variability put additional demands on the worker without additional compensation. The neo-Fordism and post-Fordism approaches to distance education are fundamentally different.

The debate about Fordism is intricate, heated, and tied in with differing political, economic, aesthetic, ethical, and educational perspectives. The issues raised in this debate are important because policymakers introduce regulations, generate institutional structures, and effectively organize workplace practices on the basis of such paradigms. How students learn, and frequently what they learn, is a product of these decisions. As the role of distance education is defined in a changing society, these issues need to be given careful consideration.

There is little involvement in the Fordism/post-Fordism debate by American distance educators. In the United States, local control, small classes, rapport between teachers and students, and highly personalized instruction are hailed as important characteristics of its highly respected educational system (Simonson, 1995). This approach to education is diametrically opposed to the mass production, centralized control advocated by a Fordist approach to distance education. Although Thach and Murphy (1994) suggest that there is a need for national coordination of higher distance education and that local and state control of education inhibit opportunities for collaboration at a distance among institutions, the U.S. traditional approach to education is prevalent. This focus on student needs, personalized instruction, and interaction is evident in the following statement by Michael Moore (1994):

> In a typical United States course that uses teleconferencing technologies to link, let us say, six sites, the curriculum problem is how to integrate the local interests and needs, as well as the local knowledge that lies at each site, into the content to be taught. (p. 5)

SUMMARY

In the rapidly changing and diverse environment in which distance education is practiced, many questions remain unanswered. In this environment it is difficult to arrive at one definition or agree on a theory of how to practice and do research in the field of distance education. New technologies, globalization, and new ideas about student learning, challenge the traditional approaches to the practice of distance education. This theme of change is evident in the discussions of distance education and its definition, history, status, and theory.

Numerous definitions of distance education have been proposed. Most include the separation of teacher and learner, the influence of an educational organization, the use of media to unite teacher and learner, the opportunity for two-way communication, and the practice of individualized instruction. The traditional definitions describe distance education as taking place at a different time and in a different place, whereas recent definitions, enabled by new interactive technologies, stress education that takes place at the same time but in a different place. The role of educational organizations in the distance education process has also been challenged. For example, open learning is a form of distance education that occurs without the influence of an educational organization. These issues will continue to be debated as distance educators seek definitions that fit a changing world.

Investigating the relatively brief history of distance education reveals both diversity and an ongoing change in its practice. Historically, diverse practices of distance education have been developed according to the resources and philosophies of the organizations providing instruction. The history also shows that advances in technology have promoted key changes in distance education. These changes have been most evident in the rapid development of electronic communications in recent decades. How the future of distance education will be shaped by the integration of its history and these new technologies is yet to be seen.

Changes in society, politics, economics, and technology are impacting the status of distance education around the world. In some cases, distance education is seen as an answer to inadequate educational opportunities caused by political and/or economic instability. In other situations, established distance education providers are being required by a changing society to convert from mass instruction to a more decentralized approach to meet the diverse needs of their students. In many countries, the need for continuing education or training and access to degree programs is accelerated by the demands of a changing society. Students in rural or isolated parts of the world look to distance education for opportunities to "keep up" with the outside world. Again, technology advances are a major influence for change in distance education worldwide. The globalization of the world enabled by these new technologies will challenge distance educators to rethink the practice of distance education to take advantage of these new opportunities.

The changing and diverse environment in which distance education is practiced has inhibited the development of a single theory on which to base practice and research. A variety of theories have been proposed to describe traditional distance education. They include theories that emphasize independence and autonomy of the learner, industrialization of teaching, and interaction and communication. These traditional theories emphasize that distance education is a fundamentally different form of education. Recent emerging theories, based on the capabilities of new interactive audio and video systems, state that distance education is not a distinct field of education. Both utilization of existing educational theory and the creation of like experiences for both the distant and local learner are emphasized. Traditional distance education theorists will need to address the changes to distance education facilitated by new technologies.

Advocates of the new theories will need to consider their impact on the traditional strengths of distance education. Specifically, the focus of the new theories on face-to-face instruction eliminates the advantage of time-independent learning that traditional theories of distance education value. The debate on these theoretical issues will only increase in the face of continued change. One indication of the impact of change in distance education theory is the Fordist/post-Fordist/neo-Fordist debate. Fordist distance education is administered centrally and involves mass production of curricula for mass consumption. Rapid changes in society have resulted in diverse market needs. The Fordist paradigm is unable to respond quickly to these needs. The post-Fordist paradigm implements a decentralized, democratic administration that focuses on the consumer. In this paradigm, teachers have a high responsibility to respond to individual needs of students. Central to the debate between Fordists and post-Fordists are changing views about how learning occurs. The Fordist approach is based in behaviorism learning theory, in which knowledge is delivered to the learner. The constructivist approach to learning, in which individuals give meaning to the world through experience, underlies the post-Fordist position. The debate on these differences will continue as distance education adapts to meet the needs of a changing society.

An environment in which technology, society, economics, politics, and theories of learning are all in transition suggests that definitions, theories, and the practice of distance education will continue to be contested. This theme of change will both challenge and motivate distance educators and researchers as they strive to understand and develop effective ways to meet the needs of learners around the world.

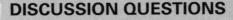

DISCUSSION QUESTIONS

1. Why are there different definitions of distance education? Discuss and develop the definition that you feel is most appropriate.
2. Discuss Desmond Keegan's five main elements of the various definitions of distance education. Write a paragraph explaining which of the elements is most critical and which is least critical.
3. Many think that in the near future the concept of distance will become relatively unimportant. What do you think this means?
4. Correspondence study is a form of distance education that developed during World War II. Is correspondence study still important today? Why or why not?
5. What might be the reasons for the founding of special distance teaching universities? Why is there no national distance learning university in the United States?
6. Distance education has a long history in European countries. Why is distance learning more commonplace in Europe than in the United States?
7. Keegan writes that the lack of an accepted theory of distance education has weakened the field. Discuss the importance of theory and how theory helps the practitioner of distance education.
8. Wedemeyer has six characteristics of independent study systems. Why would Wedemeyer's perspective be important to American educators?
9. Explain the concept of the assembly line as it relates to the industrialization of teaching. Will industrialized education ever be important in American education? Explain.
10. Simonson proposed an emerging theory of distance education. What learning experiences are different for local and distant learners?

REFERENCES

Badham, R., & Mathews, J. (1989). The new production systems debate. *Labour and Industry, 2*(2), 194–246.

Brookfield, S. (1986). *Understanding and facilitating adult learning.* San Francisco, CA: Jossey-Bass.

Campion, M. (1995). The supposed demise of bureaucracy: Implications for distance education and open learning—more on the post-Fordism debate. *Distance Education, 16*(2), 192–216.

Cropley, A. J., & Kahl, T. N. (1983). Distance education and distance learning: Some psychological considerations. *Distance Education, 4*(1), 27–39.

Delling, R. (1985). Towards a theory of distance education. Paper presented at the ICDE Thirteenth World Conference, Melbourne, Australia.

Ding, X. (1995). From Fordism to neo-Fordism: Industrialisation theory and distance education—a Chinese perspective. *Distance Education, 16*(2), 217–240.

Edwards, R. (1995). Different discourses, discourses of difference: Globalisation, distance education, and open learning. *Distance Education, 16*(2), 241–255.

Evans, T. (1995). Globalisation, post-Fordism and open and distance education. *Distance Education, 16*(2), 256–269.

Garrison, D. R., & Shale, D. (1987). Mapping the boundaries of distance education: Problems in defining the field. *The American Journal of Distance Education, 1*(1), 7–13.

Holmberg, B. (1985). *The feasibility of a theory of teaching for distance education and a proposed theory* (ZIFF Papiere 60). Hagen, West Germany: Fern Universität, Zentrales Institute fur Fernstudienforschung Arbeitsbereich. (ERIC Document Reproduction Service No. ED290013).

Holmberg, B. (1986). *Growth and structure of distance education* (3rd ed.). London: Croom Helm.

Holmberg, B. (1995). *The sphere of distance-education theory revisited.* (ERIC Document Reproduction Service No. ED386578).

Keegan, D. (1988). Theories of distance education: Introduction. In D. Sewart, D. Keegan, & B. Holmberg (Eds.), *Distance education: International perspectives* (pp. 63–67). New York: Routledge.

Keegan, D. (1995). *Distance education technology for the new millennium: Compressed video teaching.* (ERIC Document Reproduction Service No. ED389931).

Keegan, D. (1996). *The foundations of distance education* (3rd ed.). London: Croom Helm.

Knowles, M. (1990). *The adult learner: A neglected species* (4th ed.). Houston, TX: Gulf.

Moore, M. (1994). Autonomy and interdependence. *The American Journal of Distance Education, 8*(2), 1–5.

Moore, M. (2007). The theory of transactional distance. In M. Moore (Ed.), *Handbook of distance education* (2nd ed.). Mahwah, NJ: Erlbaum.

Perraton, H. (1988). A theory for distance education. In D. Sewart, D. Keegan, & B. Holmberg (Eds.), *Distance education: International perspectives* (pp. 34–45). New York: Routledge.

Peters, O. (1988). Distance teaching and industrial production: A comparative interpretation in outline. In D. Sewart, D. Keegan, & B. Holmberg (Eds.), *Distance education: International perspectives* (pp. 95–113). New York: Routledge.

Renner, W. (1995). Post-Fordist visions and technological solutions: Education technology and the labour process. *Distance Education, 16*(2), 285–301.

Rumble, G. (1989). On defining distance education. *The American Journal of Distance Education, 3*(2), 8–21.

Rumble, G. (1995a). Labour market theories and distance education I: Industrialisation and distance education. *Open Learning, 10*(1), 10–21.

Rumble, G. (1995b). Labour market theories and distance education II: How Fordist is distance education? *Open Learning, 10*(2), 12–28.

Rumble, G. (1995c). Labour market theories and distance education III: Post-Fordism the way forward? *Open Learning, 10*(3), 47–52.

Schlosser, L., & Simonson, M. (2009). *Distance education: Definition and glossary of terms* (3rd ed.). Charlotte, NC: Information Age.

Shale, D. (1988). Toward a reconceptualization of distance education. *The American Journal of Distance Education, 2*(3), 25–35.

Simonson, M. (1995). Overview of the Teacher Education Alliance, Iowa Distance Education Alliance research plan. In C. Sorensen, C. Schlosser, M. Anderson, & M. Simonson (Eds.), *Encyclopedia of distance education research in Iowa* (pp. 3–6). Ames, IA: Teacher Education Alliance.

Simonson, M. (2007a). What the accreditation community is saying about quality in distance education. *Distance Learning, 4*(2), 104.

Simonson, M. (2007b). Virtual schools. *Distance Learning, 4*(1), 76.

Simonson, M. (2009). Distance learning. In *The 2009 book of the year* (p. 231). Chicago: Encyclopaedia Britannica.

Simonson, M., & Schlosser, C. (1995). More than fiber: Distance education in Iowa. *Tech Trends, 40*(3), 13–15.

Simonson, M., & Schlosser, C. (1999). Theory and distance education: A new discussion. *The American Journal of Distance Education, 13*(1), 60–75.

Thach, L., & Murphy, L. (1994). Collaboration in distance education: From local to international perspectives. *The American Journal of Distance Education, 8*(3), 5–21.

U.S. Department of Education. (2006). Evidence of quality in distance education programs drawn from interviews with the accreditation community. Retrieved April 30, 2007, from http://www.itcnetwork.org/Accreditation-EvidenceofQualityinDEPrograms.pdf

Wedemeyer, C. (1981). *Learning at the backdoor.* Madison, WI: University of Wisconsin Press.

SUGGESTED READINGS

Albright, M. (1988). A conceptual framework for the design and the delivery of a university-level credit course by communications satellite. Unpublished doctoral dissertation, Iowa State University, Ames.

Barry, M., & Runyan, G. B. (1995). A review of distance-learning studies in the U.S. military. *The American Journal of Distance Education, 9*(3), 37–47.

Bruder, I. (1989). Distance learning: What's holding back this boundless delivery system? *Electronic Learning, 8*(6), 30–35.

Buckland, M., & Dye, C. M. (1991). *The development of electronic distance education delivery systems in the United States. Recurring and emerging themes in history and philosophy of education.* (ERIC Document Reproduction Service No. ED345713).

Holmberg, B. (1989). *Theory and practice of distance education.* London: Routledge.

Johnson, J. K. (1988). Attitudes of high school students in small rural schools toward interactive satellite instruction. Unpublished master's thesis, Iowa State University, Ames.

Keegan, D. (1988). On defining distance education. In D. Sewart, D. Keegan, & B. Holmberg (Eds.), *Distance education: International perspectives* (pp. 6–33). New York: Routledge.

Lintz, M., & Tognotti, S. (1996). Distance education on the WWW [World Wide Web]. Retrieved from http://tecfa.unige.ch/edu-ws94/contrib/peraya.fm.html

Magnus, J. (1996). Distance education in sub-Saharan Africa: The next five years. *Innovations in Education and Training International, 33*(1), 50–56.

Moore, M., & Anderson, W. (Eds.). (2003). *Handbook of distance education.* Mahwah, NJ: Earlbaum.

Riel, M., & Harasim, L. (1994). Research perspectives on network learning. *Machine-Mediated Learning, 4*(2–3), 91–113.

Rose, S. N. (1991). Collegiate-based noncredit courses. In B. B. Watkins & S. J. Wright (Eds.), *The foundations of American distance education* (pp. 67–92). Dubuque, IA: Kendall/Hunt.

Simonson, M. (1995). Distance education revisited: An introduction to the issue. *Tech Trends, 40*(30), 2.

Simonson, M. (1995). Does anyone really want to learn at a distance? *Tech Trends, 40*(3), 2.

Sorensen, C., Maushak, N., & Lozada, M. (1996). *Iowa Distance Education Alliance preliminary evaluation report.* Ames: Iowa State University, Research Institute for Studies in Education.

Tompkins, L. S. (1993). A new light on distance learning—Fiber optics. *Journal of Educational Technology Systems, 21*(3), 265–275.

U.S. Department of Education. (1995). *The Star Schools program.* (Available from Star Schools, U.S. Department of Education, 555 New Jersey Avenue NW, Washington, DC 20208-5644.)

Watkins, B. L. (1991). A quite radical idea: The invention and elaboration of collegiate correspondence study. In B. L. Watkins & S. J. Wright (Eds.), *The foundations of American distance-education* (pp. 1–35). Dubuque, IA: Kendall/Hunt.

Young, J. R. (1995, November 3). Classes on the Web. *Chronicle of Higher Education,* pp. A27, A32–A33.

CHAPTER **3**

Research and Distance Education

CHAPTER GOAL

The purpose of this chapter is to summarize the research on distance education.

CHAPTER OBJECTIVES

After reading and reviewing this chapter, you should be able to

1. Explain research dealing with learning outcomes in distance education environments.
2. Explain research on learner perceptions concerning distance education.
3. Explain research on learner attributes and other variables in distance education situations.
4. Describe research related to interaction in distance education.
5. Summarize research on distance education.

 DISTANCE EDUCATION RESEARCH: SETTING A FOUNDATION

Three quotes are central to the development and growth of the field of distance education. These statements represent the themes of classic articles written by leaders in education and remain today as guides for the field (Simonson, 2009).

The first was by James Finn, one of the founders of the modern educational technology field. In 1953, in the introductory issue of *Audio-Visual Communication Review*, he wrote:

> Finally, the most fundamental and most important characteristic of a profession is that the skills involved are founded upon a body of intellectual theory and research. Furthermore, this systematic

theory is constantly being expanded by research and thinking within the profession. As Whitehead says, " . . . the practice of a profession cannot be disjoined from its theoretical understanding and *vice versa* . . . . The antithesis to a profession is an avocation based upon customary activities and modified by the trial and error of individual practice. Such an avocation is a Craft . . . " (Smith et al., 1951, p. 557). The difference between the bricklayer and the architect lies right here. (p. 8)

The second quote is by Campbell and Stanley, who, in their classic 1963 monograph, described the experiment

as the only means for settling disputes regarding educational practice, as the only way of verifying educational improvements, and as the only way of establishing a cumulative tradition in which improvements can be introduced without the danger of a faddish discard of old wisdom in favor of inferior novelties. (p. 2)

The final quote is the controversial statement from the *Review of Educational Research* made by Richard Clark in 1983 and quoted often in this book:

The best current evidence is that media are mere vehicles that deliver instruction but do not influence student achievement any more than the truck that delivers our groceries causes changes in nutrition . . . only the content of the vehicle can influence achievement. (p. 445)

Finn (1953) attempted to encourage those in the audiovisual field to take a more professional view of themselves and their discipline by basing decisions on theory supported by research. Campbell and Stanley formalized what previously had been unclear to many—the need for the rigorous application of the scientific method to the study of education. Twenty years later in 1983, Richard Clark identified why Campbell and Stanley's admonition was so important. His article documented the failure of many educational researchers to "verify educational improvements, as demanded by Campbell and Stanley" (p. 2). Clark's article was not popular. However, it clearly and precisely showed how researchers had violated basic guidelines for rigorous research, which had led many educators to adopt "inferior novelties" at the expense of scientifically-validated "wisdom."

Each of these scholars had a message of critical importance to distance education— scientific inquiry, conducted with rigorous attention to correct procedures, is the key to success of our field. Research and theory are at the foundation of credibility and quality.

THE FOCUS OF DISTANCE EDUCATION RESEARCH

Emerging technologies have forced a redefinition of distance education. At the same time, the distance education research agenda has also evolved. The focus has shifted to a more learner-centered approach. Researchers are not merely looking at achievement but are examining learner attributes and perceptions as well as interaction patterns and how these contribute to the overall learning environment. Although there is continued interest in the technology, the focus is not on which medium is best, but on what attributes of the medium can contribute to a positive, equivalent learning experience. This chapter will provide a review of distance education research literature. In his 1987 landmark article "The Development of Distance Education Research,"

Börje Holmberg, a leading distance education theorist and researcher, suggested that the structure of distance education research should include:

■ Philosophy and theory of distance education
■ Distance students and their milieu, conditions, and study motivations
■ Subject-matter presentation
■ Communication and interaction between students and their supporting organization (tutors, counselors, administrators, other students)
■ Administration and organization
■ Economics
■ Systems (comparative distance education, typologies, evaluation, etc.)
■ History of distance education

Recently, a number of researchers have reviewed the literature on distance education and provided support for the effectiveness of instruction delivered to distant learners and guidelines for teaching and learning at a distance (Howell & Baker, 2006; Orellana, Hudgins, & Simonson, 2009; Sorensen & Baylen, 2004; Smith 2006; Tallent-Runnels, Cooper, Lan, Thomas, & Busby, 2005). Research dealing with various aspects of distance education, once characterized as anecdotal, is now more likely to be theory based and methodologically sound. Thus, research results are beginning to have a positive impact on the practice of distance education (Simonson, 2006). For example, Hirumi (2005) has examined a significant portion of the distance education literature and has analyzed e-learning guidelines "in search of quality" (p. 309). Hirumi found that there are significant differences in how industry and education view quality and approaches for e-learning. Education guidelines focus on the quality of e-learning courses and programs, but industry develops standards in order to promote reusability and interoperability of learning objects (Hirumi, 2005). Hirumi analyzed six sets of guidelines, including:

1. The Council of Regional Accrediting Commissions (C-RAC, 2000). *Statement of the regional accrediting commissions on the evaluation of electronically offered degree and certificate programs* (www.wiche.edu/telecom/Guidelines.htm).
2. The Institute for Higher Education Policy (IHEP, 2000). *Quality on the line: Benchmarks for success in Internet-based distance education* (www.ihep.com/quality.pdf).
3. The American Council on Education (ACE, 1997). *Guiding principles for distance learning in learning society* (www.acenet.edu/calec/dist_learning/dl_principlesIntro.cfm).
4. The American Distance Education Consortium (ADEC, n.d.a., n.d.b). *Guiding principles for distance learning* and *Guiding principles for distance teaching and learning* (www.adec.edu/admin/papers/distance-teaching_principles.html).
5. The American Federation of Teachers (AFT, 2000). *Distance education: Guidelines for good practice* (www.aft.org/higher_ed/downloadable/distance.pdf).
6. Open and Distance Learning Quality Council (ODLQC, 2001). *Standards in open and distance education.*

These sets of guidelines offer a basis for development of quality distance education courses and programs (Hirumi, 2005). Also of importance is a recent publication by

Lou, Bernard, and Arbrami (2006). They reported that "218 independent findings from 103 studies representing 25,320 students were analyzed in the undergraduate dataset in this meta-analysis. On average, undergraduate students achieved similarly, whether they learned in DE courses or in the traditional classrooms" (p. 161). Lou, Bernard, and Abrami went on to say, "There is consistent and reliable evidence that undergraduate students achieved equally, whether they learned at the remote site or the host site." The authors continued, "In synchronous instructor-directed undergraduate DE, when media are used to deliver the same instruction simultaneously by the same instructor and with the same course activities and materials, there is little reason to expect undergraduate students to learn differently in the remote sites than at the host site" (p. 162).

LEARNING OUTCOMES

It is likely that when different media treatments of the same informational content to the same students yield similar learning results, the cause of the results can be found in a method which the two treatments share in common . . . *give up your enthusiasm* for the belief that media attributes cause learning. (Clark, 1994, p. 28)

Hundreds of media comparison studies indicate, unequivocally, that no inherent significant difference exists in the achievement effectiveness of media (Clark, 1983). These results support Clark's position summarized in the previous quote: The specific medium does not matter. That being the case, the focus of future research should be on instruction itself since it is the truly critical factor in determining student achievement (Whittington, 1987).

Unfortunately, much of the research in distance education is still of the media comparison type. This is to be expected given the rapid development of distance education technology, especially in the area of two-way interactive television systems. With each technological advance, the temptation is to conduct media comparison research on the off-chance that the new technology might truly bring about higher student achievement.

A Recent Summary of the Research

Evaluation of Evidence-Based Practices in Online Learning: A Meta-Analysis and Review of Online Learning Studies is must reading for anyone involved in education generally, and distance education specifically. This report is a comprehensive review of 51 studies that:

- "contrasted an online to a face-to-face condition,
- measured student learning outcomes,
- used a rigorous research design, and
- provided adequate information to calculate an effect size." (p. ix)

The report's most quoted conclusion is printed in italics in its abstract and states,

The meta-analysis found that, on average, students in online learning conditions performed better than those receiving face-to-face instruction. (p. ix)

The 70-page report is well written, informative, and scholarly. It is an important document that attempts to provide a state-of-the-research report on the effectiveness of online/distance education. Unfortunately, unless carefully read, the report can be misleading.

On page 51, the report's authors, staffers from SRI International's Center for Technology in Learning under contract to the U.S. Department of Education, clearly state what *should be* the most quoted outcome of this meta-analysis where they wrote:

> Clark (1983) has cautioned against interpreting studies of instruction in different media as demonstrating an effect for a given medium inasmuch as conditions may vary with respect to a whole set of instructor and content variables. That caution applies well to the findings of this meta-analysis, which should not be construed as demonstrating that online learning is superior as a medium. Rather, it is the combination of elements in the treatment conditions, which are likely to include additional learning time and materials as well as additional opportunities for collaboration that has proven effective. (p. 51)

Learning time, materials, and collaboration—the big 3. Apparently online students spent more time, had access to more materials, and collaborated differently than did the traditionally taught comparison students—no wonder online students tended to achieve better.

What we do not know from this report is *why* some students spent more time, accessed different materials, and had more collaboration opportunities. It is somewhat unfortunate that these important outcomes were not stressed instead of the misleading conclusion that "*students in online learning conditions performed better*"(p. ix).

Many will remember the meta-analyses of the 1980s that also misled a generation of educators into thinking that computer-based instruction was superior to classroom instruction (Kulik, Bangert, & Williams, 1983; Kulik, Kulik, & Cohen, 1979, 1980). The "Kulik" studies, as they were called, concluded that students using computer-based instruction achieved better than students who were traditionally taught. More critical analyses revealed that most of the studies included in the "Kulik" studies were methodologically flawed (Clark, 1983). Unfortunately, a whole generation of educators implemented computer-based instruction, and then waited for positive effects that never materialized.

Certainly, the USDE Report is important. It represents a review of the best studies available. The study's authors made every attempt to be methodologically and conceptually rigorous—perhaps the author of the abstract was a marketing adviser rather than a researcher. At any rate, this report should be read and analyzed by all distance educators.

And finally, as George Washington said over hundreds of years ago, "Facts are stubborn things: and whatever may be our wishes, our inclinations, or the dictates of our passions, they cannot alter the state of facts and evidence."

Research Reported

Mary K. Tallent-Rennels and a team of other scholars published an interesting review that summarized the research on online teaching and learning (Tallent-Rennels et al., 2006). The review was organized into four primary categories:

- Course environment
- Learner outcomes

■ Learner characteristics
■ Institutional and administrative characteristics

This review examined 68 published papers and drew a number of interesting conclusions. They identified the failure of authors to use standardized terms and to clarify the definitions of key ideas, in this case the types of courses taught—traditional, blended, and online. Tallent-Runnels and her co-authors suggest that these three terms be used when research is conducted and reported.

The review also found that there did not seem to be a comprehensive theory guiding the design of courses taught online and used when research is conducted. This is a critical weakness of the field.

The article goes on to identify conceptual and methodological problems with the research dealing with online teaching and learning. Apparently, the problems of early research on distance education have not yet been corrected—problems related to the lack of a theory base, the ad-hoc nature of studies, and the difficulty of generalizing results from one study to other similar situations.

One important conclusion reported in this review is the research finding that students have positive attitudes about online learning, and that computer anxiety is not a problem for most students. Well-designed online courses were reported to produce more positive learning outcomes and to be related to overall student satisfaction. Design and quality are important.

Ronsisvalle and Watkins (2005) reviewed the literature dealing with K–12 student success in online learning. They asserted that online K–12 learning is growing and "here to stay." The authors reported that completion rates of online students in virtual K–12 schools were increasing; most online students received grades of B or better; and student, teacher, parent, and administrator levels of satisfaction with online instruction was high.

An evaluation of the first year showed that the achievement of students in the telecourse schools was significantly higher than that of students in the comparison schools for both listening and writing. The results for the second year were similar. The researchers observed that the older students in the distant class were highly motivated, and this had a significant impact on their achievement, much more than the fact that they learned at a distance. Additional data were collected in the third year to investigate possible effects of motivation (measured by self-efficacy rating) and differences in student characteristics of self-reported grades in school and prior language learning experience. The mean achievement test scores for the telecourse students continued to be significantly higher than those of students in the comparison schools, even when the variables of self-efficacy, self-reported ability, and prior language experience were controlled. This indicates that the achievement differences between the telecourse students and the comparison group were not related to motivational, self-reported ability, or prior experience factors.

Bramble and Martin (1995) investigated the effectiveness of teletraining in the military. Participants were 275 individuals enrolled in five different teletraining project courses. Standard multiple-proficiency, criterion-based tests were used where available, and achievement tests were developed for the other courses.

In all but one course, both pretests and posttests were administered. Students were allowed a second chance at taking the proficiency tests, and when these retakes were taken into account, all students reached acceptable performance levels. No comparison data were available from schools offering these courses in traditional settings, but knowledgeable training personnel indicated that this performance is as high as or higher than one would normally expect. In all courses where precourse and postcourse performances were measured, the gain was statistically significant.

Students in all five courses were asked if they felt the teletraining was as effective as live instruction. In all but one of the courses, 75% or more responded in the affirmative. The course that had only a 54% affirmative rate was the first course offered, and adjustments may have been made prior to delivery of the other courses. This pattern was repeated when students were asked if they felt that the instructor was in the same room. For the first class only 78% responded yes; for subsequent classes 84% or more responded in the affirmative.

Although comparison research studies on achievement tend to show no significant difference between different delivery systems and between distance education and traditional education, several recent studies indicate a significantly higher achievement level for those learning at a distance (Figure 3–1). The accepted position is that the delivery system affects no inherent difference in achievement (Clark, 1994), therefore future research needs to examine what factors do, indeed, contribute to this difference in achievement. In general, a safe conclusion is that distant and local learners will achieve at the same level, and that distance education is an effective method for delivering instruction that works. In other words, distance is not a predictor of learning. It is safe to say that learning at a distance is not related to achievement. Researchers who are interested in achievement might explore equivalency theory and attempt to identify ways to define equivalency of learning experiences and relate this to measurable learning outcomes (see Chapter 2).

FIGURE 3–1 On average, distant and traditional learners achieve about the same.

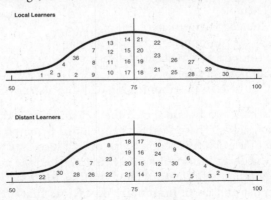

LEARNER PERCEPTIONS

Learner perceptions are an important area of research on distance education (Seok, DaCosta, Kinsell, & Tung, 2010). Ross, Morrison, Smith, and Cleveland (1991) evaluated two programs for tutoring at-risk elementary school children at a distance. One program used a local electronic bulletin board system, and the other used Applelink, a national network system featuring both electronic mail and teleconferencing. For both studies, both tutor and tutee attitudes were assessed.

In the first program, student reactions ranged from mixed to negative. More than half of the students did not understand corrections made by their tutors, received little help with their writing skills, did not have enough time with their tutors, found the assignments difficult, and said they did not learn much from their tutors. On the positive side, slightly more than half the students felt they had enough online time to complete assignments.

Most tutors felt they possessed the computer skills and content knowledge to do the work. They also felt they related well to their tutees and had the materials necessary. A need for more intensive training was expressed, and a majority (67%) said they would have liked more personal contact with their students.

More positive results were found in the second study. Tutees felt they had a positive relationship with their tutors and preferred talking to their tutors instead of their friends. They regretted the limited amount of time for online communication.

The tutors, similar to those in the first study, felt they possessed the necessary skills. They cited communication problems as a negative aspect. Many (60%) expressed indecision on whether they had found the experience enjoyable or not.

Distant learner satisfaction is an important dimension in understanding the success of interactive telecourses. Biner, Dean, and Mellinger (1994) conducted two studies to identify the major dimensions of learner satisfaction. In the first study, the telecourse evaluation questionnaire (TEQ), developed by Biner, was administered to 201 students enrolled in live, interactive, televised courses at the beginning of the last class meeting. Using factor analysis, the researchers identified students' satisfaction with the following seven factors:

- Instructor/instruction
- Technology
- Course management
- At-site personnel
- Promptness of material delivery
- Support services
- Out-of-class communication with the instructor

The second study, conducted the following year, confirmed the results of the preliminary study. The researchers concluded by emphasizing the importance of assessment of learner satisfaction to the overall success of a distance education program.

Jegede and Kirkwood (1994) investigated the anxiety level of distance education students and the factors contributing to anxiety. Two instruments, an anxiety checklist and an opinionnaire on factors that affect learning at a distance, were administered at the beginning of the semester and at the end of the semester.

Complete results were obtained from 222 distance education students enrolled at the University of Southern Queensland.

Analysis of data from the anxiety checklist indicated that participants had a high anxiety level and were generally more anxious about their studies at the end of the semester than at the beginning. Results showed a statistically significant difference between the presemester means and the postsemester means.

A factor analysis of the opinionnaire identified seven factors affecting learning at a distance: content, environment, finances, readiness, time, employment, and family support. A comparison of presemester and postsemester opinions showed that five factors were significantly different at the end of the class than at the beginning. Students' concerns related to content, finance, and readiness were higher at the beginning of the class than at the end, while concerns related to time and employment increased toward the end of the class (Jegede & Kirkwood, 1994).

The results of this study indicated that anxiety felt by distance education learners played a higher role in attrition than previously considered. The researchers suggested the need for future research on the role of anxiety, probably comparing on-campus with off-campus students, along with the introduction of other variables such as achievement outcomes and a longer period of study.

As part of a larger study, Sorensen (1995) identified the most important predictors of student satisfaction. Surveys were returned by 210 community college students enrolled in two-way interactive televised courses. In general, the students were satisfied with their distance learning experience.

Fast (1995) investigated multisite instruction of students enrolled in foreign language courses delivered by fiber optics that allowed interactive instruction. Nineteen students participated in the study, 11 at the origination site and 8 at the remote site. Postinstruction questionnaires administered to all students provided data on three variables: student motivation, perceived learning, and involvement. Remote students had a significantly more favorable attitude toward interactive TV than the origination-site students. Responses to open-ended questions requesting the likes and dislikes of interactive TV classes helped clarify this difference.

Students at both locations cited two reasons for liking the multisite instruction: human interest and facilitation of learning. Students at the remote site felt the delivery system provided opportunities for learning that would not be available otherwise.

The two groups differed strongly on their list of dislikes. A high number (over 40%) of the dislikes identified by the origination-site students were organizational issues. Of special concern was the loss of class time because of the need to transport students to the technology classroom. This was not an issue for the remote-site students.

The majority of criticisms (60%) from the remote-site students focused on problems with interaction. They disliked the lack of opportunity to interact one-on-one with the instructor. Discussions were difficult because everyone talked at once, and posing questions necessitated interrupting class. Origination-site students also identified the loss of interaction with the instructor as a problem. These results suggested that remote-site students tended to experience difficulty in being accepted as part of the discourse, whereas origination-site students found it more difficult to share their teacher with the remote-site group. Analysis of questions related to perceived learning showed no important differences between remote-site students and on-site students

A similar situation was found when data about perceptions of interaction were analyzed. Although there were no important differences between sites, there was a major difference between learning group levels. Higher-level students at the remote site indicated that having the teacher at a distance hindered learning.

Research related to learners' perceptions has focused on identifying factors related to satisfaction, attitudes, and perceived learning and interaction (Wang, 2005). Factors affecting satisfaction are often considered to be organizational and involve the environment, management, and support services. In other words, there are identifiable factors that relate to distant learners' perceptions about the effectiveness of their instructional experiences, and these factors are similar to those of local, traditional learners.

LEARNER ATTRIBUTES

Sense of community has become an important research area in distance education (Carabajal, LaPointe, & Gunawardena, 2007; Ouzts, 2006). Ouzts (2006) found that student perceptions of community related to increased satisfaction toward online learning. Coggins (1988), in a study of students associated with the University of Wisconsin System External Degree Program, examined the relationship between personal variables (learning style and demographic data) and program completion rate. She found that completers and noncompleters did not differ significantly on variables related to gender, occupation, marital status, presence or absence of children, distance from campus, or age of entry into the baccalaureate program. However, significant differences existed between the two groups for a number of other variables. Completers had entered the program with higher levels of education, and they had greater expectations of earning higher grades as well as greater expectations of earning a degree. The two groups of students differed in their preference for course content. Noncompleters tended to be more concrete learners, preferring a content that allowed them to work with things instead of people. Completers preferred a content that involved interviewing and counseling of people.

The relationship between gender and success in distance education courses was the subject of a study by Ross and Powell (1990). Data from Athabasca University, in Alberta, Canada, indicated that a greater percentage of women passed distance education courses. Further, this higher completion trend was visible irrespective of the student's general study area, the specific course selection, the course level, the mode of course delivery, the student's program status, or the number of courses the student had previously taken. An exploratory analysis assessing demographic, motivational, support, and learning style variables indicated some possible reasons for the gender differences in academic achievement. These included differences in marital status, employment, and use of institutional support between the two groups. An important difference was noted in the motivational variable. Women felt that gaining a university credential was critical and that the impact of failing was serious.

Dille and Mezack (1991) studied locus of control and learning style as predictors of risk among college distance education students. In their study, 151 students enrolled in telecourses completed the assessment instruments, which included demographic information, the internal-external locus of control scale (IELC), and the learning style inventory (LSI).

The locus of control measure was a significant predictor of two variables: success, measured as receiving a grade of C or above, and actual letter grade. Students with a more internal locus of control were more likely to be successful and to obtain a higher grade. Students with an external locus of control were less likely to persevere when faced with the perceived tougher challenge of a telecourse. An analysis of the data from the learning style inventory indicated that students who were more successful had a lower LSI average score measuring concrete experience. On the abstract conceptualization/concrete experience scale, where a lower score indicated a more concrete learner, successful students had a significantly higher score than nonsuccessful students. These findings support the idea that the less concrete one's learning style, the better suited one is to learn in the telecourse format. Although examining the abstract/concrete scale was helpful in predicting success in a distance learning environment, individual learning style was not found to be a significant predictor of success.

Wang, Foucar-Szocki, and Griffin (2003) found that the dropout rate for distance education courses they studied was about 26%. Laube (1992) examined the relationship between academic and social integration variables and the persistence of students in a secondary distance education program. Students were divided into two groups based on persistence. Completers/persisters were those who completed or still persisted in coursework 1 year after enrollment, whereas dropouts/nonstarters had dropped out during the same time.

Out of 351 surveys mailed, 181 surveys were returned, 124 in the completer/persister group and 57 in the dropout/nonstarter group. The nonreturned surveys were comprised of 44 completer/persisters and 126 dropout/nonstarters.

Two variables showed important differences between the groups. Completers/persisters were more likely than dropouts/nonstarters (1) to have higher educational goals and (2) to study more than 10 hours a week.

Three variables related to social integration were studied: self-initiated contact with the school, student attitudes toward their tutors, and student attitudes toward missing peer socialization. The two groups differed significantly only in their attitudes toward their tutors, with completers/persisters indicating a more positive attitude. Both groups indicated a positive attitude toward their tutors, but a large percentage of dropouts/nonstarters selected "undecided" as a response, which contributed to the significant results obtained. Stone (1992) examined the relationship of contact with a tutor and locus of control to course completion rates for students enrolled in print-based distance training courses. One group received weekly phone calls from the training staff, whereas the second group received only minimal feedback. Results did not show any important difference between the two groups in course completion rates. However, Stone did find that students with relatively external loci of control completed their coursework at significantly faster rates when exposed to regular telephone cues from their tutors.

How study practices and attitudes of students in a distance learning program relate to academic success was examined by Bernt and Bugbee (1993). This study examined approximately 300 students. The most important result reported was that students who were considered high passers were likely to have advanced degrees.

Several types of study strategies with distance education students were also examined. The researchers concluded that those who passed differed significantly from failers in their test strategies, concentration, and time management skills, but they were not significantly different in active processing of information, diligence, and positive attitude.

The researchers also found that students with varying education levels differed in their study strategies, notably time management, concentration, and testing strategies. This, they concluded, suggested that distance learning students who have not completed college are "at risk" primarily because they lack metacognitive or executive skills for approaching coursework and taking examinations. Distance education instructors need to be aware that, similar to traditional education students, learners are different and some need more direction and structure than others.

Garland (1993) used ethnographic procedures to identify barriers to persistence in distance education. Building on the framework of Rubenson (1986), Garland classified barriers into four categories: situational, institutional, dispositional, and epistemological. Face-to-face interviews were conducted with 47 students enrolled in primarily print-based introductory academic courses. Participants in the study included 17 students who did not complete the final exam and 30 persisting students, who took the final exam regardless of outcome.

Barriers to persistence in all four categories were encountered by both withdrawal students and persisting students. Situational barriers included poor learning environment and lack of time. Students indicated that a lack of support from both family and peers contributed to poor learning environments. They also identified resource availability and a quiet place to study as important. Students felt the course took more time than anticipated, especially as many were juggling the demands of work, home, and school.

Cost, institutional procedures, and course scheduling/pacing were reported as institutional barriers. In this study, students said that tuition was not a problem, but add-on costs of texts and labs were seen as barriers to persistence. Students who felt the university did not try to meet their needs identified both institutional procedures and course scheduling/pacing as problems. Limited office hours made it difficult to reach staff for assistance.

The largest number of barriers to persistence related to the psychological and sociological nature of the student. These barriers included (1) uncertainty of an educational or professional goal, (2) stress of multiple roles (school, work, home), (3) time management problems, (4) problems associated with learning style differences, and (5) adult pride indicated by overachievement and/or fear of failure. The study pointed to the individualness of learning, whether at a distance or in a traditional setting. Regardless of the setting, the focus needs to be on creating optimal learning conditions for each individual.

Pugliese (1994) investigated psychological variables as predictors of persistence in telecourses. Variables studied included loneliness, communication apprehension, communication competence, and locus of control. Of those urban commuter students enrolled in telecourses, 306 (a 39% response rate) responded to Pugliese's telephone survey.

The study's results were interesting. In a traditional classroom, it would be expected that the students possessing greater social interaction skills would be more likely to persist and complete the course. Results appeared to indicate that telecourses were the social equalizer. Telecourses apparently minimize the impact of social skills.

Fjortoft (1995) similarly investigated predictors of persistence in distance learning programs. Fjortoft developed a model, based on the literature of adult education, that related adult learners to persistence. The variables studied included age, gender, grade point average at the time of college graduation, satisfaction with the college experience, intrinsic job satisfaction, ease of learning on one's own, intrinsic benefits of degree completion, and extrinsic benefits of degree completion. Persistence was defined by active enrollment status.

The 395 students surveyed included those actively enrolled in a distance learning program in pharmacy and those who had been admitted but had withdrawn before completion. The response rate was 50%, with a sample size of 198.

Three variables were significant in predicting persistence in distance learning programs. Results indicated a positive relationship between perceived intrinsic benefits and continued enrollment, whereas a negative relationship between both age and ease of learning on their own and persistence was indicated. An internal desire for more satisfaction and challenge in one's career more than desires for enhanced salary and career mobility motivated adults to continue their education. The respondents ranged in age from the upper 20s to just over 60. Results indicated it was more difficult for older students to persist in the distance learning program than it was for younger students.

Fjortoft (1995) concluded that only individuals who recognized that they possessed the skills necessary to learn on their own elected to enter a distance learning program. Alternatively, adults might not be able to assess realistically their individual learning styles.

Biner, Bink, Huffman, and Dean (1995) investigated the role of personality characteristics in predicting achievement in televised courses. The Sixteen Personality Factor Questionnaire was administered to both traditional-course and televised-course students to determine how the two groups differed and also to identify personality factors predictive of success in televised courses.

The personality profiles of the two groups differed. Telecourse students tended to be more intelligent, emotionally stable, trusting, compulsive, passive, and conforming than traditional students.

Results indicated that several personality characteristics correlated significantly with course achievement. The group-oriented/self-sufficient student was more likely to have high performance, indicating that successful telecourse students tended to be self-sufficient. A negative relationship was found between the introvert/extrovert dimension and course performance. This indicated that the more introverted a student was, the better the student performed in a distance education setting.

Higher levels of expedience were associated with higher grades in the telecourse group. This was in contrast to higher levels of conscientiousness associated with higher grades in the traditional course group. Telecourse students tended to be older and were juggling responsibilities of job and home.

A review of the studies just discussed indicates that several learner characteristics have some effect on the success of the learner in a distance education environment. Although studies on the effects of gender indicated mixed results, students who were younger and had a higher level of education were more likely to complete a distance education course.

Motivation is important. Intrinsically motivated learners and those with high expectations for grades and completion of a degree tended to have higher success rates. A positive attitude toward the instructor is another factor contributing to the success of distant learners.

Dille and Mezack (1991) and Stone (1992) both found locus of control to be a significant factor. More abstract learners with internal loci of control and skills in learning alone tended to be more successful. Providing students possessing external loci of control with regular contact with the instructor increased their chances of success. Individual learning style was not a significant predictor of success. Distance education systems proved to be adept in providing for the learning needs of students with a variety of learning styles. Once again, the distant learner and the local learner are not generally different from each other.

INTERACTION

Interaction is one of the most discussed topics in distance education (Anderson & Kuskis, 2007; Moore, 2007; Sammons, 2007). Mahle (2007) reviewed literature on interaction in distance education and concluded that interaction is a primary component of any effective distance education program. Wanstreet (2006) reviewed the literature dealing with interaction in online learning and reported on the various definitions of *interaction*, including an instructional exchange, computer-mediated communication, and social/psychological connections. Beare (1989) compared the effectiveness of six instructional formats that allowed differing levels of interaction: (1) lecture, (2) lecture with videotape backup, (3) telelecture, (4) audio-assisted independent study, (5) video-assisted independent study, and (6) video on campus. Study participants consisted of 175 nontraditional teacher education students.

Not surprisingly, given the history of media comparison research, individual instructional formats had little effect on student achievement. The amount of interaction also appeared to have had no impact on student achievement.

Course evaluations yielded some interesting results, however. Analysis showed that distant learners found the course just as stimulating, were equally interested in the subject matter, and judged the instructor equally as skilled as did those receiving face-to-face instruction. The on-site students in the telecourse strongly disliked the medium. It was reported that one night, when the electronic equipment failed temporarily, the class spontaneously cheered. Bauer and Rezabek (1992) compared verbal interaction under three conditions: (1) two-way audio and video, (2) two-way audio, and (3) traditional instruction. The study included 172 students pursuing teacher certification randomly assigned to one of the three treatment groups.

No significant difference existed in total number of interactions between the audio/video group and the audio group. However, a statistically significant difference occurred between the audio/video group and the traditional group as well as between the audio group and the traditional group. Results seem to indicate that merely the addition of video in the distance education format does not increase interaction.

This could be a result of the conditioned passive response of individuals to viewing television. Simply measuring interaction may not be the answer in discovering variables contributing to increased interaction.

Souder (1993) investigated interaction and achievement of students in traditional delivery courses compared with students in a distance delivery course. Three groups of students in the same course participated in the study. One group was in a traditional classroom; the second group was on-site with the instructor while the class was broadcast to the third group at a distance. The instructor, the course content, and the course evaluation requirements were the same for each group.

There was no significant difference between the two traditionally delivered courses for evaluation questionnaire items addressing face-to-face interaction. However, the responses of the distance group were significantly different from both the on-site group and the traditional group. The students at a distance defended their distance learning experiences. They did not agree that face-to-face instruction with a live instructor was vital, nor did they believe that real-time interactions with other students were vital. The students in traditional settings disagreed and did not feel that a distance class would be of the same quality as the more traditional approach to instruction.

The results seemed to indicate that students at a distance tended to bond more with their fellow classmates and the instructor. They appeared supportive of each other and, in general, felt they performed better than the other two groups. In fact, the overall achievement of the distance group was significantly higher than that of the on-site group.

Souder (1993) concluded that:

> the distance learners in this study were observed to gain much more than a traditional education from their experiences. They gained a broadened network of valuable colleagues, skills in working with others and collaborating across distances, and many social skills beyond those offered by traditional settings. (p. 50)

Using semistructured personal interviews, May (1993) investigated the contribution of interaction to women's learning experiences in women's studies courses delivered using distance education. Nine women of varied backgrounds and experiences were interviewed. Course delivery was mostly one-way technology, and content focused on the dissemination of knowledge. There was very little interaction.

Students did not appear to miss the interaction or to recognize its potential benefits. The general feeling was that increasing student interaction required arranging face-to-face meetings. Making time for these meetings was not desirable. Distant learners questioned the value and desirability of increased collaboration.

The women in this study did not believe that isolation among distance learners necessitated a negative learning experience. The researcher concluded that increased learner interaction was not an inherently or self-evidently positive educational goal or strategy.

Fulford and Zhang (1993) examined the relationship of perceived interaction and satisfaction in an in-service training course delivered by the Hawaiian Interactive Television System (HITS). In their study, 123 students completed surveys at the beginning, midpoint, and end of a 10-week course. Participants responded to questions about three variables: personal interaction, overall interaction, and satisfaction with the value and quality of instruction.

Level of personal interaction was considered only a moderate predictor of satisfaction. Perceived level of overall interaction was almost three times more important. Learner satisfaction was considered to be attributed more to perceived overall interactivity than to individual participation. Instructors using interactive television should probably focus more on building group interaction rather than individual participation.

This study also examined the variable of time. Learners' perceptions of interaction and satisfaction decreased over the length of the course; however, overall interaction was a more stable predictor of satisfaction as learners became more experienced with the technology. In a follow-up study, Zhang and Fulford (1994) investigated the variable of time. Participants were 260 students enrolled in a course delivered by HITS. Although this study also looked at perceived interaction and satisfaction, variables were expanded to include attitude toward interaction and actual interaction time determined by analyzing videotapes of each session.

The correlation between perceived interaction and actual interaction time was nonsignificant. Reserving a considerable portion of TV time for interaction, a common strategy among TV instructors, did not seem to be quite as important as some suggest. This seems to support the work of May (1993), which indicated that more interaction was not necessarily better.

Although the correlation between actual interaction time and attitude was clear, the relationship between perceived interaction and attitude was nearly perfect. Similar relationships were found when correlating actual interaction and perceived interaction with satisfaction. Increasing interaction time merely for more time's sake is not necessary.

Communication and teaching patterns that contributed to student participation were examined in a study by Schoenfelder (1995). Schoenfelder studied 44 students and 11 teachers participating in interactive television courses. A questionnaire was used to measure teachers' and students' perceptions of ways to increase interaction and involvement.

Both teachers and students thought that an enthusiastic teacher with a sense of humor was an important factor in enhancing involvement. They also felt that addressing students by name and providing timely feedback were factors that made a positive contribution to interaction. Specific teaching habits were found to help increase student involvement. These included varying the learning activities and using a variety of visual materials.

Using observations, interviews, and videotapes, Baker (1995) examined the interactive television teaching behaviors of five faculty members teaching courses using distance education technology. Seven broad categories of teaching behaviors were identified:

- Nonverbal "immediacy" behaviors
- Verbal "immediacy" behaviors
- Behaviors that personalize the class
- Technology management strategies
- Methods for acquiring student feedback
- Methods used to manage student participation
- Active learning strategies

Nonverbal behaviors that conveyed a feeling of approachability and warmth increased involvement of students at the remote site. Specific behaviors included making eye contact with the camera, using gestures, and using camera angles and shots that allowed students to see facial expressions. Verbal "immediacy" behaviors that were found to contribute to student involvement included the use of humor, frequent positive encouragement, and the frequent sharing of personal examples. Teachers used a variety of methods for acquiring student feedback that improved student involvement. Most of the teachers relied, at least partially, on the nonverbal cues of the students at the origination site. Some used a variety of questioning techniques, whereas others used more formal, written formative evaluations.

Orellana (2006) reported on an interesting study that related class size to interaction. This study reported that the optimal class size for an online college course taught by a single instructor was approximately 20. However, it was reported that for optimal levels of interaction, as defined by Orellana, a class size of about 16 was best. Online instructors indicated that smaller class sizes (15 students) would produce more and higher-level interaction.

Research regarding interaction and distance education technologies indicates that different technologies allow differing degrees of interaction. However, similar to comparison studies examining achievement, research comparing differing amounts of interaction showed that interaction had little effect on achievement (Anderson & Kuskis, 2007; Beare, 1989; Souder, 1993). Those students who had little or no interaction as part of a course did not seem to miss it (May, 1993).

BARRIERS TO DISTANCE EDUCATION

Why some organizations adopt distance education and others do not has produced many interesting studies (Chen, 2009; Irvin, 2010; Simonson, 2001). Berge and Muilenburg (2000) reviewed the literature and identified 64 potential barriers to the implementation of distance education. They surveyed several thousand persons involved in distance education, instructional technology, and training. Of those responding, 1,150 were teachers or trainers, 648 were managers, 167 were administrators in higher education, and the remaining responders were researchers and students.

When the data were analyzed, the strongest barriers to distance education were identified. Their rank order is:

1. Increased time commitment
2. Lack of money to implement distance education programs
3. Organizational resistance to change
4. Lack of shared vision for distance education in the organization
5. Lack of support staff to help course development
6. Lack of strategic planning for distance education
7. Slow pace of implementation
8. Faculty compensation/incentives
9. Difficulty keeping up with technological changes
10. Lack of technology-enhanced classrooms, labs, or infrastructure

Additionally, Berge and Muilenburg identified the least important barriers to implementation. They were (in rank order):

54. Competition with on-campus courses
55. Lack of personal technological expertise

56. Lack of acceptable use policy
57. Lack of transferability of credits
58. Problems with vast distances and time zones
59. Technology fee
60. Tuition rate
61. Local, state, or federal regulations
62. Ethical issues
63. Existing union contracts
64. Lack of parental involvement

Berge and Muilenburg concluded by identifying the need for cultural change within organizations involved or contemplating involvement with distance education. Five of the top barriers related directly to organizational culture are as follows:

- Organizational resistance to change
- Lack of shared vision for distance education in the organization
- Lack of strategic planning for distance education
- Slow pace of implementation
- Difficulty keeping up with technological change

In South Dakota (Simonson, 2001), a series of focus groups of teachers revealed the following reasons why they were reluctant to be involved in distance education:

- Fear
- Training
- Time
- Changes needed

These same groups indicated that the impediments to implementing distance education in schools were as follows:

- Need for training
- Need for and lack of support
- Time needed
- Fear of the process
- Scheduling problems
- Technical problems

In 2009, Chen reported that the three primary barriers that prevent institutions from offering distance education are program development costs, faculty workload concerns, and the need for faculty rewards for offering courses at a distance. Effective incorporation of new technologies was considered to be one way to reduce barriers.

DISTANCE EDUCATION TECHNOLOGY

Numerous studies have described or examined the efficacy of individual forms of distance education, whereas others have examined aspects or components of those forms. Garrison (1990) used a description of audio teleconferencing to argue for an appropriate concentration on the role of the teacher and the importance of two-way communication in the education process. Along the way, he argued for the appropriate, conservative use of interactive communication technologies.

The core of Garrison's argument was the following:

> Education, whether it be at a distance or not, is dependent upon two-way communication. There is an increasing realization in the educational community that simply accessing information is not sufficient. In an educational experience information must be shared, critically analyzed, and applied in order to become knowledge. (p. 13)

A goal of some distance education programs is to make education more student centered through the prepackaging of instructional materials that students may use when convenient. However, Garrison argued that this approach ignores the essential nature of an educational learning experience. He reported that this simply risked making learning more private and therefore less likely to transform the views and perspectives of the learner in a positive developmental manner.

Garrison argued that the quality and the integrity of the educational process depend on sustained, two-way communication. Such communication, between student and teacher and between student and student, is the prime benefit of teleconferencing. When this technology is applied to distance education, the result is that distance education is no longer necessarily an independent and isolated form of learning, but instead begins to approach the interactive ideal of an educational experience.

Garrison supports audio teleconferencing, which he regards as a distinct generation of distance education capable of providing unique and varied teaching and learning possibilities. Independent and isolated study is no longer the hallmark of distance education. Egan, Welch, Page, and Sebastian (1992) examined graduate students' perceptions of three instructional delivery systems: (1) conventional delivery, (2) closed-circuit microwave system (EDNET), and (3) videotape recordings (Professor Plus). Near the conclusion of the course, 514 students evaluated the delivery systems using the Media Evaluation Survey. This instrument allows individuals the opportunity to evaluate instructional media on 10 elements:

> (1) amount of material covered, (2) level of difficulty, (3) degree to which the course content was well organized, (4) clarity of the content, (5) degree to which the various programs and instructional activities were relevant to the course objectives, (6) excellence or lack of excellence of the presenter's delivery, (7) extent to which text and weekly assignments were integrated with each week's class, (8) value of slides, films, and other visual materials, (9) value of text screens to support the presenter's delivery, and (10) degree to which the course held the student's interest. (p. 50)

Results showed 6 of the 10 variables to be different for distant learners. The conventional delivery group gave higher ratings to organization, clarity, relevance, integration, value of visuals, and value of text screens. A comparison of conventional delivery to Professor Plus yielded similar results, but with significant differences shown on the two additional variables of adequacy of presenter's delivery and student interest, which were rated higher by the conventional delivery group.

A comparison of the two television delivery systems, EDNET and Professor Plus, showed a significant difference for distant learners for only one variable. The average of the EDNET group's ratings on the value of visuals variable was higher than that of the Professor Plus group's ratings.

An analysis of the educational attributes of two forms of communication technology was reported by Tuckey (1993). The electronic white board, a form of synchronous audioconferencing, and asynchronous computer conferencing were reviewed. It was not the intent of the analysis to identify one form of communication as better than the other.

Face-to-face interaction was available in the uses of the electronic white board reviewed. Students met in small groups with the aural presence of the instructor. This element provides opportunities for social interaction, for mutual support, and for collaborative learning, and provides more possibilities for group work than does audioconferencing.

Computer conferencing permitted only text-based communication. Several negative aspects, including limits in display capabilities, contributed to difficulties in collaboration. Group work is also difficult due to the asynchronous nature of this technology. Tuckey (1993) concluded that each form of communication has its advantages. Visual channels may be more important in subject areas such as mathematics and the sciences, whereas computer conferencing may be more suitable in areas requiring extensive discourse.

Ahern and Repman (1994) examined two different delivery technologies and their relationship to interaction. They found that interaction was sometimes inhibited in distance education systems. The attributes of specific delivery technologies may contribute to both the quantity and the quality of teacher–student and student–student interactions. In the first study, the researchers analyzed videotapes of a class delivered using two-way audio/two-way video technology. Levels of teacher–student interaction were identified. Teachers talked 62% of the time, with students talking 38% of the time. The percent of questions asked was divided almost equally between students and teachers.

In the second study, Ahern and Repman (1994) evaluated computer-mediated communication systems and their impact on interaction. Two versions of software were developed for this study. The first used a graphic-based discussion map; the second was a more traditional text version. Students in the graphic interface produced significantly more messages than students using the textual interface. The students using the graphic version spent approximately 25% more time per visit.

As with any medium used for instruction, it is important to examine attributes and their contribution to the learning outcome. The previous studies suggest that different distance education technologies meet different needs. Two-way communication is an essential component of the learning environment. Collaboration with other students and with the instructor is more possible and easier today than several years ago because of advancements in technology. Continued research needs to examine the setting and context as well as the media attributes to determine variables contributing to learner outcomes.

MYTHS REGARDING DISTANCE EDUCATION RESEARCH

A *myth* is an invented story, and it does not always begin with "Once upon a time." In any field, including distance education, ideas and approaches quickly emerge that seem to gain a life of their own, even though there is little, if any, factual support for them. The myth of the media effect has been discussed for decades, making the rounds every time a new instructional technology is introduced. It implies that merely using media for instruction somehow has an impact on learning. This myth has been widely discussed and soundly rebuked (Clark, 1983). Three more myths about distance education deserve the same fate.

Myth 1: The more interaction there is in a distance education class, the better. This myth is easy to trace to its roots. Early research on distance education demonstrated clearly that the *provision* for interaction was critical. In other words, some early forms of distance education were one way, or had interaction that was so delayed that students had little if any feeling of involvement with their instructors. Students need to be able to interact with their teacher, at least to ask questions.

Interaction is *needed and should be available.* However, interaction is not the "end all and be all" of learning. It is only necessary to look at a few research studies, such as Fulford and Zhang (1995), to discover that interaction is not a magic potion that miraculously improves distance learning. Interaction is important, and the potential for all involved in teaching and training to be able to confer is essential.

However, forced interaction can be as strong a detriment to effective learning as is its absence.

Myth 2: Instructor training is required for anyone planning to teach at a distance. Naturally, the more training a person has, the more likely it is that he or she will learn, assuming education works. However, training in how to teach distant learners is only one of a collection of interrelated competencies needed by an effective teacher.

By far the most important competency of any teacher is content knowledge. Understanding a subject and the ability to break down the topic into meaningful and manageable concepts is fundamental for any effective teacher. In some distance education systems, the course delivery specialist may not need to know much about content, notably the industrialized systems of Europe where an assembly-line approach and division of labor are typical, and where different people prepare courses and course content. If there is only one person, the teacher, who is responsible for the entire process—from course design and course delivery to course evaluation—then knowledge of content is essential.

Myth 3: Using instructional technology in teaching is e-learning, and this is the same as distance education. A report by Zemsky and Massy titled *Thwarted Innovation: What Happened to e-Learning and Why* (2004) presents this myth. *Thwarted Innovation* presents research that exposes the failures of e-learning. A careful reading of this monograph shows that the idea of e-learning discussed is really a review of the use of technology in education. Distance education should not be confused with e-learning, which is considered an outdated term by some (Cole, 2004).

The definition of distance education presented in Chapters 1 and 2 clarifies what is meant by distance education. When research on the field is conducted, a clearness of definitions of terms is critical.

SUMMARY

Although it is always perilous to summarize research in a few sentences, it is also the obligation of those who have studied the literature extensively to provide others with their best estimates of what has been reported.

The distance education literature has several characteristics that make summarization difficult. The largely anecdotal nature of distance education literature, reporting results of a specific project, makes it difficult to generalize. Widely criticized comparison studies continue to be popular. Comparing the achievements of distance learners with those of traditional learners or between distance learners using different technologies continues to show "no significant difference." Students tend to be highly motivated, with adult learners providing little help in generalizing to other populations.

In spite of these limitations, it is possible to draw the following tentative conclusions from the research literature. Although these summary statements should be interpreted skeptically, they are supported by the literature.

- Distance education is just as effective as traditional education in regard to learner outcomes.
- Distance education learners generally have a more favorable attitude toward distance education than do traditional learners, and distance learners feel they learn as well as if they were in a regular classroom.
- Successful distance education learners tend traditionally to be abstract learners who are intrinsically motivated and possess an internal locus of control.
- Although interaction seems intuitively important to the learning experience, interaction should not be added without real purpose.
- Focusing on building collaboration and group interaction may be more important than focusing on individual participation.
- Each form of distance education technology has it own advantages and disadvantages in contributing to the overall quality of the learning experience.

The research clearly shows that distance education is an effective method for teaching and learning. Future research needs to focus on different populations, particularly K–12 students; psychological and social attributes of the learner; the impact of distance education on the organization; and the contributions of different media attributes to learning outcomes.

Recently, a great deal of attention has been paid to the concept of "best practices." The research in this area suffers from the same characteristics as other distance education research. It is largely anecdotal, lacks clear reference to theory, and does not use standardized measures to identify outcomes. In other words, this research is not widely generalizable. Chapter 5, "Instructional Design for Distance Education," reviews the best practices literature in depth. One striking summary of this research is summarized by the statement that "it is not different education, it is distance education," which implies that what we know about best practices in education is directly applicable to distance education.

DISCUSSION QUESTIONS

1. If only one conclusion could be made from the research about leaning at a distance, what would it be?
2. What is the trend of learner perceptions about learning at a distance?
3. Why is the recent meta-analysis report from the U.S. Department of Education important, and why might the results be suspect?

REFERENCES

Ahern, T. C., & Repman, J. (1994). The effects of technology on online education. *Journal of Research on Computing in Education, 26*(4), 537–546.

Anderson, T., & Kuskis, A. (2007). Modes of interaction. In M. Moore (Ed.), *Handbook of distance education*. Mahwah, NJ: Erlbaum.

Baker, M. H. (1995). Distance teaching with interactive television: Strategies that promote interaction with remote-site students. In C. Sorensen, C. Schlosser, M. Anderson, & M. Simonson (Eds.), *Encyclopedia of distance education research in Iowa* (pp. 107–115). Ames, IA: Teacher Education Alliance.

Bauer, J. W., & Rezabek, L. L. (1992). *The effects of two-way visual contact on student verbal interactions during teleconferenced instruction.* (ERIC Document Reproduction Service No. ED347972).

Beare, P. L. (1989). The comparative effectiveness of videotape, audiotape, and telelecture in delivering continuing teacher education. *The American Journal of Distance Education, 3*(2), 57–66.

Berge, Z., & Muilenburg, L. (2000). Barriers to distance education as perceived by managers and administrators: Results of a survey. In M. Clay (Ed.), *Distance learning administration annual 2000*. Baltimore: University of Maryland–Baltimore.

Bernt, F. L., & Bugbee, A. C. (1993). Study practices and attitudes related to academic success in a distance learning programme. *Distance Education, 14*(1), 97–112.

Biner, P. M., Bink, M. L., Huffman, M. L., & Dean, R. S. (1995). Personality characteristics differentiating and predicting the achievement of televised-course students and traditional-course students. *The American Journal of Distance Education, 9*(2), 46–60.

Biner, P. M., Dean, R. S., & Mellinger, A. E. (1994). Factors underlying distance learner satisfaction with televised college-level courses. *The American Journal of Distance Education, 8*(1), 60–71.

Bramble, W. J., & Martin, B. L. (1995). The Florida teletraining project: Military training via two-way compressed video. *The American Journal of Distance Education, 9*(1), 6–26.

Campbell, D., & Stanley, J. (1963). *Experimental and quasi-experimental designs for research*. Boston: Houghton Mifflin.

Carabajal, K., LaPointe, D., & Gunawardena, C. (2007). Group development in online distance learning groups. In M. Moore (Ed.), *Handbook of distance education*. Mahwah, NJ: Erlbaum.

Chen, B. (2009). Barriers to adoption of technology-mediated distance educaiton in higher-education institutions. *Quarterly Review of Distance Education, 10*(4), 333–338.

Clark, R. E. (1983). Reconsidering research on learning from media. *Review of Educational Research, 53*(4), 445–459.

Clark, R. E. (1994). Media will never influence learning. *Educational Technology Research and Development, 42*(2), 21–29.

Coggins, C. C. (1988). Preferred learning styles and their impact on completion of external degree programs. *The American Journal of Distance Education, 2*(1), 25–37.

Cole, A. (2004). E-learning outdated. *Educational Technology, 44*(2), 61.

Dille, B., & Mezack, M. (1991). Identifying predictors of high risk among community college telecourse students. *The American Journal of Distance Education, 5*(1), 24–35.

Egan, M. W., Welch, M., Page, B., & Sebastian, J. (1992). Learners' perceptions of instructional delivery systems: Conventional and television. *The American Journal of Distance Education, 6*(2), 47–55.

Fast, M. (1995, April). Interaction in technology: Mediated, multisite, foreign language instruction. Paper presented at the Annual Meeting of the American Educational Research Association, San Francisco, CA.

Finn, J. (1953). Professionalizing the audiovisual field. *Visual Communication Review, 1*(1), 6–17.

Fjortoft, N. F. (1995). *Predicting persistence in distance learning programs.* (ERIC Document Reproduction Service No. ED387620).

Fulford, C., & Zhang, S. (1995). Interactivity in distance education television: A constructed reality. Distance Education Symposium 3. The Pennsylvania State University.

Fulford, C. P., & Zhang, S. (1993). Perceptions of interaction: The critical predictor in distance education. *The American Journal of Distance Education, 7*(3), 8–21.

Garland, M. R. (1993). Student perceptions of the situational, institutional, dispositional, and epistemological barriers to persistence. *Distance Education, 14*(2), 181–198.

Garrison, D. R. (1990). An analysis and evaluation of audio teleconferencing to facilitate education at a distance. *The American Journal of Distance Education, 4*(3), 13–24.

Hirumi, A. (2005). In search of quality: An analysis of e-learning guidelines and specifications. *Quarterly Review of Distance Education, 6*(4), 209–330.

Holmberg, B. (1987). The development of distance education research. *The American Journal of Distance Education, 1*(3), 16–23.

Howell, S., & Baker, K. (2006). Good (best) practices for electronically offered degree and certificate programs: A ten-year retrospect. *Distance Learning, 3*(1), 41–47.

Irvin, M. (2010). Barriers to distance education in rural schools. *Quarterly Review of Distance Education, 11*(2), 73–90.

Jegede, O. J., & Kirkwood, J. (1994). Students' anxiety in learning through distance education. *The American Journal of Distance Education, 15*(2), 279–290.

Kulik, C., Bangert, R., & Williams, G. (1983). Effects of computer-based teaching on secondary school students. *Journal of Educational Psychology, 75*, 19–26.

Kulik, C., Kulik, J., & Cohen, P. (1979). Research on audio-tutorial instruction: A meta-analysis of comparative studies. *Research in Higher Education, 11*(4), 321–341.

Kulik, C., Kulik, J., & Cohen, P. (1980). Instructional technology and college teaching. *Teaching of Psychology, 7*(4), 199–205.

Laube, M. R. (1992). Academic and social integration variables and secondary student persistence in distance education. *Research in Distance Education, 4*(1), 2–5.

Lou, Y., Bernard, R., & Abrami, P. (2006). Undergraduate distance education: A theory-based meta-analysis of the literature. *Educational Technology Research and Development, 54*(2), 141–176.

Mahle, M. (2007). Interactivity in distance education. *Distance Learning, 4*(1), 47–51.

May, S. (1993). Collaborative learning: More is not necessarily better. *The American Journal of Distance Education, 7*(3), 39–50.

Moore, M. (2007). A theory of transactional distance. In M. Moore (Ed.), *Handbook of distance education*. Mahwah, NJ: Erlbaum.

Orellana, A. (2006). Class size and interaction in online courses. *Quarterly Review of Distance Education, 7*(3), 229–248.

Orellana, A., Hudgins, T., & Simonson, M. (2009). *The perfect online course.* Charlotte, NC: Information Age Publishing.

Ouzts, K. (2006). Sense of community in online courses. *Quarterly Review of Distance Education, 7*(3), 285–296.

Pugliese, R. R. (1994). Telecourse persistence and psychological variables. *The American Journal of Distance Education, 8*(3), 22–39.

Ronsisvalle, T., & Watkins, R. (2005). Student success in online K–12 education. *Quarterly Review of Distance Education, 6*(2), 117–124.

Ross, L. R., & Powell, R. (1990). Relationships between gender and success in distance education courses: A preliminary investigation. *Research in Distance Education, 2*(2), 10–11.

Ross, S. M., Morrison, G. R., Smith, L. J., & Cleveland, E. (1991). *An evaluation of alternative distance tutoring models for at-risk elementary school children.* (ERIC Document Reproduction Service No. ED335009).

Rubenson, K. (1986). Distance education for adults: Old and new barriers for participation. In G. van Enckevorrt, K. Harry, P. Morin, & H. G. Schutze (Eds.), *Distance higher education and the adult learner: Innovations in distance education* (Vol. 1, pp. 39–55). Heelern, the Netherlands: Dutch Open University.

Sammons, M. (2007). Collaborative interaction. In M. Moore (Ed.), *Handbook of distance education.* Mahwah, NJ: Earlbaum.

Schoenfelder, K. R. (1995). Student involvement in the distance education classroom: Teacher and student perceptions of effective instructional methods. In C. Sorensen, C. Schlosser, M. Anderson, & M. Simonson (Eds.), *Encyclopedia of distance education research in Iowa* (pp. 79–85). Ames, IA: Teacher Education Alliance.

Seok, S., Da Costa, B., Kinsell, C., & Tung, C. (2010). Comparison of instructors and students' perrceptions of the effectiveness of online courses. *Quarterly Review of Distance Education, 11*(1), 25–36.

Simonson, M. (2001). Examining barriers to distance education. *Quarterly Review of Distance Education 2*(1), 1–2.

Simonson, M. (2001). *Connecting the schools: Final evaluation report.* North Miami Beach, FL: Nova Southeastern University. Available online at www.tresystems.com/projects/sdakota.cfgm.

Simonson, M. (2006). Teaching courses online. *Quarterly Review of Distance Education, 7*(4), vii–viii.

Simonson, M. (2009). Scientific rigor. *Quarterly Review of Distance Education, 10*(4), vii–viii.

Smith, B., Benne, K., Stanley, W., & Anderson, A. (1951). *Readings in the social aspects of education.* Danville, IL.: Interstate Printers and Publishers.

Smith, L. (2006). Best practices in distance education. *Distance Learning, 3*(3), 59–69.

Sorensen, C., & Baylen, D. (2004). Learning online: Adapting the seven principles of good practice to a Web-based instructional environment. *Distance Learning, 1*(1), 7–17.

Sorensen, C. K. (1995). Attitudes of community college students toward interactive television instruction. In C. Sorensen, C. Schlosser, M. Anderson, & M. Simonson (Eds.), *Encyclopedia of distance education research in Iowa* (pp. 131–148). Ames, IA: Teacher Education Alliance.

Souder, W. E. (1993). The effectiveness of traditional vs. satellite delivery in three management of technology master's degree programs. *The American Journal of Distance Education, 7*(1), 37–53.

Stone, T. E. (1992). A new look at the role of locus of control in completion rates in distance education. *Research in Distance Education, 4*(2), 6–9.

Tallent-Runnels, M., Cooper, S., Lan W., Thomas, J., & Busby, C. (2005). How to teach online; what the research says. *Distance Learning, 2*(1), 21–34.

Tallent-Runnels, M., Thomas, J., Lan, W., Cooper, S., Ahern, T., Shaw, S., & Liu, X. (2006). Teaching courses online: A review of the research. *Review of Educational Research, 76*(1), 93–135.

Tuckey, C. J. (1993). Computer conferencing and the electronic white board in the United Kingdom: A comparative analysis. *The American Journal of Distance Education, 7*(2), 58–72.

U.S. Department of Education, Office of Planning, Evaluation and Policy Development. (2009). *Evaluation of evidence-based practices in online learning: A meta-analysis and review of online learning studies,* Washington, D.C. (www.ed.gov/about/offices/list/opepd?ppss?reports.html).

Wang, G., Foucar-Szocki, D., & Griffin, O. (2003). *Departure, abandonment, and dropout in e-learning: Dilemma and solutions.* Sarasota Springs, NY: Maisie Center e-Learning Corsortium.

Wang, P. (2005). Online and face-to-face students' perceptions of teacher–learner inteactions. *Distance Learning, 2*(5), 1–7.

Wanstreet, C. (2006). Interaction in online learning environments: A review of the literature. *Quarterly Review of Distance Education, 7*(4), 399–411.

Whittington, N. (1987). Is instructional television educationally effective? A research review. *The American Journal of Distance Education, 1*(1), 47–57.

Zemsky, R., & Massy, W. (2004). *Thwarted innovation: What happened to e-learning and why.* Philadelphia: The Learning Alliance at the University of Pennsylvania.

Zhang, S., & Fulford, C. P. (1994). Are interaction time and psychological interactivity the same thing in the distance learning television classroom? *Educational Technology, 34*(6), 58–64.

SUGGESTED READINGS

American Journal of Distance Education. University Park, PA: The Pennsylvania State University.

Journal of Distance Education. Ottawa, ON: Canadian Association for Distance Education.

Moore, M. G. (1995). The 1995 distance education research symposium: A research agenda. *The American Journal of Distance Education, 9*(2), 1–6.

Quarterly Review of Distance Education. Greenwich, CT: Information Age Publishing.

CHAPTER 4

Technologies, the Internet, and Distance Education

CHAPTER GOAL

The purpose of this chapter is to discuss the technologies used for distance education systems and distance education classrooms.

CHAPTER OBJECTIVES

After reading and reviewing this chapter, you should be able to

1. Describe systems for categorizing media used for distance education.
2. Explain the technologies used to connect teachers and learners for distance education, including correspondence, audio, video, and desktop systems.
3. Explain the configuration of a modern distance education classroom.
4. Understand the Internet and the World Wide Web and the relationship of both to the growth of distance education.

 A TRUE STORY

In the 1980s, the southeast African nation of Zimbabwe was founded from the British Commonwealth country of Rhodesia after a long and painful process. Before the founding of Zimbabwe the educational system of Rhodesia enrolled less than 500,000 learners, and most were located in the major cities and towns of the country. One of the first acts of the new government was to offer free and universal education to the nation's children, no matter where they were located. This meant that the enrollment in the country's schools increased tenfold overnight.

The teacher education faculty at the University of Zimbabwe in Harare and at other institutions of teacher training had to face the immediate problem of preparing the thousands of teachers needed by the many new and enlarged schools of the country. The approach selected was partly ingenious and partly based on necessity.

It was decided that teachers in training should attend one of the institutions of higher education for their first year of preparation. For their second and third years these teacher education students were assigned to a school where they taught classes of students.

College students functioned as regular educators with two exceptions. First, they were under the guidance of a more experienced colleague, and second, they continued their teacher education and higher education coursework at a distance. In other words, they enrolled in a full curriculum of coursework while they also functioned as novice teachers. Their coursework was delivered to them from a distant higher education institution. For their fourth year they returned to the university or college and completed their degrees.

In Zimbabwe, distance education became the primary technique for preparing the thousands of teachers needed to staff the new country's schools. Interestingly, the technology used to connect professors, such as those of the faculty of education at the University of Zimbabwe, and students located in the many cities, towns, and villages of the country was the postal system. Students received written assignments and printed resources from the university. They used, studied, and interacted with these materials to complete assignments, which then were returned to the faculty of education for evaluation. Follow-up assignments and materials were then posted back to students. This process continued until the second and third years of the bachelor's degree were completed. Periodic visits to the campus occurred, but the majority of the learning events and activities took place at a distance.

This system, born of the necessity of educating millions of students, used the most appropriate technology available—the postal system. Certainly, a major social, political, and ultimately educational problem was solved, even though the approach was not high-tech. However, it was efficient and effective. Whatever technology is used, the purpose is to promote communication.

 ## A MODEL OF COMMUNICATION

Communication occurs when two or more individuals wish to share ideas. Communication in a distance education environment happens when learners interact with one another and with their instructor. Communication, including communication for distance education, is possible because individuals have overlapping fields of experience. In other words, they have things in common, such as language and culture (Figure 4–1).

Communication must be based on what the senders of messages—distance educators—have in common with the receivers of messages—distant learners. Effective instructional messages are designed according to the situation, experiences, and competencies of learners. In order to communicate, instructional ideas are encoded

FIGURE 4–1 A model of communication.

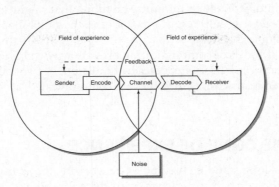

into some transmittable form, such as spoken words, pictures, or writing. The instructional message is then sent to the learner over a channel. If the receiver of the message is nearby, such as in the same classroom, the sender—the teacher—may speak or show pictures in order to communicate. If the learner is at a distance, then the instructional message will need to be sent over a wire (e.g., the telephone), hand-delivered (e.g., the mail), or broadcast through the air (e.g., television). In other words, media are used to communicate to distant learners. In fact, media extend the senses, so instructional messages can be sent over long distances or stored for learning at different times.

When the distant learner receives the message it must be decoded. This means the words spoken must be heard and defined, or the pictures shown must be seen and understood. If communication is successful, the receiver—the learner—will have the same idea or understanding as the sender—the teacher.

Effective communication requires an active audience. The response of the learners who receive messages is called *feedback*. Feedback allows the sender and receiver, the teacher and learner, to determine if the message was understood correctly. Feedback in distance education systems is often referred to as *interaction*. Feedback permits those involved in communication in a distance education system to evaluate the process.

Noise is also part of the communication process. Any disturbance that interferes with or distorts the transmission of a message is called *noise*. Audible static is one form of noise. Classroom distractions are noise, as is ambiguous or unfamiliar information.

The model of communication has been widely used to describe the interaction between message designers and audiences—teachers and learners. It is also quite relevant for distance education. Specifically, instruction must be designed in a way that capitalizes on what learners already know and what they have already experienced—their fields of experience. Then messages should be encoded so they can be effectively transmitted to distant learners.

Channels of communication, the media that connect the teacher and the distant learner, should be appropriate for the learner and the instruction. In other words, the media used to connect the learner, teacher, and learning resources must be capable of conveying all necessary information.

When instruction is designed and when feedback and interaction are planned, efforts should be made to minimize anything that might interfere with the communication process (e.g., noise). One way this can be accomplished is by sending information through multiple channels.

Models of communication provide a general orientation to the process of distance education. The model described in Figure 4–1 contains the elements to be considered when instructional messages are communicated.

THE CONE OF EXPERIENCE

One long-standing method of categorizing the ability of media to convey information is the cone of experience, introduced by Edgar Dale (1946). An adapted *cone of experience* helps organize the media used in distance education systems (Figure 4–2).

Children respond to direct, purposeful experiences, not only because they are young but also because they are learning many new things for the first time. Real experiences have the greatest impact on them because they have fewer previous experiences to look back on and refer to than do older learners. Real experiences provide the foundation for learning.

As learners grow older and have more experiences, it is possible for them to understand events that are less realistic and more abstract. Dale first stated this basic idea when he introduced his cone of experience. He proposed that for students to function and learn from experiences presented abstractly (those at the higher levels of the cone), it was necessary for them to have sufficient and related experiences that were more realistic (those at the lower levels). Learners need to have direct, purposeful experiences to draw on in order to successfully learn from more abstract events. For example, if children are to look at pictures of flowers and know what they are, they must have first seen, smelled, and touched real flowers.

Media permit the educator to bring sights and sounds of the real world into the learning environment—the classroom. However, when new information is presented, it is important that it be as realistic as possible. Similarly, when younger learners are involved, more realistic instruction is needed.

Still, one misunderstanding about the cone of experience is the belief that "more realistic" is always better. This is definitely not true. More realistic forms of learning are considerably less efficient in terms of uses of resources, and they are often less effective because of the many distractions of realistic instruction.

The critical job of the educator, especially the designer of distance education materials, is to be only as realistic as needed in order for learning to effectively occur. If instruction is too realistic, it can be inefficient. It may cost too much, it may have too much irrelevant information, or it may be difficult to use. Similarly, learning experiences that are too abstract may be inexpensive, but may not contain enough relevant information and may not be understood. To clarify the conflict between realistic and abstract experiences, Dale (1946) told a story about the life of a Greek sponge fisherman. The most realistic way to learn about the fisherman's life was to go

FIGURE 4–2   Cone of experience.

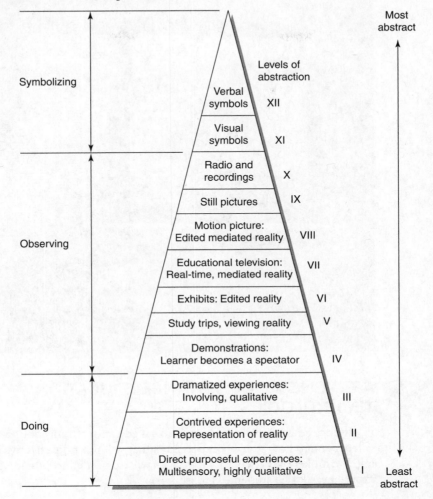

to Greece and work on a sponge boat. This approach to learning would be very realistic, effective, and authentic. It would also take a long time and cost a great deal, both in money and in learning time. An abstract way to learn about the life of a sponge fisherman would be to read about it in a book. This would take only a few hours and would cost little, even though the experience would not be overly authentic. Today, most would opt for something that is in the middle of Dale's cone, such as a 28-minute video on cable television's Discovery Channel titled "A Day in the Life of a Greek Sponge Fisherman."

© 2007 Polycom, Inc.

A TAXONOMY OF DISTANCE EDUCATION TECHNOLOGIES

In distance education, it is imperative that educators think about how communication will occur and how to apply experiences that will promote effective and efficient learning. Most likely, a variety of techniques will be needed to provide equivalent learning experiences for all students (Figure 4–3):

- Correspondence study
- Prerecorded media
- Two-way audio
- Two-way audio with graphics
- One-way live video
- Two-way audio, one-way video
- Two-way audio/video
- Desktop two-way audio/video.

Correspondence Study

The simplest and longest-lived form of distance education is generally considered to be *correspondence study*. This approach to distance education uses some kind of mail

FIGURE 4–3 Distance education technologies.

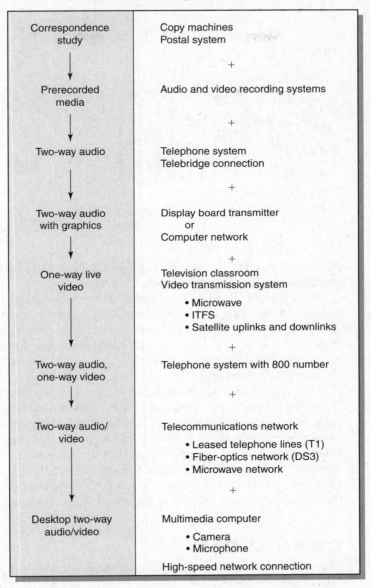

system, such as regular post office mail or electronic mail, to connect the teacher and the learner asynchronously (Figure 4–4).

Usually, lessons, readings, and assignments are sent to the student, who then completes the lessons, studies the readings, and works on the assignments, which are mailed to the instructor for grading. For a college-level course worth three credits,

FIGURE 4–4   Correspondence study utilizing the post office to connect the teacher and the learners.

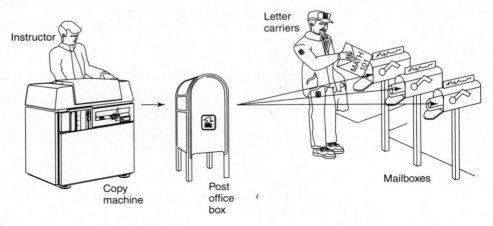

there are often 10 to 12 units to be completed. Each is finished in turn, and when all are completed satisfactorily, the student receives a grade.

Sophisticated forms of correspondence study have used techniques of programmed instruction to deliver information. Linear-programmed instruction is most common, but for a period of time a number of correspondence study organizations attempted to develop print-based branched programmed instruction.

Programmed instruction normally has a block of content, followed by questions to be answered. Depending on the answers students give, they move to the next block of text (linear programmed instruction) or to another section of the programmed text (branched programmed instruction). Sometimes remedial loops of instruction are provided to help students through difficult content, or content that supposedly had been covered in previous courses or blocks of instruction. Advanced students do not need to study remedial loops. In this manner, the rate and route of instruction are varied for students of correspondence courses. Correspondence study is relatively inexpensive, can be completed almost anywhere, and has been shown to be effective. Correspondence study has been used by millions of learners of all ages since the nineteenth century.

Prerecorded Media

The next logical step in the development of distance education technologies, both historically and conceptually, was the incorporation of media other than print media into correspondence study systems. First, pictures and other graphics were added to correspondence study texts. Then, audiotapes and finally videotapes were added to the collection of materials sent to distant learners. Usually, the correspondence study guide would direct the learner to look at, listen to, or view various media, in addition to assigning more traditional readings.

One interesting approach used by distance educators was borrowed from advocates of individualized instruction. This approach used audiotapes to guide the distant learner through a series of learning events, very similar to how a tutor would direct learning. This audio-tutorial approach was quite popular for a number of years, and it is still used by commercial organizations that present self-help materials for individual study.

MPG Files (Podcasting).   An .mpg audio file, often called an *educational podcast,* is usually a prerecorded single-concept lesson, normally audio only, but sometimes with accompanying still or motion visuals (Simonson, 2007). Essex (2006) says a podcast is a digital "radio show"—an audio program that can be downloaded from the Web. Podcasts have become a huge new information and entertainment option for Internet users. It is estimated that 4.8 million people downloaded a podcast in the last year, and in the year 2006–09 the podcast audience is estimated to be between 45 and 75 million (Essex, 2006). The podcast has been incorporated into the culture to the degree that the word *podcast* was chosen as the New Oxford American Dictionary's 2005 Word of the Year (*New Oxford American Dictionary*, 2005).

Podcasting is not a new idea. It has been around at least since the audio tutorial movement and the Sony Walkman. A podcast is really a single-concept event that is explained by an audio file, or an audio file supplemented by still pictures or video. The most widespread and current example of a type of a podcast is a song, usually 3 to 5 minutes long, available in an electronic file format, such as mpg3 or mpg4, that also might be available as a music video with singers, dancers, and actors in addition to the song. Luther Vandross's tune "Always and Forever" is a wonderful 4-minute, 54-second example. The tune is also available as a music video showing Vandross singing the song.

Individual songs work well as podcasts because most modern tunes have the characteristics of an effective single-concept event—what many now are calling a podcast, which really is a learning object that is stored in an .mpg format. The characteristics of an *effective* podcast are as follows:

■ A podcast is a single idea that can be explained verbally, or if necessary with audio and appropriate still or motion pictures (not a face talking).
■ A podcast is a recorded event that is 3 to 10 minutes long.
■ A podcast is part of a series, with each single event related to others.
■ A podcast is a learning object available in an electronic format that is easily played, most often as an mpg3 file.
■ A podcast is stored on a website or other Internet location for easy access.
■ A podcast is current and changed or updated frequently.

A recording of a lecture is a poor example of a podcast. Rather, it is best to "chunk" a 50-minute class into five or six single-concept blocks, each as a separate learning object. Effective lecturers do this already; they break up their class session into related topics. These topics can become podcasts when they are recorded electronically in an .mpg file format, especially if they are supplemented with related examples and recorded in a proper location without distracting background noises. Essex (2006) identified six tips for better podcasts:

1. *Listen.* Few of us have access to recording studios for our podcasts, but the environment that you are recording in should be as quiet as possible. Turn off

that fan, close the windows, tell your cubicle neighbor to turn off the radio, and so on. Close the door and put a "Don't Knock" sign on it.

2. *Rehearse first, but record the rehearsal as well.* Oftentimes, I find that my delivery during the rehearsal take is more lively and spontaneous than the "final" version. You may want to edit together the best parts of both attempts.

3. *Provide URLs.* Cite resources on a website or, even better, on a companion blog site, rather than tediously spelling out every underscore, dash, and dot verbally.

4. *Keep it short.* Yes, there are podcasts that last for an hour or more, but that is asking a lot of your audience. If you have more content to cover than that time will allow, give the listeners the option to download the show in multiple segments.

5. *Don't go it alone.* Find a colleague with an engaging personality, sense of humor, and clear speaking voice to join you during your recording sessions. Dialog is more interesting to listen to than monologue, and it takes some of the pressure off. It's also good to provide multiple perspectives on issues when possible. Invite guests who are experts or at least experienced in the topic at hand.

6. *Get feedback from your listeners.* In order to ensure that you are meeting your audience's information needs, you should provide them with multiple methods of providing feedback on the show.

Podcasts are a reincarnation or reinvention of what the masterly learning movement of the 1960s called single-concept files or single-concept films. They were effective then, and can be effective today (Simonson, 2007).

Two-Way Audio

Correspondence study filled a terrific void for those who wanted to learn when they could and wherever they were located. However, many wanted direct, live communication with the teacher, especially for those in precollege schools.

The first widely used live, synchronous form of distance education employed two-way audio, with either a telephone hookup, a radio broadcast with telephone call-in, or short-wave radio transmissions (Figure 4–5). In all cases, the distant learner and the instructor are interacting with some form of live, two-way audio connection. Teachers lecture, ask questions, and lead discussions. Learners listen, answer, and participate. Often, print and nonprint materials are sent to distant learners, similar to correspondence study.

The key to this approach is the participation of the teacher and learners in a class session at a regularly

FIGURE 4–5 Two-way audio—audioconferencing.

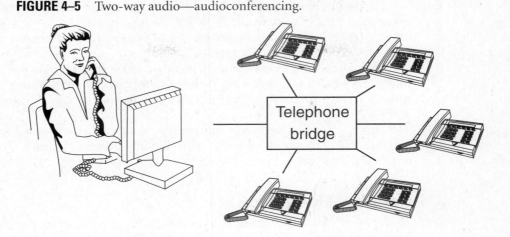

scheduled time, or a set period of time, over a predetermined number of weeks or months, such as a semester. For example, a high school class in French might be offered by telephone, radio station broadcast, or short-wave signal every weekday from 10:00 A.M. until 10:50 A.M. for 9 weeks. Students would tune in at home, assignments would be made, and activities completed. In other words, this form of distance education models the traditional classroom—except the teacher and learners can only hear one another, they cannot see each other.

Two-Way Audio with Graphics

Recently, an embellishment of the two-way audio form of distance education has incorporated electronic methods of sending graphics information synchronously to distant learners. Two general approaches are used. The first incorporates a special display board that looks like a chalkboard but that actually transmits whatever is drawn on it to a similar display board at a distant site. Since the electronic boards are connected to one another, whatever the students at the distant site draw is also seen by the instructor.

© 2007 Polycom, Inc.

Conference-table audioconferencing systems are easy to use and set up.

The main disadvantage of this approach is the limited visual capability of the system and the difficulty in connecting more than two locations. A modification of this approach uses personal computers that are connected to one another, either through a central bridge computer or by using special software. For these systems, the instructor sends graphics, visuals, pictures, and even short video clips to desktop computers located at distant sites. Members of the class are connected by telephone or some other two-way audio system, so they can discuss the visual information being sent via the computer.

This approach is relatively inexpensive and permits the visualization of the teleclass. The major problem is the availability of powerful, networked computers at distant learning sites.

One-Way Live Video

This approach is often referred to as *broadcast distance education*, popularized in the 1950s by programs such as "Sunrise Semester," which was broadcast over commercial television stations. Presently, most broadcast television approaches to distance education are offered by public television stations or are broadcast in the early morning hours by commercial stations (Figure 4–6).

Programs are broadcast in installments over a 12- to 15-week period. Often, each program is about 60 minutes in length and is accompanied by packets of printed materials and readings. Sometimes instructors are available for telephone office hours,

FIGURE 4–6 Satellite transmission—one-way audio, one-way video.

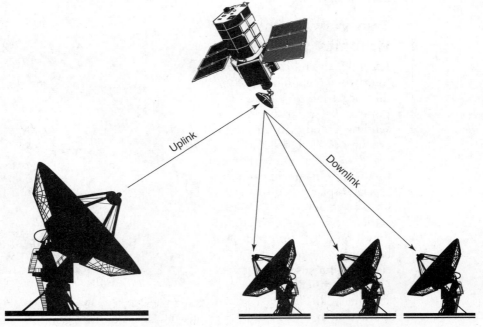

Receive sites

but most commonly students watch the programs on television and respond to assignments that are described in the course packet. Completion of the assignments depends on viewing each television program, which is often broadcast several times. For those students who miss a broadcast, DVD versions are available, or students can tape the program with their own DVD player.

One advantage of this approach is the relatively high quality of the video broadcasts. Public television stations offer excellent productions of important historical, political, and social events. Educational institutions use these broadcasts as the basis for high school and college courses related to the topics of the television shows. The *Civil War* series and the *Lewis and Clark* series are examples of public television programming that was modified into distance education courses.

Two-Way Audio, One-Way Video

In the last few decades, a number of organizations have begun to use live television to broadcast high school and college courses. Initially, this approach used microwave transmission systems, instructional television fixed service (ITFS), or community cable television networks (Figures 4–7 and 4–8).

FIGURE 4–7   Instructional television fixed service (ITFS)—two-way audio, one-way video.

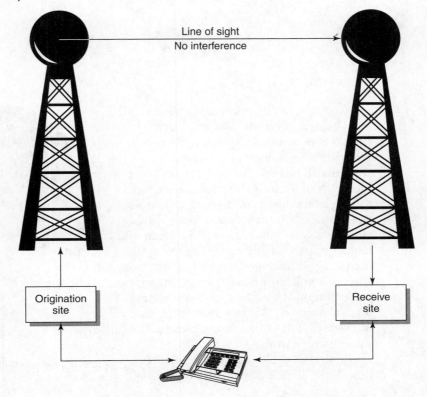

FIGURE 4–8   Cable delivery system (CATV)—two-way audio, one-way video.

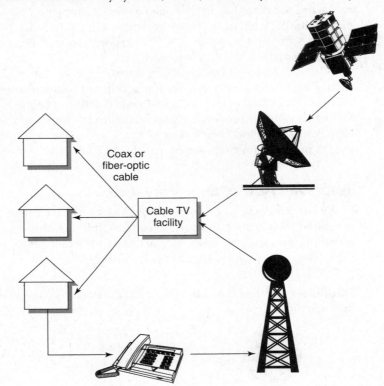

Recently, satellite communications systems have become widely available (Figure 4–9). In these systems, the courses are offered synchronously (e.g., live) to students in as few as two to as many as hundreds of locations. Students are given a toll-free telephone number to call to ask questions of the instructor both during class and after class. Normally, students have a packet of instructional materials, including interactive study guides, that they use and complete during the class presentation. Interaction between instructor and students is stressed in these kinds of courses, even ones where hundreds of students are enrolled.

In the last decade as satellite uplinks and downlinks have become more prevalent,

SWE-DISH Satellite systems

Satellite systems are small enough to place in a suitcase.

FIGURE 4–9   Satellite transmission—two-way audio, one-way video.

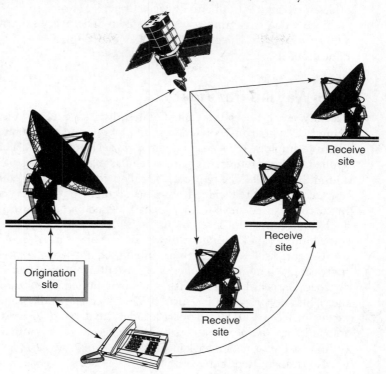

the concept of the teleconference has become more popular. *Teleconferences* are short courses on specialty topics such as copyright, classroom discipline, sexual harassment, due process, or funding strategies that are offered by an organization to individuals or small groups spread throughout a wide geographic area. Since one satellite in geosynchronous orbit in the Clarke Belt above the equator can transmit a video signal to nearly one-third of the Earth's surface, it is possible to offer satellite programming to literally thousands of learners.

A number of educational organizations have used satellite-broadcast coursework to offer entire high school and college curricula. For example, United Streaming is an archived video streaming service created by Discovery Education that contains over 4,000 full-length videos and 40,000 video clips for K–12 education (Discovery Education, 2006).

Two-Way Audio/Video

Recently, especially in the United States, distance education is being widely practiced using live, synchronous television employing one of several technologies. The prevalent technology is called *compressed video* (Figure 4–10). This approach, commonly applied in corporate training, uses regular telephone lines to send and receive audio and video signals. The approach is called compressed video because fewer than the normal number of 30 video frames per second (fps) are transmitted between the sites. In the compressed video form, usually 15 video fps are transmitted using what is called a T1 connection. This level of quality is acceptable for most instruction, except when some kind of rapid motion or movement is part of instruction.

Compressed video systems are often used in teleconferences for corporate training. Increasingly, schools and colleges are installing compressed video networks. For this approach, a special classroom is needed that has video and audio equipment to capture the sights and sounds of instruction. The video and audio signals are manipulated by a device called a CODEC (coder/decoder) that removes redundant information for transmission to the distant site. At the receive site another CODEC converts the compressed information back into video and audio signals. Camera control information is also transmitted between sites, so it is possible for the instructor to pan, tilt, and zoom cameras.

One major advantage of compressed video systems is their portability. Many systems are installed in movable carts that can be set up in almost any classroom or training site where there is a wireless connection. Recently, the size of the classroom systems has been reduced significantly. The best-selling systems are called "set-top" systems because they can be set on top of a television monitor. Set-top systems contain a camera, microphone, and the electronics necessary to compress and decompress

Industries use sophisticated videoconferencing systems that incorporate display boards and computers as well as cameras and microphones.

VTEL Products Corporation

FIGURE 4–10 Two-way audio/video—compressed videoconferencing system.

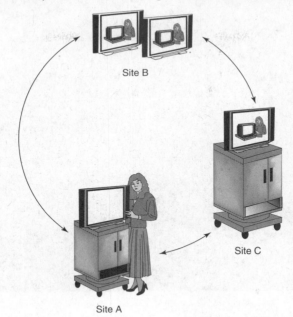

outgoing and incoming transmissions. Set-top systems cost less than 25% of traditional compressed video systems, yet are of similar quality. The Digital Dakota Network (DDN) in South Dakota is a compressed video network that links over 200 educational sites for live, two-way video and audio instruction (Figure 4–11). The DDN uses traditional "roll-around" and "set-top" systems.

A second, more technically sophisticated approach to two-way audio/video instruction uses fiber-optic cable to connect sites. Fiber-optic cable is the telecommunications medium of choice for new and updated telephone, video, and computer networking. Fiber's cost inhibits its installation in all situations, but fiber's high capacity makes it possible for one fiber (sometimes called a DS-3 connection) to carry full-motion video signals, in addition to high-quality audio signals and almost unlimited amounts of other voice and data information. One exemplary use of fiber-optics for distance education is Iowa's publicly owned Iowa Communications Network.

An Example: Two-Way Audio/Video in Iowa.   In Iowa, distance education is being redefined on a statewide basis. Iowa's approach to distance education is based on the belief that live, two-way interaction is fundamental to effective learning. The Iowa Communications Network (ICN) makes high-quality interaction possible in the state. The ICN is a statewide, two-way, full-motion interactive fiber-optic telecommunications network with hundreds of connected classrooms. It is designed to be used by teachers and students in learning situations where they can and expect to see and hear each other. Distant and local students function together and learn from and with one another.

FIGURE 4–11 Digital Dakota Network layout.

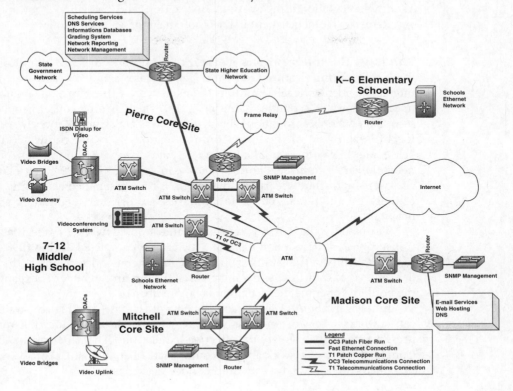

A key to Iowa's successful distance education system is the concept of sharing. Iowa's vision for distance education is being built around the development of partnerships of schools that share courses and activities. For example, a physics class originating in Jefferson, a small town in west central Iowa, may have students in Sac City and Rockwell City, schools in two other counties. French students in Sac City have distant classmates in Jefferson and Rockwell City, and a calculus class that originates in Rockwell City is shared with students in Sac City and Jefferson. All three schools provide courses to partner schools and receive instruction from neighbors. Classes are small, with enrollments of 30 to 35 or less, and are taught by teachers prepared in the skills needed by distance educators.

The use of fiber-optic technology, because of its extensive capacities and flexibility of use, provides unique opportunities for augmenting the instructional process beyond what is possible with other distance delivery technologies. The Iowa approach demonstrates the use of a system that emphasizes:

■ Local control of the distance education curriculum
■ Active involvement by educators from local school districts
■ Interactive instruction
■ Statewide alliances and regional partnerships

■ Preservice, in-service, and staff development activities to support teachers
■ Implementation using existing organizations and expertise
■ Research-based instructional decision making.

The Iowa Communications Network.   Central to distance education in Iowa is the Iowa Communications Network. The ICN is a statewide, two-way, full-motion interactive fiber-optic telecommunications network with at least one point of presence in each of Iowa's 99 counties (Gillispie, 2008). The ICN links colleges, universities, and secondary schools throughout the state and was constructed entirely with state and local funds. Part 1 of the Iowa Communications Network connected Iowa Public Television, Iowa's three public universities, and Iowa's 15 community colleges to the network. Part 2 connected at least one site in each of Iowa's 99 counties. Most Part 2 sites were high schools. Part 3 of the system is being expanded constantly. Currently it connects an additional 700 schools, libraries, armories, area education agencies, and hospitals.

The plan for the ICN was completed and adopted by the Iowa legislature in 1987. Construction of Parts 1 and 2 of the network was completed during 1993. In addition to the capability of transmitting up to 48 simultaneous video channels, the ICN carries data and voice traffic; as demand increases, the system can be easily expanded without the need for "opening the trench" to lay more fiber.

In Iowa and South Dakota, and in many other states and regions, traditional education works. Educators in these two states adopted distance education, but wanted to preserve their beliefs about effective education. The fiber-optics–based Iowa Communications Network and the compressed video Digital Dakota Network permit this since both are live, two-way audio/video networks.

Desktop Two-Way Audio/Video

One disadvantage of the video telecommunications systems described in this chapter is their cost and their cumbersomeness. In order to provide video-based distance education, special electronic devices are needed, satellite or telephone network time must be reserved, and equipped classrooms are required. Desktop systems often reduce the need for special high-cost equipment or special networking. Desktop systems use personal computers and the Internet to connect local and distant learners (Figure 4–12). Increasingly, the Internet and Internet II have the capacity to connect personal computers for the sharing of video and audio information. Inexpensive servers that function as reflector sites for connecting multiple sites are also available. Streaming video is becoming more widely used in traditional as well as distance education classes. Mullins-Dove (2006) describes *streaming video* as using the Internet to allow video and audio content to play, or stream, as it is downloaded from a remote source. A key characteristic of streaming is that there is no physical file on the viewer's computer (Reed, 2001).

Early systems used CU/SeeMe technology that was free and used very inexpensive video cameras. These systems permitted two sites to connect and to share video and

FIGURE 4–12   Computer conferencing—desktop two-way audio/video.

audio. Multiple sites could be connected if a reflector computer was available. The CU/SeeMe approach was relatively low quality and was used mostly for conferencing and meetings. However, it pioneered the use of desktop systems. NetMeeting, a Microsoft product, was another widely used desktop conferencing system, provided free with early versions of Windows operating system.

Now higher-quality cameras and even complete classrooms can be connected to a personal computer for transmission of instruction to distant learners. Horizon Wimba has a "Desktop Lecture Series" that streams short courses over the Internet using audio, graphics, and chats (www.horizonwimba.com/horizon/). It uses a simple interface that is easily set up on a personal computer. Certainly the personal computer will be the telecommunications tool of the future.

There are four categories of desktop audio/video systems: analog, high speed, medium speed, and low speed. These systems permit sharing of audio and video from the instructor's computer to a student's computer.

Analog systems use existing telephone wiring in buildings, commonly called twisted-pair wires. The major advantage of this approach is the high quality of the audio and video. Since existing wiring is used, connections are limited to relatively short distances—several thousand feet. Analog systems are limited to a campus, or a building, which significantly reduces this application in distance education.

High-speed videoconferencing sends video at millions of bits per second. Even at this high rate, the video signal is compressed using a compression protocol such as mpeg. The H.310 protocol is used for high-speed desktop videoconferencing. Currently, high-speed videoconferencing is used primarily with dedicated networks within individual schools or businesses.

Medium-speed desktop videoconferencing is the primary approach used today. This type of desktop video transmits at speeds of 128,000 or 256,000 bits per second. The video signal is compressed so it can be transmitted over the Internet (H.323 protocol). There are both hardware and software methods to compress and decompress the video signal. Since the Internet is used, medium-speed systems have considerable promise for distance education.

Low-speed desktop video includes all systems that transmit at speeds lower than 56,000 bits per second (56 kbps). This category permits conferencing using the Internet and modems at speeds of 28.8 kbps. A V32 model modem with v.80 extension is generally what is needed for low-speed desktop video. Once again H.323 protocols are used, and software and hardware compression systems are available. Very inexpensive systems are currently in use. However, the quality is quite poor and the video signal is usually limited to a small window on the computer screen. Low-speed systems are widely used for limited types of instructor/student conferencing, rather than for course delivery.

When the Internet is used, rather than a special or dedicated network, the H.323 standard is used. The primary problem with desktop video-conferencing using the Internet is the poor quality of the video and the limited capacity of the Internet to carry video signals. Since the Internet is a "packet-switched" network, a video signal is broken into packets that are disassembled and then sent to the distant site where the packets are reassembled into a signal. Obviously, this approach

© 2007 Polycom, Inc.

Special "distance learning" carts are sometimes used. These carts can be wheeled into any conference room, classroom, office, or work area.

is a limiting factor when live, interactive video is sent. Video streaming is a growing subset of this category of distance education. Video streaming is usually defined as the progressive downloading of a video file (Mallory, 2001). A storage space (buffer) that is much smaller than the video file is identified on the computer's hard drive. The video file begins to download into the file location and the file begins to display on the computer screen. The file continues to download from the origination site somewhere on the Internet to the buffer and onto the local computer screen. Often the video file is a prerecorded event, but live video can be streamed also.

The three most popular video file types are Apple QuickTime (.mov files), Microsoft Windows Media Player (.avi files), and RealNetworks RealPlayer (.rm files).

QuickTime's .mov files are very popular for standard movie downloads, but are not used as much for streamed video and audio. The most widely used formats are Flash (.flv), H.264, and MPEG 4 (Harrington, 2008). A commonly used strategy is to store video segments on a CD or DVD and ship them to the distant learner to use as part of a course or lesson. CDs can store approximately 650 megabytes (approximately 1 hour of video), and DVDs can store several hours of video.

Desktop videoconferencing is a critical area for growth in distance education. Increasingly, the Internet will be used to connect learners for sharing of video, in addition to data (text and graphics). Before this happens, however, additional advances in compression standards, network protocols, and transmission media will need to be made.

A LOOK AT BEST PRACTICE ISSUES

Wireless Canopies

A *canopy* is a roof-like covering, and *wireless* means no wires, so one would assume that a wireless canopy is a roof-like covering with no wires.

Well, most of us know that *wireless canopy* is used to refer to a "hot zone," or a wireless network area. Thus, a wireless canopy is a location where one can obtain access to the Internet through a high-speed connection using a computer's wireless networking card.

Increasingly, the wireless canopy is becoming used for global, more extensive network areas, such as a school campus, a neighborhood, or even an entire community. In many towns there are initiatives to establish, or at least begin planning for, citywide Internet access, usually wireless.

These initiatives are very reminiscent of the days when community cable television (CCTV) franchises were awarded. In the 1960s and 1970s, city councils were approached by cable TV companies asking to be awarded a monopolistic franchise to offer cable TV at a reasonable price throughout the city. Franchise agreements were drawn up and signed, and cable TV commissions were established to monitor the activities of the private company that was awarded the cable TV franchise.

Savvy communities obtained one or more local access channels on the cable network, and some even negotiated for state-of-the-art production studios where programming could be created, edited, and delivered. In many cases, unfortunately, the awarding of the CCTV franchise was an opportunity lost. Many cities and towns did not aggressively pursue the potential of a city-wide television network, and today, CCTV is not often perceived as a community resource but as an entertainment system.

Today, another opportunity is waiting. For many, Internet access is a necessity. Cities have utilities that offer essential services if those services are not offered economically by the private sector. Water, electricity, and trash collection, for example, are often city services, or at least city controlled.

Traditionally, access to information has been considered a public necessity, ever since Carnegie libraries were established in almost every town and city. The public library has always been free and open. In the last few years, Internet access has become an essential service. Certainly, there should be debate about whether the connection to the Internet is supplied by a public utility or a private provider, and this debate should begin quickly.

The image of a city sitting under the canopy of a wireless Internet network is a vision most want to see—it is the vision of a city with universal access to the power of the Internet at a reasonable cost for everyone.

DISTANCE EDUCATION CLASSROOMS

Two-Way Video/Audio Classrooms

Video-based distance education requires a classroom or studio that is equipped with the technology needed for recording and displaying video and listening to sound. Initially, studios were used as distance education classrooms. Then, as distance education became more widespread, regular classrooms were converted into distance education receive and send sites (Figure 4–13).

Video classrooms need recording, instruction, and display equipment. Recording equipment includes video cameras—usually three—one that shows the instructor, one for the students, and an overhead camera mounted above the instructor console to display printed graphics materials. A switching system is needed to permit the instructor to switch between cameras and instructional equipment, such as a computer, DVD player, mpg player such as an ipod. Several companies offer devices that attach to video cameras and cause them to follow the action in the classroom. For example, when its activation button is pushed, the student camera automatically pans and zooms to the appropriate microphone location to show the student who is talking. Also, the instructor camera has sensing devices that, when activated, automatically direct the camera to follow the instructor's movements in the classroom.

FIGURE 4–13 Distance learning classroom-teaching site, view from rear.

Push-to-talk microphones are most often used in videoconferencing classrooms.

Visual presenters allow the instructor to project and transmit flat visuals, such as book pages, pictures, and drawings.

Additionally, audio equipment is needed. Audio tends to cause more problems than video in distance education classrooms. Early classrooms used voice-activated microphones, but currently push-to-talk microphones are the most common.

Instructional media often found in distance education classrooms include a computer, and a DVD player. Laser disk players are sometimes supplied. Student equipment includes desktop computers that are networked and that can be displayed for others to see both in the local classroom and at remote sites.

Display equipment includes large LCD television monitors and audio speakers. Most often three display monitors are mounted in a classroom—two in the front of the room for students to view and one in the rear for the instructor. Audio speakers are connected to a volume control. Sometimes classrooms are connected to a control room where technicians can monitor action and even control the recording and display

Videoconferencing rooms are configured in a variety of ways.

Videoconferencing systems permit simultaneous live interaction and the display of graphics

equipment. Increasingly, however, classrooms are controlled by the teacher and students. In other words, the teacher is responsible for equipment operation and use, or students in the class are assigned these responsibilities.

Classroom Technologies for Online Instruction

The key to success in an online classroom is not which technologies are used, but how they are used and what information is communicated using the technologies.

Selecting Appropriate Technologies for Online Instruction

Step #1: Assess Available Instructional Technologies. Instructional technologies can be organized into two categories: telecommunications technologies and instructional technologies. Since *telecommunications* means to communicate at a distance, telecommunications technologies are electronic methods used to connect the instructor, students, and resources. Obviously, this chapter discusses online technologies, which means a computer and network.

However, embedded within computers and networks are capabilities permitting the delivery of instruction using a variety of media. Instructional media are ways that messages are stored, and most online applications include verbal symbols (words spoken and written), visual symbols (line drawings and graphics), pictures, motion pictures, real-time video, and recorded/edited video.

This list is similar to the one proposed by Edgar Dale (1946), discussed earlier in this chapter. The bottom levels of Dale's cone listed realistic experiences, such as actually doing something in the real world, like going to Greece. Realistic experiences are the most difficult to make available to students. It takes a great deal of time and extensive resources to provide totally authentic, real-world learning experiences continually.

Dale (1946) implied when discussing his cone that the tension between efficiency (abstract experiences) and effectiveness (realistic experiences) is at the core of instructional design. The professor should choose learning experiences that are no more realistic than necessary in order for outcomes to be achieved. Overly abstract learning experiences require the student to compensate or to learn less effectively. Overly realistic experiences waste resources. When the professor who is designing online instruction selects the correct media, it maximizes efficiency and makes available more resources for other learning experiences.

Assessing available technologies often requires that the instructor determine the level of lowest common technologies (LCT). This means that the sophistication of the computer and software of all learners and the instructor should be determined. Also, this means that the capabilities of the telecommunications technologies must be identified. Often, LCT is determined by having students complete a survey in which they clearly identify the technologies that are available to them.

Step #2: Determine the Learning Outcomes.   Learning outcomes are those observable, measurable behaviors that are a consequence of online instruction. When learning activities are designed it is important that some expectations for students be identified in order to guide the selection of appropriate technologies.

Since online environments should be media rich and strive for authenticity, it is critical that many technologies be used. It is also important that students demonstrate learning outcomes by using a variety of technology-based activities. Students may be expected to take a test to demonstrate their competence, but more likely they will be expected to offer some kind of real-world project that gives an authentic assessment of what they learned. *Rubrics*, which are simply predetermined strategies for how assignments are to be graded, should be available for students to use to guide the development of the outcome materials they produce.

One strategy used by developers of online instruction is to collect student projects and use these materials as models for subsequent students. If this strategy is used, a thoughtful and comprehensive critique of the student projects should be included so mistakes are identified and not repeated. Some developers of instruction advocate that students should begin with existing materials produced previously and redesign them to eliminate weaknesses, build on strengths, and add new concepts.

Specifically, text used in a lesson could be analyzed and replaced with graphics or word pictures that are combinations of text and graphics that represent teaching concepts. Still pictures could be modified and upgraded to animations, and synchronous chats could be made more effective by including a threaded discussion strategy that involves asking questions, collecting answers, asking follow-up questions, and selecting the most appropriate final responses. Traditionalists identify learning outcomes in terms of behavioral objectives with specific conditions under which learning will occur, a precise behavior to be demonstrated that indicates learning, and an exact standard to measure competence. Recently, learner-identified objectives have become popular: The student is expected at some point during the instructional event to identify what changes he or she feels are important indicators of learning. Whatever approach is used, it is critical that outcomes of instructional events be clearly identified at some point.

Touch panel control systems permit the easy operation of distance education equipment in videoconferencing classrooms.

Step #3: Identify Learning Experiences and Match Each to the Most Appropriate Available Technology. Usually, the content of a course is divided into modules or units. Traditionally, a module requires about 3 hours of face-to-face instruction and 6 hours of student study or preparation, and a three-credit college course would have 12 to 15 modules. In an online course, the classical approach of organizing content around teaching and study time is no longer relevant. One approach would be simply to convert a classroom-centered course's content into online modules. For totally new courses, this approach will obviously not work.

An alternative approach is to organize a course around themes or ideas that directly relate to student activities or learning activities. For example, a course in history about the Reconstruction period following the American Civil War might have 12 modules, each with 5 learning activities, for a total of 60. The learning activities would be content-centered experiences such as reading assignments, PowerPoint presentations, and audio recordings, or learner-centered experiences, such as threaded discussions on specific topics, research assignments utilizing Web search engines, or self-tests.

One example for a module dealing with a topic such as the economic redevelopment of the South in the first 5 years after the end of the Civil War might begin with a reading assignment from the textbook about the economic conditions in the South. This reading assignment would be prescribed by a Web-based assignment. The reading would be followed by participation in an online discussion with a small group of classmates. The purpose of this discussion would be to identify the five impediments to effective economic development. When the group agreed to the list, it would be posted to the course's bulletin board for grading by the instructor. The third learning experience in this module would be a review of a PowerPoint presentation with audio that was prepared by the instructor that discusses what actually happened economically in the South after the Civil War. Finally, the student would be expected to write a two-page critique of the period of

Videoconferencing is often used for meetings, but is also a valuable addition to web-based courses

economic development according to a rubric posted on the Web. This assignment would be submitted electronically to the course's instructor for grading.

Subsequent modules in this course would be designed similarly. At several points during the course, benchmark projects would be required of students, such as an individual online chat with the instructor, or the submission of a major project that synthesized work completed for module assignments.

Once the course's content is organized into modules, the next design requirement is to match learning experiences to technology–delivery strategies. The reading assignments could be delivered using the textbook, or posted as files to be downloaded, or even read directly from the computer monitor.

PowerPoint presentations could be handled the same way, and used directly from the computer or downloaded and studied later. E-mail attachments could be used for assignment submission and chat rooms or e-mail could provide ways to hold threaded discussions.

In this example, the instructional media are relatively simple ones. What is sophisticated is the design and organization of the activities and content facilitated and delivered by the media.

Step #4: Preparing the Learning Experiences for Online Delivery.   Basically, there are four strategies for organizing instruction for online delivery. They are (1) linear-programmed instruction, (2) branched-programmed instruction, (3) hyper-programmed instruction, and (4) student-programmed instruction.

In each case, the content of the course is subdivided into modules. The modules consist of topics that relate to one another or have some sense of unity or consistency,

Videoconferencing is usually instructor led in both training and educational programs

such as the economic condition of the South after the Civil War. The modules themselves, and the learning activities within the modules, are organized according to one of the four delivery strategies.

Linear-programmed instruction, a long-standing approach to individualized instruction, requires that all content be organized into concepts that are presented in blocks or chunks. Students review content, take a self-test, and if successful move to the next chunk/block of information. This happens sequentially until the content blocks are completed. Students move in the same order through the sequence of concepts. The teacher determines the order of the concepts/chunks.

Branched-programmed instruction is similar, except the self-tests are more sophisticated so students can branch ahead if they are exceptionally proficient or move to remediation if they are floundering. Similar to linear-programmed instruction, the order and sequence of instruction, including branches, is instructor determined.

Hyper-programmed instruction, widely advocated for Web-based online instruction, also organizes content into modules and concepts, but it permits students to move through the learning activities at their own rate and pace, in a route they determine themselves. In other words, learning experiences are identified and mediated, and students use them until either an instructor- or student-determined outcome is met. Often, each module has a terminal, or final, activity that must be completed before the student moves to the next course module.

Finally, the student-programmed approach uses an extremely loose structure where only the framework of the content is provided to online learners who are expected to provide the structure, outcomes, and sequence of learning activities.

For example, students who enroll in a course on the *Period of Reconstruction* would be required to organize and sequence the modules and activities, and during the course to identify personal outcomes and activities to be accomplished.

When teachers attempt to make instruction equal for all students, they will fail. Rather, the teacher of online instruction should provide a wide collection of activities that make possible equivalent learning experiences for students using an approach that recognizes the fundamental differences between learners, distant and local. Equivalency is more difficult but promises to be more effective.

WHAT IS THE INTERNET AND WHY DOES IT MATTER?

As a foundation for current approaches to distance education, it is helpful to understand what the Internet is and how it works. The Internet is not a single, clearly defined entity, but a meta-network of interconnected networks that share a common language, TCP-IP (transmission control protocol/Internet protocol). (A *protocol* is an electronic language that computers use to communicate with one another and exchange data. Protocols are roughly analogous to the languages humans use to communicate and share information.) These networks are in a constant state of evolution, with thousands of vendors making changes on a daily basis.

The Internet has no international headquarters or mailing address, no chief executive officer or board of directors, no stockholders to whom it must be accountable, and no toll-free telephone number to call for assistance or information. This is not to say that the Internet is an anarchy, although some cynical observers might disagree. Much of the planning and coordination responsibility is assumed by the *Internet Society,* an international, nonprofit organization established for the purposes of "global cooperation and coordination for the Internet and its internetworking technologies and applications." Founded in 1991, the Society facilitates the development and implementation of Internet standards and policies and holds oversight responsibilities over several important boards and task forces that address Internet issues. Membership in the Internet Society is free and open to all interested persons anywhere in the world, including the readers of this book. Further information about membership may be obtained on the Society's website. See the URL following References at the end of this chapter.

Although some national governments restrict access and practice censorship, in general the existing oversight bodies are concerned with technical and network management matters rather than what information is placed on the Internet, who puts it there, and who has access to it. This is an important issue for students and teachers using the Internet for educational purposes, because no quality-control mechanism exists to ensure that information found on the Internet is accurate and unbiased, and that it may be freely viewed by the young and innocent.

Architecture of the Internet

How is it that a fifth-grade class in Cambridge, Ohio, can participate in online interaction with counterparts in Cape Town, South Africa, and Folkestone, England? A brief look at the architecture of the Internet will help us understand the answer to that question. It will also help illustrate the enormous potential of the Internet for distance education, as well as its limitations.

Figure 4–14 is a graphic representation of the structure of the Internet. The model consists of four basic tiers of services.

Tier 1: Backbone Networks and Internet Exchange Points. The essential framework is provided by a worldwide configuration of extremely high-bandwidth networks called *backbones*. Backbones may be regional, national, or international in coverage, and are typically operated by major telecommunications carriers such as AT&T, Sprint, and Qwest on a for-profit basis. Backbones meet and transfer data at junctions called Internet exchange points (IXs). As of 2010, hundreds of IXs existed in the world. The vast majority were located in North America, Europe, Australia, and eastern Asia, but the numbers were growing rapidly in less industrialized regions.

Tier 2: Regional Networks. Regional networks operate backbones on a smaller scale in the United States, typically within a state or among adjacent states, connecting to one or more national or international backbones.

FIGURE 4–14   Graphic representation of the structure of the Internet in the United States.

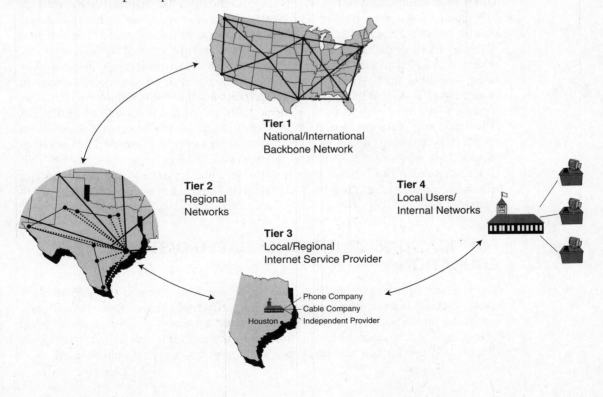

Tier 1
National/International
Backbone Network

Tier 2
Regional
Networks

Tier 3
Local/Regional
Internet Service Provider

Tier 4
Local Users/
Internal Networks

Phone Company
Cable Company
Independent Provider

Houston

Tier 3: Internet Service Providers.   This is perhaps the most important component for distance educators. The individual Internet service providers (ISPs) are connected to regional networks and provide dial-up, or direct, high-speed access to the Internet at the local level. These are the companies that provide Internet access to schools, businesses, private homes, and other community entities such as libraries, churches, and government offices, if not available through other networks. Internet service providers have been largely responsible for the worldwide Internet boom, because they have made the Internet available to almost everyone in their local communities. Companies providing these services locally may be identified by looking up *Internet access providers,* or something similar, in the telephone book yellow pages.

Tier 4: Organizational and Home Networks.   These are the local area networks that interconnect computers within an organization, such as a school, college, government agency, or company, and provide Internet access to individuals within those entities. Many persons are now installing wireless networks in their homes to extend Internet access to multiple computers via one high-speed connection.

Are the Terms *Internet* and *World Wide Web* Interchangeable?

This is another important point to clarify at the beginning of this chapter. The answer is *no.* The Internet is the network itself. The World Wide Web, accessed through web browsers such as Internet Explorer, Firefox, Safari, and Opera, is just one use of the network. Although many e-mail applications are web-based and are accessed through browsers, others, such as Microsoft Outlook, Eudora, and FirstClass, operate on a "client–server" basis. They are on the Internet but outside the Web, and users must open client software on their desktops to access their mail. (We should point out that both Outlook and FirstClass have web versions.) File-transfer protocol (FTP), which is often used to transfer files between a server and a user desktop, is another example. The FTP servers are accessible via the Web (by entering "ftp://" and the server address in the address window instead of "http://") but are more commonly accessed through FTP client software such as WS_FTP, FTP Commander, and Fetch. Generally speaking, if the application is accessed through a desktop icon other than a web browser, it is on the Internet but not on the Web.

 ## FOUNDATIONS OF INTERNET-BASED DISTANCE EDUCATION

The Internet and the personal computer in general have changed the way we think about teaching and learning. To teach and learn effectively in an online environment, we must understand the concepts of *student-centered learning* and *distributed learning.* These terms will be essential to our discussions in this chapter about web-based tools that are available for educational purposes and how they are, or should be, used.

Student-Centered Learning

The model of teaching employed during the instructional television era of distance education essentially replicated the model found in the conventional classroom. Teachers and the textbook were the two primary sources of course content. Teachers lectured and demonstrated. Students listened and took notes, and then regurgitated the same information back to the teachers on exams. This "teacher-centered" model continues in many courses delivered to distant learners via today's synchronous, video-based technologies.

With computer- and Internet-based technologies, however, have come exciting new opportunities for providing learning experiences to students. This philosophy of education has become popularly known as *student-centered learning,* because it so strongly promotes active learning, collaboration, mastery of course material, and student control over the learning process. Barr and Tagg (1995) discussed the differences between teacher-centered and learner-centered instructional models. See Table 4–1 for a summary of the transformations that have the strongest implications for Internet-based distance education.

Oblinger (1999) also observed these transitions, but from a slightly different perspective:

- From lecturing to coaching
- From taking attendance to logging on
- From distribution requirements to connected learning
- From credit hours to performance standards
- From competing to collaborating
- From library collections to network connections
- From passive learning to active learning
- From textbooks to customized materials.

We will see evidence of these transformations throughout this chapter. Successful faculty in online learning environments are able to "think out of the box" and set aside the traditional teacher-centered instructional model. It is in this context that we discuss Internet-based learning.

Distance Learning versus Distributed Learning

The concept of *distributed learning* illustrates how the learner-centered educational model is being implemented in today's schools and colleges. Not all online learning is necessarily distance learning. Much Internet-based learning activity involves students and teachers who continue to meet at least part time in conventional classroom settings. One of the earliest definitions was offered by Saltzberg and Polyson (1995):

> Distributed learning is not just a new term to replace the other DL, distance learning. Rather, it comes from the concept of distributed resources. Distributed learning is an instructional model that allows instructor, students, and content to be located in different, noncentralized locations so that instruction and learning occur independent

TABLE 4–1 ■ Characteristics of the Transition from an Instructor-Based to a Learner-Based Instructional Model

Instructor-Centered Model	Learner-Centered Model
Mission and Purposes	
Provide/deliver instruction	Produce learning
Transfer knowledge from faculty to students	Elicit student discovery and construction of knowledge
Offer courses and programs	Create powerful learning environments
Teaching/Learning Structures	
Time held constant, learning varies	Learning held constant, time varies
50-minute lecture, 3-unit course	Learning environments
Covering material	Specified learning results
Success determined by accumulated credit hours	Success determined by demonstrated knowledge and skills
Learning Theory	
Learning is teacher centered and controlled	Learning is student centered and controlled
"Live" teacher, "live" students required	"Active" learner required, but not "live" teacher
Classroom and learning are competitive	Learning environments are cooperative, individualistic, collaborative, and supportive
Nature of Roles	
Faculty are primarily lecturers	Faculty are primarily designers of learning methods and environments
Faculty and students act independently	Faculty and students work in terms with each other

Source: Adapted from Barr & Tagg (1995).

of place and time. The distributed learning model can be used in combination with traditional classroom-based courses, with traditional distance learning courses, or it can be used to create wholly virtual classrooms. (p. 10)

Distributed learning thus is a broader term that can be, and in fact most often is, associated with face-to-face (f2f) instruction that incorporates some form of technology-based learning experience, either inside or outside the classroom. In other words, students do not need to be at a distance from their instructor to benefit from distributed learning. While the primary focus of this book is distance learning, in which students and their teachers are geographically separated, many distributed learning experiences may involve only resources that are at a distance, or that occur at a different time and/or place than the conventional class meeting. Much of what we will discuss in this chapter represents distributed learning.

For example, learning materials can be located on a server anywhere in the world and accessed either by the classroom teacher as part of her presentation or independently by the students in some interactive setting. Course discussions can take place online and outside the classroom. A class activity could involve tracking a scientific expedition in real time, including interaction with the explorers and live video transmitted through the Web. High-speed networking now enables music students in Ohio to perform ensemble works with students in Pennsylvania, Texas, and Colorado. Likewise, a medical school professor in California can demonstrate unusual surgical procedures to students in Georgia and Massachusetts, complete with sophisticated graphics and audio for real-time discussion. The states identified here are for example purposes only; the participants could be almost anywhere.

Distributed learning is also represented by what are called *hybrid* or *blended* courses, in which online activities substitute for a portion of actual seat time in an otherwise conventional face-to-face course. Blended courses are more likely to be found on college campuses with significant classroom shortages, so that multiple courses can share the same classroom at the same hour, but they can be employed in any situation in which the instructor feels that online activities are more productive learning experiences. A Sloan Consortium analysis of data collected over the period from 2003 to 2009 found that almost 54% of higher education institutions surveyed offered blended courses, and that nearly 6% of all course sections were taught in a blended format (Allen & Seaman, 2010; Allen, Seaman, & Garrett, 2007). These numbers, however, were declining, apparently as more and more blended courses were converted to an all-online format.

Advantages and Limitations of Online Learning

The advantages of online learning compared with conventional face-to-face teaching are numerous.

- Unless access is deliberately restricted, courses or online course materials could be available to any qualified individual in the world with a properly equipped computer and an Internet connection. Students can participate from school, home, office, or community locations.
- Asynchronous course components are available 24 hours a day, at the learner's convenience, and are time-zone independent.
- Students can work at their own pace.
- Course materials and activities available through the Web are distributable across multiple computer platforms; it makes no difference if users are using Windows or Macintosh operating systems.
- The technology is relatively easy for students to use.
- Learning materials are available across the entire Web.
- Online course materials, once developed, are easy to update, providing students access to current information.

- The Internet can provide a student-centered learning environment, if the materials and methods are designed to take advantage of the interactivity and resources the Internet provides.
- The Internet promotes active learning and facilitates student's intellectual involvement with the course content.
- A well-conceived online course provides a variety of learning experiences and accommodates different learning styles.
- Students become skilled at using Internet resources, a factor that may improve employment options upon graduation.
- When personal identities remain concealed, all students, regardless of gender, ethnicity, appearance, or disabling condition, are on equal ground.
- Corporate training programs conducted via the Internet can yield significant savings in employee time and travel costs, and training can be conducted on a "just in time" basis.

The limitations of Internet course delivery may also be substantial:

- The Digital Divide is real, especially in rural and lower socioeconomic regions, contributing to a "haves-and-have-nots" situation. Even where the Internet is available, many potential students do not have ready access to computers, and if they do, they may not know how to use Internet resources.
- Online courses may emphasize the technology rather than the content and learning opportunities.
- Well-designed Internet-based courses may be labor-intensive to develop, requiring time and personnel resources not available to many instructors.
- Some instructors have difficulty adjusting to the learner-centered model of instruction and do little more than "shovel" their teacher-centered, lecture-based courses into an online format.
- Although today's students as a whole are more technologically literate than ever before, many are technophobes who find the Internet confusing and intimidating.
- Copyright violations on course Web pages that are not password-protected sit in plain sight for viewing by the rights holders—and their attorneys.
- Some topics may not adapt well to delivery by computer.
- Bandwidth limitations make it difficult to present advanced technologies, such as streamed video, multimedia, and memory-intensive graphics, over the Web. Too many students still connect using dial-up access.
- Online courses require students to take more responsibility for their own learning, a task that some find challenging.
- Although responses to student questions may be instantaneous in the conventional classroom, feedback may be delayed by hours or even days in an online learning situation.
- The support infrastructure, providing training and technical assistance to both students and instructor, is often minimal or nonexistent. Instructional design support during the conceptualization and development of a course is also frequently unavailable. These factors are major barriers that discourage many faculty from teaching online.

TECHNOLOGIES OF INTERNET-BASED DISTANCE EDUCATION

The Internet has its roots in the ARPANET, a network created in 1969 to link the computing systems of military and other government agencies to those of their research partners around the United States, including universities and corporate contractors. As the ARPANET grew, important technologies such as TCP-IP, tools for electronic mail and online discussion forums, and Ethernet were developed to enhance its capabilities. In 1985, the National Science Foundation (NSF) established the NSFNET, a high-speed data transmission network that interconnected a series of NSF-funded supercomputers across the United States, and invited other networks running the TCP-IP protocol to connect to it, including the ARPANET participants. This NSFNET national backbone and its affiliated networks became known as the Internet, and 1985 is regarded by many as the Internet's birth year. The ARPANET was absorbed into the Internet and ceased to exist in 1989.

A simultaneous but separate development was the evolution of the Because It's Time Network (BITNET), founded as a general-purpose academic network in 1981 by the City University of New York and Yale University. The Because It's Time Network ultimately grew to include about 600 educational institutions in the United States and was affiliated with networks in Canada, Europe, and other parts of the world. Because BITNET used a different protocol (RSCS/NJE) it technically was not part of the Internet, but it interconnected with the Internet through "gateways" that functioned as translators between the two protocols.

Mention of BITNET in this chapter is important for two reasons. First, BITNET was the first computer network available for widespread academic use. Hundreds of thousands of college faculty members and students became acquainted with international computing networks and their capabilities through BITNET. The first acknowledged online instruction was delivered via BITNET in 1981. Second, BITNET mainframes hosted the LISTSERV mailing list management software that enabled both BITNET and Internet users to participate in online, asynchronous group discussions on thousands of topics. The term *listserv* has found its way into the vocabularies of most educators and students as a euphemism for an online, asynchronous discussion forum, even though other list management software products exist and the LISTSERV user's guide specifically requests that the term not be used in a generic sense. The Because It's Time Network ceased operations in 1996, as its functions also became absorbed into the Internet.

The Internet itself continued to expand through the last half of the 1980s and into the early 1990s, but for educators its primary functions remained electronic mail and online discussion groups, file transfers (using file transfer protocol, or FTP software), and remote access to computers ("remote login," commonly through Telnet software). It is important to understand that many higher education faculty members were engaged in online instruction during this period, including completely virtual courses, using electronic mail, mailing lists, and files stored on FTP servers. Even before the introduction of the World Wide Web, this was a rich period in American distance education. (Library and Web searches on the terms *computer-mediated communication* and *asynchronous learning networks* will yield a wealth of interesting resources on pre-Web online learning.) Use of the Internet at the K–12 level was minimal at this time, primarily because of access issues and the general lack of computing resources, although some schools were engaged in innovative e-mail exchange programs with other schools all over the globe.

The World Wide Web itself was conceived by Tim Berners-Lee of the European Center for Particle Research (CERN) as a means of sharing data among scientists and was first used in 1989. It did not become the subject of a standard desktop icon until 4 years later, when the National Center for Supercomputing Applications (NCSA) at the University of Illinois unveiled Mosaic as an all-purpose World Wide Web "browser." Within a year, more than 2 million persons around the world had downloaded Mosaic, and when Netscape appeared as the next-generation Web browser in late 1994, interest in the Web spread more dramatically. As access grew, the number of websites online increased exponentially—from just 130 in June 1993 to 23,500 by June 1995 and 100,000 by January 1996 (Gray, 1996) to more than 3 million by mid-1998 and 122 million by 2007, and over 300 million today.

The World Wide Web brought the "point and click" technology of the desktop computer to the Internet. Although such objects as graphics, photographs, and audio and video files were accessible through FTP and other applications (including a technology called Gopher that was very popular in the early- to mid-1990s), the Web was the first Internet application to integrate them into a single screen along with text. The use of multifont text also became possible. Perhaps the most dynamic feature of the Web was hypertext, the ability to link words, phrases, graphics, and other on-screen objects with other files located on the same server or on someone else's server on the other side of the world. As a result, web page developers, including teachers, could easily organize information from multiple sources and make any of it accessible to users with a single click of a mouse.

The potential for commercialization of the Internet led to a radical change in the network's architecture, as the National Science Foundation decided that the federal government should not continue to fund the backbone infrastructure in competition with private telecommunications carriers. A new structure was put in place by April 1995, and the NSFNET was retired. The transition to commercial backbone operators was seamless and unnoticed by most Internet users. With the privatization of the Internet, commercial use of the network mushroomed, as reflected in the extraordinary growth in the number of websites and individual pages after mid-1995, as described earlier in this chapter. Internet service providers were established to serve virtually every community in the industrialized world. Most commercial entities developed websites for customer sales and support. And a whole new industry of vendors emerged to support Internet users. Thousands of these evolved to offer products and services to educators engaged in Internet-based distance education. We will address just a few of these in this chapter.

WEB 2.0

As the twenty-first century progressed, it became more and more evident that course management systems, and indeed the Web itself in its first decade of widespread public use, reflected the teacher-centered instructional paradigm (Brown, 2007). The Web presented information with very little interactivity and user involvement beyond pointing, clicking, and reading. Course management systems (CMS) were largely places for faculty to place lecture notes and other materials for student study, and for students to obtain those materials, take online quizzes, and check their grades, and were *very* instructor centered. Outside of opportunities for online discussions, which are rarely utilized effectively by rank-and-file faculty, CMSs were not locations that facilitated the high levels of student intellectual engagement—with content, with their instructors, and with each other—that hallmark the learner-centered instructional paradigm.

Beginning in the early 2000s, however, a new generation of web applications emerged, tools that are highly participatory and promote collaboration, networking, sharing, and the widespread generation of content, and the editing and mixing of content from diverse sources for new purposes through a model called the *mash-up*, by both groups and individuals. The term *Web 2.0* was coined by O'Reilly Media in 2003 (O'Reilly, 2005) and is now widely used in a collective sense to describe these technologies. Web 2.0 applications are not limited to education—in fact, Web 2.0 exists primarily outside the education sphere—but these technologies have extraordinary potential for education and the kinds of learner-engaging functions that should be incorporated into the next generation of course management systems. They represent the very essence of learner-centered instruction. According to Maloney (2007),

> What we can see in the Web's evolution is a new focus on innovation, creation, and collaboration, and an emphasis on collective knowledge over static information delivery, knowledge management over content management, and social interaction over isolated surfing. The jargon-laden stars of the second-generation Web—wikis, blogs, social networking, and so on—all encourage a more active, participatory role for users.

Web 2.0 technologies include, but certainly are not limited to, the following areas.

Blogging.   Web logging, or *blogging*, is a form of online reporting and journaling that gives anyone an opportunity to publish on the Internet. Blogs can be open to the public or restricted to groups of readers determined by the blogger. Blogs can be excellent tools for student reflections about course content or reporting activities in a student teaching experience, for example. See Blogger.com (URLs for sites mentioned in this section are located at the end of this chapter) for an example of a blogging site freely available for personal or academic use.

Wikis.   A *wiki* is usually thought to be a space designed to be created and edited by groups of persons. The term derives from the Hawaiian word *wiki*, which means "quick." A wiki can be an excellent tool for collaborative online writing assignments and group activities compiling information in a single online resource. The best known is Wikipedia, a free online encyclopedia being written by more than 75,000 active contributors all over the world. Wiki applications, including Wiki-Site, the same engine that drives Wikipedia, are available at little or no cost to educational institutions.

Podcasting.   *Podcasting*, which derived from the Apple product iPod and the term *broadcasting*, is the process of recording and storing audio and/or video content on the Internet for downloading and playback using iPods, MP3 players, computers, and other electronic gear that plays back audio and/or video files. College professors are now finding podcasting a convenient way to provide lectures and other course-content-related recordings to students. This concept is hardly new. We were doing this in the 1980s when the Sony Walkman came into vogue as a portable audiocassette player. Now, though, the Web provides a convenient medium for the distribution of audio content by just about anyone, including students and faculty. Audio recordings are easy to make and simple to edit, and they can easily be uploaded into course management systems.

Other Forms of Content Creation.   Until the early 2000s, only webmasters and others authorized to build websites could put information on the Web. No more. One of the defining characteristics of Web 2.0 is that literally anyone can generate "content" and place it on the Web without knowledge of web page design tools and methods. Blogs and wikis are examples of web user content generation. YouTube, founded in February 2005 as a place where anyone can upload a video file for viewing by the masses, has become one of the most frequently visited sites on the Web. By June 2006, more than 60,000 video files *per day* were being uploaded into YouTube, and over 70 million videos *per day* were being viewed (Hinchcliffe, 2006) by persons all over the world. No figures are available for how many of these uploaders are students, but a safe estimate is "plenty." Likewise, many faculty are uploading video-based lecture recordings and other course materials for convenient viewing by students. With video recording capabilities built into many digital cameras and even cell phones, and with most computers sold today pre-equipped with simple video editing tools, possibilities for video-based student learning activities, posted to the Web, seem endless.

Social Bookmarking.   Social bookmarking was described by Alexander (2006) as "classic social software . . . a rare case of people connecting through shared metadata" (p. 36). As such, social bookmarking epitomizes the collaborative and sharing aspects of Web 2.0. Most of us save lists of our frequently visited websites as favorites or bookmarks in our web browsers. In social bookmarking sites such as del.icio.us, people post their bookmarks for viewing by others. Through a sophisticated system of meta-tagging, or assignment of descriptive information, anyone is able to search for bookmarks on specific subjects and identify sites that others have found valuable. In a sense, social bookmarking is like Google or Yahoo! on steroids, because the sites located have already been prescreened and found to be useful by others with similar interests. Social bookmarking sites have high potential for students searching for web resources for class assignments. Moreover, once other users have been identified as posting a significant number of helpful sites, bookmarks posted on other topics by those users can be reviewed to identify "kindred spirits" with common interests. The sites provide contact information for purposes of social communication.

Social Networking.   Most college students need no introduction to social networking, and according to a recent study by the Pew Internet and American Life project (Lenhart & Madden, 2007), 55% of precollege Americans ages 12 to 17 were active on social networking sites in 2006. According to the online competitive intelligence service Hitwise, MySpace was the single-most frequently accessed website in the United States in June 2007, well ahead of runners-up Google and Yahoo!, and Facebook was also in the top 10. Social networking sites promote the development of online communities through posting of personal information, journals, photos, likes and dislikes, and provide communication channels for persons with similar interests to meet virtually. Considerable research is needed on the relationship between social networking and distance education (Simonson, 2008a, 2008b).

Virtual Worlds.   Virtual reality is hardly a new concept. Virtual reality in the form of computer-generated simulations dates back to the mid-1950s and has long been used for corporate, health science, and military training purposes. More recent

A LOOK AT BEST PRACTICES—WEB 2.0

We all know what it means to be a friend. We learn early in life that, as Emerson said, "the only way to have a friend is to be one." A *friend* is a person who is admired and respected, and whose company is enjoyed.

The idea of friends has recently changed, however, at least in social networking applications. According to Boyd and Ellison (2007), social networks are Web-based services that allow persons to construct a public or semipublic profile within a system, to articulate a list of other users with whom they share connections, and view and move through a list of links made by themselves and others. Most often these locations are called *social networking sites.* Social network sites such as MySpace and Facebook have attracted millions of participants who blog, share messages, post photos and videos, and list their friends, all in personally constructed profiles.

To participate in a social network site, a user constructs a profile and by this act the social networker becomes real in a virtual world. They "type oneself into being" as Suden (2003) stated. One characteristic of most social networking sites is the listing of friends, or *friending.* Social networkers name those they want to list as friends, and in most cases the request to be a friend requires an affirmative response. Some sites even allow top eight or top ten lists of friends; as Boyd (2006) said, "In a culture where it is socially awkward to reject someone's Friendship, ranking them provides endless drama and social awkwardness" (p. 11).

Many who study the phenomena of social networking refer to the idea of *Web 2.0,* a trend in the use of the Internet and the Web that is based on collaboration and information sharing. Web 2.0 is not a new network, nor a "thing." Web 2.0 is an idea in people's heads, based on the interaction between the user and provider. Examples are eBay, Wikipedia, Skype, and Craigslist.

So, what does this all mean to the distance educator? Certainly it is nice to have friends, even virtual ones, and social networks seem to have reached the point of "critical mass" and are here to stay, at least until a new innovative use of the Web evolves.

The importance of social networking makes the concept important to distance. At the least, a modest understanding of social networking is a must for distance educators. And, it is likely that more depth of understanding will be needed. The taxonomy of social networking for distance learning might look like this:

Level 1: Learning about social networks—definitions, history, background, and examples

Level 2: Designing for social networks—profiling, blogging, wiki-ing, and friending

Level 3: Studying social networks—ethics, uses, misuses, policing, supporting

Level 4: Learning from and with social networks—social networks for teaching and learning, science, research, and theory building

projects, such as Second Life and Active Worlds, have brought these technologies to the World Wide Web and made them accessible to much broader populations, including educators. Although the instinct among some has been to put classroom lectures into virtual worlds so they can be experienced by students via 3-D animation, virtual worlds appear to have (as they have for several pre-Web decades) exciting potential for placing students in real-life applications of course content; for example, in problem-solving situations, and especially experiences in other places and times that would otherwise be inaccessible, such as visiting Mars, traveling through the human body's circulation system, or witnessing rituals at Stonehenge. Limitations at this time include the need for significant bandwidth at the user's end, and the skills, time, and effort needed to plan and develop the animations. It is likely, however, that virtual worlds will represent the standard learning environments at some point in our future. More immediately, Schroeder (2007) believes that virtual environments "built on the very premises of online engagement and interaction" will ultimately replace the World Wide Web.

PEDAGOGIES OF INTERNET-BASED DISTANCE EDUCATION

In their widely read, if criticized, report entitled *Thwarted Innovation: What Happened to E-Learning and Why,* Zemsky and Massy (2004) concluded that online learning was a good thing but had fallen way short of its promise (Simonson, 2004).

E-Learning Adoption Cycles

While their research was questioned, Zemsky and Massy's thoughts on e-learning adoption cycles are relevant. They noted that technology applications in both on- and off-campus instruction follow four distinct adoption cycles, each requiring pedagogical and cultural changes within the educational organization (Zemsky & Massy, 2004, p. 11). Any or all of these cycles may be operating simultaneously in different parts of the same campus.

- **Cycle 1: Enhancements to traditional course/program configurations.**   In this cycle, faculty introduce basic-level technologies into their courses, such as e-mail, Web resources, and PowerPoint slides, without fundamentally altering their instructional strategies.
- **Cycle 2: Course management systems (CMS).**   Here, faculty use some of the basic tools a CMS offers and shift resources and course activities to an online format. Some use these tools completely in lieu of face-to-face class meetings. (Zemsky and Massy [2004] noted that more than 80% of all online course enrollments at the institutions they studied consisted of on-campus students.) Recall what we said earlier about course management systems reflecting a teacher-centered instructional paradigm.
- **Cycle 3: Imported course objects.**   This cycle involves embedding electronic learning objects within a course to further promote student understanding of the course material. These objects could range from photographic slides and audio and video files to complex 3-D animations and simulations.
- **Cycle 4: New course/program configurations.**   In this cycle, courses are reconceptualized and redesigned to take advantage of the power of technology and the Internet in enhancing learning and increasing student engagement. "The new configurations focus on active learning and combine face-to-face, virtual, synchronous, and asynchronous interaction in novel ways. They also require professors and students to accept new roles—with each other and with the technology and support staff" (Zemsky & Massy, 2004, p. 11). Use of Web 2.0 applications is most likely to occur in a course in Cycle 4.

Zemsky and Massy (2004) felt that faculty in general were well into the first two cycles but that this interest has not expanded to Cycles 3 and 4. Specifically in the case of distance education, they observed

> good use of the presentation enhancement tools represented by PowerPoint; heavy reliance on the kind of course infrastructure that a good course management system provides; computerized assessments; and threaded discussions. At best, it would include the importation and use of elementary learning objects; in reality, it has prompted almost no development of new course/program configuration beyond taking advantage of the Web's capacity to promote self-paced and just-in-time learning. (p. 12)

Other obvious reasons for the failure of educational organizations to realize the potential of online learning were not discussed in this report. These "barriers" are long-standing and are firmly entrenched in institutional culture, and they have power-ful effects. Many faculty simply do not have the time or the instructional design skills for, let alone the interest in, completely redesigning their courses per Cycle 4. Campus reward systems governing promotion and tenure discourage instructional innovation among junior faculty. Faculty training is minimal to nonexistent and typically focuses upon basic PowerPoint and CMS "how-to" tutorials rather than the pedagogies of teaching online. Most educational institutions do not employ trained, professional *instructional* technology consultants whose functions are to assist faculty in online course development and the creation of learning objects. Many of those that do offer such consultants instinctively target these positions for elimination when budgets get tight. Many faculty with interests in teaching online have to deal with obsolete computers, minimal software, and no funding for upgrades. Until fundamental infrastructure issues such as these are addressed, e-learning will never reach its potential, nor will any other instructional technology.

Fundamentals of Teaching Online

What advice can we offer to instructors who teach online? What kinds of processes can faculty follow to advance their online courses to Cycles 3 and 4? Here are some suggestions that are intended to supplement Chapters 5 and 7 on instructional design and teaching in a distance education environment, respectively.

Avoid "Dumping" a Face-to-Face Course onto the Web.   Many faculty operating in Zemsky and Massy's Cycle 2 do little more than transfer course handouts and selected discussion topics to the CMS. The term *shovelware* has evolved to describe this practice: Shovel the course onto the Web and say you are teaching online, but don't think about it much. Online activities for students should have specific pedagogical or course management purposes.

Organize the Course and Make the Organization and Requirements Clear to Students.   Many students have never before studied in an online educational environment. If they have, chances are good that it was not a positive experience. One student quoted by Zemsky and Massy referred to "the fairy tale of e-learning" (2004, p. 50). Instructors of online courses must make the course organization, calendar, activities, and expectations as clear as possible. Students need this kind of structure and detail to help them stay organized and on task. A detailed syllabus is a good starting point.

The calendar tools provided in CMSs generally are adequate for showing students the big picture, but instructors should also provide more detailed information on a topic-by-topic basis, or week-by-week or even day-by-day in more compressed classes, to guide students and keep them on track. Each "weekly schedule" page should include (1) inclusive dates; (2) topics; (3) learning outcomes; (4) identification of readings and other preparatory activities; (5) schedule of activities, including quizzes or exams; (6) topics and/or specific questions to be discussed in the online forums; (7) identification of assignment(s) and due dates; and (8) any other relevant information. Let students know exactly what is expected of them, and when.

Detailed assignment instructions are imperative. Each component of an instructor's grading scheme should have its own document easily locatable within the course website. The instructions could include any of the following, as appropriate. Certainly not all these components may be necessary for all assignments.

- Stated purpose of the assignment
- Identification of the intended audience for the assignment (e.g., "Write the proposed business plan as if it would be read by a senior executive within the company. Your instructor will assume that role during grading.")

- Examples of acceptable and unacceptable topics
- Hot links to relevant online resources
- Caveats (e.g., "The proposed business plan must be realistic within the current budget climate. Do not propose eight new positions without explaining how the funds for these positions would be generated.")
- Identification of the required components of the assignment (e.g., "The proposal should include the following: introduction and justification of need, project goals, proposed budget, timeline . . .")
- Grading criteria, including areas of special emphasis
- Due date
- Point value
- Instructions for submitting the assignment, such as in the CMS drop-box or as an e-mail attachment sent directly to the instructor
- Any other special instructions or information (e.g., "Your paper will be posted on the course website.")

Keep Students Informed Constantly.   The announcements tool in a course management system is an excellent means for instructors to get new information to students. Use announcements to introduce new topics, remind about deadlines, announce schedule changes, and provide a wide variety of other timely information. Many online instructors prefer to send direct e-mail to their students for these purposes in the form of weekly updates/introductions to new topics. Constant contact is essential.

Think about Course Outcomes.   This is the first step in truly transforming a course. What knowledge, skills, and feelings does the instructor really want the students to gain in the course? In what ways do students need to be prepared for subsequent courses or for application of the course content in the real world (the real bottom line)? These are the course outcomes. Bloom's (1969) taxonomy of educational objectives is extremely useful in this process. Course activities then need to be structured to enable students to achieve those outcomes. In almost every discipline, activities can be conducted in an online environment to facilitate student learning at each of these levels. It is imperative to activate higher-order thinking skills.

Test Applications, Not Rote Memory.   Student assessment must be designed to reflect the specific behaviors identified in the course outcomes. The chapter author recently encountered a completely online Art Appreciation course that had noble student outcomes at the comprehension and appreciation levels. Yet, almost the totality of student assessment came from a pool of 1,600 objective quiz items, hardly any of which were higher than the knowledge level in Bloom's taxonomy. For all practical purposes, this course had one outcome: "Recall from memory 1,600 simple facts, some of which may actually be somewhat relevant."

Although it is possible to design multiple-choice quiz items that assess students at the analysis, synthesis, and evaluation levels of Bloom's taxonomy, these are not likely to be typical applications of the course material in the real world. Assessing students in a manner consistent with the behaviors identified in course outcomes also helps combat student academic dishonesty. Techniques such as question pools and randomization are used within CMSs to minimize cheating, but creative students can devise many ingenious ways to beat the system. Avoiding objective online testing altogether may be the best strategy.

Integrate the Power of the Web into the Course. This is essential for purposes of student intellectual engagement—with course content, with each other, and with the instructor and other resource persons involved in the course. The Web offers powerful opportunities for resource utilization, collaboration, and communication. Many highly valuable primary sources are now available online.

For example, in the early- to mid-1990s, an agricultural economics professor at a land-grant university in the Midwest was involved with extensive economic development projects in the newly independent nations in Eastern Europe that had been Soviet republics. In the process, he collected an enormous volume of documents and videotaped interviews with numerous local, regional, and national officials of those countries, which he then had digitized with dubbed translations. As the number of websites exploded later in the decade, he identified hundreds of related sites, from United Nations and World Bank resources to countless local and national sites describing conditions in those areas related to agriculture and local economic drivers such as tourism. He then organized this information by selected country and community on his course website and asked his students to study the resources and create economic development plans based on the information available. This was truly learning at the higher cognitive levels. The real-world learning experience was emphasized when local officials in those communities assisted in the assessment of the plans for grading purposes.

In particular, the power of the Web can be employed through the use of Web 2.0 applications. These tools are all about student engagement and higher-order learning.

Apply Adult Learning Principles with Nontraditional Students. If students enrolled in a course are working adults, the course design should incorporate the basic principles of adult learning. Adults are more self-directed and have specific reasons for taking the course. Many have their own learning goals in mind and expect the instructor to help them achieve those goals. Activities and assignments should be relevant to the students' immediate needs, rather than the deferred needs of traditional college-age students, and should contain options for customization. Online discussions should build on the students' personal and professional experiences. Adult students can learn as much or more from each other as from the instructor. They have many commitments in their lives in addition to the course, involving work, family, church, and community. Therefore, the instructor may need to exercise more flexibility regarding timelines and deadlines than with a class of traditional college-age sophomores. These are but a few examples.

Extend Course Readings Beyond the Text (or to Replace the Text). Many instructors are conditioned by their own college experiences and years of practice to allow the textbook to dictate the course content and to organize course activities around the textbook. This is fine if the instructor wrote the textbook for the course, perhaps not so otherwise. The step of selection of course readings occurs about in the middle of a course development model, not at the beginning. Nowhere is it written that a course has to have a textbook. The Web is positively rich with outstanding primary sources that can be used effectively to promote outcomes achievement. The Zemsky and Massy (2004) report cited earlier is an example of a possible required reading in a distance education course, as is the plethora of online resources used by the agricultural economics professor identified earlier to supplement his personal collection of documents and media. In addition, more than 10,000 professional journals and other periodical publications are now available online and in full text. Almost every profession has online newsletters available free or at low cost that allow students and faculty to stay abreast of current developments. These resources are what professionals in the field use; students need to get acclimated to using them at the beginning of their respective careers.

Train Students to Use the Course Website.   Students cannot use course web tools effectively if they do not know how. It is essential that training be provided at the beginning of the course, through online tutorials in the case of virtual courses and in a face-to-face setting if available. Instructors should consistently monitor to detect if students are having difficulty navigating the course website and using its components.

FUTURE OF INTERNET-BASED DISTANCE EDUCATION

When the chapters for the first edition of this book were written in 1998, course management systems were new on the market and not widely used. Little attention was paid to CMSs in the Internet chapter. The Web was just beginning to be exploited as a means of commerce. Few homes had broadband Internet access. Virtual schools were just starting to appear. So much has changed in such a relatively short period of time that both the third and fourth editions of this chapter required significant updates. And we are already seeing nationally distributed reports about the *failure* of online learning! By the sixth edition, another major overhaul likely will be necessary.

So, it is with some trepidation that we discuss the future of Internet-based distance education. Here are four trends to watch.

Growth of Virtual Schools and Universities

Many teachers incorporate technology into their daily activities, but despite the emergence of a new, student-centered approach, most education today still follows fundamentally the same instructional model as it has for the past 200 years. Students sit in a classroom, teachers stand in the front and control the learning activities, students listen and take notes, and periodically some form of in-class assessment is conducted. How long will this model persist? Is this the way students will be learning in the year 2100? Probably not, although the historically glacial pace of educational change may lend doubts. The growth of virtual schools and colleges gives us a glimpse into a possible educational model of the future.

K–12 Initiatives.   Virtual schools at the K–12 level are now seeing significant growth. As a matter of fact, the state of Florida has mandated that every school district in the state must have a virtual K–8 and 9–12 virtual school (Simonson, 2008).

Enrollments and program quality will be the subject of much public (and undoubtedly legislative) interest and scrutiny in the years to come. A study conducted by Picciano and Seaman (2007) for the Sloan Consortium estimated that nationwide about 700,000 students at the K–12 level engaged in completely online courses or hybrid/blended learning experiences during a recent school year. In 2006, the Michigan legislature approved a requirement for all high school students in the state to take an online course as a graduation requirement (Michigan Department of Education, 2007). More than a dozen states have established statewide virtual schools to reach their K–12 populations. "Cyber" schools are also being operated by universities, school districts, consortia, and private companies. The state of Ohio alone had more than 40 virtual schools operating (Stephens, 2004).

Virtual schools can have many benefits for students, districts, and states. They can supplement existing curricula, promote course sharing among schools, and reach students who cannot (for physical reasons or incarceration) or do not (by choice) attend school in person. Virtual schools enable districts and states to provide advanced placement courses and enrichment courses to rural schools and those in other smaller, less affluent locations. Such courses are particularly advantageous in enabling these schools to meet. Home-schooled students, in particular, stand to benefit from courses and curricula offered online. The Web can help overcome two of the main limitations of homeschooling—the lack of interaction with other students and, as with many alternative schools, limited access to high-quality learning materials (Owston, 1997).

Higher Education Initiatives.   At the postsecondary level, interest in establishing virtual colleges and universities (VCUs) was stimulated by the creation in 1996 of the Western Governor's University, a collaboration of 13 western states, and by the dawn of the twenty-first century had spread across the country.

The report noted at the outset that the economic climate for VCUs changed dramatically after the turn of the century, when state budget shortfalls led many higher education administrators and legislatures to reexamine the costs and realities of virtual education before payoffs had been demonstrated. A high-profile example of a virtual university flameout was the rather spectacular demise of the California Virtual University (CVU) in 2000, although some of the CVU's functions have emerged in the California Virtual Campus (CVC), formerly a venture of the state's community colleges. The SHEEO/WCET report was cautiously optimistic about the future of VCUs. It noted that although VCUs have been somewhat successful in increasing access to previously underserved populations, the foremost goal for many, 42% of the institutions surveyed identified on-campus students as their primary users. This was seen as an unintended side effect but an illustration of expanded access. The report also observed that although VCUs are new and have yet to become firmly established, some are already beginning to build sustainable revenue streams that take pressures off the need for state funding (Epper & Garn, 2003). It is also likely that more regional and national consortia of virtual higher education institutions will need to be established in order to better leverage resources.

Advances in High-Speed Networking

By the mid-1990s, it had become evident at many universities that the Internet as it existed at that time was woefully inadequate for the kinds of bandwidth-intensive research, development, and instructional activities that they wished to conduct, particularly in collaboration with other organizations. The Internet2 (I2) project was initiated in 1996 and now has more than 300 members, including educational institutions and corporate partners. Internet2 also has an interesting cast of affiliate members, representing the diversity of potential applications of high-speed networking. For example, I2 affiliate members range from the NASA Jet Propulsion Laboratory and the Oak Ridge National Laboratory to the New World Symphony, the Cleveland Institute of Art, the Philadelphia Children's Hospital, and the Smithsonian Institution. Internet2 has three goals:

- Create a leading-edge network capability for the national research community.
- Enable revolutionary Internet applications.
- Ensure the rapid transfer of new network services and applications to the broader Internet community.

Note that replacement of the existing Internet is not one of them. Internet2 was never intended to supplant the Internet, but rather to demonstrate the applications of a faster, wider bandwidth network and to work with its corporate partners in research and development endeavors that would lead to a vastly improved Internet, which is estimated to be about 3 to 5 years behind Internet2 technologically.

The implications of I2 for distance education are particularly relevant to this chapter. An Internet that reaches speeds approaching those of Internet2 offers tremendous potential for real-time delivery of instruction in broadcast-quality video format, as well as greatly enhanced streaming capabilities in asynchronous online instruction. The obvious limitation is the "final mile" dilemma that has plagued distance education since experiments with satellite-based instruction in the 1970s. High-speed networking may be available in the student's community but is problematic without an extension to the student's home or work location. This barrier is also being overcome with the increased availability of cable-modem and digital subscriber line (DSL) high-speed Internet access through Internet service providers at the local level, and Internet service provided through electrical power lines is likely to be available in many communities at some point in the near future. Internet2 also has extraordinary potential for conventional classroom-based instruction in the form of distributed learning activities.

Development of Standards and Learning Objects

When a consumer buys a DVD of a recent movie release, does she wonder if it will play on her home DVD player? When she buys a conventional 60-watt light bulb, is she afraid that it won't screw into her table lamp? When she buys gasoline at a gas station, is she concerned that it won't fuel her car? Unless the products themselves are defective, the answer is *no*, because the world has established technical standards for such things. Most countries in the world have national standards institutes that work closely with the International Organization for Standardization (www.iso.org/) to ensure worldwide compatibility to the greatest degree possible.

Enter the matters of learning objects and learning management. If an instructor developed an online course using one type of course management system and the institution then licensed a different system, the course would not easily port over to the new platform. The manner of tracking student performance is not consistent from one CMS or student assessment software product to another. We currently have no easy way of identifying existing courseware to meet a specific learning need. The Masie Center (2002) has captured the nature of the problem:

> As we have seen historically with battles over such things as railway track gauge, telephone dial tones, video tape formats, email protocols, and the platform battles between Microsoft, Apple, Sun, HP, and others, companies often start out with proprietary technology that will not work well with others. However, these technologies often do not meet the needs of end-users, and thus, the market typically drives the various leaders from business, academic, and government to work together to develop common "standards." This allows a variety of products to co-exist. This convergence of technologies is very important for the consumers of these technologies because products that adhere to standards will provide consumers with wider product choices and a better chance that the products in which they invest will avoid quick obsolescence. Likewise, common standards for things such as content meta-data, content packaging, question and test interoperability, learner profiles, run-time interaction, etc., are requisite for the success of the knowledge economy and for the future of learning. (p. 7)

The Masie Center (2002, p. 8) identified five "abilities" that e-learning standards should enable:

1. *Interoperability:* Can the system work with any other system?
2. *Reusability:* Can courseware (learning objects, or "chunks") be re-used?
3. *Manageability:* Can a system track the appropriate information about the learner and the content?
4. *Accessibility:* Can a learner access the appropriate content at the appropriate time?
5. *Durability:* Will the technology evolve with the standards to avoid obsolescence?

This, very briefly stated, is the background for a number of collaborative efforts to develop standards for e-learning. The general process followed is that a designated organization conducts research and development activities and generates "specifications" that are a preliminary form of standards. The specifications are then put through extensive testing and continued development until they are accepted by the developer and user communities, at which time they become standards.

The Advanced Distributed Learning (ADL) initiative, sponsored by the Department of Defense, has taken on the overall coordination role for developing e-learning standards in the United States, working with several organizations that develop specifications. Advanced Distributed Learning is responsible for conducting the testing, review, negotiation, and further development activities that transform specifications into standards. Accepted standards collectively form the Sharable Content Object Reference Model (SCORM) for product developers and users that ensures conformance with the five "abilities" just listed. When vendors describe their products as "SCORM-compliant," they are referring to this.

The IMS Global Learning Consortium is the organization with its focus on developing specifications for distributed learning and CMSs. Originally oriented toward higher education only, IMS now addresses a multitude of distributed learning contexts, including K–12 and corporate and government training. The IMS Global Learning Consortium's specifications currently in various stages of development cover the following areas: accessibility, competency definitions, content packaging, digital repositories, enterprise, learner information, learning design, meta-data, question and test interoperability, simple sequencing, and vocabulary definition exchange. The value of having technical standards in each of these areas should be self-evident.

The specifications for digital repositories are particularly important as they relate to learning objects. The definitions of *learning objects* vary considerably from one source to another. The simple explanation is that a learning object is an object used for the purposes of learning. Some authorities consider the "old" media such as overhead transparencies and videotapes to be learning objects. Others say that learning objects have to be in digital format. To be truly useful in a standards-based context, learning objects must be digital and have certain characteristics that give them added value. One is that learning objects are meta-tagged; they carry coding containing descriptors that enable the objects to be identified during searches. Another is that learning objects should be reusable. In other words, they should be indexed in a digital repository that adheres to IMS specifications, so that they can be accessed by any instructor, anywhere, at any time.

Only a few such repositories exist at this time. For example, one of these repositories is the Multimedia Educational Resource for Teaching and Online Learning (MERLOT). Others are beginning to appear under the "open courseware" concept, the publication on the Web of course materials developed by higher education institutions and shared with others. Two high-profile open courseware projects are the Massachusetts Institute of Technology's Open CourseWare initiative, through which MIT has placed materials from over a thousand courses online, and Rice University's Connexions project; at least 30 others are either already public or are under development. As digital asset management technology evolves, we can expect to see many more. These will greatly expand the number and range of instructional resources available to instructors teaching online.

Potential Impact of Open Source

Open source software is intended to be freely shared and can be improved upon and redistributed to others. The code in which the software is written is free and available to anyone to do just about anything with it, as long as the uses are consistent with a 10-part definition maintained by the Open Source Initiative (OSI). *Open source* does not mean "unlicensed." Open source software typically has a license, but the terms of the license should comply with the OSI definition before the software is truly open source. Nor does *open source* mean "free." The code may be free, but the costs involved in implementing the application within an organization (e.g., hardware and personnel) can be significant.

The concept of open source is relevant to this chapter because a number of initiatives have evolved to create open source CMSs that can be licensed by educational institutions without a license cost. This option is appealing to many campuses that already have technical support staffs in place that can manage open source software applications. For example, the Australian open source CMS product called Moodle has become so widely adopted that it is now available in 75 languages and has produced a worldwide grassroots network for development and peer support numbering more than 200,000 persons. In the United States, the Sakai Project, a collaboration among Stanford University, the Massachusetts Institute of Technology, Indiana University, the University of Michigan, and a group of partners, has consolidated the individual efforts of the four institutions to develop an open source, standards-based CMS that interoperates with other campus systems and emphasizes pedagogy over course management (Simonson, 2007).

As we noted earlier, more than half the course management systems currently available are open source or otherwise made available to educational institutions without charge. During the 2004 to 2006 period, Blackboard itself, through a series of actions largely viewed by the educational community as arrogant, may have driven some if not many of its current and potential customers to reconsider open source CMS products. Blackboard first purchased and absorbed its primary rival, WebCT, then it secured a patent for electronic learning technology that many professionals in the field viewed as "prior art," then it sued its next most prominent competitor, Desire2Learn, for patent infringement. These moves infuriated Blackboard's main customer base, with the long-term fallout yet to be assessed. Overall, the degree to which open source course management systems cut into the market share of commercial CMS vendors, or force them to improve their product quality, change their pricing models, and bolster customer relations, will be a focus of much interest over the next few years.

SUMMARY

The technologies used for distance education fall into two categories: telecommunications technologies that connect instructors to distant learners and classroom technologies that record, present, and display instructional information. Increasingly, video- and computer-based systems are being used.

Most often, teachers and students use classrooms that have been designed and installed by others. However, the effective utilization of distance education classrooms requires a new set of skills for most educators and learners. Teaching with technology to learners who are not physically located in the same site where instruction is taking place requires a different set of skills and competencies than traditional education. Technologies are tools that must be mastered to be effective.

DISCUSSION QUESTIONS

1. According to Dale's Cone of Experience, which is the most realistic, a video of a museum, or a field trip to the museum? What would make one experience more appropriate than the other?
2. Define noise and explain how noise influences the communication process. Put noise in the context of an online course.

3. Should traditional classrooms also be equipped to be distance classrooms? Why?
4. What are the most significant advantages of Internet-based instruction? Why?
5. Explain how an online course can be structured to be student centered. Give specific strategies.
6. What is one significant trend in online learning? Why?

REFERENCES

Alexander, B. (2006). Web 2.0: A new wave of innovation for teaching and learning? *EDUCAUSE Review, 41*(2), 32–44. Available online at http://www.educause.edu/apps/er/erm/erm06/erm0621.asp

Allen, I. E., & Seaman, J. (2010). Learning on demand. Online Education in the United States, 2009. Needham, MA: Sloan Consortium.

Allen, I., Seaman, J., & Garrett, R. (2007). Blending in: The extent and promise of blended education in the United States. Needham, MA: Sloan Consortium. Available online at http://www.sloan-c/org/publications/survey/pdf/Blending_In.pdf

Barr, R. B., & Tagg, J. (1995). From teaching to learning: A new paradigm for undergraduate education. *Change, 27*(6), 13–25.

Bloom, B. S. (1969). *Taxonomy of educational objectives: The classification of educational goals.* London: Longman Group.

Brown, M. (2007). Mashing up the once and future CMS. *EDUCASE Review, 42*(4), 8–9. Available online at http://www.educase.edu /apps/er/erm07/erm0725.asp

Boyd, D. (2006). Friends, Friendsters, and MySpace Top 8: Writing community into being on social network sites. *First Monday, 11*(12). Retrieved July 21, 2007 from http://www.firstmonday.org/issues/issues11_12/boy

Boyd, D. M., Ellison, N. B. (2007). Social network sites: Definition, history, and scholarship. *Journal of Computer-Medicated Communication, 13*(1), article 11. http://jcmc.indiana.edu/vol13/issue1/boyd.ellison.html

Dale, E. (1946). *Audiovisual methods in teaching.* Hinsdale, IL: Dryden Press.

Discovery Education. (2006). About United Streaming. Retrieved on March 28, 2006, from www.unitedstreaming.com/publicPages/about Us.cfm

Epper, R. M., & Garn, M. (2003). Virtual college & university consortia: *A national study.* Denver: State Higher Education Executive Officers. Available online at http://www.wcet.info/resources/publications/vcu.pdf

Essex, C. (2006). Podcasting: A new delivery method for faculty development. *Distance Learni 3*(2), 39–43.

Gillispie, J. (2008). Meeting the shifting perspective: The Iowa communications network. *Learning: For Educators, Trainers, and Leaders, 5*(1), 1–12. Charlotte, NC: Informa

Gray, M. (1996). *Web growth summary.* Available online at http://www.mit.edu/people/mkgray/net/web-growth-summary.html

Harrington, R. (2008). Producing video podcasts. Burlington, MAS Focal Press

Hinchcliffe, D. (2006). *"User" generated content and YouTube.* Available online http://web2.socialcomputingmagazine.com/user_generated_content

Lenhart, A., & Madden, M. (2007). *Social networking sites and teens: An* Pew internet & American Life Project. Available online at http://www.pewinternet.org/pdfs/PIP_SNS_Data_Memo_Jan

Mallory, J. (2001). Creating streamed instruction for the deaf and hard-of-hearing online learner. *DEOSNEWS, 11*(8), 1–6.

Maloney, E. J. (2007, January 5). What Web 2.0 can teach about learning. *Chronicle of Higher Education.* Available online at http://chronicle.com/weekly/v53/i18/18b02601.htm (login required)

Masie Center. (2002). *Making sense of learning specifications & standards: A decision-maker's guide to their adoption.* Saratoga Springs, NY: The Masie Center. Available online at http://www.masie.com/standards/S3_Guide.pdf

Michigan Department of Education. (2007). *Michigan merit curriculum guidelines: Online experience.* Available online at http://www.michigan.gov/documents/mdcd/Guuidelines__for_Online _Experiences_180515_7.pdf

Mullins-Dove, T. (2006). Streaming video and distance education. *Distance Learning, 3*(4), 63–71.

New Oxford American Dictionary announces word of the year: 'Podcast' (2005, December 6). *MacDaily News.* Retrieved December 7, 2006, from http://macdailyNews.com

Oblinger, D. G. (1999). Hype, hyperarchy, and higher education. *Business Officer, 33*(4), 22–24, 27–31.

O'Reilly, T. (2005). *What is Web 2.0? Design patterns and business models for the next generation of software.* Available online at http://www.oreillynet.com/pub/a/oreilly/tim/news/2005/09/30/what-is-web-20.html

Owston, R. D. (1997). The World Wide Web: A technology to enhance teaching and learning? *Educational Researcher, 26*(2), 27–33.

Picciano, A. G., & Seaman, J. (2007). K–12 online learning: *A survey of U.S. school district administrators.* Needham, MA: The Sloan Consortium.

Reed, R. (2001, August). Streaming technology: An effective tool for e-learning experiences. *National Association of Media and Technology Centers Bulletin,* pp. 1–3.

Saltzberg, S., & Polyson, S. (1995). Distributed learning on the World Wide Web, *Syllabus, 9* (1), 10–12.

Schroeder, R. (2007, May). Web 2.0: Enhancing engagement in online education. Sloan-C View, 6(5), 1. Available online at http://www.sloan-c.org/publications/view/v6n5/viewv6n5.htm

Simonson, M. (2004). Thwarted innovation or thwarted research. *Quarterly Review of Distance Education. 5*(4), vii–ix.

Simonson, M. (2007). Podcasting: Or, seeds floated down from the sky. *Distance Learning, 4*(2), 104.

Simonson, M. (2007). Course management systems. *Quarterly Review of Distance Education. 8*(1), vii–ix.

Simonson, M. (2008). Virtual schools mandated. *Distance Learning: For Educators, Trainers, and Leaders, 5*(4), 84–83.

_____. Will you be my friend? *Distance Learning: For Educators, Trainers, and*

. New York: Peter Lang.

king for distance Education: Where's the research. *Quarterly* 2), vii.

hwarted innovation: *What happened to e-learning and why.* iance, University of Pennsylvania. Available online at e.info/Docs/Jun2004/Weatherstation_Report.pdf

SITES REFERENCED IN THIS CHAPTER

ICN/icnsites/prices/contents.html
Standardization

http://wikipedia.org/
Wiki-Site
http://www.wiki-site.com/
YouTube
http://youtube.com/
del.icio.us
http://del.icio.us/
MySpace
http://www.myspace.com/
Facebook
http://www.facebook.com/
Second Life
http://secondlife.com/
Active Worlds
http://www.activeworlds.com/
Advanced Distributed Learning Initiative
http://www.adlnet.org/
ADL is the entity that has taken on the overall coordination role for developing e-learning standards
    known as the Sharable Content Object Reference Model (SCORM).
Connexions, Rice University
http://cnx.org/
Connexions is the Web site maintained by the Rice University providing free and open access to a wide
    variety of learning objects and other course materials available for use by faculty at other institutions.
IMS Global Learning Consortium
http://www.imsglobal.org/
The IMS Global Learning Consortium is the organization with its focus upon developing specifications
    for distributed learning and course management systems. Approved specifications become
    standards and are incorporated into SCORM (see Advanced Distributed Learning entry).
Internet II
http://www.internet2.edu/
The Internet II project conducts research and development intended to enhance the performance
    and capabilities of the Internet.
Internet Society
http://www.isoc.org/
The Internet Society is an international nonprofit organization that assumes much of the manage-
    ment, coordination, and oversight responsibility for the Internet.
Moodle
http://moodle.org/
Moodle is a highly popular open source course management system that has been
    Translated into at least 75 languages and has a worldwide user community of over 200,000 persons.
Open Course Ware, Massachusetts Institute of Technology
http://web.mit.edu/ocw
Learning objects and other course materials from over 1,400 MIT courses are available for down-
    loading and academic use by faculty without permission.
Open Source Initiative
http://www.opensource.org/
The Open Source Initiative maintains standards and sample licenses for open source software.
Sakai Project
http://www.sakaiproject.org/
The Sakai Project is a collaborative effort among a group of prominent U.S universities to develop
    and distribute an advanced open source course management system and related products.

PODCASTING . . . OR "SEEDS FLOATED DOWN FROM THE SKY"

Bud-like seeds floated down from the sky, from space actually—they were not noticed at first but soon the seeds grew into pods, plant-like oblong objects that when ripe disgorged a terrible creature, a creature that killed and eliminated humans and replaced them with exact physical replicas that were identical in appearance but lacking in any emotion—podpeople.

This sentence could be the plot-line to one of the four motion pictures made over the last 50 years based on Jack Finney's 1955 book, *The Body Snatchers*. The film that most people remember was released in 1979 starring Donald Sutherland, who was one of the last on earth to remain free of will and independent of the pod menace.

Another explanation of this sentence might be a teacher's lament about the students in class constantly putting the tiny "buds" in their ears to listen to the tens of thousands of rap tunes on their personal iPod, hidden in a backpack.

The iPod became an icon in the first decade of the twenty-first century, and podcasting has become one of the most talked about applications in distance education. Podcasting and iPods are written about in the popular press, in journals, and even in the prestigious *Chronicle of Higher Education*. The *Chronicle* recently published a long article with the unfortunate title "How to Podcast Campus Lectures."

Podcasting is not a new idea. It has been around at least since the audio tutorial movement and the Sony Walkman. A podcast is really a single concept event that is explained by an audio file, or an audio file supplemented by still pictures or video. The most widespread and current example of a type of a podcast is a song, usually 3 to 5 minutes long available in an electronic file format, such as mpg3 or mpg4, that also might be available as a music video with singers, dancers, and actors in addition to the song. Luther Vandross's tune, "Always and Forever" is a wonderful 4 minute and 54 second example. The tune is also available as a music video showing Vandross singing the song.

Individual songs work well as podcasts because most modern tunes have the characteristics of an effective single concept event—what many now are calling a podcast, which really is a learning object that is stored in an .mpg format. The characteristics of an *effective* podcast are as follows:

- A podcast is a single idea that can be explained verbally, or if necessary with audio and appropriate still or motion pictures (not a face talking).
- A podcast is a recorded event that is 3 to 10 minutes long.
- A podcast is part of a series with each single event related to others.
- A podcast is a learning object available in an electronic format that is easily played, most often as an mpg3 file.
- A podcast is stored on a website or other Internet location for easy access.
- A podcast is current and changed or updated frequently.

In spite of what the *Chronicle* says, a recording of a lecture is a poor example of a podcast. Rather, it is best to "chunk" the class into 5 or 6 single concept blocks, each as a separate learning object. Effective lecturers do this already; they break up their class session into related topics. These topics can become podcasts when they are recorded electronically in an .mpg file format, especially if they are supplemented with related examples and recorded in a proper location without distracting background noises. Podcasts are a reincarnation or reinvention of what the masterly learning movement of the 1960s called *single concept files* or *single concept films.* They were effective then, and can be effective today.

And finally, let's call them something other than podcasts. MPGcast doesn't have the same cachet as podcast, but then MPGcast doesn't remind everyone of Donald Sutherland pointing his finger at the last normal person, either.

Sources: B. Read, "How to Podcast Campus Lectures," *Chronical of Higher Education* (January 26, 2007): A32–A35. J. Fenney, *The Body Snatchers.* New York: Dell, 1955.

2

Teaching and Learning at a Distance

Chapter 5
Instructional Design for
Distance Education

Chapter 6
Teaching and Distance
Education

Chapter 7
The Student and Distance
Education

Chapter 8
Support Materials and
Visualization for Distance
Education

Chapter 9
Assessment for Distance
Education

Instructional Design for Distance Education

CHAPTER GOAL

The purpose of this chapter is to present a process for designing instruction at a distance.

CHAPTER OBJECTIVES

After reading and reviewing this chapter, you should be able to

1. Explain why it is important to plan ahead when teaching at a distance.
2. Describe a systematic design process for instructional design.
3. Describe the types of learner information to be collected for planning.
4. Explain the decisions about content that need to be made.
5. Explain why it is important to examine teaching strategies and media.
6. Discuss how technology and resources influence the distance learning environment.
7. Discuss the literature dealing with "best practices."
8. Design a course using the Unit–Module–Topic model.
9. Describe the process for assessment of learning.

"SIGNAL FIRES?"

In one of the greatest Greek tragedies, *Agamemnon*, Aeschylus begins his drama with word of beacon fires carrying news of the fall of Troy and the return of the king—news that set in motion Clytemnestra's plan to kill her husband in long-delayed revenge for his slaying of their daughter. These signal fires would have required a series of line-of-sight beacons stretching 500 miles around the Aegean Sea.

Line-of-sight communication has a long history. Most broadcast television applications require line of sight; even communications satellites orbiting in the Clarke Belt thousands of miles above the equator are "in sight" of the uplinks and downlinks on Earth.

Communication with someone you can see has a visceral element that is missing when that person or group of people is not "in sight." Certainly, considerable communication in distance education does not involve face-to-face instruction. The heart of distance education is the concept of separation of teacher and learner. Many say the meeting of students with teachers will soon be a relic of the past, like signal fires. This group touts the convenience of "anytime, anyplace" learning and the power of modern communications technologies to unite learners with instructional events no matter when they are needed and no matter where students may be located.

Others advocate the need for face-to-face instruction. This group stresses the importance of seeing and being seen, and the personal nature of the teaching/learning environment. Some even say that you cannot really learn some topics without being in a specific place with a select group of collaborators.

A third position is advocated by others who say that education should occur using a combination of instructional strategies. Schlosser and Burmeister (1999) wrote about the "best of both worlds," where courses and programs would have varying percentages of face-to-face and distance-delivered learning experiences. Blended or hybrid approaches are probably the most widespread applications of distance education (Daffron & Webster, 2006; Epstein, 2006; Orellana, Hudgins & Simonson, 2009).

To date, however, no clear and verified process for determining whether face-to-face instruction, distance instruction, or a combination of the two is best. Most instructional designers and instructional technologists know that Richard Clark (1983) was correct when he said that media are "mere vehicles," but when courses are designed and instruction delivered, what are the templates, the processes, the approaches to be used to determine whether a module, course, or program should be delivered face to face or online? Or, what percentage of each is "best"? Where is the research? Certainly, decisions about how a course is to be delivered should not be based solely on the "beliefs" of the instructor or the mandates of administrators. Signal fires told of the fall of Troy probably because that was the most appropriate technology available. Today, many technologies are available for instruction of the distant learner. Instructional design processes help the instructor make informed decisions about technology use.

WHY PLAN FOR TEACHING AT A DISTANCE?

Just like other kinds of teaching, teaching at a distance requires planning and organizing. However, teaching at a distance, whether synchronous or asynchronous, requires that greater emphasis be placed on the initial planning phase.

Instructional design should consider all aspects of the instructional environment, following a well-organized procedure that provides guidance to even the novice distance instructor. (See, for example, Figure 5–1.) The instructional environment should be viewed as a system, a relationship among all the components of that system—the instructor, the learners, the material, and the technology. Especially when planning for distance education, the instructor must make decisions that will affect all aspects of the system (Moore & Kearsley, 2005).

FIGURE 5–1   The instructional systems design model.

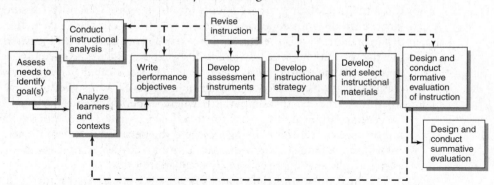

Source: Dick, et al., *Systematic Design of Instruction*, pp. 90–91, 2009 by Walter Dick and Lou Carey. Reproduced by permission of Pearson Education, Inc.

This chapter presents background information about an organized and systematic way to go about planning instruction. Central to this chapter's organization is the Unit–Module–Topic model for course design (UMT approach). This model is based on best practices in course design and delivery, which will also be presented. This design process allows the instructor to consider elements such as the content, the nature of the learner, the process by which the learning will take place (methodology), and the means for assessing the learning experience. By following through with this process, the instructor will find that teaching at a distance is an exciting and dynamic experience, one that will be welcomed by both the instructor and the learners.

PRINCIPLES OF INSTRUCTIONAL DESIGN SYSTEMS

Systematic Process

The process of systematic planning for instruction is the outcome of many years of research (Dick, Carey, & Carey, 2009). An analysis of the application of this process indicates that when instruction is designed within a system, learning occurs. The process of instructional design is a field of study. Instructional design is considered the intellectual technique of the professional who is responsible for appropriate application of technology to the teaching and learning process. In other words, instructional design is to the instructional technologist as the rule of law is to the lawyer, the prescription of medicine is to the medical doctor, and the scientific method is to the chemist—a way of thinking and solving problems (Thompson, Hargrave, & Simonson, 1996).

A critical part of the process is to consider the components of a successful learning system (Dick et al., 2009). These components are the learners, the content, the method and materials, and the environment, including the technology. The interaction of these components creates the type of learning experience necessary for student learning.

The components must interact both efficiently and effectively to produce quality learning experiences. There should be a balance among the components—none can take on a higher position than the others. The attempt to keep the components equally balanced while maintaining their interaction effect is essential to planning quality instruction. Simply stated, a series of activities alone cannot lead to learning; it is only with the careful planning for their balance and interface that learning is the result.

Another critical part of the process is evaluation. For successful learning to take place, it is vital to determine what works and what needs to be improved. Evaluation leads to revision of instruction, and revision of instruction helps secure the final outcome of helping students learn (Smaldino, Lowther, & Russell, 2007). Because of an emphasis on planning and revising, well-designed instruction is repeatable. This means that the instruction can be applied again in another class. For example, instruction designed for a televised, multisite class can be used again with a new group of students at different sites. Because it is "reusable," the considerable initial effort is well worth the time and energy.

Planning for Instruction at a Distance

The process of planning and organizing for a distance education course is multifaceted and must occur well in advance of the scheduled instruction. To eliminate trial-and-error preparation, distance learning faculty should:

- Keep in mind that courses previously taught in traditional classrooms may need to be retooled. The focus of the instruction shifts to visual presentations, engaged learners, and careful timing of presentations of information.
- In revising traditional classroom materials, consider ways to illustrate key concepts, or topics, using tables, figures, and other visual representations.
- Plan activities that encourage interactivity at all the sites. It is a common pitfall to focus on only one site during the process of managing the class and operating technology. Planning for interactivity reduces this problem and helps learners. Not only does the instructor have to plan for interaction but students may require training to participate actively in these types of activities.
- Plan activities that allow for student group work. This helps construct a supportive social environment. For example, the instructor could present case studies related to theories and concepts covered in the course, and then groups of students, perhaps in different sites, could discuss case study questions and reach consensus on a solution to the problem.
- Be prepared in the event that technical problems occur. If the equipment fails, it is important for students to have projects and assignments independent of the instructor and alternative means of communication (e.g., fax, phone, e-mail). Discussing with students ahead of time alternative plans in case there is a technological problem will eliminate confusion and loss of productive class time when a problem occurs (Orellana, Hudgins, & Simonson, 2009).

In addition to considerations related to planning for instruction, there is also a need to examine issues associated with the separation of instructor and some or all of the students. Time constraints for class delivery, lack of eye contact, visualization of the materials, and planning for interaction require a reconsideration of classroom dynamics. Often instructors use visual cues, such as student facial expressions, within the traditional classroom and conversations with students after class to decide quickly to adjust the instructional approach for a course. These cues give instructors insights that help them personalize the instruction for the students and ensure a quality learning experience for all.

In an online course, it is more difficult to acquire visual clues about students. Even when using desktop conferencing technologies, the visual component provides limited information to the instructor. Students who incorporate emoticons into their writing do not help the instructor get a better view of the student within the nonvisual online environment.

Teaching at a distance eliminates many of these cues. Alternative approaches to ongoing evaluation of instruction must be incorporated. If instructors ignore this area of preparation, planning to teach as they always have, they will feel frustrated. Likewise, students may feel alienated and will begin to tune out the instructor. The instructional development process must be based on the unique characteristics and needs of students, meshed with the teaching style of the instructor and the course goals and content. Interaction must be maximized, the visual potential of the medium must be explored, and time constraints must be addressed.

ISSUES TO ADDRESS IN THE PLANNING PROCESS

Who Are the Learners?

There are several reasons for bringing students together in a distance learning setting. Students can be pooled into classes of sufficient size to create a critical mass. Students can aggregate for advanced courses in subjects that might not otherwise be available on-site. Distance education can be an important approach to responding to the growing pluralism of learners' backgrounds, characteristics, or unusual learning needs that may require or benefit from specialized instruction.

Taking the time to learn about the learners in the class yields a more productive learning environment. Knowledge of general learner characteristics can inform the instructor of the nature of the students at origination and distance sites. This knowledge can aid the distance education instructor in overcoming the separation of instructor and students.

Along with the general information about the learners, an instructor needs to know the number of students in the class. Knowing how many students are at each site and the number of sites involved in a face-to-face class can influence the level of inter-activity. For example, in an Internet-based class (e.g., on the Web) with a large number of participants, it is likely that some students will fail to interact in discussions. Thus, an instructor needs to know how many students are enrolled, how many sites are there, and what technologies are available to them to plan effectively for interactive learning. Also, it is essential to know the nature of the audience. Are students from an urban area? A rural area? What is their age range, grade range, and educational background? All this can have a marked impact on the levels of interaction among students. The instructor may have to plan more carefully for the types and levels of interaction to ensure a quality learning experience for all members of the class. The cultural, social, and economic backgrounds of the students also constitute important information for the instructor. In addition, educational expectations of learners can influence the quality of the learning experience. The attitudes and interests students bring to the class will impact the learning environment. Thus, an instructor who wants to create a quality learning experience for all members of the class, with the ultimate goal of learning as the outcome, will be certain to account for these variables in planning.

Analyze the General Abilities of the Class.   Analysis of the cognitive abilities of the class allows the instructor to observe how students relate to the content of the lesson. Such issues as clearly defining the prerequisite knowledge or skills for the specific learning experience are important to ensure a successful learning experience. The students' prior experience with similar types of cognitive tasks is important.

Further, learning styles have once again become an important area of consideration. With the introduction of Gardner's multiple intelligences has come the resurgence of an examination of learning styles (Gardner, 1993). How students approach learning is as important as how well they can function in the classroom. So knowing more about how students interact with information is important in creating a valuable learning environment.

An instructor can determine students' general knowledge and ability in a number of ways. Pretests and portfolio reviews can provide information about learners' abilities. Because students are coming to the class from a variety of backgrounds and learning experiences, they may be underprepared for the content intended for a particular course, and thus will be frustrated and even unsuccessful in the learning experience. Or, conversely, they may already be familiar with the content and will be bored and uninterested in participating in the class.

By knowing more about students, the instructor can develop supporting materials to individualize instruction. Varying the presentation of materials to match different learning styles (e.g., animation, text, verbal descriptions, visual messages) can also ensure the greatest potential for reaching all learners.

The instructor can present complex cognitive content in ways that give learners various tags for understanding the fundamental concepts, and thereby reach a wider range of individuals. People can remember complex material better if chunks of information are grouped into spatially related locations. Placing similar ideas in a logical sequence can aid retrieval of information at a later date.

Analyze Potential for Learner Interactivity.   Students who are less social may find the distance education environment more comfortable for them. Students may become more expressive because of the perception of privacy and the informative nature of mediated communication. They may perceive the increased and varied interactivity and immediate feedback as a positive input to their interface with the learning experience.

Additionally, students can benefit from a wider range of cognitive, linguistic, cultural, and affective styles they would not encounter in a self-contained classroom. The emphasis should not be on the inherent efficiency of the distance learning, but on the values and services offered to students through their exposure to others (Herring & Smaldino, 1997). Relationships can be fostered, values can be expanded, and shared purposes or goals can be developed. Distance learning experiences can serve as windows to the world by providing extended learning experiences.

When special efforts are made, distance education actually can enhance learning experiences, expand horizons, and facilitate group collaboration (Dede, 1990). Students can have more direct experiences with the information (e.g., close-up viewing of an experiment is possible). Time for reflection is possible before responding to the prompts presented, and the ability to work with peers or experts enhances the potential for learning. One of the most effective techniques to promote interaction in distance education is the *threaded discussion*—instructors post questions related to reading, viewing, and/or listening to assignments, then students post comments in a discussion area. Wade, Bentley, and Waters (2006) have identified 20 guidelines for successful threaded discussions. One critical guideline is the division of large classes into subgroups of 10 to 15 students so that discussions are manageable. A rule of thumb for the instructor's involvement in threaded discussions recommends that early in a course, the instructor should post once for every 4 or 5 student postings, then as students take more responsibility for their own learning later in the course, the instructor might post once for each 10 to 12 student postings—primarily to keep the discussions on track (Simonson, 2007).

Understand Learner Characteristics.

To be effective, it is necessary to understand the learners in the target audience. Willis (1994) suggested that the following questions should be asked prior to development of distance learning environments:

- What are students' ages, cultural backgrounds, interests, and educational levels?
- What is the level of familiarity of the students with the instructional methods and technological delivery systems under consideration?
- How will the students apply the knowledge gained in the course, and how is this course sequenced with other courses?
- Can the class be categorized into several broad subgroups, each with different characteristics?

These questions are not easy ones to answer. An instructor should attempt to find the answers prior to the first class meeting. Asking a few well-chosen questions of individual students will help the instructor understand their needs, backgrounds, and expectations. Additionally, students will feel they are important to the instructor. It may also be beneficial to discuss the learners with the remote-site facilitator. That person may be a valuable resource to the instructor by providing information about students prior to the instruction, or by observing students at work. In an online environment, it is often more difficult for the instructor to get information about students; thus it is essential that the instructor plan a way of inviting students to share information about themselves. Be careful to respect their right to privacy, while trying to learn as much as you can about them.

Help Learners Understand the Context of the Learning Experience.

Morrison, Ross, and Kemp (2004) refer to three types of context: orienting context, instructional context, and transfer context. They suggest that the learners need to grasp the intent of the instructor when participating in various types of learning experiences. When the learners have an understanding of the reasons why they are participating in a particular type of instructional activity, they are better able to use that experience to expedite their own learning.

Each of these contexts serves a particular purpose for the learner. The *orienting context* refers to the students' reasons for being in a course. These reasons vary among the students. For example, a student may be participating in a course for credits toward a pay raise. Or, a student may wish to change positions within a company, which is dependent on completing the particular study area.

Instructional context addresses the learning environment. Scheduling a course to meet at a certain time and location or specifying specific dates for completion of assignments also impact the manner in which the student interacts with the class. Knowing how convenient it is for students to access the resources or to rearrange their own personal and work schedules is important when planning instruction. The third context, *transfer context,* refers to the way in which the knowledge will be used by students. It is critical when planning that the instructor considers what information is important so the students will relate it to work or school applications. Students will value that information they perceive as useful. Knowing the students and their interests or needs will help the instructor plan useful learning experiences to ensure transfer of learning.

What Is the Essential Content?

The content of a course needs to reflect where this content relates to the rest of the curriculum. It is essential to examine the nature of the content, as well as the sequence of information. In any distance learning environment, one particular issue, that of time constraints, impacts other planning areas. *Time constraints* refer to the actual online time for delivery, which is often limited and inflexible. The issue of limited time makes it necessary to closely examine the essential elements of the course content. The instructor needs to balance content with the limited time for learning activities and possibly remove extraneous, nonessential information.

Generally speaking, the scope of the content for a course needs to be sufficient to ensure the entire learning experience will lead to the desired outcomes. Concepts, knowledge, and specific skills need to be identified (Dick et al., 2009). Supporting information or knowledge is important to the scope of content analysis. Follow-up and applications of the content should be considered.

The instructor's time is best spent on content analysis if the content is organized within a hierarchy. Starting with the general goals, followed by more specific goals and objectives, the nature of the structure of the content can be made to fall into place. The resulting framework of information about content helps the instructor decide the value and importance of specific information to the total instructional package. It is important to remember that no matter which technological formats are used in distance education, the trend is to reduce the "amount" of information delivered and to increase the "interactive value" of the learning experience. Thus, the instructor may need to throw out content that had been included in a traditional presentation of a course. Or, the instructor may need to consider delivering information through alternative means, such as additional readings or booklets designed specifically for the tasks.

The instructor also needs to examine the sequencing of information. A number of variables—for example, characteristics of the learners, their prior knowledge, content, time, and number of sites involved—are critical when deciding the order of presentation of information. Because the instructor and some or all of the members of the class are separated, the material must be sequenced in a logical fashion for the students.

Goals and Objectives for Instruction.   The challenge of education is to match the content of the subject to the needs of the learners. Broadly stated goals are a helpful starting place for the instructor. The instructor must decide what is appropriate for a group of students and for the individuals within that group. Each instructor constantly must face the challenge of adapting instruction to the student who is expected to learn it. Although content is important, instructors must remember that their focus is on the students. This is critical when establishing goals for any course.

The traditional approach for writing objectives is also effective for distance education courses. Specifically, objectives should state the conditions under which learning should occur, the performance expected of the learner, and the standard to which the performance will be matched. One way to write objectives is as follows:

Given: *the conditions under which learning occurs,*
the learner will: *meet some predetermined level of performance*
according to: *a minimum standard.*

The objectives of a particular lesson may not necessarily change simply because an instructor teaches at a distance. Good instructional goals should form the basis for instruction, regardless of the medium used. Instructional goals and objectives always should be shared with the students, helping both the origination and remote-site students to focus on the parameters of the instruction. This information may be included in course outlines, presentation handouts, or materials presented at the beginning of the course.

What Teaching Strategies and Media Should Be Used?

Students can provide insight into the design of the learning experience. They can give feedback in lesson design and instruction delivery. Using a simple feedback form, students can describe or indicate in some other way their expectations and perceptions of the class structure and the delivery mode. The instructor can examine the information from both origination and remote-site students to determine if the mode of presentation was effective for both types of locations. Evaluating these responses, the instructor can gain an understanding of how the learners perceived the class experience. An instructor's personal philosophy will influence the approach to teaching at a distance. An individual's philosophical belief will affect selection of goals and curricular emphases, and influence how that individual views himself or herself as a classroom instructor. The instructor who believes in the philosophical arena of realism, idealism, essentialism, or perennialism will see the instructor as the central figure in the classroom, delivering knowledge and modeling to the student—an instructor-centered approach. On the other hand, the instructor who believes in the philosophies of pragmatism, existentialism, progressivism, constructivism, or social reconstructionism believes that the student is the central figure in the classroom. The instructor is viewed as the facilitator of learning by guiding, rather than directing, the students, thus modeling a student-centered approach.

Although the dynamics of a philosophy will not predict an instructor's success in the distance education classroom, successful teaching at a distance places the recipients' needs before organizational convenience and at the center of planning and decision making. The individual needs of the learners are brought to the forefront in education that uses electronic technology because separation of learners from the instructor requires students to take more responsibility for learning. Consequently, the learner's opinions and needs play a more important role in decision making than is usual in an instructor-centered environment (Macfarlane & Smaldino, 1997). It is oversimplified to suggest that there is one best way to teach at a distance. In any given content area, there are several potential ways of providing a quality learning experience for the students (Smaldino, Lowther, & Russell, 2007). However, the one thing that has been repeatedly demonstrated through research is that lecture, or the "talking head" approach, is the least successful strategy to employ in distance education (Schlosser & Anderson, 1994). What is essential in deciding which strategy or strategies to employ is the issue of engaging the learner.

The instructor needs to focus on selecting instructional strategies that engage all the learners in active learning. To do this, the instructor may need to de-emphasize the "informative" part of the instruction for more "discovery" of information. The emphasis on keeping the learners engaged in learning ensures that students will be in tune with the class.

Media Selection.   Several models are often used in selecting media (Dick et al., 2009; Holden & Westfall, 2006). The common theme among these models is the learning context, which is the content, the intended outcome, and the nature of the students. Practical considerations such as available resources for creating media and the technologies for delivery of instruction also play a hand in the selection process. Mainly, though, the goals and objectives will influence the selection of media. McAlpine and Weston (1994) have come up with a set of criteria for selecting media, whether they are commercial media or media developed specifically for a particular course. The first criterion is to match the medium to the curriculum or content. Other criteria include the accuracy of information, motivational quality, engagement quality, technical quality, and unbiased nature of material. These should be considered in selecting media in order to match student needs to the strategies employed.

Media that are "off the shelf" are often considered sufficient for a quality learning experience in the traditional classroom (Heinich, 2004). However, in a distance learning environment, the "ready-made" materials may need to be adapted or modified to accommodate the technologies involved. Some materials may need to be enlarged or enhanced to be seen by students at a distance. With others, the format may need to be changed to allow access.

Because of the nature of distance learning and the separation of the instructor from the students, it is essential that the instructor begin to think visually. Too often, instructors do not place enough emphasis on designing and using quality visual materials. Taking the time to develop good visual media will enhance the quality of the learning experience (Heinich, 2004).

Visualizing Information.   Visuals provide a concrete reference point for students, especially when they are engaged in a nontelevised learning experience. Even if the visuals are lists of concepts and ideas, they can help students. Visuals also help learners by simplifying information. Diagrams and charts often can make it easier to understand complex ideas. A visual that breaks down a complex idea into its components can show relationships that might otherwise be confusing to students. Also, visuals that serve as mnemonics can assist student understanding. Students find that visuals are helpful in their studies as well as in their preparation for tests and other means of assessing their learning.

When creating visuals, the instructor needs to keep certain things in mind. First is legibility. In a televised distance learning environment, even with the close-up capabilities of the cameras, the choice of font and size can influence how easily students can read the text. Several "rules of thumb" should be applied:

- Use a large font (e.g., 24 or 36 point).
- Use a sans serif font (e.g., Helvetica).
- Use just a few words per line of text (e.g., six words per line maximum).
- Use only a few lines of text per visual (e.g., six lines per visual).
- Use a combination of both uppercase and lowercase letters; all uppercase is difficult to read.
- Use plenty of "white space" to enhance the readability.

Second, color also plays an important role in designing visuals. Color can increase the readability of text or graphics. However, the key to good use of color is in the contrast. Use a dark background and light lettering, or vice versa. Make certain to select colors that will not be compromised by the technology used for transmission (e.g., red vibrates in a televised environment). Further, select colors that will not be a problem for students who might be color-blind.

The third important issue is that of copyright. No matter what technologies are incorporated in the distance environment, the instructor needs to respect the copyright restrictions that might apply. For example, in a televised class, the instructor may not be able to use a video without first obtaining permission to display it to the class. In a Web-based class, the instructor may need permission to post a journal article. An instructor needs to be responsible in obtaining copyright permissions where appropriate.

And last, the instructor cannot assume that all students at a distance have equal access to resources. Students may not have the technologies available. Also, students may not have the facilities at hand. The instructor needs to be certain that all students have similar learning experiences, including access to the materials. For example, if the instructor wishes students to use certain books or journals for outside reading, it is important to check with local libraries to be sure these materials are available.

What Is the Learning Environment?

Educators are familiar with classroom settings. They are comfortable with using the space available to enable learning to take place. It is when the classroom shifts into a distance learning setting that the environment often becomes a challenge to the instructor. Several important elements must be addressed within the distance learning environment.

Technology.   The type of setting, be it place- or time-shifted, will influence planning decisions. Environments that are place-shifted are those that are synchronous but are not in the same location (e.g., a live, video-based distance class). Those that are time-shifted are asynchronous, where students access the class at different times. Assessing the use of technology in a distant setting is essential. In any distance learning environment, the technology becomes the element of most concern for the instructor. The instructor must become familiar with the hardware and the nuances of the technology to use them effectively. The instructor needs to balance concern for the operation of the equipment with effective teaching. Once the technology becomes transparent in the educational setting, the instructor can reflect on the lesson quality, the outcomes, and the plans for subsequent lessons.

Several issues are associated with technology when teaching in a distance learning mode. First is the basic operation of the equipment. In a televised distance learning setting, switching between sites is usually a simple procedure, but it does require time to acquire the finesse to operate the switching buttons smoothly. Second, using additional cameras in the classroom can create some concern for the instructor. The overhead camera needs to be focused and materials lined up to ensure that learners in all sites can see the material. Third, the instructor should always consider what the student should be viewing during the lesson. Is it better to see the instructor, the visuals, or other students? When an instructor has had experience teaching with the equipment, these decisions become automatic, making learning the foundation for the decisions made (Herring & Smaldino, 2001).

In an Internet-based learning environment, the instructor needs to be concerned with the layout of the courseware and the types of resources available to the students at the distant sites. The instructor needs to be certain the material is designed in a way that is intuitive for the various types of learners who may be interacting with it. The instructor also needs to be concerned about student access to the appropriate hardware and software to be successful in connecting to the courseware. Further, the instructor needs to be concerned that the students can complete the tasks expected of them. Finally, the instructor needs to be certain that the students understand the terminology being used.

It is essential that the instructor be prepared with alternatives for each lesson in case of system problems. What will the students do during the lesson time if the technology is not operating properly—or at all? Preplanned contingencies should continue the learning process even though the technology is malfunctioning. Alternative lessons must always be ready, but, it is hoped, never needed. Students need to be prepared to know what to do with those materials. The materials must be designed to be used without instructor intervention.

Resources.   The second element to consider in the instructional environment is the resources available to students. What materials will they have at hand? What materials will be available in libraries and laboratories? Will students have access to resources for easy communication with the instructor?

A LOOK AT BEST PRACTICE ISSUES

Course Management Systems

Course management systems (CMSs), also called learning management systems or virtual learning environments, are software systems designed to assist in the management of educational courses for students, especially by helping teachers and learners with course administration. The systems can often track the learners' progress. Although usually thought of as primarily tools for distance education, they are also used to support the face-to-face classroom.

A course management system allows teachers to manage their classes, assignments, activities, quizzes and tests, resources, and more in an accessible online environment. Students can log on and work anytime, anywhere. Ullman and Rabinowitz (2004) more succinctly define *course management systems* as "Internet-based software that manages student enrollment, tracks student performance, and creates and distributes course content." Commonly used proprietary course management systems are WebCT and Blackboard.

Proprietary versus Open Source

In addition to the two ways CMSs are used, there are two categories of CMSs—proprietary and open source. *Proprietary*, single-vendor systems (such as Blackboard) are software products that are purchased or licensed from one vendor. These systems are installed and used by the school, college, or university. On the other hand, *open-source* course management systems are free educational software that are maintained by users who implement, even modify, and ultimately support their system to meet local, specific needs. Two major open-source systems are the Sakai Project and Moodle, although there are dozens of open-source CMSs (www.Edupost.ca/pmwiki.php).

The Sakai Project is of particular interest because of its scope and its approach. The project is named after Iron Chef Hiroyuki Sakai, and was started with the purpose of creating an open-source/free course management system that completes and complements proprietary systems.

Five institutions that had created their own CMS met in 2004 and invited other institutions to join in a "Sakai Partners Program." The five institutions—Indiana University, Massachusetts Institute of Technology, Stanford University, the University of Michigan, and UPortal and the Open Knowledge Initiative—were the founders of the Sakai Project. There are now over 70 educational institutions involved. Members contribute financially and develop programming code for the project and the CMS.

The Sakai CMS has most, if not all, of the features common to course management systems, including course materials distribution, gradebooks, discussion areas, chat rooms, testing, and assignment drop boxes. There are announcement areas, e-mail systems, forums, presentation systems, and a variety of teaching tools such as syllabus posting, content delivery, and editors. The Sakai

Project is reported to be growing rapidly as more organizations join. Moodle is another popular open-source system.

Course management systems are not just for distance education. They are becoming critical components of possible benefit for almost any course. Also, CMSs can be purchased from a single vendor that provides the product and supports its implementation, or CMSs can be obtained free, or at low cost, by adopting one of the many open-source systems that are available. Although currently the domain of the CMS is the college or university, it is apparent that the potential of the CMS for K–12 education is real and offers solutions to the many instructional and managerial problems of the school. Additionally, the impact of course management systems is yet to be determined. Anecdotal reports indicate there are changes in instructional organization and delivery associated with the use of CMSs. Certainly, a CMS is an essential tool of the distance educator. More generally, the CMS may be one of the most important technological tools now available to education and training.

Another consideration is the quality of the instructional setting. Is the room comfortable? Can students get to the room easily? Will the room accommodate the nature and type of learning activities planned? Can students move the tables and chairs about in ways to make learning easy?

These are the types of concerns that an instructor needs to address when thinking about the learning environment. It is difficult to plan for a particular type of learning activity if the room cannot be adapted or changed in any way. For example, if the instructor plans a group activity in which students will need to move chairs and tables, can they do it without causing technical problems?

Planning to Teach on the World Wide Web

Much of what has been suggested in the planning process is not specific to a particular type of distance technology or delivery mode. Rather, the instructional design process is relatively open to any instructional setting. But, when planning to teach on the Web, an instructor needs to address some essential considerations. One very important issue is that the instructor is "ready" for the course to begin. It is frustrating for students who begin an online course only to find that all the materials are not prepared or not accessible at the time they need them. It would be an advantage for the instructor planning an online course for the first time to consider working 3 to 5 months in advance of the beginning date. This will ensure that the materials will be planned and prepared in a timely fashion. Another important issue when teaching online is that of establishing the communications framework. All too often, instructors of online courses "complain" that students expect them to be available all the time. If you do not intend to check your course materials daily, indicate that with the initial materials that are distributed. Tell students they can expect a response within a day or that you intend to be online checking the course on specific days of the week. That way both students and faculty will not be frustrated by the interrupted communications process.

Instructors have found that to ensure quality and promptness with online coursework, it is necessary for the students to know exactly when assignments are due. A calendar or timeline is very important. Providing students with rubrics or guides for how to complete assignments well is also very important. The more information students have about completing assignments, the fewer problems the students and instructor will experience during the course.

Finally, when planning to teach online, advise students (and this is a good piece of advice for the instructor as well) to set aside specific periods of time during the week to work on the course. It is so easy to "let it slide" that often the complaint is that there is never enough time to get all the work done. This usually results from someone letting the work pile up before getting to it. With an online course, it is best to plan two shorter periods per week, rather than one longer one. This helps to check things out, do work offline for a period of time, and then to finish up before the time period is up. Part of the initial materials presented to the students should provide guidelines for students to ensure a successful learning experience. When it is noted that a student is falling behind in the work or is not participating at an acceptable level, the instructor should contact that student privately, either by e-mail or by phone, to check to see if there is a reason for nonparticipation. This takes time, but the instructor will find it beneficial for a successful distance learning experience.

How Do You Determine the Quality of the Instruction?

Assessment will be discussed in Chapter 10, and evaluation will be discussed at greater length in Chapter 12. However, there is a need to look at questions an instructor might consider as part of the planning process. These questions revolve around considerations related to the strategies selected, the learners' interaction with the learning experience, and the learning environment.

In the instructional design process, formative evaluation becomes an important aspect. Two questions need to be considered. The first relates to reflection on the action or activity: "Is this approach going to work?" (Schon, 1987). To be an effective educator, it is important to consider what can happen within an instructional event. All experiences, both positive and negative, have some element of surprise. Perhaps expectations were not achieved; perhaps a serendipitous event led to an altogether different, but pleasant, outcome. Whatever the nature of the event, it is essential to reflect upon what has happened.

Reflection may take the form of critical assessment of the events, satisfying curiosity about the nature of those events. Reflection may focus on the success of the learning situation. It helps the instructor understand the learning event. Once the instructor has reflected on what took place, it is time to move on to the second question of the formative evaluation process.

The second question is, "How can I make this better?" The instructor needs to examine the instructional event in terms of what worked and what appears to have been a problem. This second phase of the formative evaluation is concerned with helping the instructor ensure a more successful educational experience for students.

The instructor needs to consider the learning task, the instructional materials, and the teaching strategies, and also the role that the technology may have played in the instruction.

The instructor needs to consider the elements of technologies and their effect on the students. Did the hardware components of the system cause the problem? If so, what was the nature of the problem? Was there a temporary interference with the transmission? Was weather or some other noncontrollable phenomenon causing problems with the transmission? Can the hardware be improved? Can changes be made in the interactive instructional classroom to aid instruction in the future? If the problem did not relate to the hardware, then what was the problem? Perhaps students needed to be better informed about how to use the equipment. It may be that students needed preparation for the lesson. Perhaps the instructor needed to prepare other types of handouts or manipulatives to ensure that the students could accomplish the tasks. Maybe the instructor needed to select an alternative teaching strategy to improve interactivity and student outcomes. Because so many different factors affect the interactive learning environment, reflective teaching practices play a vital role in developing effective teaching practices. The process of determining what has transpired and how to change it creates a dynamic educational experience for both the instructor and the learners. Formative evaluation is essential for successful interactive distance learning experiences.

A LOOK AT BEST PRACTICE ISSUES

What the Accreditation Community Is Saying About Quality in Distance Education

In March of 2006, the U.S. Department of Education's Office of Postsecondary Education released an interesting report titled "Evidence of Quality in Distance Education Programs Drawn from Interviews with the Accreditation Community." What is interesting and important about this document is the approach used to collect information—12 accrediting organizations were asked to identify representatives who had served on evaluation teams for schools offering distance education programs. These representatives were asked to identify "good practices" and "red flags." Their comments make great reading for anyone interested in identifying quality strategies for teaching and learning at a distance.

The report is organized into six sections, each dealing with various indicators of quality: Mission, Curriculum, Faculty, Students, Sustainability, and Evaluation and Assessment. In each category they are dozens of indicators of quality and red flags—danger signs that often indicate a weak or ineffective distance education program.

Some of the most interesting positive indicators are:

■ The mission statement contains an explicit statement of the purpose of distance education.
■ The regular faculty have oversight of the distance education curriculum.

- The regular faculty are actively involved in course design.
- There is a strong and active faculty development process.
- The university provides instructional design support for distance education.
- There is 24/7 technology support.
- There are academic advisers for distance education students.
- A systematic approach is applied to the growth and management of the distance education program.
- There are clear plans for the future of distance education.
- Evaluation of distance education courses and programs is used for continuous improvement.
- Input from faculty and students is used for program improvement.

Of equal interest and importance are some of the most noteworthy "red flags":

- There are two separate approaches, even mission statements, for traditional and distance education.
- There are two target populations for traditional and distance education.
- There are two course approval processes for traditional and distance education.
- Distance education courses are designed using a "cookie-cutter" approach.
- Faculty attempt or are encouraged to directly convert traditional courses to distance-delivered courses.
- There are two course evaluation systems, one for traditional and one for distance education.
- Some student services must be accessed face-to-face by distant students.
- Distant students are often confused about contact people at the institution.
- The institution has a history of starting and then stopping distance education programs.
- Few, other than administrators, know about the institution's distance education program.
- A large number of distant students drop out.
- There are many complaints from distant students.

OTHER ISSUES TO BE CONSIDERED

As with any planning, some of the aspects of the system that need to be considered are outside of the content, learners, and instructional setting. Three of these issues relate to student handouts, materials distribution, and the site facilitator.

Student Handouts

Even though the topic of student handouts is discussed at greater length in Chapter 8, it is also mentioned here because it is important for the instructor to think about handouts within the context of the planning process. The types of handouts will vary according to the age of the students and the content of the course. But whatever the type, it is important that the instructor realize that in a distance course, handouts are an essential communication link with students. Therefore, during the planning process, the instructor needs to invest time and energy in creating quality handouts for students.

Distribution of Materials

Even within a traditional class, the instructor is concerned with getting materials to the students. Frequently papers and books are distributed at the beginning of the class period. But when teaching at a distance, this task is rarely an easy one. Often the majority of the class is at a distance, and distribution of materials becomes a logistical nightmare.

An instructor needs to consider the following:

■ *Getting the materials to the distant sites on time.* A distribution network must be established for getting tests and other materials to the remote sites. The technology can be useful in transferring materials.
■ *Communicating with the students.* Geographic separation between instructor and students does affect this communication.
■ *Dealing with time delays in material transfer.* Students may have to wait a longer time than normally expected to receive written feedback. Instructors may elect to use other forms of telecommunications to facilitate this feedback.

Site Coordinators and Facilitators

The presence of a coordinator or facilitator at the distant sites is often an option. For many instructors and students, the presence of such a facilitator is important. Other instructors may consider the extra person to involve more work than necessary. The decision to have a coordinator or facilitator might be best made as it relates to the context of the course, the students, and the types of technology being used.

For example, if the students are on the young side or are unfamiliar with the distant learning environment, a facilitator might be valuable to get them started with the class. The facilitator can serve as an extension of the instructor. This person can help distribute materials, maintain organization, and keep order, as well as proctor. This person can also help with the instruction.

Students need to understand the facilitator's role in the learning environment. They need to know what is expected of the facilitator. Further, the instructor needs to have input into the selection and evaluation of the on-site facilitator to ensure a quality experience for all.

MODELS FOR DESIGNING WORLD WIDE WEB COURSES

Traditionally, there are four approaches for the instructional design of courses that are to be delivered asynchronously using the Web. These four approaches are not entirely new. Two are based directly on the individualized instruction movement of the 1950s and 1960s. The four models are:

1. Linear-designed instruction (Figure 5–2)
2. Branched-designed instruction (Figure 5–3)

3. Hypercontent-designed instruction (Figure 5–4)
4. Learner-directed design (Figure 5–5)

These four designs are depicted graphically. Although they are different in approach and use, they have several similarities. To begin, instruction is divided into units.

FIGURE 5–2   Linear design for instruction.

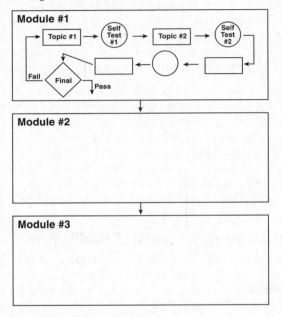

FIGURE 5–3   Branching design for instruction.

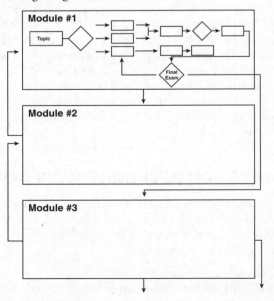

FIGURE 5–4 Hypercontent design for instruction.

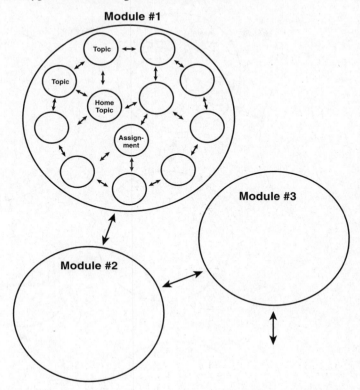

Different instructional designers use terms such as *units* or *blocks* instead of *modules,* but all refer to a subdivision of a course's content. Generally, a three-credit college course would have about three units divided into 12 modules, each taking about a week to complete. Designers further divide modules into topics that directly relate to the module. Topics then can be divided into concepts. An example of a unit of instruction—a course—that is divided into units, modules, or topics, would be this book. This book has 12 chapters that identify the major subheadings of content. Each chapter is divided into modules, and modules are supported by major topics.

    Linear-designed instruction is based on linear-programmed instruction. First, major subdivisions of a course are identified—usually three for a three-credit college course. Next, a content area such as distance education foundations is divided into important ideas. These ideas are called *modules.* Modules of instruction are divided into topics. Each topic has an instructional event, or learning experience, followed by some kind of an assessment. Before students are permitted to continue to the next topic within a module they must successfully complete the assessment. If the assessment is an objective test, they must pass the test. The sequence of topic-related instructional events followed by assessments continues until all topics in a module have been studied. Often, a module-ending assessment must be completed before the student moves to the next module. Similarly, there are often midcourse assessments and

FIGURE 5–5   Learner-directed design for instruction.

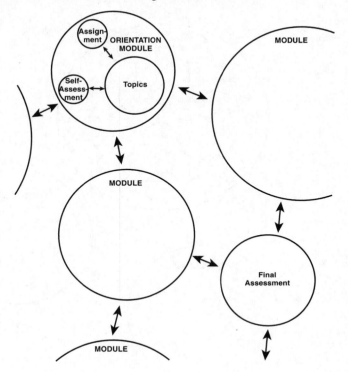

end-of-course assessments that require the student to synthesize learning related to many modules. The Unit–Module–Topic (UMT) model is explained in greater detail at the end of this chapter.

Linear-designed instruction is sequential. Students move in the same path through the concepts, topics, and modules, and complete the same assessments and tests.

Branched-designed instruction is similar to linear with two major exceptions. First, assessments are more sophisticated in order to diagnose a student's progress and understanding of concepts and topics. If a student shows a propensity for topics in a module, it is possible to skip ahead, or branch forward. Similarly, if a student has difficulty, the assessment process will require that the student branch backward, or to remedial instruction, before moving forward in the lesson.

The second distinguishing characteristic of branched-designed instruction is the use of alternative instructional events or learning experiences. In other words, students may interact with different instructional content depending on the results of assessments. Just as a human tutor might decide that an algebra student needs more practice with mathematics, a branched-designed lesson might require a student to complete a drill-and-practice lesson on long division. Branched-designed instruction is difficult and time consuming to produce effectively.

Hypercontent-designed instruction also has units, modules, and topics. First, modules are identified and organized into units of similar content. Next, topics related to the module are identified and learning experiences are designed and produced. These topics are presented using text, audio, graphics, pictures, and video. Finally, a module assessment activity is developed. This assessment is designed to determine if a student has successfully completed and understands the module satisfactorily. If so, the student moves to the next module in the sequence.

Within the module, there is little instructor-determined sequencing of topics. Rather, the topics and corresponding learning experiences are studied in an order determined by the learner. In other words, the student has control and topics can be studied in a random, nonsequential manner, or in a hypercontent order. Often a course-ending assessment, such as a major paper, presentation, or product, is required.

The final design module is the *learner-directed design*. For this approach, the instructional designer identifies units, modules, and topics, including learning experiences, but places no sequence or order on the topics within modules, or among the modules themselves. Learners decide in what order the topics are studied, and sometimes even the topics themselves. Learners construct their own instructional strategies and even their own instructional design. Students move through modules in any order they choose. Few, if any, requirements are placed on the student by the instructional designer.

To be successful, this approach requires considerable talent and effort on the part of the learner. Direction is given to students by module goals and by outcome assessment activities. Some constructivists who advocate learner-directed design procedures ask students to construct their own outcome assessments.

Instructional design models for online instruction are evolving. These four approaches draw on the experience and research of the programmed instruction efforts of the past. Some teachers mix and match the four approaches into amalgams of design procedures. The four approaches just described are something of a starting point for course design. Next, literature dealing with what is commonly referred to as "best practices" will be reviewed, and finally the UMT model for course design, a more prescriptive design recommendation, will be explained.

 ## BEST PRACTICES IN COURSE DESIGN FOR DISTANCE EDUCATION

One key to effective distance education is correct instructional design, a systematic process that applies research-based principles to educational practice. If the design is effective, instruction will also be effective.

Distance education has been practiced for more than 150 years, passing through three phases: first, correspondence study, with its use of print-based instructional and communication media; second, the rise of the distance teaching universities and the use of analog mass media; and third, the widespread integration of distance education elements into most forms of education, and characterized by the use of digital instructional and communication technologies. Peters (2002) has suggested that "the swift, unforeseen, unexpected and unbelievable achievements of information and communication technologies" will require "the design of new formats of learning and teaching and [will cause] powerful and far-reaching structural changes of the learning-teaching process" (p. 20). Peters's views are well accepted, but there is also consensus that the most fruitful way of identifying elements of quality instruction may be to reexamine "first principles" of distance education and mediated instruction.

Perhaps the first of the "first principles" is the recognition that distance education is a system, and that the creation of successful courses—and the program of which they are a part—requires a "systems" approach. Hirumi (2005) identified a number of systems approaches but noted a concept common to all: "A system is a set of inter-related components that work together to achieve a common purpose" (p. 90). He described a system that involved the efforts of faculty, staff, administrators, and students, and consisted of eight key components: curriculum, instruction, management and logistics, academic services, strategic alignment, professional development, research and development, and program evaluation.

Bates (in Foley, 2003) proposed 12 "golden rules" for the use of technology in education. These rules offer guidance in the broader areas of designing and developing distance education:

1. *Good teaching matters.* Quality design of learning activities is important for all delivery methods.
2. *Each medium has its own aesthetic.* Therefore professional design is important.
3. *Education technologies are flexible.* They have their own unique characteristics but successful teaching can be achieved with any technology.
4. *There is no "super-technology."* Each has its strengths and weaknesses; therefore they need to be combined (an integrated mix).
5. *Make all four media available to teachers and learners.* Print, audio, television, and computers should all be available.
6. *Balance variety with economy.* Using many technologies makes design more complex and expensive; therefore, limit the range of technologies in a given circumstance.
7. *Interaction is essential.*
8. *Student numbers are critical.* The choice of a medium will depend greatly on the number of learners reached over the life of a course.
9. *New technologies are not necessarily better than old ones.*
10. *Teachers need training to use technology effectively.*
11. *Teamwork is essential.* No one person has all the skills to develop and deliver a distance learning course; therefore, subject-matter experts, instructional designers, and media specialists are essential on every team.
12. *Technology is not the issue.* How and what we want the learners to learn is the issue and technology is a tool. (p. 833)

A number of these guidelines are overlapping. Three of them (1, 2, and 11) address course and program design. Any examination of "first principles" should first examine instructional design. Although it has been noted that instructors, even those new to distance education, can learn to adapt courses and create materials for online delivery (Ko & Rossen, 2010), and the author-editor model has long been an element of correspondence study programs, "what is strikingly missing in these arrangements, usually, is an instructional designer and many good features of the instructional design approach" (Moore & Kearsley, 2005, p. 103). The team-based approach to distance education course development is generally regarded as more likely to result in high-quality materials, experiences, and, hence, more satisfactory teaching and learning experiences (Hirumi, 2005).

Bates's triumvirate of subject-matter expert, instructional designer, and media specialist is the standard core of the course design team, which may be expanded—one source (Hanna, Glowacki-Dudka, & Conceicao-Runlee, 2000) has suggested as many as eight members—based upon the particular needs of the program and the media employed. No one approach to course design is ideal; as Moore and Kearsley (2005) observed, the course team approach results in "materials [that] are usually much more complete and effective. Furthermore, [it] tends to emphasize the use of multiple media in a course" but is "very labor-intensive and therefore expensive, and it involves a lengthy development period" (p. 106). Of the two approaches noted by Moore and Kearsley, "the author-editor approach is the only one that makes economic sense if courses have very small enrollments or short lifetimes, while the course team approach is justified for courses with large enrollments and long-term use" (p. 107).

Foley (2003) has stated "there are general principles of good design that can be applied to all distance learning activities" (p. 831), but noted the following influences:

■ The target audience of the activity
■ The content of subject matter to be delivered
■ The outcomes or objectives desired (p. 831)

Other considerations having "profound effects on the design of the learning activities" (p. 831) include:

■ The cost effectiveness of the system
■ The opportunity costs of alternative systems and methods
■ The availability of technology to the provider and to the learners
■ The geographical location of the learners
■ The comfort level of the learners with any technology that is used (p. 834)

Foley notes that these factors apply equally well when designing instruction for any given audience, from children to adults. When designing the World Bank's Global Development Learning Network, "results of more than 30 years of research on adult learning were applied to the distance learning programs" (p. 832). The criteria included:

1. They are based on clearly established learning needs and built around succinct statements of outcome.
2. They are based on a variety of teaching and learning strategies and methods that are activity based.
3. Effective distance learning materials are experiential . . . they address the learner's life experience.
4. Quality distance learning programs are participatory in that they emphasize the involvement of the learner in all facets of program development and delivery.

5. Successful distance learning programs are interactive and allow frequent opportunities for participants to engage in a dialogue with subject-matter experts and other learners.
6. Learner support systems are an integral part of any successful distance learning program. (p. 832)

The Indiana Partnership for Statewide Education (IPSE, 2000) proposed "Guiding Principles for Faculty in Distance Learning":

- Distance learning courses will be carefully planned to meet the needs of students within unique learning contexts and environments.
- Distance learning programs are most effective when they include careful planning and consistency among courses.
- It is important for faculty who are engaged in the delivery of distance learning courses to take advantage of appropriate professional developmental experiences.
- Distance learning courses will be periodically reviewed and evaluated to ensure quality, consistency with the curriculum, currency, and advancement of the student learning outcomes.
- Faculty will work to ensure that incentives and rewards for distance learning course development and delivery are clearly defined and understood.
- An assessment plan is adapted or developed in order to achieve effectiveness, continuity, and sustainability of the assessment process. Course outcome assessment activities are integrated components of the assessment plan.
- Learning activities are organized around demonstrable learning outcomes embedded in course components, including course delivery mode, pedagogy, content, organization, and evaluation.
- Content developed for distance learning courses will comply with copyright law.
- Faculty members involved in content development will be aware of their institution's policies with regard to content ownership.
- The medium/media chosen to deliver courses and/or programs will be pedagogically effectual, accessible to students, receptive to different learning styles, and sensitive to the time and place limitations of the students.
- The institution provides appropriate support services to distance students that are equivalent to services provided for its on-campus students.
- The institution provides its students at a distance with accessible library and other learning resources appropriate to the courses or programs delivered via technology. It develops systems to support them in accessing and using these library and other learning resources effectively.
- It is important to provide the appropriate developmental experiences for faculty who are engaged in the delivery of distance learning experiences.
- The institution implements policies and processes by which the instructional effectiveness of each distance learning course is evaluated periodically.
- Timely and reliable technical support is vital to the success of any distance learning program.
- It is recommended that a system of faculty incentives and rewards be developed cooperatively by the faculty and the administration, which encourages effort and

recognizes achievement associated with the development and delivery of distance learning courses.

■ The institution will communicate copyright and intellectual property policies to all faculty and staff working on distance learning course development and delivery.

■ The institution complies with state policies and maintains regional accreditation standards in regard to distance learning programs. (www.ihets.org/learntech/ principles_guidelines.pdf)

Commonalities between these principles and those suggested by other authors and organizations may be readily perceived. For instance, careful planning and the need for teacher training are cited by Bates (in Foley, 2003), and the emphasis on the unique needs of students in a variety of contexts is mentioned by Foley (2003). The IPSE principles make an important contribution by highlighting the need for consideration of copyright law and policies, intellectual property ownership, faculty incentives, and state policies and accreditation standards.

Because education (including distance education) is a system, each of its elements interacts with other elements, making difficult the isolation of elements. Interaction (its type, quantity, quality, timing, etc.), for instance, cannot be separated from instructional philosophy, choice of media, and other factors.

Whatever media are selected to facilitate instructor–student and student–student interaction, it should be recognized that these forms of mediated discussion should not completely replace the face-to-face element in courses. As Peters (1998) stated, those who believe that new, digital media will "supply the interactivity and communication lacking in distance education . . . cherish a hope here that will prove to be serious self-delusion" (p. 155). Peters's comments on the topic (in the context of video-conferencing, a relatively rich, "high-bandwidth" form of communication), trenchant and incisive, are worth quoting at length:

> Communication mediated through technical media remains mediated communication and cannot replace an actual discussion, an actual argument, the discourse of a group gathered at a particular location. Mediated communication and actual communication stand in relationship to one another like a penciled sketch and an oil painting of the same subject. What takes place in a discussion between two or more people can only be transmitted in part electronically. . . . A virtual university that does without face-to-face events by referring to the possibility of videoconferencing can only ever remain a surrogate university. . . . There is no doubt that to a certain extent [videoconferencing] will improve the structure of communication in distance education—but it cannot ever take the place of personal communication in distance education. (p. 155)

Peters's views on virtual communication have not been significantly modified with time.

> They reduce, surround, parcel out, spoil or destroy experiences gained at school or university. For this reason, it may be concluded, learning in virtual space will never be able to replace completely teaching in real spaces. (p. 104)

The effective use of a variety of media to facilitate communication, combined with critical quantities of well-structured face-to-face instruction and learning, have characterized many distance-delivered programs. They are two key elements of the

NSU/ITDE Model of Distance Education, what has been called "the best of both worlds" (Schlosser & Burmeister, 1999).

As important as is the appropriate selection and use of technologies of instruction and communication, technologies are not critical elements in shaping students' satisfaction with their distance courses. Rather, satisfaction is determined by "the attention they receive from the teachers and from the system they work in to meet their needs." Those needs, "what all distant learners want, and deserve" include:

- Content that they feel is relevant to their needs
- Clear directions for what they should do at every stage of the course
- As much control of the pace of learning as possible
- A means of drawing attention to individual concerns
- A way of testing their progress and getting feedback from their instructors
- Materials that are useful, active, and interesting

At the same time, it should be noted that frustration with the use of complex, inadequate, or malfunctioning equipment, as well as perceptions of emotional distance engendered by the use of distance education technologies, have negatively affected students' attitudes toward—and, in some cases, achievement in—distance education.

Bates's seventh "golden rule," that "interaction is essential," is well accepted by the field, and is a central element in most definitions of distance education (see, for instance, Keegan [1996] and Schlosser & Simonson [2009]). Keegan (1996) noted that distance education must offer "the provision of two-way communication so that the student may benefit from or even initiate dialogue" (p. 44). Initial provisions for interaction were primarily for student–instructor interactions, but with the availability of expanded communication technologies in the 1990s came an increasing emphasis on additional forms of interaction. Three forms of interaction are widely recognized by the field: student–content, student–instructor, and student–student. It is this third form of communication, reflecting, in part, andragogical and constructivist perspectives, that has increased dramatically with the rise of online education.

Concurrent with the expansion of online education and the diffusion of new communication technologies, there arose the mistaken belief that if interaction is important, "the more interaction there is in a distance education class, the better" (Simonson, 2000, p. 278). He noted that early research in the field had "demonstrated clearly that the provision for interaction was critical," but later research indicated as clearly that "interaction is not a magic potion that miraculously improves distance learning." Indeed, "the forcing of interaction can be as strong a detriment to effective learning [as is] its absence" (p. 278).

When quantifying and qualifying student–teacher and student–student interaction, perceptions may be less than reliable. In a study comparing distance students' perceptions of interaction (as compared with observations of their interaction), Sorensen and Baylen (2000) remarked that students accurately noted that: across-site interaction was very low, within-site interaction was very high, interaction changes with instructor location, remote-site students participate less, and group activities increase interactions. However, students perceived that less interaction occurred over time (when, in fact, interaction increased), and that technology inhibits interaction when, more accurately, it seems to create different patterns of interaction (p. 56).

Although Sorensen and Baylen (2000) examined interaction in the context of an interactive television course, their findings have implications for other distance education modalities. The researchers concluded that a sense of community formed among students at the distant sites, but interaction increased when the instructor was present at a given distant site. Having instructors rotate among sites encourages interaction. Interaction was hampered when students were unable to see or hear their distant classmates. Allowing constant displays of distant students would likely increase interaction. Maintaining distant students' attention "appears to be a more difficult task than perhaps in the traditional class" (p. 56). Sorensen and Baylen noted that "varying activities and including hands-on exercises and small and large group discussions were instructional methods appreciated by the students" (p. 56). Students in the Sorensen and Baylen study expressed satisfaction with the "distance learning experience" but suggested that the course include "at least one opportunity for students to meet face-to-face" (p. 57).

Distance teaching institutions (and their students) have a wide variety of instructional and communication media from which to choose. These two categories (instructional and communication) may be, to some extent, addressed separately, but they are often one and the same. Bates's fourth "golden rule," that there is no "super-technology," is well accepted and understood by experienced instructional technologists and distance educators, but often less so by those new to the field (and many, many of today's practitioners fall into this latter category). For this reason, it is important to invoke the findings of Clark (1983) explained in an earlier chapter, who noted, more than two decades ago, that "media do not influence learning under any conditions" (p. 446).

If, as Clark (citing hundreds of studies and decades of research) maintains, the application of any particular medium will neither improve student achievement nor increase the speed of learning, what criteria might a distance teaching institution apply in the selection of media for the delivery of instruction and the facilitation of communication? Cost (to both the institution as well as to the student) is an obvious criterion. Less obvious, perhaps, are the culture of the institution and expectations of students (or potential students).

At a very practical level, Ko and Rossen (2010) suggested that, prior to selecting media and instruction for online education, the institution's resources should be assessed and the following questions should be asked:

■ What's already in place (what, if any, courses are being offered online; who is teaching them, etc.)?
■ What kind of hardware and operating system does your institution support?
■ What kind of network has your institution set up?
■ What kind of computer support does your institution provide? (p. 19)

As Ko and Rossen noted, "the tools an institution uses and the support it offers very much influence the choices [the instructor will] need to make" (p. 18).

Other guidelines for selection of media for synchronous communication, in the context of one "best practice" in distance education—collaborative, problem-based student work groups—have been offered by Foreman (2003). Foreman notes the usefulness of a wide variety of synchronous technologies: chat, telephone conference, Web conferencing and application sharing, voice-over-IP, virtual classrooms, and videoconferencing. Of the technologies at either end of the spectrum—chat and video conferencing—"neither works especially well as a tool for collaborative teamwork" (para. 5) because chat is slow and awkward, and because videoconferencing is expensive, is frequently of low technical quality, and often fails to capture many of the visual cues so helpful for communication.

Telephone conferencing, however, "is highly effective for organizing small-team distance learning experiences" (Foreman 2003, para. 6), as it "provides immediacy, a high rate of information exchange, and complex multi-person interaction facilitated by a familiar audio cueing system." Foreman recognizes that telephone conferencing can be expensive, but counters that significant savings may be realized through inexpensive three-way calling options—which, "despite its name, four or more people can use . . . at once" (para. 7)—available through most telecom providers.

Commercially provided Web conferencing, combining telephone and Web technologies, overcomes the limitations of voice-only technologies through the provision of "application sharing," but its telephone component is costly. Virtual classrooms focus on synchronous teacher–student and student–student interaction through application-sharing and voice over IP. Virtual classrooms have been available for several years, but only recently (as with Elluminate's "V-Class" product) has usability advanced to a level considered acceptable by many. Foreman (2003) suggests that this final category is most promising, as it can:

> create inexpensive cyberspaces where geo-distributed students can perform their learning work through the preferred medium for intense communication-talk. Their talk will focus on shared screen objects . . . that facilitate the dialogue. . . . Under the best circumstances, the students will divide the work, perform it separately, and then gather online to share their findings and integrate them into a deliverable product that can be assessed by the instructor. This is the decentered classroom taken to a logical extreme by an emerging technology. (para. 21)

Adams and Freeman (2003) have noted the benefits of the virtual classroom, noting that the interactions within them "in addition to allowing for the exchange of information, provide participants with a shared feeling of presence or immediacy that reinforces their membership in the community."

In the end, all of the criteria just mentioned are considered and, frequently, a pragmatic approach is adopted. As Bates recommends in his fourth "golden rule," "each [medium] has its strengths and weaknesses, therefore they need to be combined (an integrated mix)" (Foley, 2003, p. 843).

The literature abounds with guidelines for distance education and identified "best practices" of distance education. Sometimes these are based on careful research but are, in the overwhelming majority of cases, the products of practitioners relating practices that have proven successful for that author. Still, some common threads have emerged.

Graham, Cagiltay, Lim, Craner, and Duffy (2001) offered seven lessons for online instruction:

1. Instructors should provide clear guidelines for interaction with students.
2. Well-designed discussion assignments facilitate meaningful cooperation among students.
3. Students should present course projects.
4. Instructors need to provide two types of feedback: information feedback and acknowledgment feedback.
5. Online courses need deadlines.
6. Challenging tasks, sample cases, and praise for quality work communicate high expectations.
7. Allowing students to choose project topics incorporates diverse views into online courses. (http://ts.mivu.org/default.asp?show+article&id=839)

In his eighth "golden rule," Bates notes that "student numbers are critical." Although this observation is made in the context of cost and media selection, student numbers are, indeed, critical in at least two other respects: class and working- (or discussion-) group size. Distance education has been embraced, in some quarters, as an opportunity to reduce costs by increasing class sizes. The literature clearly indicates that there are practical limits beyond which the quality of instruction and learning are compromised. As Hanna, Glowacki-Dudka, and Conceicao-Runlee (2000) noted, "Demand for interaction defines the size of face-to-face classrooms and the nature of the interactions within those classrooms; the demand for interaction has a similar effect upon online classrooms" (p. 26). Palloff and Pratt (2003) suggested that experienced online educators can handle 20 to 25 students in an online course, but "instructors who are new to the medium, or instructors teaching a course for the first time, should really teach no more than fifteen students" (p. 118). Chat sessions should be smaller, with perhaps 10 to 12 students (Palloff & Pratt, 2003), and work/discussion groups might have 4 or 5 members (Foreman, 2003; Hanna et al., 2000).

On a larger scale, institutions of higher education should understand that distance education is not the "cash cow" that some have mistakenly suggested (Berg, 2001). Indeed, the development and support of distance education courses and programs is normally more expensive than similar traditional courses and programs. When exceptions are occasionally noted, it is usually found that a difference in scale could explain the savings, as in the University of California–Davis study that found that preparing and offering a large (430 students) general education course at a distance cost less than the cost of the same course delivered traditionally (Sloan, 2002). Another exception is the instance of the very large distance teaching universities, such as the British Open University, where large enrollments and a long "product cycle" reduce the unit cost per student to about half that common among traditional graduate programs (Moore & Kearsley, 2005).

Care should be taken when schools search the field for suitable models. As Garon (2002) has noted, "Academic attempts at providing universities online have been marketing failures and academic distractions." Garon cites two successful for-profit institutions—the University of Phoenix and DeVry University—while noting that their success may be because, given their model for instruction, they "are much closer to large, national community colleges than traditional four-year colleges, but the model serves their community of adult learners well" (para. 6). Schools, then, should clearly identify the type of students they wish to attract, the needs of those students, and the type of university they aspire to be. Distance education is a broad field with a long history. It is important to remember that, the views of some authors notwithstanding, there is no one "right" way to conduct distance education. At the same time, it would be foolish to ignore the insights and recommendations of longtime practitioners of distance education, as well as those whose field is the study of distance education. Distance education has experienced a marked expansion and, to a certain extent, reinvention in the past few years (coinciding with the rise of the Web and entrepreneurial forces in education). However, it should be borne in mind that online education is not the sum of distance education, that the field existed long before the Web, and that enduring principles of education did not become obsolete with the development of new, electronic technologies.

RECOMMENDATIONS FOR DISTANCE DELIVERED INSTRUCTION—THE UNIT–MODULE–TOPIC MODEL

The recommendations that follow are based on the current literature of the field of distance education (Simonson, 2005, 2008). These recommended guidelines are intended to provide ways to organize courses and be guiding principles that will make courses with equal numbers of semester credits equivalent in terms of comprehensiveness of content coverage, even if these courses are offered in different programs, cover different topics, and are delivered using different media.

Organizational Guidelines

In traditional university courses, the 50-minute class session is the building block for courses. Usually, 15 classes are offered for each semester credit. Distance delivered courses often do not have class sessions. It is proposed that the *topic* be the fundamental building block for instruction. Topics are organized into *modules* that are further organized into *units* that are roughly equivalent to a semester credit traditionally offered using 15 50-minute class sessions (Orellana, Hudgins & Simonson, 2009).

When courses are planned, the designer might want to use the Unit–Module–Topic approach or model (UMT approach), as explained next.

Unit–Module–Topic Guideline

- Each semester credit = 1 unit
- Each unit = 3–5 modules
- Each module = 3–5 topics
- Each topic = 1 learning outcome

A typical three-credit course has 3 units, 12 modules, 48 topics, and 48 learning outcomes. Working definitions of *unit*, *module*, and *topic* are as follows:

Unit. A *unit* is a significant body of knowledge that represents a major subdivision of a course's content. Often, one unit of a course would represent 4 or 5 weeks of instruction, and would be equivalent to a semester credit. For example, a unit in an educational statistics course might be Descriptive Statistics.

Module. A *module* is a major subdivision of a unit. A module is a distinct and discreet component of a unit. Generally, a unit such as Descriptive Statistics might be divided into three to five major components, such as Statistical Assumptions, Measures of Central Tendency, Measures of Variation, and the Normal Curve. Modules generally are the basis for several class sessions and are covered in about a week of instruction and study.

Topic. A *topic* is an important supporting idea that explains, clarifies, or supports a module. A topic would be a lesson or an assignment. Topics in a module on Central Tendency might be Median, Mode, and Mean.

These three terms can be used in a variety of ways. Of importance is the idea that topics form modules, modules form units, and units are the main subdivisions of courses.

Assessment Guidelines

Assessment is defined as the determination and measurement of learning. Ultimately, assessment is used for grading. Assessment is directly related to learning outcomes. Normally there is at least one learning outcome for each topic.

- 1 major assignment per unit
- 1 minor assignment per two to three modules

A typical three-credit course has the following assessment strategy:

- 1 examination
- 1 ten-page paper
- 1 project
- 3 quizzes
- 3 small assignments (short paper, article review, activity report)
- graded threaded discussions, e-mails, and chats

Learning Outcome. A *learning outcome* is observable and measurable. Learning outcomes are a consequence of teaching and learning—of instruction and study. Often, learning outcomes are written with three components: conditions under which learning is facilitated (instruction), observable and measurable actions or products, and a minimum standard of expectations. Usually, there is at least one learning outcome for each course topic. For example, a learning outcome for a topic dealing with the median might be:

After studying the text, pages 51–53, reviewing the PowerPoint with audio presentation on measures of central tendency, and participating in synchronous chats, the Child and Youth Studies student will satisfactorily complete the objective test dealing with measures of central tendency at the 90% level.

Content Guidelines

Traditionally, instructors have offered content by making presentations during face-to-face instruction. Additionally, readings in textbooks and handouts are required of students.

FIGURE 5–6 Online courses should use more media.

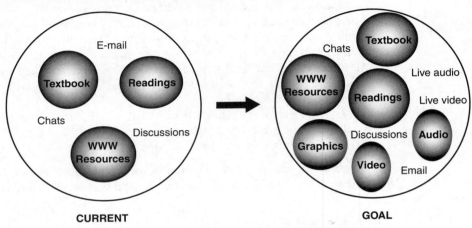

In distance teaching situations, readings in texts, handouts, and information on the Internet are often used to deliver content. For high-quality courses, there should be an emphasis on the use of various forms of visual media to offer instructional content. Videos, visual presentations with accompanying audio, and other graphical representations of important topics are important to the well-designed course. A variety of delivery systems for content should be considered, including the use of compact discs, electronic files posted to websites, and streaming. Content is organized for students into *topics*. Topics are combined into *modules* of similar topics, and modules are used to form *units* (Figure 5–6).

Modules might have three to five topics presented in the following ways:

■ Readings in the text or other written materials
■ Videos supplied on CD, DVD, or streamed
■ Audio recordings of speeches or presentations supplied on a CD, as an e-mail attachment, or streamed
■ Recorded presentations using PowerPoint with prerecorded audio
■ Synchronous chats with content experts

Instruction/Teaching Guidelines

The pace of instruction for learners is a critical concern to the distance educator. Because many distance education students are employed full time, it is important to offer instruction in a way that complements their other responsibilities. These guidelines relate to the pace of instruction and the need for continuing interaction between instructors and students:

■ 1 module per week
■ Instructor e-mail to students each week
■ 1 synchronous chat per week

- 2 to 3 threaded discussion questions per topic, or 6 to 10 questions per week
- Instructor comments on discussions as part of threaded discussion board
- Progress reports (grades) submitted to students every 2 weeks

These course design guidelines are based on the literature of distance education and are derived from an analysis and review of quality courses delivered at a distance.

The simplicity of the Course Unit (also referred to as the Carnegie Unit) has made it the standard for course design, primarily because it is easy to apply. The Course Unit requires 750 minutes of class time for each semester credit, which translates into 15 50-minute class sessions. A three-credit college course would meet three times a week for 15 weeks, according to most interpretations of the Course Unit. It is easy to count class sessions in order to determine if a course "measures up." If traditional students are in class for 3 hours per week, they probably spend about 6 hours per week outside of class doing homework, reading, completing assignments, and viewing course materials. Thus, a typical student might be expected to be involved in a typical college three-credit course for somewhere between 100 and 150 hours, or 5 to 10 hours each week in a 15-week semester. This rule of thumb is also explained in Chapter 7. The Unit–Module–Topic approach to course design can be used to meet this "time standard."

COURSE MANAGEMENT SYSTEMS

With the rapid growth of the Web in the mid-1990s and keen interest in Web technologies on college and university campuses, it was inevitable that products that ultimately would become known as course management systems (CMSs) would appear—and they did. By 1997, Web course authoring and management systems in various stages of development included CyberProf, Mallard, and Virtual Classroom Interface (all from the University of Illinois), QuestWriter (Oregon State University), Web Course in a Box (Virginia Commonwealth University), World Wide Web Course Tools (to become WebCT, University of British Columbia), and CourseInfo (to become Blackboard, Cornell University) (Albright, 1997). At that time, no tested CMS product was available on a nationwide basis, so it was common for universities with programming expertise to develop their own. Numerous others besides those listed here were created. The Wikipedia page on "The history of virtual learning environments" (http://en.wikipedia.org/wiki/History_of_virtual_learning_environments) provides a fascinating history of CMS development and has been offered into evidence to combat Blackboard's claim to a patent on electronic learning technology, which will be discussed near the end of this chapter.

Course management systems, which are known as virtual learning environments (VLEs) in Europe, have now become the de facto standard by which the vast majority of asynchronous distance education courses are delivered. Course management systems are also commonly used for distributed learning purposes, enabling teachers of conventional face-to-face courses to provide learning resources and conduct course-related activities, such as discussions and testing, outside of normal class time.

More than 40 different products promoted as course management systems were available at the time this chapter was revised for the fifth edition, although some of these focused on specific tools, such as online discussions or real-time delivery of instruction, rather than providing the full array of CMS tools described in this section. More than half of the course management systems available today are either open source, meaning that adopting organizations can download, install, and modify the software for their own needs without payment of a license fee, or are otherwise free to educational institutions.

Course management systems are often erroneously identified as "learning management systems." Learning management systems (LMSs) are an entirely different genre of product. The primary difference between the two is that the focus of a CMS, as its name implies, *is on the delivery of courses,* while an LMS focuses *on an individual and tracks the learning needs and outcomes achievement of that person* over periods of time that can be several years in length. Learning management systems first emerged in the corporate and government training sectors as tools that could compare a worker's existing skills with the job skills required for the position, and then guide and/or provide the specific training to enable the employee to become fully qualified. The training itself is often provided via products called learning "content management systems" (LCMSs), which are the corporate world's equivalent of CMSs.

Learning management systems are also now common at the K–12 level as a means of providing learning experiences and tracking student achievement toward state and No Child Left Behind standards. At the higher education level, LMSs would seem to have excellent potential for tracking student achievement in outcomes-based educational programs, as well as for faculty and staff professional development, but colleges and universities have been slow to adopt these tools. For the purpose of this chapter, know that a CMS is not an LMS, and vice versa.

Components of a Course Management System

The major course management systems all provide essentially the same basic set of components. A CMS typically includes the following tools. The actual pedagogical content for each tool needs to be created and installed by the individual teacher and/or technical support staff, unless it is acquired from a publisher or other third-party vendor.

Course Management.   Course management components may include a syllabus, course calendar, announcements, assignment instructions, learning objectives, a student roster, and a glossary. Some faculty elect not to use the CMS calendar tool and install a detailed calendar that incorporates much more information about course activities, including weekly or daily assignments and due dates for all student work that must be completed online or otherwise submitted. Course management systems also typically provide gradebook tools for faculty to post grades (or for the CMS to post grades in the case of system-scored exams and quizzes) and for students to review their progress. Tools for attendance record keeping are also common and may be linked to the gradebook in the case of courses with face-to-face components.

Readings.   CMSs typically provide a tool for listing required and recommended course readings, with hot links to those readings that may be found online. These may include links to readings that have been copyright cleared and reside in library electronic reserve collections or in electronic coursepacks, which will be discussed later in this chapter. References may be listed by topic according to the course schedule.

Content Presentation.   Many faculty maintain archives of lecture notes online for student review. Links to embedded media, such as streamed audio and video, graphics, photographic slides, and PowerPoint presentations, may also be maintained to assist students in their studies outside of the classroom. Course management systems also typically provide pages for annotated hot links to relevant websites that can be organized by course topic.

Course Communications.   Communication tools normally packaged with CMSs include asynchronous e-mail capabilities at several levels—one-to-one, one-to-several, one-to-all, and within groups. With some CMSs, e-mail is self-contained within the system and is separate from the institution's enterprise-level e-mail system, whereas with others, CMS mail is *only* integrated with the campus e-mail system and is not self-contained within the course. Most CMS systems also contain chat forums for real-time discussions, typically with white boards and other presentation tools. Some systems now provide instant messaging tools and tools for online journals called weblogs or "blogs."

Group Project Space.   The need for self-contained work space for groups within the course site has become evident to some CMS vendors. The system allows the instructor to create groups and assign students to groups. Within the group space, the members can chat or exchange e-mail and share documents for group discussion and revision. Some CMS systems even provide tools for groups or individual students to make presentations to the rest of the class in an online environment.

Student Assessment.   Almost all CMSs provide tools for exams and quizzes. Some also enable self-help or practice quizzes that are not part of the grading scheme. Built-in tools allow the instructor to generate questions in a variety of formats (e.g., true–false, multiple choice, multiple answer, matching, short answer, essay), maintain banks of questions, and stipulate that questions be selected randomly from the bank for each student as a means of enhancing security. The instructor can specify windows of time for quizzes to be available to students and set a time limit once a student starts taking the quiz. (Some of the hazards of testing students online will be discussed later in this chapter.) A very helpful tool packaged with some CMSs is the ability to draw posttest statistical analyses and reports summarizing student performance.

Digital Drop-Box for Assignment Submission.   Many course management systems contain digital drop-boxes for student submission of assignments within the CMS.

Course Evaluation Tools.   Course evaluation tools are relatively uncommon but are included in some CMSs. These tools are specifically for the course itself and not for student assessment. Instructors are able to customize the question sets. The system compiles the evaluations and provides statistical analyses and reports.

Course and System Statistics.   Some systems contain tracking tools that enable the instructor to find out precisely when each student accessed course components (for example, content pages), how often, and how much time was spent on task. These tools are extremely helpful to faculty in identifying students who are falling behind in the course. On a broader perspective, some CMSs offer to system administrators detailed information such as total number of courses, instructors, enrolled students, and "hits" on the server. This information can be compiled for a single day, a month, a year, an academic term, or any other specified date range, and can be tremendously helpful in reporting system use and troubleshooting problems such as server overloads.

Figure 9.2, on page 284, illustrates an instructor view page in a typical course management system. Note the variety of tools available to the faculty member for customizing the course and obtaining information.

Products for Enhancing Course Management Systems

Instructors are not limited to the tools provided within a CMS, nor must they generate all the content themselves. Products for enhancing course management systems are available from a wide range of vendors.

Course Supplements.   Often CMS providers partner with textbook publishers to provide online course materials that supplement the texts and can be integrated into course shells set up on those CMS platforms. These supplements typically contain such features as learning goals and objectives, amplification of the text content to provide learning guidance, updates to the text (which may not contain current information), annotated links to relevant websites, additional course readings, case studies and other types of vignettes for use in class discussions, digitized video and other media, quizzes and tests, discussion questions, and a host of other resources. All components are already copyright cleared by the publisher for use within the course.

Electronic Coursepacks.   Electronic coursepacks are different from Course Cartridges and E-Packs, although Course Cartridges and E-Packs may include electronic coursepacks. Most readers are familiar with the conventional paper coursepack. These are (hopefully) copyright-cleared readings for a course that have been compiled, duplicated, and sold or given to students. The Copyright Clearance Center, XanEdu, and University Readers (see URLs at the end of this chapter) are companies that can provide electronic coursepacks to support both distance education and traditional face-to-face courses. Electronic coursepacks can be accessed in digital form through links provided in the course management system or can be sold to students in paper form via partnering area bookstores.

Other Tools Supporting the Management of Online Courses

Other products provided by third-party vendors assist instructors with the management of online courses. They may interoperate with the CMS or be used independently. These occur in many genres. We will discuss the most common here.

Homework Collection and Grading.   This product category includes products that enable teachers to collect, grade, and return assignments online. As of this chapter revision date, few vendors beyond those that provide course management systems had entered into this market. For one example, see WebAssign. (See the URLs for each of the companies listed in this section at the end of this chapter.) WebAssign is also developing a large database of chapter-end questions from popular textbooks, from which teachers can select questions for homework assignments.

Electronic Gradebook.   The gradebook has also gone online. Gradebooks are built into course management systems such as Blackboard and Desire2Learn, as well as enterprise management systems like PeopleSoft and Banner. Now we are seeing stand-alone gradebook products that interface with administrative student information systems so that students can view their grade reports and transcripts. These systems also have features by which parents can be sent e-mail messages for reasons such as grade slippages and absences not verified by the parents. See, for example, Pinnacle Plus (primarily a K–12 product) and GradeQuick.

Electronic Testing.   Various products outside of CMSs allow instructors to build and store question databases, construct exams, and distribute them to the students; permit students to download and take the exams in a secure environment, then upload them to the teacher; and then score the exams, analyze and report the results, and archive the data. These products are available in a variety of formats and price ranges, and often extend beyond traditional formats for student assessment. Respondus was identified previously in Chapter 4. Other examples include ExamSoft, Quia, Perception from Questionmark, and IntelliMetric from Vantage Learning IntelliMetric.

Plagiarism Detection.   Oh my. You think student academic dishonesty was a problem *before* the Internet? The Web has provided global access to an unfathomable cornucopia of term papers, essays, and other scholarly works, right there out in the open for purchase or outright theft. The situation is much broader than the acquisition of schoolwork from dubious sources and extends to cheating on virtually every form of student assessment. Studies (e.g., by ABC News, 2004; Bushweller, 1999; McCabe & Drinan, 1999) have repeatedly shown that about three-fourths of both high school and college students cheat at least once, and that the majority do so without feelings of guilt or remorse. McCabe (cited in Mengers, 2004) found that the highest cheating rates were among students majoring in business, education, and journalism, three professions in which college graduates should be expected to have high levels of integrity. It is a serious issue, one for which instructors of online courses must maintain a high level of awareness.

Fain and Bates (2003) identified more than 250 "term paper mills" on the Internet, providing various services to students. However, a number of other vendors have seen this situation as an opportunity to market plagiarism detection services, such as Turnitin.com.

In addition to the use of plagiarism detection services, faculty have a number of options at their disposal for combating plagiarism. For example:

- Require students to write papers in stages, so that drafts can be reviewed and revisions required along the way.
- Require students to submit copies of their references along with the paper.
- Require students to write papers in groups, with each contributing sections.
- Give students enough advanced warning that they have time to do the research and complete the assignment, which may not deter procrastinators.
- Make the guidelines for paper submissions so specific that it is difficult to purchase a paper that meets the requirements.

SUMMARY

It is essential that the instructor take the time to plan and organize the learning experience when engaged in teaching at a distance. The instructional design process provides the framework for planning. Instruction must be at a standard that is acceptable in all venues. The students should be engaged, and the instructor should be satisfied. Planning makes the difference in a successful learning environment.

DISCUSSION QUESTIONS

1. Why is the concept of instructional design so important to the field of distance education?
2. Why is it important to write performance objectives using the three components described in this chapter?
3. Discuss the building blocks for an online course—starting with units, then progressing to modules, and finishing with topics—the U–M–T approach.

REFERENCES

ABC News. (2004). A cheating crisis in America's schools. Available online at http://abcnews.go.com/Primetime/story?id=132376&page=1

Adams, E., & Freeman, C. (2003). Selecting tools for online communities: Suggestions for learning technologists. *The Technology Source.* Available online at http://ts.mivu.org/default.asp?show+article&id=994.

Albright, M. J. (1997). Web course authoring and management systems. *Journal of Academic Media Librarianship, 5*(1), 14–23. Available online at http://wings.buffalo.edu/publications/mcjrnl/v5n1/inter.html

Berg, G. A. (2001, April–June). Distance learning best practices debate. *WebNet Journal,* 5–7.

Bushweller, K. (1999). Generation of cheaters. *American School Board Journal, 186*(4), 24–32. Available online at http://www.asbj.com/199904/0499coverstory.html

Clark, R. E. (1983). Reconsidering research on learning from media. *Review of Educational Research, 53*(4), 445–459.

Daffron, S., & Webster, E. (2006). Upon reflection: A case study of a simultaneous hybrid classroom. *Distance Learning, 3*(3), 25–34.

Dede, C. (1990, Spring). The evolution of distance learning: Technology-mediated interactive learning. *Journal of Research on Computing in Education,* 247–264.

Dick, W., Carey, L., & Carey, J. O. (2009). *The systematic design of instruction* (7th ed.). New York: Longman.

Epstein, P. (2006). Online, campus, or blended learning: What do consumers prefer and why. *Distance Learning, 3*(3), 35–37.

Fain, M., & Bates, P. (2003). Cheating 101: *Paper mills and you.* Available online at http://www.coastal.edu/library/presentations/papermil.html

Foley, M. (2003). The Global Development Learning Network: A World Bank initiative in distance learning for development. In M. G. Moore & W. G. Anderson (Eds.), *Handbook of distance education.* Mahwah, NJ: Erlbaum.

Foreman, J. (2003, July/August). Distance learning and synchronous interaction. *The Technology Source.* Available online at http://ts.mivu.org/default.asp?show+article&id=1042.

Gardner, H. (1993). *Multiple intelligences.* New York: Basic Books.

Garon, J. (2002, August). A new future for distance education. *Interface Tech News.* Available online at www.interfacenow.com/syndicatepro/displayarticle.asp?ArticleID=180.

Graham, C., Cagiltay, K., Lim, B-R., Craner, J., & Duffy, T. M. (2001, March/April). Seven principles of effective teaching: A practical lens for evaluating online courses. *The Technology Source.* Available online at http://ts.mivu.org/default.asp?show+article&id=839.

Hanna, D. E., Glowacki-Dudka, M., & Conceicao-Runlee, S. (2000). *147 practical tips for teaching online groups: Essentials for Web-based education.* Madison, WI: Atwood.

Heinich, R. (2004). Technology and the management of instruction. Charlotte, NC: Information Age Publishing.

Herring, M., & Smaldino, S. (2001). *Planning for interactive distance education: A handbook* (2nd ed.). Bloomington, IN: AECT Publications.

Hirumi, A. (2005). In search of quality: An analysis of e-learning guidelines and specifications. *The Quarterly Review of Distance Education, 6*(4), 309–329.

Holden, J., & Westfall P. (2006). Instructional media selection for distance learning: A learning environment approach. *Distance Learning, 3*(2), 1–11.

Indiana Partnership for Statewide Education. (2000). *Guiding principles for faculty in distance learning.* Available online at www.ihets.org/learntech/principles_guidelines.pdf.

Keegan, D. (1996). *Foundations of distance education* (3rd ed.). London: Routledge.

Ko, S., & Rossen, S. (2010). *Teaching online: A practical guide* (3rd ed.). Boston: Houghton Mifflin.

Macfarlane, C., & Smaldino, S. (1997). The electronic classroom at a distance. In R. Rittenhouse & D. Spillers (Eds.), *Modernizing the curriculum: The electronic classroom.* Springfield, MO: Charles Thomas.

McAlpine, L., & Weston, C. (1994). The attributes of instructional materials. *Performance Improvement Quarterly, 7*(1), 19–30.

McCabe, D. L., & Drinan, P. (1999) Toward a culture of academic integrity. *Chronicle of Higher Education, 46*(8), B7.

Mengers, P. (2004, August 9). Keeping it honest as schools battle plagiarism problems. *Delaware County Times.*

Moore, M., & Kearsley, G. (2005). *Distance education: A systems view* (2nd ed.). Belmont, CA: Wadsworth.

Morrison, G., Ross, S., & Kemp, J. (2004). *Designing effective instruction* (4th ed.). New York: John Wiley and Sons.

Orellana, A., Hudgins, T., & Simonson, M. (2009). *Designing the perfect online course: Best practices for designing and teaching.* Charlotte, NC: Information Age Publishing.

Palloff, R. M., & Pratt, K. (2003). *The virtual student: A profile and guide to working with online learners.* San Francisco: Jossey-Bass.

Peters, O. (1998). *Learning and teaching in distance education: Pedagogical analyses and interpretations in an international perspective.* London: Kogan Page.

Peters, O. (2002). *Distance education in transition: New trends and challenges.* Bibliotheks und Informations sytem der Universitat Oldenburg.

Schlosser, C., & Anderson, M. (1994). *Distance education: Review of the literature.* Ames, IA: Research Institute for Studies in Education.

Schlosser, C., & Burmeister, M. (1999). The best of both worlds. *Tech Trends, 43*(5), 45–48.

Schlosser, L. A., & Simonson, M. (2009). *Distance education: Definition and glossary of terms* (3rd ed.). Greenwich, CT: Information Age Publishing.

Schon, D. (1987). *Educating the reflective practitioner.* San Francisco: Jossey-Bass.

Simonson, M. (2000). Myths and distance education: What the research says and does not say. *Quarterly Review of Distance Education, 1*(4), 277–279.

Simonson, M. (2005). Planning the online course. *Distance Learning, 2*(5), 43–44.

Simonson, M. (2007). Rules of thumb, or DeRoTs. *Distance Learning, 3*(4), 92.

Simonson, M. (2008). And finally . . . designing the perfect online course. *Distance Learning: For Educators, Trainers, and Leaders, 5*(3), 82–84.

Sloan, C. (2002). *Practice: Comparing the cost-effectiveness of online versus traditional classroom cost per student pass rates.* Available online at www.aln.org/effective/details5.asp?CE_ID=21.

Smaldino, S., Lowther, D., & Russell, J. (2007). *Instructional technology and media for learning* (9th ed.). Upper Saddle River, NJ: Prentice Hall.

Sorensen, C., & Baylen, D. (2000). Perception versus reality: Views of interaction in distance education. *The Quarterly Review of Distance Education, 1*(1), 45–58.

Thompson, A., Hargrave, C., & Simonson, M. (1996). *Educational technology: Review of the research* (2nd ed.). Washington, DC: Association for Educational Communications and Technology.

Ullman, C., & Rabinowitz, M. (2004). Course management systems and the reinvention of instruction. Available online at http://thejournal.com.the/printarticel/?id=17014.

U.S. Department of Education. (2006). Evidence of quality in distance education programs drawn from interviews with the accreditation community. Retrieved April 30, 2007, from www.itcnetwork.org/Accreditation-EvidenceofQualityinDEPrograms.pdf.

Wade, D., Bentley, J., & Waters, S. (2006). Twenty guidelines for successful threaded discussions: A learning environment approach. *Distance Learning, 3*(3), 1–8.

Willis, B. (1994). Distance Education: Strategies and tools. Englewood Cliffs, NJ: Educational Technology Publications.

ADDITIONAL WEB SITES REFERENCED IN THIS CHA

Blackboard
http://blackboard.com
Desire2Learn
http://www.desire2learn.com/
The companies listed above provide services and products related to course management in an
    online environment.
Copyright Clearance Center
http://www.copyright.com/
XanEdu
http://www.xanedu.com/
University Readers
http://www.universityreaders.com/
WebAssign
http://www.webassign.net/
Pinnacle Plus from Excelsior Software
http://www.excelsiorsoftware.com/solution/sys_pinnPLUS.aspx
GradeQuick
http://www.gradequick.com
ExamSoft
http://www.examsoft.com/
Quia
http://www.quia.com
Perception from Questionmark
http://www.questionmark.com/
Intellimetric from Vantage Learning
http://www.vantagelearning.com/intellimetric
Turnitin
http://www.turnitin.com/

Best Practices for Distance Education: Designing the *"perfect*"* Online Course

Structure (for a 3 semester credit course)

- Instructor time: ~120 hours
- Student time: ~120 hours
- 3 Units, 15 modules,
  45 Learning Experiences
- Unit = 5 weeks
- Module = 1 week
- Learning Experience = 1 day

Contents (of a 3 semester credit course)

- Syllabus
- Course Management System — WebCT

- ■ Instructor Guidance
  - ■ Introductory Statement
  - ■ Monday Morning Memos
  - ■ Emails
  - ■ Telephone Calls
  - ■ Live Presentations
- ■ Textbooks
- ■ Media
  - ■ Videos
  - ■ Audios
  - ■ Visuals
  - ■ Animations
- ■ Virtual Materials
  - ■ Discussions
  - ■ Chats

Artifacts of Learning

- ■ 3 Major Graded Assignments
  - ■ Exam
  - ■ Problem/Scenario/Situation Solution
  - ■ Research Paper/Portfolio/Blog/Presentation
- ■ 10–15 Minor Graded Activities
  - ■ Discussion Posting
  - ■ Chat Participation
  - ■ E-mails
  - ■ Wiki Postings
  - ■ Blog Entries

Unit Contents

- ■ Introduction to Unit
- ■ Readings
- ■ Viewings
- ■ Listenings
- ■ Discussions
- ■ Chat Debates

Teaching and Distance Education

CHAPTER GOAL

The purpose of this chapter is to provide guidance for the instructor when teaching at a distance.

CHAPTER OBJECTIVES

After reading and reviewing this chapter, you should be able to

1. Describe the responsibilities of the instructor in distance education.
2. Explain the importance of creating a learning community.
3. Discuss issues related to course organization.
4. Identify ways to enhance delivery of instruction.
5. Discuss policy issues important to the teacher of distant learners.
6. Estimate the time needed to teach a course delivered at a distance.

QUALITY INSTRUCTION AT A DISTANCE: COAL SLURRY PONDS

Recently, there was a program on the History Channel dealing with something called coal slurry ponds—those ponds used by coal mines to hold the water runoff from coal cleansing operations. Apparently there are hundreds of these ponds in the coal mining regions of Pennsylvania and West Virginia. The program on this "dirty" topic was presented in such an interesting way that those who were "channel surfing" probably were captivated and watched the entire program—and in the process became knowledgeable about coal slurry ponds.

Actually, there is something relevant for distance educators in programs like the History Channel's "Coal Slurry Ponds." Most of us have watched the History Channel—a polished editing of video tied together with an artful narration. Almost always the programs are informative, persuasive, and entertaining—they are well done, and by TV production standards, at a very low cost.

Recently in distance education, there has been an interest in what some call "best teaching practices" and others label as "quality instruction indicators." Research by Kidney, Cummings, and Boehm (2007) suggests that attributes of quality can be characterized within three groups:

- Learners
  - ease of access and usability
  - accurate instructions
  - intuitive navigation and well-integrated tools
- Faculty
  - ease of instruction and consistent with standards
  - intuitive and customizable course management system
  - ease of preparation and updating
- Administration
  - comparable rigor to nondistance classes
  - increased enrollment
  - maintenance of institution's reputation (p. 18)

Lists of "best teaching practices" are often concluded with summary statements about the course being informative, interesting, even inspiring, and certainly memorable. Well-designed courses, like programs on the History Channel, draw the learner in and keep them engaged. The story is interesting and keeps the learner motivated. High-quality distance teaching is *obvious*. You really do not need checklists or rating scales. When you see quality you know it. If coal slurry ponds can be presented in a way that is informative and interesting, then so can instruction delivered at a distance (Simonson, 2004).

TEACHING THE DISTANT LEARNER

Teaching in general has moved away from the more traditional approaches we have experienced in classrooms. Today, schools, universities and training organizations are looking for more effective learning approaches that focus on the students' learning and less on the delivery of content. Well-designed courses provide students with engaging learning experiences.

A shift in location suggests that the participants are not in a single setting, whereas a shift in time implies that the instruction is not "live." Both of these aspects of distance learning present instructional challenges to even the most experienced educators. Distance education is an opportunity to revisit the role of the instructor in the learning environment. Moreland and Saleh (2007) identified faculty concerns related to distance education. The six concerns they identified were:

Concern 1: Faculty size and job security.
Concern 2: Quality of distance education.
Concern 3: Interactivity in distance education.
Concern 4: Plagarism.

Concern 5: Assessment and dishonesty.

Concern 6: Credits, clock hours, and student contact requirements.

Moreland and Saleh concluded that effective institutional policies should be in place that deal with these issues of faculty concern.

From Teacher-Centered to Student-Centered Learning

Student-centered learning is not a new concept. It dates to times when education pioneer John Dewey advocated the personal experience of the learner in the learning process (Conrad & Donaldson, 2004). Further, Dewey supported student collaboration as a way of defining the learning situation. Although Dewey focused on junior and senior high students, Knowles (1980) expanded Dewey's ideas into ways to approach adults in learning settings. He proposed that adults enter the learning setting as self-directed learners who expect to be engaged.

The movement toward online distance education advanced the ideas suggesting active learning for the student. When television was the primary vehicle for delivery, it essentially replicated the traditional classroom. And, by its very nature, it allowed for a passive student experience, whereby the instructor lectured and the student listened, took notes, and completed tests. This teacher-centered model continued for many years with the use of video-based technologies. However, there is a shift away from the instructor's "talking head" as more faculty begin to recognize the need for engaging their students throughout the learning experience.

With the advent of online resources, the student-centered approach to learning fits well into distance education environments. By its very nature, online education demands that students become engaged in the learning process. They cannot sit back and be passive

Mitch Wojnarowicz/The Image Works

When teaching at a distance, the role of the instructor is often that of facilitator rather than presenter.

learners; rather, they must participate in the learning process. The need to interact with the instructor and other students is important to enhance student learning. The online resources promote active learning, collaboration, mastery of material, and student control over the learning process. The addition of technology as part of the learning process means that the learner actively communicates within the instructional setting.

Barr and Tagg (1995) discussed the differences between teacher-centered and student-centered instructional models (see Table 4.1 on page 124). Oblinger (1999) viewed the transformation between teacher-centered and student-centered differently:

- From lecturing to coaching
- From taking attendance to logging on
- From distribution of requirements to connected learning
- From credit hours to performance standards
- From competing to collaborating
- From library collections to network connections
- From passive to active learning
- From textbooks to customized materials.

The transformation from teacher-centered to student-centered can be seen when the instructor sets aside traditional ideas about teaching and begins to "think out of the box." A successful online environment moves away from the teacher to the student as the key to the learning process.

Just-in-Time Learning

Just-in-time learning is a phrase used most often by trainers in private business. In the workplace, required skills change frequently. Just-in-time learning most often provides instruction in the form of online modules specific to the topic. The modules are available at all times and easily accessed. This way, employees can access the training module they need, when they need it, to learn the new information. Just-in-time learning makes work-related instruction available for new employees who need to gain a skill or as a refresher for those who have been working at a task for a period of time. It serves well for those who find themselves with a new and novel situation and need to explore their options for solutions.

Distance Learning versus Distributed Learning

The concept of *distributed learning* illustrates how the learner-centered educational model is being implemented in today's schools and universities. Not all online learning is necessarily distance learning. Much online learning activity involves students and instructors who continue to meet at least part of the time in conventional classroom settings. Saltzberg and Polyson (1995) offered an early definition of this phenomenon:

> Distributed learning is not just a new term to replace the other DL, distance learning. Rather, it comes from the concept of distributed resources. Distributed learning is an instructional model that allows instructor, students, and content to be located in different,

noncentralized locations so that instruction and learning occur independent of place and time. The distributed learning model can be used in combination with traditional classroom-based courses, with traditional distance learning courses, or it can be used to create wholly virtual classrooms. (p. 10)

Distributed learning thus is a broader term that can be, and in fact most often is, associated with face-to-face (f2f) instruction that incorporates some form of technology-based learning experience, either inside or outside the classroom. In other words, students do not need to be at a distance from their instructor to benefit from distributed learning. Although the primary focus of this book is on distance learning, in which students and their teachers are geographically separated, many distributed learning experiences may involve only resources that are at a distance, or that occur at a different time and/or place than the conventional class meeting.

For example, learning materials can be located on a server anywhere in the world and accessed either by the classroom teacher as part of a presentation or independently by students in some interactive setting. Course discussions can take place online and outside the classroom. A class activity can involve tracking a scientific expedition in real time, including interaction with explorers using live video transmissions. High-speed networks enable sophisticated audio, video, and graphics for real-time learning experiences.

Distributed learning is also represented by what are called *hybrid* or *blended* courses, in which online activities substitute for a portion of actual "seat time" in a conventional face-to-face course. Blended courses can be employed when the instructor feels that the online activities are more productive learning experiences for students. As the technology resources expand to allow more video and audio capabilities, there is a shift from a blended to a fully online course format.

ASPECTS OF INSTRUCTION

The design of instruction captures those elements that create a learning environment that facilitates student learning. Content is organized and sequenced with an orientation toward prescribed outcomes (Dabbagh & Bannan-Ritland, 2005). Often, decisions related to the content are closely aligned with curriculum or professional standards. Standards alignment is one aspect of the design of instruction.

Another aspect of the design of instruction is the instructor's level of comfort with a variety of methods. Common in higher education is the lecture approach, which serves to provide the same instruction to all participants. In its early years, the lecture approach was common in distance education. The "talking head" is frequently the image brought to mind when thinking about televised instruction. In online settings, long documents of text equate to the talking head image. With the transition to more student-centered instructional approaches, the lecture is being used less as a method of instruction. However, instructors need to assess their own comfort levels with the various methods available.

Structuring the Instruction

In any instructional setting, students benefit when they have a clear view of such issues as class organization and student responsibilities. The instructor's responsibility involves organizing the course, including such items as class schedule, grouping for activities, and expectations for interaction. What is essential is that students understand how the course will function so that they can be better prepared to participate. The more informed the students, the greater the chances for success.

In this book, the Unit–Module–Topic approach for course organization is presented in Chapter 5. This method for structuring courses is simple to apply and is applicable to almost any instructional situation.

Sorensen and Baylen (2004) have suggested that there are good instructional practice principles that provide a guideline for involving students in quality learning experiences. Their guideline includes such things as:

- Communication with students
- Collaboration among students
- Active learning experiences
- Prompt feedback
- High expectations
- Respecting diversity.

These principles seem logical to most educators, but can become lost in the development of distance learning courses due to the complexities of designing an environment that often involves complex technology. The technology can often afford the instructor options for engaging learners in unique ways that adhere to these principles, but these strategies may apply in traditional classrooms as well. Often, you will find that in blended classes, where the instructor incorporates technology to facilitate communication and interaction among students, these principles enhance the learning opportunities for students.

Organization of the Instruction.   Issues of format or structure are important to help students quickly and easily become involved in learning rather than students trying to puzzle through how the course is delivered (Herring & Smaldino, 2001). The instructor needs to make decisions as to the best way to communicate how the course is structured with students and content in mind. When considering how to approach learning, does the instructor begin with an activity that requires students to interact with each other? Or, should the instructor begin each class with a brief overview of content? And, at the end of each class should the instructor consider closing with student questions?

The instructor needs to consider how to begin each session or module. Is a text-based lecture or a short streamed video possible for presenting the content? Should the instructor post prompts or questions prior to the actual "beginning" time for discussion so students can preview them? Or, should students be expected to post questions or prompts prior to beginning the learning experience? The instructor needs to consider how and when to respond to each student's postings. Will the instructor interject comments along the way without specifically responding to all the individual comments? Or, will it be valuable to the discussion to remain quiet, only interjecting comments when necessary to facilitate the discussion or to bring students back on track?

Students are more comfortable with distance learning when instructors adhere to predetermined course schedules (Macfarlane & Smaldino, 1997). For synchronous settings, instructors need to maintain a class schedule that is congruous with the transmission schedule. For asynchronous distance learning settings, they need to post information and assignments in a timely fashion, ensuring that students have ample time to complete the tasks before moving to the next phase of the course. Instructors need to provide practice at the beginning to allow students experiences to use time wisely and to maintain the schedule of activities. Students need to know about the importance of the available materials if they are used and how to use them to benefit their learning. It may be necessary to adjust the schedule; however, it needs to be done with the students involved in making the decision to adjust the time line.

Students need a clear understanding of their own responsibilities (Kiliç-Çakmak, Karatas, & Ocak, 2009). They need to know what is expected of them in terms of preparation for class and participation in class activities. Expecting students to read assignments prior to the learning activity means the instructor must expand on the information, not merely repeat within the experience (Herring & Smaldino, 2001). Students will not read in advance if their learning experience does not expand their understanding of the content or helps them explore additional options. If the instructor has assigned a specific reading selection, then incorporating interactive activities related to that reading assignment would reinforce the need to be prepared in advance.

The Syllabus to Ensure Communication.   The syllabus is the single-most important document an instructor can prepare. This is the primary communication with students at a distance. An instructor needs to provide enough information within the syllabus that students are able to understand the structure of the course, expectations and assignments, and the assessment process.

The syllabus helps students understand their role in the distant setting. They need to know what they are to do when having technical or personal difficulties with the course. Students need to assume responsibility for initiating contact with the instructor. Because of the distant setting, the instructor and students may not meet in person, but rather must meet via the technology. If students are having difficulty with the course or need additional information or assistance, it is their responsibility to contact the instructor. But the instructor must provide them with contact information as part of the syllabus. It is crucial that students have convenient and reliable means of connecting with the instructor. An e-mail address or a toll-free phone number is desirable, as it will not impose much expense on the students. But if neither of these is available easily, then an office or home phone number needs to be shared.

In addition, it is appropriate on the syllabus to provide some framework for contacting the instructor. If the instructor wishes to receive phone calls, then it is important to indicate when and what number to use. An instructor who shares a personal or home phone number needs to be aware that students may well use that number. So if the instructor has preferred times to communicate with students, the students need to know that information. The instructor needs to be clear as to response time when receiving communication from students. For example, an instructor needs to state that e-mail communication will be within 24 hours and not on Saturday or Sunday if that's the desired time frame for the instructor. That way, a student will know if he or she does not receive a reply to a message it is because the instructor may be busy or it is the weekend. And, if the instructor is going to be at a conference or unable to be in contact for a few days, it is best to let students know in advance of the changes in the routine communication patterns.

Another related issue to include on the syllabus is what to do when there are technical difficulties. Provide students with alternatives; students need to know what is expected of them. If, in a televised class, there are transmission problems, students need to know what to do about the session and assignments. If there are problems with an online class, students need a way to follow through with the learning tasks without penalty. When teaching with technology, always assume the worst and be pleasantly surprised when everything goes well.

Creating the Learning Community.   Creating a learning community involves both the instructor and the students (Palloff & Pratt, 2007). Everyone must take an active role in the development of a collegial learning situation. Students must understand their role in the progress of the learning experiences (Luppicini, 2007).

Respect for others is an important part of working in groups, especially at a distance (Herring & Smaldino, 2001). Students may need training in communication protocols. They may need to be aware of any cultural issues that might be important. In an audio setting, students must be prepared to use microphones or other audio equipment. Further, they need to understand their responsibilities to be courteous and well-mannered, in both audio- and text-based communication formats. In an online setting, students must be sensitive to their peers and select appropriate language to express themselves. They should also be cautious in the use of humor. Gentle guidance is often all that is necessary to ensure respect for others.

Icebreakers, or sessions in which students get to know each other, serve as a positive experience in developing the community of learners especially in the distance learning environment. The class is often comprised of a diverse geographic collection of unique individuals. Sometimes an institution can create a cohort of students who study together through the length of their program. The cohort model allows students a greater opportunity to become a community of learners. The single course comprised of a diverse population that may not appear together again brings about a greater challenge to creating the learning community.

Several authors have suggested icebreakers as a means to developing a community among the participants in the class (Conrad & Donaldson, 2004; Herring & Smaldino, 2001). What is fundamental to the concept of an icebreaker is that it serves to humanize the new learning situation. The icebreaker's role is to help build a sense of trust among the members of the group. By gaining knowledge about each member of the class, the opportunities for communications and collaborations are enhanced. An activity as simple as having each student introduce himself or herself and perhaps share favorite books or television programs, personal highlights like honors or awards, or something that the student hopes for in the future, can be a way to help foster a sense of community among the members of the course. As they move through the course, students often build on that initial information to continue building their community.

Facilitating Active Learning Practices.   Learners who are engaged in learning are actively participating in their own understanding of the content. The "kiss of death" for any distance course is the lack of student participation. Strategies for active learning range from giving students opportunities to think about a topic and respond to actual hands-on manipulation of learning objects (Sorensen & Baylen, 2004). The students who are engaged in learning are reported to remember the content better and for a longer period (Dobbs, Waid, & del Carmen, 2009). In the video-based distance education setting, active learning experiences can include such things as small group discussions, hands-on experiences with materials available in advance of the class period, presentations, or similar types of classroom strategies. In an online environment, active learning may take on a different format. Such strategies as case study analysis, structured discussions or debates, or virtual field trips can be incorporated. The list of possible strategies for engaging learners in active pursuit of their own knowledge is unlimited. The key to active learning is to keep the learners involved in their own learning, not just keeping them busy.

Engaged learning involves collaboration among the members of the learning community (Conrad & Donaldson, 2004). Essential to the success of the active learning paradigm are such things as clearly articulated goals, timelines, essential questions, and authentic assessment practices. The instructor needs to work with learners to establish goals for learning, ensuring that the standards or requirements are being met. Further, while it is important to plan in advance of the beginning of any distance learning experience, it may be necessary to negotiate with students the timelines for assignments. Flexibility is critical to successful distance educational experiences, for both the instructor and the learner.

Besides answering student questions and providing authentic learning experiences that lead to products for assessment, learners need to feel comfortable with the expectations (Conrad & Donaldson, 2004). An engaged learning setting assumes that both the instructor and the students are open to adopting strategies that form a dynamic learning community.

Using Instructional Materials to Assist Learning.   Instructional materials are an essential element to ensuring quality learning experiences (Herring & Smaldino, 2001; Smaldino, Lowther, & Russell, 2011). Media formats for instruction continue to advance with the development of newer technologies. The key to using quality instructional materials is that the appropriate media is selected. To select an instructional tool because it is the latest version or the newest idea for instructional materials is not sufficient. Instructional materials need to enhance the learning opportunities for students.

The instructor can design instructional materials to direct students in their exploration of content and to actively engage them in the learning activities. Students learn to rely on these materials as an integral component of their learning process. But not all instructional materials need to be developed by the instructor as new resources; instructors can rely on existing media to help enhance learning experiences. A word of caution: Copyright rules must be recognized when using existing materials.

Further, instructors can design instructional materials to help students as they participate in the class. While it is often desirable to have all instructional materials prepared at the beginning of a course, it might be wise to consider distributing them over the life of the course. This allows the instructor to make minor changes or adjustments to the directions or resources within the materials to reflect the needs of students.

A simple rule of KISS—"keep it short and simple"—applies to the use of any instructional material. It is better to divide the information into shorter packets than to prepare one long document for students. Some instructors find that giving their students a "condensed" version of their instructional PowerPoint slides facilitates note taking during a video "lecture," and ensures that students will attend to the content as not all the information is contained in the handouts. Others advocate providing templates and other types of resources for students as they engage in course activities or assignments. By providing students with the outline or learning guides, it is possible to help them understand the expectations for assignments and facilitating the grading process.

Addressing Assessment.   Students need to know how their participation in class discussions is measured. Students who are reluctant to engage in discussion or are unprepared should be ready to accept the consequences of nonparticipation if a portion of assessment depends on a certain level of participation. Effort needs to be made to provide shy students with nonthreatening means for participating that serve to ease them into feeling confident about their abilities to participate in discussions. Instructors must assume responsibility to meet the needs of students who might be reluctant learners.

Students who are not performing according to the identified standards need to receive private communication from the instructor. Even when students are performing well, it is important for educators to inform students of their successes. Feedback provides students with guidelines for how to continue to improve their performance in a course (Conrad & Donaldson, 2004). Timeliness for feedback is also critical to successful learning experiences (Herring & Smaldino, 2001). Distance cannot be an excuse for failure to communicate with students. Students need to be informed as quickly as possible how well they are doing. Online technologies facilitate this process and might be incorporated into any distant learning course to enhance the communication process with students.

Types of feedback also provide students with the knowledge they need to improve their performance (Conrad & Donaldson, 2004; Herring & Smaldino, 2001). The types of feedback necessary to communicate with students go beyond a simple grade. Feedback should be informative to the student. Feedback that provides guidance on what was done well and on areas for improvement adds to the success of the distance learning experience. For example, a short paper that has been reviewed can include comments and edits by the instructor, which can help the student understand writing expectations for the next assignment that requires a paper. The earlier the information for improvement of performance is provided, the greater the possibilities students have for success as they move through the course.

Instructional Methods

Teaching methods should be chosen based on the characteristics of the instructor, students, content, and delivery system (Herring & Smaldino, 2001). Because of the increased responsibility for learning placed on the students at a distance, methods that focus on the learners and incorporate interactivity have been shown to be most successful (Miller, 2007; Smaldino, Lowther, & Russell, 2011). Traditional methods for instruction have a place in distance education. What is of importance when considering instructional choices is that the methods selected for a distance learning setting match the outcomes defined by the objectives and the assessments to be implemented.

Range of Instructional Methods. The instructor needs to determine the appropriate instructional methods to be used in delivering the content. Among the issues to consider is how the choice of a particular method can be used to involve the students in all the instructional settings. There is no ideal way to accomplish this. With some adaptations, the same methods and techniques that are successful in a traditional classroom setting can work as well in distance instruction. One key to selection is the way in which a strategy can be used to encourage student interaction.

It has been suggested that if a strategy works in a regular classroom, it probably will work in distance instruction with some adjustment (Herring & Smaldino, 2001). The instructor is responsible for the learning environment created in the instructional setting. Technology used in distance learning should be considered as a tool to deliver the instruction and not as a method. Whatever the choice for creating the learning environment, the instructor should include the fundamental elements of planning, including the effects of the technology in design. Using the distance education technologies should not limit the choice of strategies used by instructors, but should open new possibilities for those wishing to enrich their teaching (Smaldino, Lowther, & Russell, 2011; Westbrook, 2006).

Selecting a variety of techniques is important to creating an interesting instructional environment. An instructor must remember to think of strategies that engage learners in active rather than passive learning experiences (Conrad & Donaldson, 2004; Dabbagh & Bannan-Ritland, 2005; Palloff & Pratt, 2007). Combining techniques is useful, and instructors should not be afraid to experiment, explore, and be creative in their approaches to teaching at a distance. The more actively engaged the students, the more likely learning will occur in the distant setting.

Application of Instructional Methods to Distance Instruction. The type of instructional setting will dictate the appropriate choices for instructional methods. With live instruction (synchronous), such as television-based or audio/video teleconferencing, some approaches are more effective. When teaching online in an asynchronous format, other approaches facilitate learning. Both environments suggest the need for careful design of instruction (Herring & Smaldino, 2001).

Electronic white boards are convenient ways for teachers to quickly visualize concepts for students—local and distant.

VTEL Products Corporation

Synchronous.   When teaching in a synchronous environment, many traditional classroom instructional approaches can be incorporated. Lectures, of short duration, are often effective in helping to facilitate the instructional situation. Small and large group activities such as discussions and hands-on activities can fit into the audio and video components of the synchronous situation. A key to instruction in a synchronous environment is that the learners cannot remain passive for a length of time. Thus, using a variety of teaching strategies seems to work best.

Asynchronous.   An asynchronous environment requires consideration of the types of instructional strategies that work best to engage the learners. Without the convenience of face-to-face instruction, the instructor needs to consider ways of facilitating the learning process and encouraging students to assume responsibility for their learning. The challenge is to select methods of teaching that provide learners with enough interaction to keep them on task while encouraging them to explore their learning experiences. Strategies such as problem-based learning, collaboration, and student-led discussions work well in asynchronous settings (Smaldino, Lowther, & Russell, 2011).

TECHNOLOGY CONSIDERATIONS

With any instructional activity heavily invested in technology for the delivery of content, the choice of types of tools is important. There are expanding options available to the instructor. What follows is a brief description of the types of technology tools that can be incorporated into a distance learning experience.

Course Management Systems

In many formal learning settings, course management systems (CMS) have been available for many years. There is a migration away from these more structured online resources to less formal systems but there are aspects of the CMS that make them an easy-to-use and valuable resource for designing instruction.

Course management systems offer components that structure the resources for delivery. Built into the systems are such resources as the course calendar, announcements, assignment and discussion areas, student rosters, communications, Web links, and grade books. Some faculty elect not to use all the resources, but others have found many of them to be valuable in helping students to be engaged in their learning rather than frustrated with trying to locate and use less formalized resources. The layout for the CMS can be limiting, although as faculty develop more online learning experiences, they are requesting more options to be available.

For example, to facilitate a dialog, the instructor or a student can post a topic and as the members of the class engage in the discussion, it is possible to read postings and respond, review earlier postings by others, and to facilitate a lively conversation. Testing resources are available as well, with options for multiple choice, true–false, and short answer. Tests can be timed so that they open and close for students on a designated day. The results of the tests are automatically placed in the gradebook.

The instructor can find it easier to use the assignment tools to upload assignments, grade them, and return them to students with extended feedback. The CMS can connect the grading process to the gradebook, which means the instructor spends less time with mechanics and more time with the actual instruction.

Another major benefit to using a CMS is that all of the material for the course, the syllabus, student assignments, and communications, are managed on a server, which means less chance of loss of information or technology issues. Also, because the CMS utilizes a Web-based format, the instructor and students can access it from any location where they can connect to the Web.

Managing Distance Learning Courses

There are a number of issues related to design of a distant learning course that will facilitate the management of it during implementation. A well-designed distance education course can be as easy to deliver as a traditional face-to-face course.

Guide Students at the Beginning. Even though most students come to distance learning situations with vast experience using technology, do not assume they can transition directly into a course delivered at a distance. At the beginning of the course, it is important to guide students as to expectations for their participation, use of the tools, and location of resources. It helps to provide examples or exercises that model what will be expected in terms of performance. By giving students activities that get them using the resources as part of their introductions or community building activities, they learn to use the tools that will be part of their later learning experiences.

Communicate Regularly. Communication is an important component of ensuring successful distance learning experiences. Although you may have provided a schedule of tasks and assignments within the syllabus, regularly remind students of upcoming due dates and activities. By regularly posting announcements of things happening within the next few weeks, even the less organized student will stay on track. One technique demonstrated to be effective, especially for asynchronous courses, is the MMM: the Monday Morning Memo (or Saturday Morning Memo). The MMM is a weekly e-mail that summarizes the previous week's class activities and explains in detail what students should be expected to accomplish in the next week. The MMM becomes a guide and progress report that students can count on to direct their learning (Orellana, Hudgins, & Simonson, 2009).

Assignments and Grading.   Because the instructor is often unable to meet with students, it is critical that feedback be an integral component of the grading process. Thus, it might be wiser to develop fewer, but more complex, assignments that allow students to demonstrate their knowledge and skills about the topics. Or, tests can be generated and delivered automatically, which can save the instructor some time.

Rubrics for grading assignments are important to facilitate the communication process and to help outline expectations for assignments. Well-developed rubrics can serve to guide students as they prepare their assignments and can make the grading and feedback easier. The trick is to balance the amount of information within the rubric and keep it a reasonable length for students to use.

Plagiarism.   The Web has opened many doors to possibilities, including ready access to information that is easy to copy into documents. It is not appropriate to think that all students will plagiarize, but it is wise to be prepared to deal with the issue before it happens.

Most universities have policies regarding plagiarism. And, resources are now available to help forestall such practice. Software such as *Turn-It-In* allows the student to preview a paper before turning it in to the instructor. The software identifies where a portion of a paper might border on not being a well-prepared paraphrase and more of a near direct quote. Faculty can also use the software if there is any doubt about the honesty of the students' work.

Faculty have a number of ways to deal with the potential for plagiarism. Among them are to provide enough time to complete a paper, require students to submit drafts of their papers in stages for review, expect copies of the sources to be made available with the paper, and make the requirements for the assignment unique to the course such that it would be difficult to purchase a ready-made paper or to copy the works of others.

POLICY ISSUES RELATED TO TEACHING AT A DISTANCE

Academic

In any academic setting there are issues that need to be addressed related to instruction—issues related to course assignments, loads, expectations, and other institutional matters (Simonson, 2007).

Faculty Issues.   Faculty—or labor–management—issues can easily be the most difficult for policy developers, especially if instructors are unionized. Increasingly, existing labor–management policies are being used to cover distance education.

Clearly, faculty need to be recognized for their efforts and expertise in working with distant learners, and until distance education becomes mainstream and expected of all teachers, policies need to be in place that clarify distance teaching responsibilities.

Key issues include class size, compensation, design and development incentives, recognition of intellectual property of faculty, office hours, staff development for teachers, and other workload issues. Some have recommended that labor–management issues be kept flexible since many of these issues are difficult to anticipate. However, faculty issues should be resolved early on in order to avoid critical problems later. Once again, the concept of integration is important. Integrating distance education faculty policy with traditional labor–management policy seems most often to be the best strategy.

Compensation and Support. An issue that has been ongoing since the onset of distance education is related to faculty compensation. In many institutions, the expanse of distance education has not been recognized as additional work, but rather something that can easily be assumed within existing instructional expectations. Thus, faculty are often not given appropriate compensation for the workload associated with teaching a course at a distance. This needs to be recognized and, where appropriate, faculty need to negotiate ways of being recognized for the additional work responsibilities. This compensation can be in the form of additional pay, release from other responsibilities such as committee work, or reduced class sizes (Wolcott & Shattuck, 2007).

Support is an additional issue that needs to be addressed. Instructors teaching at a distance not only have to deal with delivery of content, but have to consider the technologies involved in that process. Their expertise in the use of technology may not be sufficient to capitalize on the nuances of the resources. By providing technical support, faculty can gain the comfort level necessary to use the technologies as appropriate to expand learning opportunities. And technical support is essential for the distant student as well. Instructors need the assurance that students will have a resource that will help them when encountering technical difficulties in accessing instructional materials or resources.

Another support issue is access to resources. Faculty need assurance that students will have access to the appropriate resources necessary for their learning. Library resources have been changing with the advent of online technologies, thus providing students at a distance with the types of materials they might need. The instructor needs the assurance that these types of support structures exist within the institution when planning the learning activities within a course.

Qualifications. The qualifications of a distant instructor are not always articulated. Each institution needs to create guidelines for instructional practice or experience essential for quality teaching at a distance. First-time distant instructors can be highly successful, whereas others who have taught for many years in the traditional classroom may be unable to adapt to a distant learning environment. Key to a quality instruction is a teacher who demonstrates flexibility and creativity.

One additional benefit of teaching at a distance is that the instructor often translates the experience into face-to-face classrooms. The result is a better traditional class experience for students. Someone who has taught at a distance often understands the needs of students better and is able to bring that appreciation into the classroom setting.

One thing that an institution can do to help faculty become better distance instructors is to provide them with training in effective instructional practice and the technology resources to be used. Faculty who have taken advantage of this resource have found their experience with teaching at a distance to be both positive and successful. They have been concerned with the time issues related to the extra work associated with distance instruction, so any help with time management within the training is essential.

Intellectual Freedom and Ownership/Property Rights

In the realm of intellectual freedom, many issues come to bear. Copyright ownership is often in dispute if there is not a clear agreement between the faculty and the institution sponsoring the distance class. Faculty who invest time into the design and development of distance coursework may be compensated for their work by the institution. When this occurs, the perception is that the organization is the owner of the content and the coursework.

Faculty who are not compensated for their efforts in designing courses may find it appropriate to consider the ownership of the course to be theirs. Again, it is important to clarify the position of the institution regarding the ownership of any of the materials designed for the course.

Course Integrity

The veracity of any course is contingent on the quality of the design and the format for implementation. Faculty who design courses need to have qualifications in the content area. It helps to have experience with teaching at a distance; however, such experience is not as important as some other issues that need to be considered.

Accreditation.   Faculty who teach at a distance need to be aware of how a particular course fits into the structure of a program of study for students. Official courses through an institution should address the standards for programs of study. Students need to know that when taking a course, they are enrolled in coursework that will match their personal and academic goals.

Curriculum and Standards.   One way to ensure quality in the coursework offered within a program of study is to ensure that the standards or critical criteria are being met (Herring & Smaldino, 2001).

Expectations are clarified for students when the curriculum has included the appropriate standards. Further, assessments are often easier to design and implement when the curriculum is aligned to standards.

Individual courses can also address the standards that may be critical for particular professional or academic areas. Although not necessarily a part of a whole program of study, courses aligned to standards often match with whole curricular areas within a field of study.

Course Rigor.   An area of concern among institution administrators has been that of the academic rigor or quality. Many administrators have expressed concern that courses taught at a distance do not have the same standard of quality associated with the on-campus courses. Wyatt (2005) found in his study that students reported their perception of the quality of online instruction as it related to regular face-to-face instruction to be more academically demanding. Faculty may be overcompensating for the issue of assuring the institution of the rigor of distance learning experiences by making the courses more difficult or requiring additional work from students. Wyatt also found that students were very satisfied with their academic experience in an online setting.

Calendar and Schedules.   When distance courses are arranged, the issue of scheduling may become a factor. When multiple institutions work collaboratively to offer courses or programs across a distance, they must learn to coordinate their calendars. If this is not possible, then the instructor needs to find ways to compensate for the differences in institutional schedules. For example, a group of schools may cooperate in the delivery of a particular course but may have different spring break schedules. When this happens, the students cannot be penalized for these differences. However, with a limited time frame for offering courses, it may be necessary to consider offering independent study activities or providing online experiences that take a block of time to complete.

Another issue that can occur with an institution new to the distance education delivery process is that of ensuring that students meet "in class" for the required number of hours. This concern is often heard regarding online courses. How can the instructor ensure that students have been engaged in the course for the required number of class hours? Although students will complain that they have done more than the usual seat-time of a face-to-face class, the institution may not recognize an asynchronous environment in the same light. Instructors need to consider how they might address this issue.

When conducting an online course, one technical option is *chat*, which is a live dialog among the members of the course. Whereas chat can be fast paced and seem a bit hectic, it is often an easy way to bring groups of people together for engaged dialog. One problem with arranging chats is that people who enroll in online courses may be from a variety of locations, including international locations. Trying to find an acceptable time to meet in a chat location may prove to be very difficult.

Student Support

Students need to know that they are able to function successfully within a course. They must be able to complete the requirements of the course without undue stress. Considerations such as access to resources and services need to be addressed when designing the course.

Access to Resources.   When preparing to work with students at a distance, it is necessary to consider the resources available to students. Resources that should be assessed include:

1. Equipment available for student use (e.g., computers with sufficient memory, scanners, video equipment, cameras, projection devices)
2. Available computer software and resource people to assist students at a distance
3. Communication resources students can access (e.g., e-mail, toll-free phone numbers, fax machines)
4. Library and course resources for homework and outside-of-class work
5. Availability of means for distribution and collection of coursework materials

This information will provide an instructor with the data necessary for creating equal educational opportunities for all students in the distance education setting. It is important for students to feel they all have equal status in the class regardless of where they are located. If this means creating new, different ways of achieving the same tasks, then the instructor must engage in creative endeavors. For example, one instructor liked to begin each class period with a quick quiz to assess student knowledge of basic facts that had been assigned. However, in her television-based distance class, quick quizzes were not practical because of the time needed to send and receive quiz papers. The instructor decided on a timed recitation exercise in which students worked in pairs to check their knowledge of the facts (Macfarlane & Smaldino, 1997). The instructor found this to be such a successful means for checking students that she began to incorporate this technique in other classes, even those offered in traditional settings.

Whereas many of the items previously identified deal with the mechanical side of the resources, course resources also have a human side. The presence of a facilitator in a television-based course is often considered optional, but this person can be important for the success of the distant instruction (Herring & Smaldino, 2001). A facilitator is generally an adult who has been hired by an educational institution to be a local contact for students. Facilitators' roles vary depending on their capabilities. They may be on-site during instruction, they may be available prior to and following transmissions, or they may be responsible for hardware and software performance.

Several issues should be considered when deciding if a facilitator is appropriate. What role will the facilitator have in conducting the class? Can facilitators assist with the teaching and learning process, or are they responsible for noninstructional aspects of the class? Can facilitators team-teach with the instructor, or is their duty to monitor the classroom, pass out papers, proctor exams, or manage online discussions?

No matter what the role of the facilitator, it is important to set up a time for discussion about expectations of each member of the team prior to starting the course, to avoid misunderstandings once the course begins. Further, it is important to share this information about the facilitator's role with students.

Another issue to consider is who will select the facilitators for the distant sites. If the facilitators are to be actively involved in the teaching and learning process, the instructor may wish to have input in the hiring. A good working relationship is essential for a successful distance learning experience.

Finally, the instructor must consider the issue of facilitator evaluation. Should the instructor have a say in the end-of-instruction evaluation of the facilitator? If the facilitator is an integral part of the teaching and learning process, there should be an opportunity for the instructor to identify the contributions of the facilitator.

For online courses, instructors should consider ways to communicate with students prior to the beginning of the course. A letter or e-mail to each participant in the class will help to clarify how a student can access the course and the initial information regarding timelines. Many successful online instructors have found that a simple letter to students with essential information can alleviate many frustrations on the part of the instructor and the students.

In the online setting it is helpful for students to know how to access resources to help them with technical problems. A contact person who is knowledgeable about technical issues can make it easier for the student to acquire the connections needed for the course. Students need to know about issues such as minimum memory requirements for their computers, versions of software necessary, and passwords. The earlier the students are aware of how to access the online environment, the more likely they are to start on time and be successful in their educational experience.

Special Services. There are some times when it is important to know about any special needs of students. Students are not required to provide this type of information, and in fact, there are stories of successful distance learning experiences where the instructor was unaware of special needs of students. But, instructors should provide comfortable ways in which students can identify their special needs.

In a television-based class, students who have visual or auditory problems can be accommodated; however, the technologies need to be placed in the appropriate locations. The earlier an instructor knows about these needs, the easier it will be to provide them.

In an online setting, students may find it necessary to communicate via e-mail or other electronic means with the instructor. If the instructor has contacted students with a letter, one thing that can be included is information on how to obtain special services. It is the student's responsibility to identify any needs.

Institutional

Within the institution there are policies related to issues of delivery for courses and programs of study. The responsibilities for these policies lay principally with the offices that contract for outreach education. These policies cover a range of topics, from tuition to types of expenses included in the charges. The central issue behind most fiscal, geographic, and governance (FGG) policies is one of ownership—ownership of the course, the student, and the curriculum. *Ownership* is defined in this context as the institution that has ultimate responsibility, and whose decisions are final.

Most of time, the institution offering the unit, course, or program has ownership, but if a student is taking only one course as part of a locally offered diploma, then in most respects the diploma-granting institution is the one responsible. Most often, several policy statements need to be in place that relate to various situations where courses are delivered or received.

Fiscal and Governance.   The key issues in this area deal with tuition rates, special fees, full-time equivalencies, state-mandated regulations related to funding, service area limitations, out-of-district versus in-district relationships, consortia agreements, contracts with collaborating organizations, board oversight, administration cost, and tuition disbursement.

With ownership comes the question of costs. Certainly the institution offering a unit, course, or program has considerable expenses, but so does the receiving site and even the student. In sharing relationships, the hope is that costs will average out over a period of time. In other words, if three institutions enter into a relationship to share courses, and do so uniformly, the costs of offering and receiving courses will be fairly equal for the three schools. Conversely, if one setting does most of the offering of units, courses, or programs, then that institution will have disproportionate expenses. Policies are needed to clarify how to deal with situations such as this.

Other fiscal policies for institutions offering instruction include those related to tuition, network fees, room and equipment expenses, administration of student files and records, and troubleshooting. Schools receiving courses have costs for room maintenance, library and media support, reception equipment, and student support. Technology fees are often levied to support distance education costs. If fees are implemented, policies need to be in place to determine who collects and distributes this money, and how expenditures are monitored.

Finally, agreements to regularly review costs and to share revenues are important. Often it is difficult to anticipate costs, so if agreements can be made in good faith to yearly or quarterly review expenses and income, it is easier to establish working consortia.

Geographic Service Area.   Geographic service areas are also difficult administrative issues. Traditionally, schools had clearly designated areas they served, such as districts, counties, or regions. With electronic distribution of instruction, these boundaries are invisible. Regulations that set particular geographic limits for schools may need to be clarified or altered when distance education programs are started.

Governance is closely related to geography. What school board is responsible for courses delivered at a distance—the receiving or the sending board? Policies need to clarify this issue before problems emerge.

Legal Issues

Copyright.   Copyright presents a complexity of issues within a distance education environment. It is imperative that the instructor and students understand the copyright laws and the institution's policies. The TEACH Act provides guidelines related to the use of multimedia in courses offered at a distance (Dabbagh & Bannan-Ritland, 2005). An institution may have an office that has the responsibility of clearing copyright issues for instructional materials. If there is not a specific office for this purpose, the librarian can provide information related to copyright.

Copyright does not restrict students from using materials for their projects. What is important is that they understand the restrictions related to the use of copyrighted materials. Further, they need to be certain to provide the appropriate credit in recognition of the authorship of the materials.

And, finally, plagiarism is an issue that might need to be addressed within the syllabus. Students need to understand the difference between quotations and paraphrases and the appropriate citations regarding the use of material. Most institutions have a policy regarding plagiarism that can easily be applied to the distance setting.

With copyright, ignorance of the law is not sufficient. The laws are very specific and there are no excuses regarding infractions. It is best to request permission to use materials rather than find oneself in violation of the law.

Technical Policies

Usually, an organization owns the distribution network used for distance education or is responsible for its reliability. If a private-sector business is the provider, then clear expectations must be in place, and all members of a consortium should be part of the relationship. If a public agency such as a state education department or educational organization is the telecommunications service provider, then a very clear chain of command of responsibilities should be in place. Often, telecommunications policies are not the same as other policies related to the distance education enterprise because they are not related to the educational mission of the organizations involved, and often the private or public provider of services mandates them. However, telecommunications procedures should be understood by all involved with managing distance education.

Policies related to student and faculty technical needs, such as the quality of personal computers needed by students who learn at home, should be established. Hardware, software, and connectivity minimum requirements should be clearly explained.

Reliability of Resources. Certainly for those resources provided by the institution, there needs to be access to reliable technology. If necessary, arrangements need to be made in advance to assure that the technology will be appropriate and available at the beginning of the course.

Students who provide their own technology, such as in an online course, need to understand where the responsibility of the institution lies regarding reliability. It may be that the student will be held accountable for acquiring additional hardware or software at personal expense. Policies need to be articulated so that all parties are clear about responsibilities.

Technology Requirements. Instructors must be clear about their requirements for delivering distance courses. If they have particular technology needs, they need to identify those requirements prior to the beginning of the course. Also, instructors should be reasonable and specific in their requests. And just because a certain technology resource is available does not mean that it has to be implemented. Sometimes the use of certain technology resources can inhibit the quality of instruction. Choose carefully.

It is when the technology expectations are dependent upon individual resources (e.g., an online course), that complications arise. Students need to understand the expectations for the types of hardware and software resources they will need to supply. For example, in an online course that uses streaming video, it may be necessary for students to acquire additional memory for their computers. Versions of software can also be important variables that require student access. Communication with students prior to beginning the course is valuable to ensure they can prepare their technology for the learning experiences.

A LOOK AT BEST PRACTICE ISSUES

Intellectual Property

Carol Twigg, Executive Director of the Center for Academic Transformation, has written and spoken extensively in the area of intellectual property and ownership of online courses and course materials. A reading of the abstract of her excellent monograph "Intellectual Property Policies for a New Learning Environment" is a requirement for any serious distance educator (Twigg, 2000). It is well written, informative, and thought provoking.

Reading Twigg's monograph got me to thinking about the two words *intellectual* and *property*. *Intellectual* has a number of definitions, but most deal with the idea of the use of the intellect, and the showing or possessing of intelligence. *Intellect*, by the way, is the power of knowing and understanding.

Property, on the other hand, refers to things that are owned or possessed. Usually *property* means things like land or objects that a person legally owns.

So, intellectual property is "intelligence that is legally owned." Or, is it? Wikipedia defines intellectual property (IP) as

> a legal entitlement which sometimes attaches to the *expressed form* of an *idea*, or to some other *intangible* subject matter. This legal entitlement generally enables its holder to exercise *exclusive rights* of use in relation to the subject matter of the IP. The term *intellectual property* reflects the idea that this subject matter is the product of the *mind* or the intellect, and that IP rights may be protected at law in the same way as any other form of *property*.

Somehow, the Wikipedia definition seems different than what is meant when the two words are defined separately.

Twigg writes eloquently about course and course materials ownership, and draws several conclusions. Of the most interesting is the statement that "there is a radically different—and infinitely simpler—solution if we treat the intellectual property issue not as a legal issue but as an academic issue" (2000, p. 29). The question of ownership becomes less contentious and more collegial when the rights of faculty and institutions are satisfied equally.

TEACHING AND DISTANCE EDUCATION—THE TIME COMMITMENT

Time, specifically the saving of time, may be one of the most significant contributions of distance learning to formal education. College students save time when they do not have to drive to campus. High schoolers save time when they access resources in class online and do not have to walk to the media center. Doctors save time when they interview distant specialists about an illness, and sales staff save time when they learn about new products on the sales floor rather than in the training room.

Most who study distance education are beginning to document the potential and real savings in time for distant learners but what about teachers and trainers? The conventional wisdom is that teaching at a distance takes more time than conventional teaching or training, but other than anecdotal reports, where is the evidence to support this "wisdom"?

For example, let's talk about the college course. According to the century-old standard of the course unit, sometimes called the Carnegie Unit, a one-credit course should have 750 minutes of instruction by a teacher to students in a classroom. This equates to 15 50-minute classes. A three-semester class would have 2,250 minutes of classroom instruction, or 45 50-minute classes often scheduled over a 15-week semester—3 classes each week for 15 weeks. Typically, a student would be expected to spend two hours outside of class for every hour in the classroom—time spent studying or completing assignments.

What about instructors? Well, if students are in the classroom for 45 50-minute sessions, the instructor probably is also. And most agree that for every hour the college professor or teacher is in class she or he probably needs to spend two hours preparing and grading—so teacher and student time required to complete a typical college course is roughly equivalent.

Obviously, in a distance-delivered course, instructors do not attend class—there often is no class, especially in an asynchronous course. Thus, instructor time can be reallocated from presenting to preparing, from lecturing to posting, and from explaining to interacting.

Therefore, the typical teacher in a typical college class should expect to allocate about 8 hours per week during a 15-week semester. Training organizations do not have semesters, so thought must be given to the amount of time an employee spends in online activities and during study and development (Orellana, Hudgins, & Simonson, 2009).

SUMMARY

Distance education may be as new to the students as it is to the instructor. Preparing students for instruction is important in any teaching mode to maximize learning from class participation. But it is especially important to prepare students for settings where class participants are separated across distances. Students need to understand their responsibility to ensure a successful learning experience.

Teaching at a distance is a challenge. The instructor needs to be creative and imaginative in the design and structure of the course. One rule of thumb is that successful interactive learning experiences that work in a traditional classroom may be adaptable to the distant learning environment. But they will require more than just some changes to the visuals or the handouts. They will likely require inventiveness and innovation.

Teaching at a distance can be a pleasurable experience for everyone involved, instructor and student alike. Keeping it interesting, and motivating the learners to remain active, can make it a valuable learning experience as well as fun.

DISCUSSION QUESTIONS

1. What are some of the organizational factors that a teacher must consider when preparing to teach at a distance?
2. What strategies might be used to facilitate introductions among students?
3. What elements of class structure need to be included when preparing to teach at a distance?
4. Why is it necessary to determine resources available at distant sites when preparing to teach at a distance?
5. What factors need to be considered when deciding to use a facilitator at a distant site?
6. How is the teacher's role affected in a distance education environment?

CASE STUDIES

1. Carol Johnson wishes to begin teaching her high school algebra at a distance. Her students have no experience taking courses with distance education. What technology resources should Carol investigate? What are some of the decisions she needs to make when planning to teach her course? What organizational factors does Carol need to consider when preparing to teach this course at a distance?
2. Tim Wallace will be teaching his philosophy course using the video-conferencing system at the regional community college. His course will involve three sites, which are quite a distance apart geographically. He has been teaching the same course on campus for several years and wants to ensure that his students at a distance will engage in discussions and work together on group projects. What can Tim do to facilitate student collaboration? What strategies might he incorporate to help his students work together?
3. Bill Cunningham has been teaching Introduction to Literature and incorporates a very directive style of teaching. After 15 years of face-to-face teaching, Bill has been informed that his course will be offered online. What does Bill need to consider when moving his course online? How will his teaching style need to be altered to address the new format? What issues does Bill need to consider as he moves his course online? What resources does he need to identify in advance?

REFERENCES

Barr, R. B., & Tagg, J. (1995). From teaching to learning: A new paradigm for undergraduate education. *Change, 27*(6), 13–25.

Conrad, R., & Donaldson, A. (2004). *Engaging the online learner: Activities and resources for creative instruction.* San Francisco: Jossey-Bass.

Dabbagh, N., & Bannan-Ritland, B. (2005). *Online learning: Concepts, strategies, and application.* Columbus, OH: Merrill/Prentice Hall.

Dobbs, R., Waid, C., & del Carmen, A. (2009). Students' perceptions of online courses: The effect of online course experience. *Quarterly Review of Distance Education, 10*(1), 9–26.

Herring, M., & Smaldino, S. (2001). *Planning for interactive distance education: A handbook* (2nd ed.). Bloomington, IN: AECT Publications.

Kidney, G., Cummings, L., & Boehm, A. (2007). Toward a quality assurance approach to e-learning courses. *International Journal on E-Learning, 6*, 17–30.

Kiliç-Çakmak, E., Karatas, S., & Ocak, M. (2009). An analysis of factors affecting community college students' expectations on e-learning. *Quarterly Review of Distance Education, 10*(4), 351–361.

Knowles, M. (1980). *The modern practice of adult education: From pedagogy to andragogy* (2nd ed.). New York: Association Press.

Luppicini, R. (2007). *Online learning communities.* Charlotte, NC: Information Age Publishing.

Macfarlane, C., & Smaldino, S. (1997). The electronic classroom at a distance. In R. Rittenhouse & D. Spillers (Eds.), *Modernizing the curriculum: The electronic classroom* (pp. 171–195). Springfield, MO: Charles Thomas.

Miller, C. (2007). Enhancing Web-based instruction using a person-centered model of instruction. *The Quarterly Review of Distance Education, 8*, 25–34.

Moreland, P., & Saleh, H. (2007). Distance education: Faculty concerns and sound solutions. *Distance Learning: For Educators, Trainers, and Leaders, 4*(1), 53–59.

Oblinger, D. G. (1999). Hype, hierarchy, and higher education. *Business Officer, 33*(44), 22–24, 27–31.

Orellana, A., Hudgins, T., & Simonson, M. (2009). *The perfect online course: Best practices for designing and teaching.* Charlotte, NC: Information Age Publishing.

Palloff, R., & Pratt, K. (2007). *Building learning communities in cyberspace: Effective strategies for the online classroom* (2nd ed.). San Francisco: Jossey-Bass.

Saltzberg, S., & Polyson, S. (1995). Distributed learning on the World Wide Web. *Syllabus, 9*(1), 10–12.

Simonson, M. (2004). Coal slurry ponds and quality indicators. *Distance Learning: For Educators, Trainers, and Leaders, 1*(2), 50.

Simonson, M. (2007). Institutional policy issues. In M. Moore (Ed.), *Handbook of distance education* (2nd ed.). Mahwah, NJ: Erlbaum.

Smaldino, S., Lowther, D., & Russell, J. (2011). *Instructional technologies and media for learning* (10th ed.). Columbus, OH: Merrill/Prentice Hall.

Sorensen, C., & Baylen, D. (2004). Learning online: Adapting the seven principles of good practice to a web-based instructional environment. *Distance Learning: A Magazine for Leaders, 1*(1), 7–17.

Twigg, C. (2000). *Intellectual property policies for new learning environments.* Retrieved June 3, 2010, from www.center.rpi.edu/pewsym/mono2.html.

Westbrook, V. (2006). The virtual learning future. *Teaching in Higher Education, 11*, 471–482.

Wolcott, L., & Shattuck, K. (2007). Faculty participation. In M. Moore (Ed.), *Handbook of distance education* (2nd ed.) (pp. 391–402). Mahwah, NJ: Erlbaum.

Wyatt, G. (2005). Satisfaction, academic rigor, and interaction: Perceptions of online instruction. *Education, 125*, 460–468.

CHAPTER 7

The Student and Distance Education

CHAPTER GOAL

The purpose of this chapter is to describe the characteristics and responsibilities of the distant learner.

CHAPTER OBJECTIVES

After reading and reviewing this chapter, you should be able to

1. Identify characteristics of the distant student.
2. Explain responsibilities of the learner for ensuring student participation.
3. Describe the factors that are important for student success.
4. Describe the responsibilities of the student in a synchronous/asynchronous class.

 AN EMPHASIS ON THE STUDENT

Often in a distance learning situation, much emphasis is placed on the technology, ensuring the operations end of the process. The audience, or the distant learner, is often considered after the planning and organizing of the hardware, the content, and the instructional plan. But it is the learner who is the crucial member of the distance learning system. It is the learner who needs to be considered early in the planning and implementation of a distance learning experience. The more an instructor understands the members of the audience, the better the distance learning experience will be for all involved (Moore & Kearsley, 2005).

The distance learner can be of any age, have attained any educational level, and have a variety of educational needs. One pervasive characteristic of the distance learner is an increased commitment to learning. For the most part, these learners are self-starters and appear to be highly motivated. Distance learners live in a variety of areas, from rural to metropolitan sites located sufficiently away from where a class is traditionally offered. The students' educational needs are usually specific and may represent low-incidence content subjects (e.g., learning a foreign language or technical content knowledge). Further impetus for distance learning can result from limited statewide resources (e.g., a specialized teacher training program) that must be shared across diverse geographical regions.

One can conclude, after examining the various tools and approaches for distance learning, that there is one primary purpose: to provide a valuable learning experience to students who might not otherwise have access to learning. Dede (1990) suggests that distance education can be useful to the academic institution in a number of ways. One way is to bring together a group of students from various locations to create a class of sufficient size to ensure its economic viability. Offering courses at a distance can also provide a limited resource to students in a low incidence topic of study. Simply stated, there are a number of reasons to bring learners together at a distance. And, because of this idea of bringing together students and resources from an array of different locations to address a common need, it may be necessary to find ways to encourage these students to appreciate the value of a distance learning setting. They will need to be motivated to participate and to engage in the types of learning experiences in which they may have little experience.

It is equally important to understand the intent of those learners when planning the process for delivery. In any instructional situation, it is important for the instructor to know as much as possible about the students in the class. Knowing the students in a class provides the instructor with an understanding of how to best approach instruction to ensure an optimal learning experience for all. In a distance learning setting, the instructor must learn about students at all the sites if working in an audio or video setting. In an online setting, it is even more challenging to get to know the students. Knowledge of students can assist the distance educator in overcoming separation of teacher and student and can ensure that the learning experience will be positive for all (Bergmann & Raleigh, 1998). It will also facilitate the design by the instructor to optimize the learning experience.

To begin, the instructor needs to acquire some basic information about the class as a whole. In a synchronously timed delivery course, knowing the number of sites and the number of students at each site gives the teacher the "big picture." Equally important is information about subgroups such as urban or rural students, as well as students from various cultural or social backgrounds represented within the class. Economics also plays a part in the nature of the class. Together, these factors provide the instructor with an overview of the class, which then can lead to learning about individuals in the class. Even in an asynchronous delivery mode, knowledge of the members of the class, even though they do not meet together, is crucial to design and delivery.

Each member of a class is an individual, although each individual may belong to one of the subgroups mentioned earlier. Each individual has a cultural identity, as well as a socioeconomic "standing" in the community. However, each individual is unique and needs to be recognized for those unique characteristics. When the individual is

Students of all ages benefit from distance education.

considered, characteristics such as attitude or interest, prior experiences, cognitive abilities, and learning styles will all have an impact. Taking the time to learn about the individual will enhance the learning experience for that individual and for the class as a whole.

TRAITS OF THE DISTANT LEARNER

Students of all ages are engaging in distance education. As more technology resources are becoming available to educational settings, more students are becoming involved in learning at a distance. There are similarities among the learners, but differences do exist and those differences need to be addressed when planning instruction.

Adult Learners

Although there are some who would suggest little difference among the distance learners, adults bring a unique characteristic to a distance learning setting. Theirs is a world of experiences related to learning, life, and their profession. To believe that adults bring little to the "classroom" is limiting the contributions that adult learners can make to any learning situation.

Further, as Benson (2004) would suggest, there are differences among the adult learners in an educational setting. She refers to two categories of what she calls busy adults: "white-collar" and "blue-collar" workers. She further defines the two types of adult learners in terms of their ease of access to distance learning situations. For the white-collar workers, Benson proposes that access is easier and more flexible. For the blue-collar workers, she states that access to distance learning is more complicated, both by work schedules and by limited access to the resources necessary to participate in distance learning. Although this difference is abating a bit, it is still an essential issue to address. Benson advocates that an instructor needs to be cognizant of these factors when designing distant learning experiences.

Sullivan (2001) further suggests that inasmuch as there is little difference between adult males and females, there is one area in which the difference is noteworthy. He maintains that both genders identify flexibility, academic achievement, and opportunity for shy students to participate as important reasons for their decisions to enroll in distance education classes and programs. He does note that both genders identify self-discipline and self-pacing as important characteristics, although more females than males suggest that this quality is essential. But, it is in the area of family and children where a significant difference in gender appeared in his study. More women mentioned family and children as a primary reason for selecting a distance education setting over a face-to-face setting. He suggests from this that the nontraditional female college student often is juggling work, school, and family responsibilities. The opportunity to study at a distance makes it possible for members of this group to accomplish their academic goals.

A standard assumption is that adults are more interested in participating in a distance learning situation because of their motivation to apply learning to their work (Moore & Kearsley, 2005). And although this is prevalent in most distance learning situations, it is still necessary to consider how to motivate adults to stay active in learning (Conrad & Donaldson, 2004). In addition, most adult learners are self-starters and thus require little to get them interested in the course of study, but their focus seems to be on only getting what they need from the learning situation. They have little patience for irrelevant information or activities that do not lead them to their intended outcomes.

P12 Learners

The younger learners, those in P12 settings, provide an even more interesting challenge to a distance education instructor. Young people are not necessarily involved in a distant class by choice. They are often seeking a particular course of study, but do not have ready access to a face-to-face class in their current location. Thus, they are often put into distance learning situations without consideration of their motivation or self-reliance as a learner.

Further, younger learners bring to the learning setting a wealth of literacy related to "information navigation" described by Brown (2000). Students of all ages have more in-class experiences with using the Internet for seeking information. They are more facile at moving about in online situations. They are less likely to be patient with instructional settings where they are not motivated or engaged.

It is more likely to find greater diversity among younger learners (Dabbagh & Bannan-Ritland, 2005) and it is more probable to find students from a variety of locations participating in an online class. With the advent of the virtual high school, groups of students from around the world can be brought together into one class. This shift in the nature of the younger distance student presents unique instructional design requirements for the instructor.

The digital divide identified by Benson (2004) in the adult population has a similar characteristic among the P12 population. As this is becoming less of an issue for younger students, access to resources outside a school building may be limited. To require students to participate in an educational experience beyond the normal school day may put undue burden on those students to locate easy access to resources. It is essential that an instructor understand individual access issues within the distance learning group when preparing assignments and out-of-class expectations.

FACTORS INFLUENCING LEARNER SUCCESS

A number of factors affect the way in which students approach learning at a distance. Their learning success is dependent on not only understanding those factors but also addressing them as part of the instructional delivery.

Attitude Factors

Much of what educators know about a classroom applies to a distance learning setting. The student brings to the classroom setting, whether face-to-face or virtual, a set of characteristics that can influence the success of the instructional plan. Many variables come to play in this situation—factors that can be addressed by the instructor when planning the learning experiences.

Classroom Culture at a Distance.   Palloff and Pratt (2007) have devoted much of their scholarship on the development of "learning communities." They advocate that without establishing a community of learners in a distance setting, the potential for success is limited. Palloff and Pratt present a strong argument for taking the time to create a classroom culture that promotes shared learning experiences and team-work. They suggest that the responsibility for creating this culture in the classroom is the responsibility of all participants, not just the instructor. They feel it is essential to take the time to create the opportunities for social interactions. Palloff and Pratt provide evidence that this time is well spent in the learning rewards identified by the participants.

Although many distance students are cited as being independent learners, they derive value from collaborative learning experiences (Dabbagh & Bannan-Ritland, 2005). The presence of other learners can benefit from the learning experiences of all members of the class by providing social and information interactions. By collabo-rating, all students expand their knowledge, skills, and ability to self-assess their own progress. Working together creates a richer learning experience for the individual participant.

Kanuka, Rourke, and Laflamme (2007) suggest that engaging the learner requires instruction that is well structured, with clear responsibilities for students, and that provokes students to join in deeper levels of discussion. In looking at student interac-tions in several types of active-learning instructional strategies, they found that students who were involved in debates or WebQuests were more likely to be challenged by the learning activity and more likely to evidence higher levels of collaboration or contributions to discussions. The other instructional strategies they identified—nominal group, invited expert, and reflective deliberation—did not seem to elicit the same levels of engaged involvement as did the other two strategies.

Etiquette.   More than ever, it is essential that students understand the complexity of the distance education setting in order to be certain to participate in an appropriate manner. With the introduction of a more diverse population, students must become sensitive to all members of the class. It is the responsibility of the instructor to establish the protocols for communications within the course. Students can be held accountable for their actions only if they know what is expected of them. Such things as humor and grammar need to be addressed early in the course. The tone of responses means that it is important for members of the class to refrain from using inappropriate or unacceptable language. This is general courtesy among students, but it is particularly important when these types of responses become archived, as might happen in an asynchronous online setting. The syllabus can become an important communication vehicle for the instructor in clarifying expectations related to appropriate use of language in all communications.

Humor is one of those communication aspects that creates the largest challenge. When in a face-to-face setting, humor can often be the "icebreaker" that opens avenues of conversation, but it frequently falls flat in a distant setting. Without all the cues associated with humor—inflection, facial and bodily gestures—the joke is often "lost." Even using such little devices as the emoticons used in text-based communications—such as :-) or :- (—humor can often go astray. If students wish to use humor, they might begin by stating something to alert others as to the intent, for example, "A NOTE OF HUMOR."

It may become necessary to take a student "aside" and have a private communication related to inappropriate use of language or humor. When working with the variety of students who are enrolled in a distance setting, the instructor needs to be aware of any sensitivities and considerations as early as possible to ensure there is a perception of respect for all participants.

Experience

As has already been mentioned, students today bring an array of experiences to the classroom, even those at a distance. Some have prior experience with distance learning; others have had experience with random Internet explorations, and still others may have not had any distance learning experiences at all in any mode, audio, video, or online. Knowing about the backgrounds of students is essential for a successful distance learning situation.

Learning Experiences.   All students bring to a class experience with learning. Especially with adults, it is important to consider how these prior experiences will impact the current learning situation. By knowing more about the learners (i.e., their background knowledge, their interests, their goals), it will be possible to design instruction to facilitate successful learning.

Further, if the intent is to facilitate collaborative learning experiences, knowing about prior experience with this type of learning situation is essential. Adult learners who are unfamiliar with the benefit of working with others may not perceive it as a valuable part of their learning. Often, adult learners find working in groups to be unproductive from their perspective and might express concern that they are expected to work with others who may not be nearby. This attitude can create difficulty for the other learners and the instructor if not clearly articulated at the onset of the course. It might be of benefit to scaffold the collaborative learning experiences for these types of students, starting with less involved collaborative interactions before forging into full-blown group projects (Bergman & Raleigh, 1998). For example, in an online course putting students into a group of collaborative learners to do an activity that is not academic in nature will help the students build their confidence in the group collaborative experience. In other words, an activity, such as one that asks the students to design a new computer input interface (e.g., a better keyboard), will provide them with the collaborative experience without having to impinge on each student's personal goal of academic success.

Finally, the experience brought to the class in terms of technologies used is of importance. Some students may have experience with Web-based searching, but little with an actual complete course offered in the Web environment. The syllabus may be a valuable communication tool to define necessary skills and to identify where to obtain those skills. It may be useful to arrange an optional class in which students are oriented to the resource tools necessary for success in the class. This orientation to the technology tools can supply those who are unfamiliar with the technologies the necessary skills to ensure their success in the class (Bergmann & Raleigh, 1998).

Distance Learning Experiences.   Many students bring to the classroom informal learning experiences using the Internet (Daggabh & Bannon-Ritland, 2005). Their explorations of the Web for personal gain have grown significantly over the past few years. This informal type of experience may be of value in a distance learning situation, but the instructor needs to determine how to guide the learners to build on their exploration experiences, channeling them into more structured learning situations.

Students who experience a distance learning situation for the first time may indicate to the teacher a discomfort with the learning situation. Others students may not be participating as willing members of the class. For some, learning at a distance may be an undue burden. All of this must be known when preparing for instruction. And, it may be necessary to take time to establish vehicles for communication that allow students to share their concerns, and their questions might prove to be a valuable initial step in easing non-experienced students into a distance setting.

An indicator of preference by students is prior experience (Bozik, 1996; Smith & Dunn, 1991). Students reported that once they took a distance course, they were willing to enroll in additional classes. Students felt satisfied with the quality of their learning experience, and the convenience factors reinforced their participation. These same students also indicated they would, if necessary, drive to a centralized campus to attend classes; however, this was not their preference. They wanted to continue as distance students. An effective educator who utilizes technological tools in a nonintrusive manner can allay these fears and encourage students to take advantage of a unique and dynamic learning experience. But this takes time and patience on the part of the instructor. It also assumes much in the way of the student's responsibility to grow and adapt personal learning characteristics to distance learning situations.

Readiness for Learning at a Distance. Students who are new to distance learning sometimes express concern about their ability to complete the perceived amount of work required to be successful (Dobbs, Waid, & del Carmen, 2009). Students who have not taken a distance learning course, synchronous or asynchronous, need guidance as to what they are expected to do within the activities, using the technology, how to efficiently and effectively communicate with peers and with the instructor, and how to demonstrate their knowledge. It is the responsibility of the instructor, when designing the course, to be certain that there are hints and suggestions, clearly articulated expectations, and information presented in multiple locations for easy access. It helps students by creating redundancy in the presentation of information (e.g., providing the course schedule in the syllabus, displaying an online calendar, and providing weekly reminders of things that will be happening within a two-week block of time). Although this presents more work for the instructor, the success of the first-time learner will be evident. And, when learners have successful experiences with learning at a distance, they will take additional courses. As they become more familiar with the tools and resources not only will these students require less support, they will also provide help for their classmates.

Elements for Success

To ensure that students in a distance setting are successful, it is important to consider those elements that can serve as indicators for achievement.

General Ability. To be successful it is important that students are in the correct educational setting. Another indicator of success is cognitive abilities (Smith & Dunn, 1991). Students of average or high ability at distance sites have demonstrated achievement at levels similar to or better than those of students in origination sites. In fact, this is true of students in distance education classes as a whole compared with students in traditional classrooms. This is not to suggest that students in distance classes are smarter, but capable students tend to succeed in distance learning situations. Students at a distance seem to assume more responsibility for their own learning earlier in the process than do those students who are enrolled in traditional classes.

Many authors have indicated the need to assume responsibility for learning by the student (Dabbagh & Bannan-Ritland, 2005; Moore & Kearsley, 1996; Smith & Dunn, 1991; Tuckman & Schouwenburg, 2003). Students need to have the ability to understand their tasks in learning. Palloff and Pratt (2007) suggest that the instructor's role is that of facilitator, which implies that the student must assume responsibility for learning. Since this is not different than what is currently being advocated in the face-to-face setting, there is a complexity of responsibility on the part of the instructor to ensure that learners have a clear understanding of expectations and opportunities for participation.

Prior Knowledge.   When an instructor accounts for the background and prior knowledge of students, the learning setting is more successful. Students of all ages come to the educational setting with some knowledge and skills in topics and areas related to the topic of study. To prevent boredom or frustration for students, it is essential that the instructor have an understanding of what students know and how that relates to the intended instruction.

Sometimes an instructor has high expectations of prior students' knowledge that can lead to difficulty in the learning setting. Often, because of the nature of distance education, students enter into classes with varied learning experiences. It is inappropriate to assume that all students have equal prior learning. A pretest of knowledge or a survey of content covered might be a way of gaining information about what students know to date. Another way of gaining this information would be to contact the educational agency or instructor who worked with the students prior to the course being planned. Whatever the means of learning about students' prior knowledge, it is clear that this is an important step in preparing a quality learning experience.

Learning Styles.   Finally, one more indicator of successful learning at a distance is learning styles. For some students, the unique characteristics of distance learning tools facilitate better instruction than educational tools generally used in a traditional classroom. For example, in a distance classroom the instructor should place greater emphasis on providing visual cues, whether the technology is synchronous (such as audio only or audio/video) or asynchronous (such as a complete Web-based course). When the instructor provides more visual cues, the visual learner may perform better in a distance education class. Auditory learners can focus on the instructor's words and generally listen better because there are fewer distractions, especially at sites with only one student. With the addition of newer technologies, audio streaming is an option open to an auditory learner in Web-based environments—as long as students have access to those technologies. Students who display a reluctance to speak out or join discussions during class can find their "niche" by utilizing text-based communications through computer conferencing or completing written assignments (Dabbagh & Bannan-Ritland, 2005).

All of this speaks to the need for the instructor to understand the characteristics of the members of the class. The more the distance education teacher knows about the individual student within the whole class, the more elegant the application of education tools to the learning situation. The instructor can learn about members of the class in a number of ways. Contacting instructors who have taught students previously is one way of getting information. This works particularly well if a cohort group is moving through an extensive program of studies. As always, caution must be exercised when providing information about previous students in order not to pass on confidential information or to prejudice the instructor. Another way of getting information is simply to ask students directly about their own sense of what works for them. Students often know what works best for them and will openly express their needs.

A survey or similar type of information-gathering device could be distributed to the students before the start of the class. This provides the instructor with information that might not be available through school records or other teachers. An additional way to get to know students is to create class-time opportunities for getting to know them (Conrad & Donaldson, 2004). Not only does this provide additional information to the teacher but it also gives the students a chance to get to know the other members of the class. For example, Macfarlane (Macfarlane & Smaldino, 1997) had four or five students bring a "me bag" to her television-based class. Following her example, students shared photos, examples of hobbies, and objects portraying various interests (e.g., a recently read book). Each student spent approximately 5 minutes doing this activity. In addition to learning more about each other, the students utilized classroom technology (e.g., document camera) to share the contents of their "bags." The outcome of this activity resulted in the class as a whole developing a strong sense of support for one another in the learning process. Finally, if possible, an instructor can meet students in person at an optional meeting before class begins or at a conference where the students will be participating. If not possible, private phone conversations and electronic mail are alternatives to spending individual time with students.

In an online setting, whether using synchronous or asynchronous technologies, there is a similar need to have students share information about themselves. Some of the same strategies used in an audio or video setting work as effectively in the online situation. Adaptations of these activities can serve well to provide students who may otherwise not see or hear each other learn more about classmates.

In essence, what is crucial is to become familiar with the students in the class and to address their needs as they have identified them. Further, by putting time into this type of discovery of information, the instructor will find that the class will function more as a unit than it otherwise would have. This makes it easier to engage learners in the activities and in the learning outcomes designed into the class structure.

LEARNER RESPONSIBILITIES

Just as the instructor must take responsibility for learning about students, learners in the distance education classroom must assume ownership in their learning experiences (Macfarlane & Smaldino, 1997). The type of distance instructional setting will dictate the kinds of student responsibilities. Students will need to know how to respond in a synchronous class or to post responses in the correct forum, ask questions, or make presentations as the result of assignments; therefore, it is imperative that distant students learn to use the tools available in the distant classroom.

Audio and Video-Based Settings

Usually a synchronous class allows for two-way transmission via audio. Thus, the first tool any student will need to learn to use is the technology being used to relay verbal responses to the teacher and other students in the class as a whole. A few comments about appropriate audio protocol are essential to managing this technology. In general, whoever speaks first "controls the airwaves." That is, no one else can make a comment that will be heard by the entire class until the first speaker has stopped talking. Thus, students need to remember to limit their remarks so that others may also contribute to the discussion. Background noise can also interfere with the audio exchange. When background noise becomes a factor, there may be little that can be done if the instructor or student has no control over the source of the noise.

Student roles change when they learn from distant instructors, but the advantages of being able to enroll in classes in otherwise unavailable topics, such as biology outweigh problems.

Even though voices are distinct, students must learn to identify themselves by name and site (e.g., "This is Bob at Mason City") when they start to speak to ask a question or make a comment. Eventually, most participants in the class will learn to recognize individual voices; however, the initial courtesy is necessary and should continue in order to avoid confusion and enhance recognition. One unique difficulty often occurs with learners in the origination-site classroom where they can see and hear the instructor without the need for audio or visual transmission: When they need to ask a question or make a comment, they often forget to use the audio equipment so classmates at distance sites can also hear. In fairness to other students, learners in the origination classroom must remember to use the technology and to identify themselves if that is the given protocol of the class.

Other equipment, such as document cameras, video players, and fax machines may be used by students in video-based classrooms. Despite the sophistication of some technology found in a distance classroom, the instructor or a trained technician, even at a distance, can talk most students through operating instructions. Early exposure to the technology being used (e.g., during student personal introductions) and modeling by the instructor can reduce anxiety and alleviate problems later on when students must use the equipment to present information as part of an assignment.

Online Settings

In an online setting, the students need to understand the nuances of the various types of resources available to them. Many students bring a wealth of experience with e-mail and with Web surfing, but may not have experience with posting to bulletin boards or discussion forums (Bergman & Raleigh, 1998). Also, they may know how to word process a document, but many do not understand how to save it into a format that is readable by all members of the class (e.g., saving in RTF format). The instructor's use of the Web-based course tools, such as the dropbox, assignment feature, or the online chat, may cause students' frustration or confusion as to how to proceed.

The syllabus can provide students with details on how to operate certain types of equipment. It can provide students information about the tools and expectations regarding their use. A technical assistant or the instructor may need to be available to handle specific individual issues related to connectivity and use of equipment and tools. Often a practice experience, without academic consequence, at the beginning of the course will allow students the opportunity to learn to use the tools without worry of a grade issue.

Students are responsible for contacting the instructor when there is difficulty with an assignment or with the technologies. The instructor can anticipate many of the probable issues that might arise, but cannot plan for all of them. Even the most carefully planned class will have situations where an individual learner will need extra assistance. Thus, the instructor is wise to provide multiple means for seeking assistance when technologies are an issue for the students.

Time for Class

With any course of study, there is a "time" for class. Students need to be aware of their responsibility related to distance class time and how to best balance their personal time. It is appropriate for the instructor to provide students with guidance on how to balance their on-task time for class with their other responsibilities.

Synchronous. Synchronous class time is similar to the on-campus, face-to-face arrangement familiar to many students. Students can go to a nearby site for a televised class or sit at home to participate in an audio conference or Web-based video conference. Whatever the type of technology used, what is important to note is that all the members of the class are together at the same time. This presents certain types of instructional opportunities for students.

Although this is desirable for some types of class activities, it can still present a problem when trying to ensure equal access. Students from different time zones may be participating in the class, which may cause unnecessary burden on some to attend the class if it might overlap with other responsibilities (e.g., work or family). The instructor needs to be aware of these issues when planning a class. It might be helpful to use the first half-hour of the scheduled time as "hall or office time," which would allow students who have to travel a distance the chance to get to the site without having to rush. The hall time would be arranged to address questions or to chat informally about recent events.

Asynchronous. In an asynchronous class, the class meeting time is a unique issue. The fact that everyone does not have to be at the class at the same time is one of the advantages of this type of class for very busy people who are unable to rearrange their schedules. It is important that students understand the need to arrange a time within their weekly schedule to "attend" class on a regular basis, however. This might be on a Saturday night, or early on a weekday morning. The time selected is not important. What is important is that students log in to the course and complete the class activities on a regular basis.

There are a number of reasons for this. If the course requires continual input from the students as part of participation in a discussion, then students must be online on a regular basis. If there are assignments, they must be completed in a timely fashion. It is imperative that the instructor make it clear what students are expected to do to complete a course, but it is the student's responsibility to adjust his or her schedule accordingly.

Communication

Connecting with the Instructor.   Distance education includes both learning and teaching. Thus, the involvement of the instructor in the educational process is critical, if changed. It needs to be very clear to the student how to contact the instructor at any point in time through the course of study. The student may need to let the instructor know of a technical or personal issue that delays the submission of an assignment, or perhaps the student will need clarification about an assignment or a comment made by the instructor comment. But it remains the responsibility of the student to make that contact. An instructor can provide information about e-mail and phone contact, with suggestions as to appropriateness for making the contact (e.g., "Please don't call between midnight and 5:00 a.m"). Another means for students to be able to contact the instructor is through a course management tool such as Blackboard or WebCT. Here, the instructor can provide an FAQ section in the discussion area. Students can post questions and the instructor can respond; however, in this format the questions and answers are available for the whole class to read. Sometimes this is a very efficient means for communicating about questions that may arise during the course.

Whatever the means of communication with the instructor, students need to provide sufficient information to the instructor so that it is clear who is making the contact. "A student in your class" may be insufficient to the instructor, especially when he or she may be teaching multiple courses at a distance. Students need to know that it is their responsibility to make the contact.

Also, the instructor needs to be clear as to the timeframe for responses. For example, if you are not going to be available due to travel, let the students know. If you don't want to be interrupted during the weekend, let students know. If you plan to respond quickly, provide a timeline for your response to inquiries (e.g., "I'll reply to your emails within 24 hours" or "I'll respond to your emails within one working day").

Connecting with Other Students.   Students need to have a sense of community within their classes. Group work is common and an excellent way for students who are working in isolated locations to be connected with others in their class. Once a group is formed and an assignment begun, each student needs to communicate with the other group members. Course management tools provide ways to create group collaboration through the system. Students are given access to several ways to connect with their classmates. As with connecting with the instructor, it is the student's responsibility to initiate the communication.

Attendance and Class Participation

As in any instructional setting, class attendance is imperative. However, on occasion, learners may not be able to attend class because of conflicts, illness, or technical difficulties. The instructor needs to be clear about expectations for attendance and participation. It may also be appropriate to provide some guidelines for ways of maintaining participation; for example, in an online class, the instructor might suggest how many times per week a student should log in to the class.

Synchronous.   In an audio or video-based class, when a student is unable to attend, one solution is to record the class and send the copy (video or audio) to the learner who missed class. Although no interaction is possible, at least the learner does not lose out on content. It may be necessary to obtain the permission of all the class participants before making any recordings. It is best to obtain this permission in written form (Macfarlane & Smaldino, 1997).

Class participation, be it in a traditional class or a distance class, always enhances learning for students (Conrad & Donaldson, 2004). The nature of the environment in distance sites has a significant impact on class participation. As mentioned earlier, some students do not like to respond, either because of learning style or perhaps because of intimidation by the technology. Some students may ask fewer questions than in a traditional class. Instructional strategies that encourage all students to provide answers can increase class participation. Teachers have also experimented with alternative answering strategies—for example, strategies such as voting on choices for decisions or activities, building consensus through small group discussions, answering a question privately either through an IM or email or if available, visually showing each individual's answer on the screen.

During discussions, some students may need a brief period to prepare an adequate answer to a question. Advance warning that a question is headed their way can ease discomfort and give the students time to think of an answer. Some learners feel intimidated by technology and are reluctant to respond to the teacher or initiate comments. The instructor needs to engage in strategies early in the course to alleviate this level of nonparticipation.

It is often the case that students at distance sites will talk with each other during class without sharing with the class. In a television-based environment, without a visual check the instructor may not know students are talking, a situation that would not happen in a traditional class or at the origination site. These "sidebar conversations" may occur as a result of a provocative piece of information presented during the class—that is, the content of the class can provoke an "in-house" discussion on the topic. The use of IM during a chat can be another form of sidebar.

Unfortunately, these comments are made to one person or a few others when the whole class might benefit. Students must be encouraged to share valid comments with the entire class. Occasionally, when participants engage in unrelated topics of conversation, others may be distracted by the comments. Out of respect for learners who are concentrating on the presentation or discussion, these conversations, whether task related or not, should not occur. We refer to this as *netiquette*—showing courtesy for the learning needs of others with respect to the technology.

Asynchronous.   In an asynchronous text or graphical-based class, similar types of considerations are related to the students' responsibilities. Although they are not as specific, the directions will require some time. It is important that students' responsibilities be made clear.

In the asynchronous setting, students need to understand their responsibilities related to participation in class discussions. Online forum discussions are valuable only when all members of the group participate. Logging in to the class the night before the final due date for postings is not contributing to the dialog. Occasionally students encounter problems getting to their online classes, but as a rule, reserving a few hours several times a week is sufficient to be able to actively participate in the class discussion. Some instructors suggest to students they treat this class as if they are going to be on campus and "lock" themselves away in a quiet area of home or office to participate in the class. Too many distracters may contribute to poor participation.

Assignments

It is the responsibility of the learner to complete assignments in a timely manner and find an appropriate means to dispatch them to the instructor. Delay in sending them in will result in delays in grading and in receiving feedback. Some instructors use a point penalty approach to discouraging delays in submitting materials. It is essential that the student inform the instructor if there is an issue with submitting an assignment on time.

Dealing with the Factors Affecting Completion of Assignments.   An instructor can anticipate some issues related to completion of assignments. These can be identified in the syllabus or in the course overview at the beginning of the class. What is important is that timelines be clearly set and that students understand how to meet them. One suggestion for the instructor is to provide "advance" warning on due dates in calendars or communications with students. Reminding students of an anticipated due date for an assignment might help them with getting the tasks done on time.

Addressing the Grading Issues.   Students like to receive good grades. Often they work hard to deliver what they believe is the right response to an assigned task. When they do not meet the expectations of the instructor, there is a need to improve the communication processes.

One way of addressing successful completion of the assignment is for the instructor to provide students with complete instructions on what is expected. Providing rubrics, outlines, and samples often helps to eliminate confusion or poorly completed materials.

Further, it is imperative that the instructor consider available resources for students when preparing assignments. If the assignment requires use of a college library, then the instructor needs to be certain that students have reasonable access to the library or that an online version of the resources are accessible. This might mean that dates are extended to allow students travel time to campuses, or that the instructor will allow more online resources than previously extended.

Students need to have a clear understanding of the grading structure and how the assignments fit into that structure. They need to know the balance of expectations so that they can expend the appropriate energies on their tasks. One idea suggested by Herring and Smaldino (2001) is to use a point structure that adds up to 1,000 rather than 100. By "adding a zero" to all the assignments within the point structure, students have the perception that there is value to their contributions. In other words, an activity that would have earned 5 points on a 100-point scale now earns 50 points on a 1,000-point scale. It is amazing the differences in students' attitudes toward completing assignments, even if they understand how the point structure works!

Assuming Responsibility for Own Learning

In any student-centered learning environment, students must assume responsibility for their own learning (Kiliç-Çakmak, Karatas, & Ocak, 2009). It is important that students know the expectations of the instructor and the requirements to complete a course of study. Further, students need guidance and assurance when they are beginning a course of study at a distance, especially if this is their first time to engage in learning at a distance. They must understand the nuances of the amount of time, the manner of communication, and the means for submitting and retrieving materials. They must focus on their own learning and be able to judge whether they need additional assistance and how to proceed to request it. Generally, students are comfortable with technology for social interactions, but they may not be as comfortable with transferring that level of skill and knowledge to learning settings. It is essential in the design of the course that the information is clear to students. It is often wise to post information in multiple ways to ensure that all students have access to it.

Equipment Requirements and Use

Regardless of the distance instructional setting, it is essential that students know how to use the equipment involved. Students might need to seek assistance from a local vendor or neighbor due to distance issues. The instructor can anticipate some issues and make suggestions as to ways of getting help when necessary.

A student who is planning to participate in an online class must be certain that the equipment requirements match what is available to use. If a student wishes to participate in a class that has very specific technical requirements, then those need to be clearly stated. But it is the student's responsibility to inquire if the requirements have not been identified. Also, it is the student's responsibility to obtain the technology required (e.g., extra memory to handle streaming video).

Technical Know-How. For some online classes, students need to know how to use certain software packages (e.g., Blackboard or SPSS), to use specific types of equipment (e.g., scanners), or to follow technical procedures (e.g., uploading a file to a website). The instructor may assume that students have this type of knowledge. The student may be required to attend special workshops or classes just to prepare for this type of class. It is ultimately the student's responsibility to know how to do these things to ensure full participation in a class.

Technical Difficulties.   In any situation where so much technology is involved, problems are bound to occur. When tools do not work, the learner has the responsibility to notify the instructor so that adjustments can be made. Sometimes, a technician can provide information to clear up the problem. At other times, the system manager must be notified to provide assistance. It is the student's responsibility to let the instructor know about problems. If the student does not assume this responsibility, the instructor might continue under the assumption that the student is not participating because of other reasons. Students should not let a technical problem delay their participation in a course—nor should they let it alter their desire to participate.

GENERATIONS OF LEARNERS

Recently, there has been considerable discussion of generations of learning and how they are different with a special emphasis on the current generation of learners, sometimes called the *millennial generation* (Simonson, 2010). A millennial is thought to be a person born between the years 1982 and 2005—the latest generation of learners to enter schools and attend college.

In 2000, Neal Howe and William Strauss published *Millennials Rising: The Next Great Generation* and a new stereotypic phrase was coined—and a new consulting industry was begun. Certainly, the popularity of the stereotype of the millennial makes it almost mandatory that distance educators know something about this group.

Millennials are the current learners in virtual K–12 schools and online college courses, and they will be the employees trained in businesses' e-learning courses. According to Howe and Strauss, millennials are typecast as rule followers who are engaged, optimistic, and pleasant. Howe and Strauss assigned millennials core characteristics using the words sheltered, confident, team-oriented, conventional, pressured, and achieving. Millennials have been prophesized as builders of new institutions that actually work, and as a generation that does not worry about tearing down old institutions. In other words, this latest generation has been characterized as being "almost too good to be real."

Eric Hoover, in a recent article titled "The Millennial Muddle" in the *Chronicle of Higher Education* reviewed the "hype" about the concept of the millennial learner and concluded that if millennial students are a maze, there are specialists that sell maze maps. Consultants who talk about millennial learners offer many insights—many accurate and some fanciful (Hoover, 2009). With that said, learning about students and learners is never a bad idea, and if even a portion of the generalizations about millennials are accurate, then distance educators have a lot to learn.

Certainly there is ample evidence that generations are different. We know of the silent generation, also called the greatest generation, the baby boomer generation, generation X, and now the millennial generation—all different in obvious ways, and similar in others. What may be important to the distance educator is the need to establish a level of understanding about millennial learners so distance-delivered instruction can capitalize on the capabilities of "tech-savvy" millennials and build learning environments that challenge them in relevant ways.

For example, millennials are considered to be multitasking experts—they use their smart phones to text, talk, search, and post. Some from older generations would consider this multitasking as "not paying attention," but perhaps there is a maximum of attentiveness that makes multitasking effective—and probably not just for younger learners.

Millenials are thought to be addicted to social networking services—they post to their friends, they tweet to their twibes, and they pretend in their profiles. Are social networking activities educationally relevant? And if they are, does social networking have a role to play in the delivery of online instruction? The research is still anecdotal: multitasking and social networking are only two obvious activities of millennial learners that need investigation—at least investigation is needed if you are a baby boomer teacher or Gen X trainer.

28 FREQUENTLY ASKED STUDENT QUESTIONS ABOUT DISTANCE EDUCATION

1. *What are the differences between distance education and those correspondence schools seen in the infomercials?* Distance education means that a recognized educational organization offers instruction to learners separated by time and/or location. Correspondence schools require self-study, which means that there is no instructor and the student directs his or her own learning.

2. *Are there any educational prerequisites for taking distance education classes?* The key here is the requirements for those taking a course offered at a distance generally are similar to what traditional-setting students must possess. If a class on statistics for students requires two years of mathematics and one semester of algebra, then similar requirements should be expected of the distance education student.

3. *What is just-in-time learning?* Just-in-time learning is a catchphrase used most often by trainers in private businesses and corporations. In the workplace, required skills change constantly. Just-in-time learning most often provides modularized, online instruction so that it is continuously available. In this way, employees can access the training module when they need the information. Just-in-time learning makes work-related instruction available for refresher courses, new employees, or when a problem is encountered.

4. *How can I assess my knowledge in particular subject areas before choosing a course?* This is a concern for many students. There are three distinct actions that potential students can take to determine if they are "ready" for a course. First, identify the prerequisites or requirements expected of students and match them to your background. Second, talk with current and former students in the course. And finally, talk with the course instructors. This is especially important for distance learners because both the course content and learning format will be new.

5. *How do I choose a distance education program?* Programs are chosen the same way courses are chosen, with one additional step: find out if the organization offering the program is recognized. This usually refers to accreditation. Most accreditation agencies review the curriculum, facilities, support services, and faculty and certify their quality. An accredited organization is one that has been reviewed and found to meet prestablished criteria for quality.

6. *What can I do about my poor computer skills?*   Specific prerequisite skills, such as basic computer skills, are best acquired by self-study. Buy books, tapes, and manuals and read, listen, and review them. Practice and explore. Many computer vendors will set your computer up for you, connect it to the Internet, and give basic training for little or no fee. After that, just practice.

7. *What is a virtual classroom?*   A virtual classroom is most often a computer environment that attempts to approximate a real classroom. There is often a lecture hall with seats that show computer-generated figures of the students that are participating in the class. There will be chat boards where messages can be typed, and even display capabilities so the teacher can post visuals such as PowerPoint slides.

8. *How can I make sure I receive credit for distance training?*   Any reputable institution offering distance education will have a system for registration, instruction, assessment, grading, and reporting. Check this before your enroll or start a formal distance education course.

9. *How can I make sure I'm getting my money's worth?*   As with any educational event, the best experience is one where you are actively involved. The more involved you are the more likely it will be that you will learn. Ask questions, participate in discussions, and get to know the instructor and your fellow students. Remember, education is an activity, not a product. You are not given education; you learn it.

10. *Is there any way to convince my employer to pay for my distance training?*   Many companies and organizations provide qualified employees with support for education. If an employer is reluctant to accept distance education, try providing them with as much information about your proposed course of study as possible. With a little extra work, it is often possible to convince a skeptical employer that distance education not only provides quality learning that makes employees more qualified, it also permits the employee to stay in the workplace and not have to take days, weeks, or even years away from the job. You might also point out to your employer that many distance education programs stress workplace-oriented applications of coursework.

11. *What should I do if I am not satisfied with a distance education program?*   As with any educational experience, if you are not learning what you expected, contact the instructor, talk with her or him, and ask for help. Don't just criticize, but offer suggestions—become an active learner by participating in the learning events of the course. Next, talk to the supervisor of the instructor. Dropping out should only be a last resort.

12. *Can distance education courses be applied to a degree?*   The answer to this question is yes, if the course is taught by an accredited institution. If the course fits your academic program then it should count toward the degree. The requirements of the degree-granting institution determine the acceptability of transfer credits, including course credits received via distance education.

13. *What should I do if I start a distance education class and realize it is too difficult/easy for me?*   The answer to this is the same as for any traditional course. Do your background work so you do not get into the wrong course, but if you find yourself in this kind of a situation, talk with the instructor. Perhaps there are

remedial activities that you can take to get "up to speed." For an easy course, see if there is a way to test out of your current course and into a higher level.

14. *In a virtual classroom, how can I make up a missed class?* Online classes may permit recording of the interactions and instructional events that have occurred. You will need to be certain to request the recording of class events.

15. *What does the expression real time mean?* *Real time* almost always refers to distance education that is offered to learners in multiple locations, at the same time. Usually, when you see instruction advertised as real time that means you must participate at a specific time, using a telecommunications technology such as audiobridge/telephone, interactive television/compressed video, or online computer-based chat rooms or video conference technologies.

16. *Who teaches online courses?* Online courses are usually taught by teachers, professors, or industry experts hired as trainers—the same people who teach traditionally.

17. *What can I do to take an online course if I don't have a PC?* There are several options for those who want to enroll in online courses but do not have a PC. Your best option is the public library. Increasingly, libraries are equipped with modern computers that are linked to the Web with high-speed connections, and these systems are available for free use. Local community colleges often have open computer laboratories that can be used, although sometimes for a small fee. Additionally, the local high school may open its lab after school hours. Finally, it is possible to lease or rent a computer and purchase a network connection for it. However, if you are considering a more long-term degree or certificate-oriented online education, then purchasing a computer system is advisable.

18. *For distance learning classes, how is homework usually submitted?* Assignments can be sent as attachments to e-mails, submitted to an online course site, or posted on to a student's website where they can be viewed or retrieved by the instructor.

19. *What do I do if I need help with my homework or have a question about an assignment?* The most obvious place to seek assistance is from the course instructor. Contact him or her routinely and be proactive in seeking advice about homework or assignments. Most quality distance education programs also have help desks or counselors to assist students.

20. *How do I know how well I'm doing in an online course?* A well-run online course should provide regular feedback to students. If you do not receive feedback, then you should contact your instructor and ask for information about your progress.

21. *What kind of structure do online courses typically use?* Many times a course is divided into modules, usually 10 to 15. A *module* can have other names such as *unit* or *topical area,* but module seems to be the term used most often. Modules are sometimes compared to chapters of books and are further divided into *concept areas.* A concept area is a specific unit of information, sometimes also compared to sections within a textbook chapter. Finally, courses have homework and assignments. Most of the time there is an assignment for each module, so, for example, a three-semester college course might have about 12 assignments, 1 for each module in the course. Assignments could be quizzes, reports, presentations, discussions, or papers. Homework usually relates to concepts within modules. An online course might last 12 to 15 weeks, 1 week for each of the 12 to 15 modules.

Students might have an assignment for each module in addition to homework that would contribute to their course grade, and homework would be expected regularly.

Increasingly, instructors incorporate audio and video into online courses. Audio and video streaming (sending the audio and/or video information over the Internet) is growing in importance. This in turn requires the student to have a relatively fast Internet connection. Instructors can also save audio and video segments to DVDs, which are sent to students to use as part of online instruction. In these instances, the DVD is placed in the student's computer and accessed to retrieve segments at appropriate points during instruction.

22. *Can I combine distance learning with a traditional degree program?*   Learning experiences, courses, and programs are being developed using an amalgam of live instruction, online instruction, and real-time distance instruction.

23. *Are there certain features in a course that I should look for to get a good fit with my learning style?*   For the person who learns best by interactively participating with other learners, the ideal distance education program is one that permits students to work collaboratively in teams or with partners. This enables the student to regularly interact with other students.

24. *If online courses are supposed to mean I can learn "anytime, anywhere," how does that work with "real-time" instruction?*   Most often, one of three approaches is used when offering real-time instructional events. First, they may not be required. In other words, a real-time chat between the instructor and students may not be a course requirement, but only attended by students if needed, desired, or convenient. In this instance, these real-time events act as "office hours." Second, real-time events are almost always offered at multiple times in order to accommodate students with different schedules. This places a burden on the teacher, but permits greater learner flexibility. Finally, some instructors record real-time instructional events for those students who cannot attend or participate. Instructors preserve chat room conversations and post them for later review; audio conferences can be tape-recorded and mailed to students; real-time video sessions can be videotaped and sent out. Video and audio can also be recorded and stored on a server for downloading at a later date.

25. *Are there any distance learning programs that allow students to pay on a monthly basis rather than the entire tuition up front?*   Payment schedules vary by institution. There is no set rule for payment schedules, but many if not most institutions have a variety of tuition payment schedules.

26. *Is it possible to continue my studies even if I move out of state or out of the country?*   Certainly most institutions that offer courses and programs to distant learners do not limit enrollment to any one country or location. This is part of the attraction of distance education programs. It may be less convenient to take a course or program in a country different than the one where the institution is located, but it is certainly possible in most cases. Synchronous learning events may be offered at inconvenient times (e.g., the middle of the night), and some face-to-face sessions may require long airplane flights, but the beauty of distance education is in the ability to reach learners virtually at any time and in any place.

27. *Are there any subjects not well suited for distance learning?*   Virtually any educational event, course, or program can be redesigned for distance delivery.

There are dozens of success stories about chemistry, physics, music, art, and physical education courses that have been offered to distant learners. And not surprisingly, there are dozens of failure stories about distance-delivered courses in history, psychology, statistics, sociology, and education. The key to success and failure is not the topic, but the design of the course. Appropriate instructional design is critical to the success of any course, especially one offered at a distance.

28. *Is it easier to cheat in distance learning courses?* Cheating has always been fairly easy for the determined person, and distance education is no different than regular education in this respect. Increasingly, we are seeing quality programs that offer education to distant learners moving away from objective testing (such as a multiple-choice exam) to more comprehensive methods of student assessment. Objective tests have always been the target of cheaters. There is a growing body of scientific literature that indicates that objective tests measure only a portion of learning. Activities such as projects, portfolios, and reports measure learning also.

When objective tests are given, they can be delivered online in either a timed or untimed environment. Some instructors ask on-site verifiers, such as school administrators, librarians, or work supervisors, to certify that the student took the test according to the rules of the examination. Increasingly, objective tests are being used for self-testing purposes and other assessment activities are being used for grading.

SUMMARY

The students are the core to successful distance learning experiences. Quality learning experiences of students not only depend on the efforts and preparation of the instructor but they are also largely determined by the efforts and preparation of the distant learner. This chapter identified many of the characteristics, responsibilities, and expectations that students may have when learning at a distance. Also, a learning experience is provided by an instructor and used by a student. Teaching and learning are two sides of the same coin, often referred to as a *learning experience*. Remember, learning experiences for learners should be equivalent, not necessarily equal.

DISCUSSION TOPICS

1. Describe some characteristics of the distant learner. Discuss why these characteristics are important and how they relate to the characteristics of the traditional-setting learner.
2. Why is it important for an instructor to obtain information about distant students?
3. What are some responsibilities of the distant student in a synchronous distance education class? Why are these responsibilities important?
4. What are some responsibilities of the distant student in an asynchronous distance education class? How are these different from those in a synchronous distance class?

CASE STUDIES

1. As Tracey Nielson prepares to take her first online course, Introduction to Teaching, she discovers that there are a number of things being expected of her. She notes there are technical expectations, assignments and due dates, and the use of a course management tool she's not used before. What can Tracey do to make it easier on herself to get started? What can her instructor provide in the way of assistance to help her get started?

2. Ruth Downer and Phyllis Alterman are middle school state history students who are enrolled in a special videoconferencing class for accelerated students. This is their first time taking this type of class. They are very good friends and like to talk with each other, sometimes even in class, which does lead to them getting detention. What do they need to consider when taking this class related to their studies and their classroom behaviors? Why is it important for them to address their tendency to talk with each other?

3. Carl Morris has been enrolled in a program at a nearby university. His program has taken on a blended approach with some courses offered only face-to-face, although others are totally online. He is aware that because he is a part-time student it will take him longer to complete his program. At this point in his program, he is taking a completely online course. What are his responsibilities as a student to be successful? How are his interactions in the online course different than those of the face-to-face classes? What should he expect in this class regarding his performance, that of his classmates, and the instructor's responsibilities?

REFERENCES

Benson, A. D. (2004). Distance education: Ready and willing to serve the underserved? *Quarterly Review of Distance Education, 5*(1), 51–57.

Bergmann, M., & Raleigh, D. (1998). Student orientation in the distance education classroom. *Distance Learning '98: Proceedings of the Annual Conference on Distance Teaching and Learning,* pp. 61–66.

Bozik, M. (1996). Student perceptions of a two-way interactive video class. *T.H.E. Journal, 24*(2), 99–100.

Brown, J. S. (2000). Growing up digital: How the web changes work, education, and the ways people learn. Available online at http://walker.ed.usu.edu/publications/brown_article.pdf.

Conrad, R., & Donaldson, A. (2004). *Engaging the online learner.* San Francisco: Jossey-Bass.

Dabbagh, N., & Bannan-Ritland, B. (2005). *Online learning: Concepts, strategies, and application.* Columbus, OH: Merrill/Prentice Hall.

Dede, C. (1990). The evolution of distance learning: Technology-mediated interactive learning. *Journal of Research on Computing in Education, 22,* 247–264.

Dobbs, R., Waid, C., & del Carmen, A. (2009). Students' perceptions of online courses: The effect of online course experience. *Quarterly Review of Distance Education, 10*(1), 9–26.

Herring, M., & Smaldino, S. (2001). *Planning for interactive distance education: A handbook* (2nd ed.). Bloomington, IN: AECT Publications.

Hoover, E. (2009). The millennial muddle. *The Chronicle of Higher Education.* Retreived April 8, 2010 from http://chronicle.com./article/The-Millennial-Muddle-How/48772/.

Howe, N., & Strauss, W. (2000). *Millennials rising: The next great generation.* New York: Vintage Books.

Kanuka, H., Rourke, L., & Laflamme, E. (2007). The influence of instructional methods on the quality of online discussion. *British Journal of Educational Technology, 38*, 260–271.

Kiliç-Çakmak, E., Karatas, S., & Ocak, M. (2009). An analysis of factors affecting community college students' expectations on e-learning. *Quarterly Review of Distance Education, 10*(4), 351–361.

Macfarlane, C., & Smaldino, S. (1997). The electronic classroom at a distance. In R. Rittenhouse & D. Spillers (Eds.), *Modernizing the curriculum: The electronic classroom* (pp. 171–195). Springfield, MO: Charles Thomas.

Moore, M., & Kearsley, G. (2005). *Distance education: A systems view* (2nd ed.). Boston: Wadsworth.

Palloff, R., & Pratt, K. (2007). *Building learning communities in cyberspace: Effective strategies for the online classroom* (2nd ed.). San Francisco: Jossey-Bass.

Simonson, M. (2010). Millennials. *Distance Learning: For Educators, Trainers and Leaders, 7*(2), 80–79.

Smith, P., & Dunn, S. (1991). Human and quality considerations in high-tech education. *Telecommunications for Learning, 3,* 168–172.

Sullivan, P. (2001). Gender differences and the online classroom: Male and female college students evaluate their experiences. *Community College Journal of Research and Practice, 25,* 805–818.

Tuckman, B., & Schouwenburg, H. (2003). Behavioral interventions for conquering procrastination among university students. In H. Schouwenburg et al. (Eds.), *Counseling the procrastinator in academic settings.* Washington, DC: American Psychological Association.

CHAPTER 8

Support Materials and Visualization for Distance Education

CHAPTER GOAL

The purpose of this chapter is to present information about the effective use of support materials in distance education.

CHAPTER OBJECTIVES

After reading and reviewing this chapter, you should be able to

1. Develop a distance education course syllabus.
2. Use interactive study guides.
3. Apply graphic design principles.
4. Develop word pictures.
5. Develop visual mnemonics.

 PRINTED MEDIA

Distance education has its roots in print-based correspondence study. The printed lesson was used to convey content information as well as to assess learning in correspondence study. Today, many people give little credit to the effectiveness of printed materials. Educators sometimes use technological media to replace printed media, even though there is no real need to do so.

Printed materials can enhance teaching, learning, and managing in distance education. In particular, two kinds of instructor-created print media can significantly improve the distance education environment—the course syllabus and the interactive study guide. Additionally, graphic design principles can be applied to develop study guides that use visual mnemonics and word pictures for the visualizations of key instructional ideas.

DISTANCE EDUCATION SYLLABUS

The typical distance education course syllabus is similar to the syllabus used in any other course. The primary difference is in the specificity and completeness of the distance education syllabus as compared with a more traditional one. Normally, the distance education syllabus contains the following:

Course Logistics

- Course title
- Course meeting dates, times, and locations
- Instructor information, including name, office address, telephone number, e-mail address, biographical information, and emergency contact information
- Office hours
- Textbook and course materials

Course Policies

- Attendance policies
- Homework policies
- Participation information

Instructional Activities

- Class schedule with topic list (if the course is a synchronous one with regularly scheduled class sessions)
- Topic list and topic organizational concept map (if the course is an asynchronous one with topics that can be studied at the learner's discretion)
- Course goals and objectives
- Reading assignments with links to topics
- Discussion questions for readings (if special discussion sessions are scheduled online, then the timeline for discussing certain topics can be included)
- Assignments
- Test and examination information
- Interactive study guides

Assessment Information

- Grading scheme
- Project evaluation criteria

- Grading contracts, if used
- Student precourse assessment
- Student postcourse assessment

Additional Information

- Student biographical information
- Project/assignment examples

The distance education syllabus should be available to students no later than the beginning of the first class, and probably should be distributed much earlier to prospective class members. Often, the syllabus is a recruiting tool for the distance education course. If the syllabus is available online, then the distant learners can access it from wherever they are located. The syllabus is a guide for the student, and can serve as an organizing document for the entire course. Many designers of asynchronous distance education courses use the syllabus to provide the overall structure for the content, delivery, and evaluation of the course.

THE INTERACTIVE STUDY GUIDE

Tom Cyrs and Al Kent (Cyrs, 1997) are often credited with proposing the interactive study guide (ISG) as an essential tool of the distance educator. Certainly, they (especially Tom Cyrs, 1997) are staunch advocates of this technique. Basically, the interactive study guide is a structured note-taking system that leads the learner through a series of concepts, and that requires some active and interactive involvement by the student (Figure 8–1).

There are several reasons why the handout, generally, and the ISG handout, specifically, are important to the distance educator. First, the use of handouts improves student note taking and makes it more efficient. Second, the ISG is a management tool that directs course activities before, during, and after instruction. Finally, the ISG handout can be used in any classroom, including all categories of distance education systems. The ISG is a handout designed to be used by students. It is a highly organized set of student notes, graphics, pictures, graphs, charts, clip art, photographs, geometric shapes, activities, problems, and exercises. It is planned before a teleclass to assist students with note taking and to guide students through a variety of instructional events so they understand the structure of the content of the lesson. Interactive study guides are also meant to show the relationships among ideas and data presented during a class (Cyrs, 1997; Stuart, 2004).

The ISG is different from other handouts because it is more organized and more systematically sequenced than other types. It consists of two parts—the display (with the word picture) and the notes section (Figure 8–2). A series of displays is sequenced (numbered) in the order that each will be discussed in class. Each display corresponds to one idea or one visual element of the lesson. Sometimes a display is equated to a concept, but most often, displays are less general and more specific than a concept.

FIGURE 8–1 The interactive study guide (ISG) is a critical tool of the distance educator.

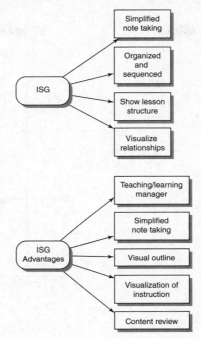

Well-designed displays are made up of word pictures that are graphic representations of concepts, principles, and information derived from various patterns to organize a lesson. The best word pictures are visual mnemonics that relate to the key ideas of the lesson. Mnemonics are ways to remember things, so visual mnemonics are visual ways to remember things.

The interactive study guide is a series of displays presented from the top to the bottom on the left side of the handout page. Normally, three to five displays are presented on each page of the ISG. A display is sometimes referred to as a "chunk" of information that is numbered and then referenced by the student (Cyrs, 1997). A display is similar to a paragraph of information in a written document, but the display attempts to present ideas visually rather than verbally, or at least with a combination of visual elements and words.

Displays can consist of the following:

■ Word pictures with fill-ins completed by the student
■ Activities or exercises
■ A set of directions
■ A quote, poem, definition, or other short written item
■ Problems—either verbal or numerical
■ Summaries of data
■ Tables or figures
■ Photographs

FIGURE 8–2 Interactive study guide components.

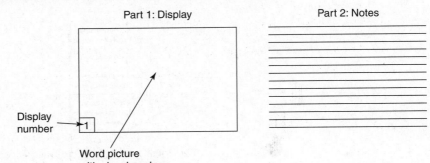

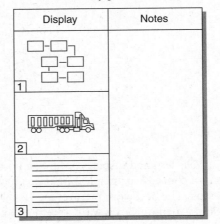

- Drawings
- Self-test questions
- Lists

An ISG display can contain directions for students to accomplish a task outside of class that is external to the ISG itself. An effective display is clear, easy to understand, and useful to the learner.

Normally, a 50-minute class session would require approximately 10 displays in an ISG. In other words, displays should be complex enough to require about 5 minutes to explain, or conversely, simple enough to cover in 5 minutes. This is an estimate. Some displays may take much longer to deal with, and others much less time, but the 5-minute estimate is good for planning purposes.

The steps necessary to produce an ISG are as follows:

- Identify the behavioral objectives for the lesson.
- Create a detailed outline of topics that relate to each objective.
- For narrative sections, identify the key words.

- Use geometric shapes to show relationships or visuals to assist the learner in understanding each section.
- Create word pictures for the narrative sections by leaving blanks in the narrative where students will fill in the key words.
- Sequence the displays in the order that they will be presented or that they will be discussed.
- Develop subdisplays for topics that have more than one visual or word picture.
- Produce the ISG using proper graphic design principles.

The production of the ISG requires considerable planning. Once it is developed, the distance education course is considerably easier for the instructor to prepare for and to teach, and is more organized and easier for learners to follow, especially those in distance education courses where live, two-way interactive television is not available.

GRAPHIC DESIGN PRINCIPLES

Interactive study guides are often used as the basis for interactive television graphics in distance education courses. For this reason, it is important to design ISGs to conform to appropriate graphic design principles. The size, font, color and contrast, alignment, and use of uppercase and lowercase in written graphics are critical to successful design (Zelanski & Fisher, 2008).

- **Size.**   Letter size is very closely related to legibility. Large, bold lettering is easier to see and read than is smaller lettering. Certainly lettering should not be smaller than 24 point (1/3 inch), and 32 to 36 point is preferable, especially if computer output is to be displayed on regular television monitors (Figure 8–3). Five words per line and five lines per page are a maximum for an ISG display or a screen of television information.
- **Font.**   Sans serif fonts should be used instead of fonts with serifs, the thin extensions to letters often used in textbooks and printed documents. Serifs tend to be too fine for display on television. Bold fonts with thick stems display the best. Also, the same fonts should be used throughout a presentation, and no more than three different fonts should be used for any single display. Two font types work the best, for example, when one is used for one category of information and the second is used for background or secondary information. Fancy typefaces and italics should be avoided unless there is an overriding reason for using them.
- **Color and Contrast.**   Color is often misused in television. Colors should be bold and simple and should not be overdone. Some combinations, such as green and red, do not work well together. Avoid saturated colors such as red. Use dark letters with a light background, or vice versa. Many television instructors like to use bright colors on a black background for displaying computer screens of information. This approach produces very readable displays.
- **Alignment.**   Centering text for television display is not as effective as aligning text to the left. Left-justified text seems to be most legible.
- **Capitalization.**   The literature on readability is quite clear that uppercase and lowercase lettering, rather than all uppercase or all lowercase, reads the best.

FIGURE 8–3   The type must be large enough to be easy to read.

	Univers Bold Caps	Univers Bold Caps and Lowercase
9 point	LEGIBILITY	Legibility
12 point	LEGIBILITY	Legibility
14 point	LEGIBILITY	Legibility
18 point	LEGIBILITY	Legibility
24 point	LEGIBILITY	Legibility
36 point	LEGIBILITY	Legibility
48 point	LEGIBILITY	Legibility
72 point	LEGIBILITY	Legibility

Elements of Design

Literate, effective visuals for display as part of ISGs or for instructor-led presentations can be developed by applying the elements and principles of design. The elements of design (Figure 8–4) are line, shape, space, texture, value, and color.

- *Line* is generally considered to be one-dimensional. Line has length but not width. Line portrays direction, presents objects, and defines the outer shape of something.
- *Shape* is used to symbolize objects or to show large or small spaces. Shapes have two dimensions: height and width.

FIGURE 8–4 Elements of design.

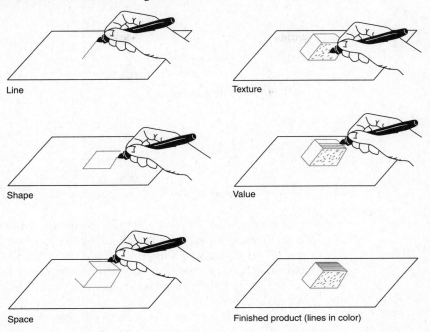

Line

Texture

Shape

Value

Space

Finished product (lines in color)

■ *Space* is either positive or negative. The outline of an object in a visual signifies its positive space. The most common negative shape of something is its background.
■ *Texture* is the perceived or actual roughness or smoothness of a surface. Texture is used to help define shape or space.
■ *Value* is the degree of lightness or darkness of a surface; it is accomplished through shading. Value shows changes in space, and is often used to create the illusion of volume or solidity in a graphic object.
■ *Color* is related to value and is used to visualize an object realistically or to differentiate one object from another. Colors have hue, value, and intensity. *Hue* describes a specific color, such as red, green, or blue. *Value* is the lightness or darkness of a color—yellow has the highest value. *Intensity* is the strength of a color, such as bright yellow or dull red. Intensity is determined by the purity of a color.

Principles of Design

The elements of design are combined according to the guidelines provided by the principles of design. There are six principles: balance, center of interest, emphasis, unity, contrast, and rhythm (Graer, 2006; Ocepek, 2003, Simonson & Volker, 1984).

■ *Balance* is the sense of equilibrium in a visual. The two kinds of balance are formal and informal (Figure 8–5). Generally, a visual should be balanced left to right and top to bottom. Formal balance means that objects of equal size and

FIGURE 8–5   Formal and informal balance.

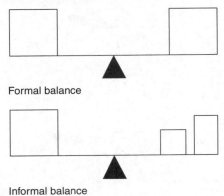

Formal balance

Informal balance

importance are placed at equivalent distances from the center of the visual (Figure 8–6). Informally balanced visuals are often more interesting to create and to view. Careful planning is important when informally balanced graphics are created. Several small images can be used to balance one large object, or words can be used to balance pictures (Figure 8–7). Small, brightly colored objects will balance larger, duller items.

■ The *center of interest* is the visual focal point of the graphic and should relate to its purpose. Historically, well-designed visuals did not place the center of interest at the center of the picture. However, television places restrictions on the graphic designer. Since the area displayed on a television screen is relatively small and varies between television sets, it is probably safest to place the center of interest of a graphic at or near the center of the picture (Figure 8–8).

FIGURE 8–6   Formally balanced display.

FIGURE 8–7 Informally balanced display.

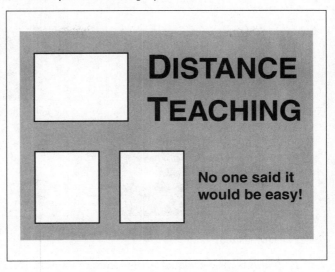

FIGURE 8–8 Rule of thirds, center of interest & How people look at images.

FIGURE 8–9   Emphasis has to do with making the key item stand out.

Arrows or pointers are effective.

A contrasting value can emphasize an area.

The placement of an item can cause it
to be emphasized.

Size can be used.

■ *Emphasis* is closely related to the center of interest. The key object should be
   emphasized so it is apparent to the viewer what is most important (Figure 8–9). There
   are several ways to emphasize the key element in a graphic, including the following:

   1. Use pointers, such as arrows.
   2. Use color to emphasize.
   3. Use large objects at the center of interest.
   4. Use different shapes for the center of interest.
   5. Use more elements of design to create the center of interest for a graphic and
      fewer for less important elements.

■ *Unity* means that a visual holds together to convey its purpose (Figure 8–10).
   If several graphics are used as part of a display, they should all convey or pertain
   to one meaning. Overlapping is a simple technique for promoting unity. Trees
   overlap buildings and each other. Houses overlap shrubs and people. A single
   background also promotes a feeling of unity. Another technique to promote the
   concept of unity is to place an outline or border around the elements of a
   display. Repetition of shapes, forms, and objects also can promote unity.

■ *Contrast* refers to the characteristics of an object that cause it to stand out (Figure
   8–11). Contrast is closely related to emphasis. Most often, it is achieved by the
   use of light- or dark-valued objects. Shapes, forms, and textures can be used to
   create contrasts and make one object stand out while others seem to recede.

■ *Rhythm* comes from repetition through variety and is used to draw a viewer
   through the various objects in a visual (Figure 8–12). A row of houses in a display
   can present a sense of rhythm. The rhythm of a graphic helps tell the story of the
   picture by leading the viewer's eyes.

An effective graphic should provide visual information related to the topic being
learned. The elements of design combined according to the principles of design can
assist the distance educator in the development of effective ISGs and handouts that
visually explain ideas and that facilitate understanding.

FIGURE 8–10   Unity involves "oneness" or a trying together of ideas.

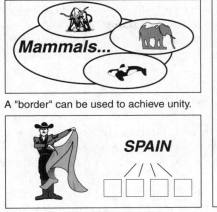

A "border" can be used to achieve unity.

Another technique is to use lines to unify.

Perhaps the most effective method is to overlap a common shape.

FIGURE 8–11   The important part of a display can be made to stand out (contrast) mainly through the use of color, size, value, and shape.

When light and dark values are used, contrast results.

Differences in size can create contrast.

FIGURE 8–12   Rhythm results when an element is repeated in some systematic manner.

WORD PICTURES

A *word picture* is a graphic representation of concepts, principles, and information. Each concept, principle, or item of information usually contains key words that can be shown in nodes. A *node* is a symbol that contains words or stands alone to represent some idea. A node is the central point around which subnodes originate (Cyrs, 1997). The best word picture is a visual mnemonic that helps the learner remember the concept, principle, or item.

Word pictures do not need to be self-explanatory. Rather, they often require additional verbal information. Key words are usually shown in the nodes. *Key words* are the most significant words in a statement that provide clues to the idea the statement is communicating. Word pictures are graphic organizers that put elements of ideas together in a visual way so the learner can understand the relationship between the elements.

Cyrs does an excellent job of explaining how word pictures differ from other ways of organizing information. Cyrs (1997) says the following about effective word pictures:

1. Emphasis should be placed on the types of symbols used.
2. They should cover chunks of information rather than entire documents.
3. Student attention can be maintained through the use of fill-ins.
4. They emphasize the logical sequence of the class presentation.
5. They provide a complete review of the class content.
6. They can also be used for display by overhead video cameras.
7. They are inexpensive to produce and duplicate.
8. They condense ideas into a few key words.
9. They should be designed to fit the format of television.
10. They apply principles of graphic design.
11. They emphasize communication via the visual sense.
12. They require the instructor to think visually rather than verbally.

Cyrs (1997) discusses various graphic organizers that can be incorporated into word pictures: semantic maps, mind maps, cognitive maps, structured overviews, outlines, patterned note taking, webbing, pyramiding, and information mapping.

■ *Semantic maps* are two-dimensional diagrams that use arrangements of nodes and links to communicate ideas and to show the relationships among ideas. Semantic maps use primarily two structures—top down and bottom up (Johnson & Peterson, 1984).
■ *Mind maps* use key words or phrases organized in a design that is nonlinear. Mind maps are based on the idea that individuals mentally organize information in a variety of structures, not just top down or bottom up. Rather, mind maps usually start at the center of a page and branch out as individual ideas are presented. Mind maps have the following characteristics (Buzan, 1982):

  1. The main ideas are clearly defined and placed in the center of the graphic.
  2. The relative importance of a subidea is indicated by its proximity to the main idea.

   3. Links between ideas are clearly indicated.
   4. New information is easily added to a mind map because of its nonlinear structure.

■ *Cognitive maps* (Diekhoff & Diekhoff, 1982) are organized around the relationship between ideas, and they provide a graphic expression of the structure of a body of knowledge. Many people confuse cognitive maps and mind maps. Cognitive maps are more structured and organized than mind maps and are usually developed by the instructor of a class.

■ *Structured overviews* use graphics and hierarchical structures showing the relationship of key ideas, concepts, and other information (Figure 8–13). Structured overviews are commonly used for readings or lectures. Austin and Dean-Guilford (1981) define the structured overview as a conceptualized visual–hierarchical type of diagram used to show concept interrelationships within written material.

■ *Outlines* are visual displays that are useful in presenting concurrent ideas. Outlines are largely verbal but use visual elements to present clusters of ideas in one display.

■ *Patterned note taking* (Norton, 1981) is related to mind mapping. A key word or phrase is placed in the center of a space, and arrows and lines radiate out to subideas. Key words and phrases are used extensively. Lines are used to show relationships.

■ *Webbing* is a graphic representation similar to other techniques discussed here. The main idea is at the center, and subordinate ideas radiate out like the spokes of a wheel. Webbing resembles semantic maps.

FIGURE 8–13   Word picture: structural overview.

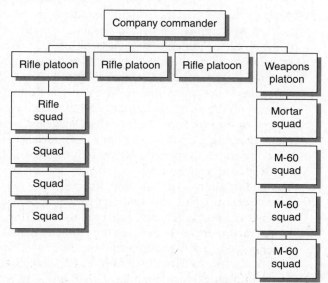

FIGURE 8–14   Word picture: Pyramiding—Bloom's taxonomy of the cognitive domain.

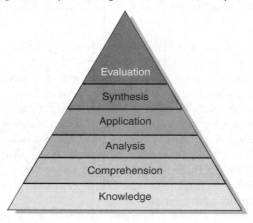

- *Pyramiding* shows the levels of ideas in a graphic way using a bottom-to-top model (Figure 8–14). Information is grouped according to a hierarchy, such as details at the bottom, concepts in the middle, and principles at the top.
- *Information mapping* is a method of bringing together current research into a comprehensive materials development and presentation approach. Maps are arranged hierarchically into blocks of information. Each block serves a separate purpose, but all relate to some central theme or idea.

Cyrs (1997) provides an excellent list of organizational patterns for distance education classes. The strategies listed by Cyrs are wonderful starting points for those beginning to develop a personal approach to distance teaching. Several of the most useful approaches are as follows:

1. *Problem solution.*   In this situation, students are presented with a real or contrived problem with elements provided about the situation that caused or had an impact on the problem. Students are then asked, often in collaborative groups, to make observations about the situation and then propose alternative solutions, including the consequences of each alternative. One effective technique for dramatizing the problem is to use *trigger films/videos,* which are short (2–4 minutes) scenarios dealing with the events that produced the problem. Students are then asked to respond to the problem. The film/video "triggers" a response. For example, a trigger film might dramatize a family in financial crisis with a stack of bills that are due at the end of the month. After watching the scenario unfold, financial counseling students would be required to work in small groups to develop a proposed solution to the situation depicted.

2. *Time sequence.*   This presentation involves organizing information in a list or sequence of events that unfold chronologically. The sequence can be presented by the instructor, or the elements of the sequence can be presented visually and students can be asked to help order the elements and then explain the rationale for their decision. Examples of time sequences include developing film, completing a tax return, building a doghouse, and baking a cake.

FIGURE 8–15   Word picture: Cause and effect—water cycle.

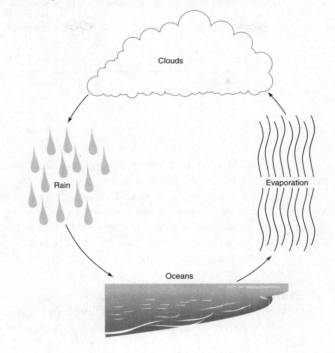

3. *Definitions.*   When a presentation is based on definitions, there is usually a statement of the concept to be defined; a listing of its attributes; and examples of how the term, phrase, or item is used. For example, terms in a chemistry laboratory exercise might first be defined by the instructor before students work together to complete the sequence of activities involved in the laboratory experience. Definitions lend themselves particularly well to sequential ISG.

4. *Cause and effect.*   In this approach an event and its causes or antecedents are presented (Figure 8–15). For example, the heavy rains in California would be discussed and would be followed by an exploration of why the rains occurred, such as the influence of El Niño water in the central Pacific Ocean. Actual or historic meteorological records could be used, as could weather reports in California newspapers.

VISUAL ANALOGIES

An *analogy* is a way to describe something that is unfamiliar by comparing it to something familiar. The two things that are being compared seem to be different but have some similarities. Analogies help improve thinking and help learners understand new ideas by giving insights and by allowing new relationships to be explained.

According to Cyrs (1997), analogies have four parts (Figure 8–16): the new subject, the analog, the connector between the analog and the new subject, and the ground.

FIGURE 8–16   Components of an analogy.

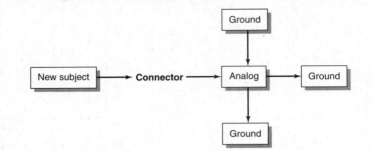

The *new subject* is the topic that is unfamiliar. The analogy is designed to help provide understanding of the new subject. Subjects normally are described by only a few words. The *analog* is familiar and is something that has been experienced by the learner. It is crucial that the learner knows the analog—the previously understood idea or concept. The *connector* shows the relationship between the two concepts: the new subject and the familiar idea, or analog. The connector is the critical element in the analogy and demonstrates the creativity of the author of the analogy. Connectors can be structural or functional.

■ *Structural* relationships show the similarity in appearance and design of the two concepts. Examples of structural relationships include (1) Sharon is as creative as Leonardo da Vinci. (2) Norman is as soft as a marshmallow. (3) Raindrops looked like balloons.
■ *Functional* relationships describe what concepts do or how they work. Functional relationships show not only what the subject and the analog have in common but also what they do that is similar.

Connectors that often are used include the following:

tastes like . . .
resembles . . .
is comparable to . . .
feels like . . .
looks like . . .
is related to . . .
is like . . .

The *ground* relates to the specific set of similarities and differences between the unfamiliar and the familiar. The ground can be verbal or visual, but the more concrete the ground, the more hints it provides and the more likely it will be that the analogy will work. Pictures are often used to help make the analogy realistic (Figure 8–17). Some examples of a ground include these:

■ Football is like war—it requires strategy, tactics, planning, and trained individuals.
■ Distance teaching is like singing and playing the piano at the same time. It requires simultaneous verbal skills and physical dexterity.
■ Media are like delivery trucks, since media carry ideas.

FIGURE 8–17 Example: A visual analogy.

Media are like delivery trucks. They permit the delivery of
ideas to learners.

When constructing visual analogies one should follow five steps. First, identify clearly what the new subject is, the idea that is not clearly known. Second, identify the appropriate connector, such as " . . . is like . . . " or " . . . is similar to . . . ." Third, identify the known analog—the familiar concept or thing that can be compared to the new idea. Fourth, provide a ground for the comparison of the new and familiar ideas. Describe the similarities and differences between the ideas. Finally, develop a visual way to demonstrate the analogy and provide learners with a visual mnemonic to help them remember the relationship and understand the new subject.

Analogies are difficult to develop. When a good analogy is identified, especially a visual one, it can be the center of an elegant discussion of instructional content. Naturally, the visual analogy should be incorporated as a word picture for an ISG.

SUMMARY

Printed handouts and teaching and learning materials are critically important to the effective practice of distance education. First, the course syllabus is the "glue" that holds the course or the learning experience together. Sometimes the syllabus is expanded into the course study guide, which is a document that provides the student with a level of orientation to the distance education experience. Second, the interactive study guide (ISG) is a very important tool that provides the distant learner with a logical sequence for the distance education lesson. The ISG is especially important when the student and instructor communicate asynchronously or when fully interactive two-way television is not used.

Interactive study guides are made up of two ingredients—the display and the notes section. The display is made up of a series of word pictures, which are visuals and words that involve student interaction and that attempt to provide the learner with ways to remember the key ideas that are to be learned. In essence, the word pictures are visual mnemonics to help learners remember things. Naturally, for visuals to be meaningful and instructional they need to be designed effectively. The guidelines for effective visual design should be followed.

Finally, printed materials are critical to the practice of distance education (Figure 8–18). Documents provide background information, amplify concepts, and give a sense of direction to instructional events. Printed materials are an important component of the distance education program.

FIGURE 8–18   Speaking of distance education, this is a graphic display attached to the *Pioneer 10* spacecraft that is hurtling into space. The designers of this display wanted to convey three ideas to whomever or whatever might find it thousands of years from now: (1) where the spacecraft came from: the Earth; (2) who inhabited the Earth: men and women; and (3) that men and women are friendly.

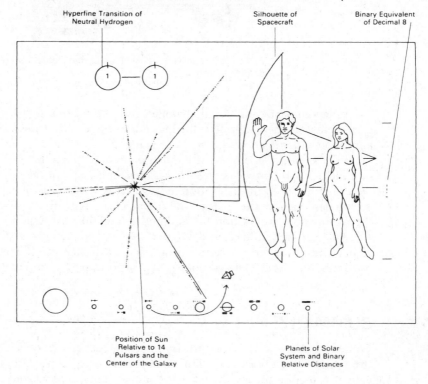

DISCUSSION QUESTIONS

1. Define *visual analogy*. Why are analogies important?
2. Develop a visual mnemonic or word picture for these concepts:
   ■ Technology as productivity enhancer
   ■ Pythagorean theorem
   ■ Definition of distance education
3. Write an analogy for these ideas:
   ■ Teaching
   ■ Golf
   ■ Learning
   ■ A pet dog
4. Why are interactive study guides important to the distance educator?

REFERENCES

Austin, R., & Dean-Guilford, M. (1981). Crashing content reading problems with reading strategies. Paper presented at the meeting of the Western College Reading Association, Dallas, TX. (ERIC Document Reproduction Service No. ED204703).

Buzan, T. (1982). *Use your head.* London: British Broadcasting Corporation.

Cyrs, T. (1997). *Teaching at a distance.* Las Cruces, NM: Center for Educational Development.

Diekhoff, G., & Diekhoff, K. (1982). Cognitive maps as a tool in communicating structural knowledge. *Educational Technology, 22,* 28–30.

Graer, M. (2006). *Inside/outside: From the basics to the practice of design* (2nd ed.). Berkeley, CA: Peachpit Press.

Johnson, D., & Peterson, D. (1984). *Teaching reading vocabulary* (2nd ed.). New York: Holt.

Norton, L. (1981). Patterned note-taking: An evaluation. *Visible Language, 15,* 67–85.

Ocepek, L. (2003). *Graphic design: Vision, process, product.* Upper Saddle River, NJ: Merrill/Prentice Hall.

Simonson, M., & Volker, R. (1984). *Media planning and production.* Columbus, OH: Merrill.

Stuart, D. (2004). A picture is worth a thousand megs: Developing music-listening skills by using technology to engage the senses. *Distance Learning, 1*(6), 15–20.

Zelanski, P., & Fisher, M. (2008). *The art of seeing* (7th ed.). Upper Saddle River, NJ: Merrill/Prentice Hall.

SUGGESTED READINGS

Carrier, C. (1983). Notetaking research: Implications for the classroom. *Journal of Instructional Development, 6,* 19–26.

Kiewra, K. (1987). Notetaking and review: The research and its implications. *Instructional Science, 16,* 233–249.

Smith, P., & Tompkins, G. (1988). Structured notetaking: A new strategy for content area teachers. *Journal of Reading, 32,* 46–53.

CHAPTER 9

Assessment for Distance Education

CHAPTER GOAL

The purpose of this chapter is to present approaches for assessment of student learning.

CHAPTER OBJECTIVES

After reading and reviewing this chapter, you should be able to

1. Discuss the role of assessment in the instructional design process, especially for distance education.
2. Describe the characteristics of several types of assessment activities and the appropriate uses of each within a distance education environment.
3. Implement practical strategies for assessing learner progress in a distance education course.
4. Discuss issues related to academic misconduct and describe how cheating, plagiarism, and other forms of unethical behavior may be preempted or alleviated in a distance education course.

ASSESSING LEARNING GAINS

In preparation for a transfer to his employer's Dubai office, Cameron spends part of each afternoon practicing useful phrases in Arabic by listening to audio clips from his language tutor and recording his responses online. This morning before going to work, Courtney logged on to a website that presents a series of urban planning simulations where she practiced working with GIS data, then checked her understanding with a self-test. Tomorrow night, Carlos will set aside 30 minutes to participate in an audioconference with his professor and three other students in his media ethics class as they prepare for their final group presentation. What do these individuals have in common? They're all involved in some form of learning assessment and are demonstrating, through observable behaviors, how well they understand the course or program content. The above activities reflect the learning gains the individual students have made, and let their instructors know how well the students are progressing.

Although this chapter focuses on assessment in distance education, much of the discussion is not exclusive to distance education. Just as exemplary "distance teaching" closely resembles our best models of face-to-face teaching, assessing student achievement has a core of good practice that remains constant across a multitude of teaching–learning configurations. In addition, although many of the examples provided will refer to institutionally based (formal) education, most of the issues related to assessment could also be applied in a workplace training program, technical certification course, or professional development workshop.

PURPOSES FOR ASSESSMENT

In this text, *assessment* is defined as the process of measuring, documenting, and interpreting behaviors that demonstrate learning. Notice that we've referred to "behaviors" rather than presuming to measure learning directly. The best evidence of learning is found in learner behavior and will likely remain so until cognitive scientists discover a reliable way to determine what knowledge and skills we carry around between our ears just by looking there. So, once we've measured, documented, and interpreted, what can we do with that information? A few of the administrative purposes of assessment results include program evaluation and improvement, facilitation of student placement in programs, justification for funding priorities, and reporting of long-term trends to state, federal, or corporate entities. In a distance education environment, assessment outcomes may sometimes be used to compare the academic performance of remote students with the performance of learners in a more traditional (i.e., face-to-face) classroom. Although not a particularly helpful comparison (we know that even if we could control potentially confounding variables, the results would very likely show "no significant difference" between the groups), it is sometimes necessary simply to demonstrate the validity of unfamiliar course structures or instructional strategies. Note that although the terms *assessment* and *evaluation* are sometimes used synonymously by other authors, in this text they are treated as activities with distinctly different purposes. This chapter is focused on the assessment of student learning.

Possibly the most important purpose for assessing learning gains is to provide feedback to learners and instructors. Students gain a sense of control and can take on greater responsibility for their own learning if they know how well they're doing, compared with an established set of criteria. Feedback from frequent assessments, informal or otherwise, provides that scale. When students encounter an assessment activity, they not only recall the needed concepts or skills, they also reinforce them through application. This is especially important if course content is highly sequential or hierarchical in nature. Frequent assessments help learners to identify the important points within a course module, while practicing the skills necessary to advance through subsequent material. For an instructor, once armed with assessment data, he or she can provide remediation or coaching where necessary and determine if a student needs additional assistance. At the same time, this feedback helps the instructor to monitor the effectiveness of the instruction. Many learners struggling with the same concept or skill might signal an instructional design problem. By using assessments carefully, the teacher can identify and address weaknesses or gaps in the instruction.

Assessment activities presented throughout a course or training module can be useful for identifying learner misconceptions that could present obstacles to further progress. Research related to learners' misconceptions (sometimes referred to as *naïve conceptions*) suggests that these erroneous cognitive constructions are frequently stable, persistent, and potentially difficult to dislodge (Hare & Graber, 2007). By incorporating assessments throughout a learning module, especially those that are specifically intended to induce cognitive dissonance in learners holding such misconceptions, errors are more quickly detected and resolved. Waiting until midterm exams are given, for example, to gather feedback about learner understanding increases the likelihood that misinterpretations of important course content will be solidly embedded and difficult to dislodge.

Assessing a learner's readiness to begin an instructional unit can be particularly important in a skills-training environment. Time, effort, and money can be wasted if students do not have important entry-level abilities or if, conversely, they have already mastered many of the class's final objectives. By designing effective entry-level tests (to determine readiness) and pretests (to determine placement), workforce training becomes more efficient and reduces time spent by employees in activities that are either too advanced or an unnecessary review of previously learned material.

Assessments often function as a motivational activity. Most learners want to do well, and knowing that they will be held accountable for a body of knowledge or set of skills can be the nudge that keeps them on track. Astute teachers have long known the value of group discussions, pop quizzes, or in-class exercises to ensure that required readings or out-of-class assignments are completed on time. Additionally, in countries such as the United States, where competitive activities (in school and out) constitute a large part of the culture, testing is often seen as an opportunity to pit one's abilities against those of others, while hoping to excel (or at least measure up). Competitive games are a frequently used assessment technique that can motivate, provide opportunities for teamwork, and reinforce important concepts or skills.

Probably the first reason that comes to mind for learner assessment, however, is to enable the instructor to assign grades or sign off on certification/licensure at the end of a course, unit, or lesson. Grades, in and of themselves, provide limited information about learning and although they can be important and may prove helpful in determining how to improve the instruction for future students, there are other, more direct ways of applying assessment techniques for enhancing teaching and learning before a course or learning module ends.

Verification of Online Learners

Verifying students who are learning at a distance has become an important issue. Specifically, there are concerns that distant learners are actually doing the work that they are submitting. The Higher Learning Commission of the North Central

Association of Colleges and Schools has issued a report in reference to the Higher Education Opportunity Act of 2008 dealing with verification of students in distance learning classes and programs.

> The revised law requires that the accreditor require institutions offering distance education . . . have processes through which the institution establishes that the student who registers in the distance education . . . course or program is the same student who participates in and completes and receives the academic credit.

The Commission requires that "institutions offering distance education . . . shall have processes through which the institution establishes that the student who registers in the distance education . . . courses or programs is the same student who participates in and completes and receives the academic credit."

The Joint Conference Committee of Congress and the US Department of Education have confirmed that "initially institutions may use simple efforts already in use at most institutions to verify the identity of students. Such efforts may include the use of IDs and passwords" and that

> as time progresses, better processes for verifying the identity of students come into existence, and final regulations develop, this policy may need to be updated . . . in the meantime, institutions should be examining more sophisticated approaches to verifying the identity of their students and making plans to incorporate such approaches in their distance education [courses and programs].

ASSESSMENT AND INSTRUCTIONAL DESIGN

The role of assessment in the instructional design process is as a corollary to the development of learning objectives, and a precedent to the development and implementation of instructional strategies. In this way, the assessment activities are matched to expectations and instruction is then based on assessment plans. A less formal way of expressing this is: Figure out what learners should get out of the instruction, determine how you'll know whether they were successful, and then decide what they should do to reach that point. In this manner, "teaching to the test" becomes a desirable basis for instruction because the test (in whatever form it takes) is a measure of what is considered important.

Unfortunately, this ideal is realized only occasionally, and assessments typically are created after the instruction is planned and often after it has been implemented. This doesn't preclude the use of objectives as a basis for determining progress, but care must be taken to ensure that the instruction has also been based on the same expectations and has not wandered from the original goals. If students prepare for an examination, thinking, "What's going to be on this test?" or face an out-of-class project wondering what is expected of them, that may indicate that the objectives have been forgotten along the way. Those desired outcomes must act as a continuous thread that binds the instructional process together from beginning to end.

It makes sense when designing assessment measures to focus on the cognitive domain. "What do students need to know and how will we know if they know it?" Unfortunately, however, this means that affective domain considerations are sometimes ignored or relegated, at best, to an afterthought during the implementation of assessment activities. This is particularly regrettable for distance education programs, where students may be presented with learning tasks and environments strikingly different from those with which they're familiar, potentially resulting in motivational problems.

When learners lack the confidence that they will be able to master the course content, their motivation drops and they are less likely to persist in their efforts to grasp new material. Keller's ARCS model (of which "confidence" is the "C") suggests that reinforcing expectations for success, providing opportunities for success, and attributing success to effort and ability will enhance learner motivation (Keller & Suzuki, 2004). Expecting a successful outcome requires that students understand how they'll be assessed and what performance criteria will be applied. Opportunities for success might include tasks that are challenging but achievable, scheduled early in a course or module, at which learners will succeed if they honestly try. To prevent attribution of their success to luck or instructor bias, feedback offered about individual performance should be specific and clearly tied to the efforts and abilities of the learner. Reinforcing student confidence will allow later assessment activities to represent accurately student mastery of course content, by removing obstacles posed by low motivation and anxiety related to fear of failure.

Another "confidence promoting" strategy deals with the technology skills of the learners. Students enrolled in their first distance education course may need practice utilizing the technological resources necessary for a class, or they may be unfamiliar with some forms of assessment. Instructors would be wise to require students to practice using tools such as an online drop box for assignments, asynchronous discussion platforms, or Web-based quizzes, well before their use during a point-generating event. In addition, in-class or real-time simulations of performance-based assessments can provide students with exposure to these activities in a nonthreatening setting; this is especially important for those more accustomed to traditional objective measures.

Once a student completes an assessment and it is scored or rated, the result may be reported in one of two ways. *Criterion-referenced* scoring is used when the rater compares the learner's performance with that of a predetermined set of standards, drawn from the learning objectives, and is sometimes referred to as *outcomes based*. The rater asks, "Did the learner demonstrate mastery of the skills identified in the objectives?" The reported score reflects the learner's level of expertise by specifying how closely the student's performance matches the ideal. *Norm-referenced* scoring uses the same outcomes but is intended to compare each student with others who have completed the same assessment (and who, theoretically, had the same instruction). The term *grading on a curve* reflects this type of scoring, and in this case the rater asks, "How well did the learner perform compared with the others?"

There are appropriate uses for each type of scoring. If our concern, as teachers, trainers, or instructional designers, is that each student master the course content, then their performance compared with one another is irrelevant; we need to ensure that they have performed well compared with our expectations by using criterion-referenced scoring. Norm-referenced scoring is used, appropriately, to report long-term trends and comparisons of extremely large groups of learners (e.g., statewide, nationwide, or worldwide, in the case of some university preadmission examinations), but should never be used to determine grades, award certification or licensure, or determine mastery of content. Grading on a curve tells the teacher and learner how well students did relative to one another, but does not offer useful information about whether any of them mastered some or all of the content.

Finally, the topic of grade inflation has captured the attention of the popular media, although the relationship of assessment to grades has largely been ignored. The critical question, then, is, "If grades have gone up over time, while actual learning has remained relatively stable, does this indicate that grades, in fact, may not be terribly useful indicators of performance?" Until a reasonable substitute for grades comes along, formal education will continue to expect teachers to distill a complex range of learner abilities, attitudes, and experiences into a single letter. This may suffice for administrative or accountability reasons, but offers relatively little useful information to improve teaching and learning over the long term, and for these purposes educators may look to what the assessment of learning gains offers, instead.

CHARACTERISTICS OF USEFUL ASSESSMENTS

As described in the previous section, assessment is one element of the teaching and learning process that evolves from the determination of desired performance outcomes. It follows, therefore, that one of the characteristics of a good assessment tool is that it matches the objectives; learners know what to expect because they have already been made aware of what is important and how they will be expected to demonstrate their mastery of this knowledge or skill. This characteristic is often referred to as *alignment*, indicating an acceptable degree of synchronicity among objectives, instructional activities, and assessment measures. The objectives, ideally, specify what the students will do to demonstrate their mastery of the content, how well they will be expected to perform this task, and under what special circumstances, if any, they should perform it. Occasionally, instructors will find that a test item or exercise they have created does not match the objectives, although they believe it to be an important skill or concept for learners to grasp. In this case, it makes sense to return to the list of objectives and consider the possibility that there are gaps or missing items. Herein is an excellent reason for creating assessment measures before implementing instruction. If there are gaps in the objectives list that become apparent only when developing an assessment activity, it is likely that the missing material will not have been included in the planned learning activities.

An assessment may, on the surface, match the objectives but still not reflect the student's progress. This characteristic, the degree to which an assessment provides an accurate estimate of learning gains, is known as *validity*. If a learner who has mastered the specified body of knowledge does poorly on the test, exercise, or project intended to measure this mastery (or, conversely, if learners who have not mastered the material perform well), that particular assessment would be said to have low content validity. For example, test items intended to measure analogical reasoning may, instead, reflect the learner's reading ability if vocabulary level is not considered in test design. Or if a project is supposed to demonstrate the learner's ability to design process controls in a laboratory environment, but an unrealistic time limit for completion is imposed, this assessment may indicate that some learners have not mastered the concepts when in fact they simply were not given adequate time to demonstrate their expertise.

Criterion-referenced validity, also called *predictive validity,* has significant implications for workforce training. If an employee successfully completes a series of training units on using a new software package but then can't apply those skills on the job, the instrument that assessed his or her performance had low predictive validity. This is also important if the content being taught is part of a hierarchically organized series of learning modules in which foundational concepts or basic skills must be mastered before the learner moves on to more advanced tasks.

Reliability refers to the stability of an instrument or activity; this could be thought of as how consistently the assessment measures learning gains. If students perform poorly as a group on one occasion and then do much better later, the predictability of this assessment is called into question. Or if learner mastery is measured by observation and scored by several different raters, the scores must be highly correlated to ensure consistency (also known as *interrater reliability*). Low reliability signals that the results are not dependable and could vary significantly from day-to-day, rendering them potentially meaningless.

Another characteristic of good assessments that is especially important in distance education settings is *clarity of expectations.* This refers to how easy the assessment is for the learner (or others) to understand, whether the instructions are clearly written, and whether any special conditions are to be met. For many distant students, examinations will be proctored by someone other than the instructor ("Is this supposed to be an 'open book' test?"), projects may be completed based only on the directions initially provided ("We weren't told we had to use both print and online resources!"), and papers will be written according to instructions provided in the course syllabus ("Was that 10 to 12 pages double-spaced or single-spaced?"). If directions are not comprehensive, specific, and clearly worded, the assessment activity quickly loses its value.

Finally, although there are many other criteria for judging the merits of a particular assessment, all are meant to help answer the question, "Does this assessment activity measure learning gains and allow an accurate generalization of results beyond the immediate situation?" In other words, a useful assessment reflects the learner's progress and understanding, as well as the transferability of skills and knowledge. The obvious purpose of an assessment is to document the direct results of instruction, but if a student successfully performs a task in a learning environment but isn't able to replicate it in a real-world setting, what's the point?

CATEGORIZING ASSESSMENT MEASURES

There are more ways to categorize assessments than there are useful reasons to do so, but it may be helpful to consider two schemas in particular: objective/subjective and formative/summative. The first is based on attributes of the assessment itself and the second is related to how the results are used.

Objective/Subjective

Classifying an assessment as either objective or subjective depends not only the activity itself, but more specifically on the nature of the product that results from student performance. Will every successful student end up with the same result? Or will the

With planning, almost any technique for assessment possible in a regular classroom is also possible for distant learners.

outcomes offer equivalent information regarding student performance but be reflected in individual results? For example, we can assume that if two students complete a multiple-choice test and each scores 100%, their tests (the deliverables) will be virtually identical. However, if those same two students submit term papers, we hope that those products are not identical! *Subjective* assessments are those that are designed to result in products quite similar from one student to the next, yet demand individual scrutiny to determine the learner's progress and/or score. In contrast, *objective* measures—the identical results type—do not require human intervention (or, at least, knowledgeable intervention) to determine whether students achieved mastery. With objective measures, we expect all of the right answers to match.

Objective measures offer significant advantages in ease of implementation. Tests incorporating multiple-choice, true–false, matching, or other types of "machine-scorable" questions can be an efficient way to measure learning, especially if the instructional objectives are written at a low level of cognitive effort, such as knowledge or comprehension, where students are merely expected to recall previously memorized information (e.g., state capitals or vocabulary words). As objectives move up the cognitive processing scale toward analyzing and synthesizing (inferring relationships or creating models), multiple-choice test items get more difficult and time-consuming to create. Writing multiple-choice test items that require higher-order thinking skills demands creativity and careful attention to the course or unit objectives. For example, a question at the analysis, synthesis, or evaluation levels might present learners with a written paragraph and then expect them to identify gaps in logical reasoning, recognize data elements relevant to the solution of a problem, or judge which statement presented fits a set of given criteria. The students would need to apply their comprehension of the course content to demonstrate these skills, but would not merely select a correct answer from rote memory.

Besides the obvious time-savings advantage of machine scoring, objective tests also enable a teacher or trainer to ascertain specifically which concepts within a course, module, or lesson are being mastered and which are not. Item analysis can quickly identify questions missed by many students, for example, and also indicate the likelihood that students simply hadn't learned the intended concepts, or whether the test items in question appear to be poor discriminators (i.e., items frequently missed by students who know the material and/or items frequently answered correctly by students who do not know the material). Additionally, objective tests created with assessment software (whether specialized or as part of a course management system) can include options such as individualized branching, adapted content presentation, and selective release of test items based on performance. For disciplines requiring meticulous classification of skill attainment and feedback of precise granularity, such customization is highly valued.

Short-answer test items (sometimes called *free-response items* or *supply items*) straddle the fence between objective and subjective assessments. These items are written either as direct questions requiring the learner fill in a word or phrase or as statements in which a space has been left blank for a brief written answer. Because students can fill in any response, care must be taken to create items that are precise and not open to a wide variety of interpretations. This is crucial in many distance education environments; test proctors at remote sites cannot be expected to answer questions about particular test items or what the instructor meant to say. Like multiple-choice tests, short-answer items are easiest to write when students are expected to recall information from memory, rather than analyze complex concepts.

Although objective assessment activities are especially attractive for use in large-enrollment courses, they rarely provide a comprehensive picture of learner progress. Subjective measures (i.e., those requiring human judgment for scoring) include such familiar learning tasks as research papers, essay tests, and projects, as well as more recently introduced strategies such as online discussions, e-portfolios, and graphic organizers (such as concept maps). By providing a mix of assessment types, measurements of student learning are less likely to be confounded by individual learner characteristics or environmental factors that might differentially affect some students.

Subjective assessment methods can work especially well in the distance education environment. For example, although many K–12 school systems have initiated distance education programs, adult learners make up the majority of students involved in distance education overall, whether affiliated with an educational institution, as part of a privately administered training sequence for certification or licensure, or professional development activities offered through their employer's human resources department. These students may have been away from the traditional classroom for several years, and assessment methods typically associated with that environment—pencil-and-paper objective tests, for example—may seem irrelevant or trivial. Many distance education programs (especially those designed for adult learners) have, therefore, adopted a wide array of subjective assessment practices. These might include traditional measures such as term papers or essay tests, but also incorporate a group of tasks collectively referred to *as alternative assessments*. As implied, this a method of gauging student progress in ways unlike those used in more traditional course configurations. Three approaches—authentic assessment, performance-based assessment, and constructivist assessment—have come to the forefront of this movement, although these categories often overlap and the terms may be used interchangeably by some writers.

Authentic assessment refers to tasks that simulate real-world challenges. Mueller, in the *Authentic Assessment Toolbox* (2010), described an effective authentic activity as one in which students "perform real-world tasks that demonstrate meaningful application of essential knowledge and skills." These types of assessments frequently emphasize the transfer of skills to unfamiliar situations beyond the classroom and are often embedded in case-based or situated instructional modules.

Performance-based assessment is, in fact, what it sounds like—expecting the learner to perform a skill. In addition, it may include determining what the learner knows about the skill itself, or focus on higher-order thinking and critical reasoning. Simply requiring that students perform a science experiment, however, does not guarantee that critical thinking about the process or about the applicable scientific concepts will occur. Exploring how learners arrive at their answers or why they performed a specific task in the manner they did will provide evidence of the desired cognitive activity. Some performance assessments will reflect a process (preparing and presenting a speech, for example) and some may have no tangible outcome (speaking a foreign language).

Assessment activities that reflect a *constructivist*, or learner-centered, approach encourage students to choose their own mode of expression, to work collaboratively with others, to think about their learning, and to rethink and revise their ideas as they build their cognitive structures (Rust, O'Donovan, & Price, 2005). The emphasis is on the creation of personal meaning and divergent thinking, which poses some interesting challenges for the instructor who has experience only with more traditional forms of testing or with projects bounded by clearly defined criteria. This need not mean that assessment activities lack scholarly rigor, however, and allowing for variance in developmental pace or individual preference may actually require learners to take on greater responsibility for their progress toward the instructional goal.

The distinction between objective and subjective assessments is useful to the extent that we consider the reason for creating and implementing an assessment activity. *Objective assessments* are more convenient to administer, easier to score, and frequently are easier to create, as well. They are useful when looking for trends over time (for example, looking at test scores over a multi-year period) or when making comparisons among disparate groups (freshmen biology students at five different universities). *Subjective assessments,* on the other hand, are more useful when the transfer of skills to environments outside the classroom is important, or if the process of identifying the correct answer is as important as the answer itself. The next section will examine another way of categorizing assessments.

Formative/Summative

Another means to categorize assessment measures is to sort them by purpose, based on how the results will be used. *Formative* assessments are those activities that lead to the refinement of the instruction itself. For example, if an instructor rewrites the directions for an assignment after noticing that several students misunderstood the task, this would be an example of formative assessment. This is a somewhat limited definition, especially since it's not always clear at the outset if an assessment activity will eventually provide feedback indicating that revision is needed. Instead, many instructional designers use a more inclusive definition for formative evaluation that includes any assessment that provides information about a learner's progress toward mastery of the objectives. In this sense, the feedback allows the learner to shape (i.e., "form") his or her efforts at accomplishing the goal and the teacher to provide customized assistance when it's needed.

Many instructional activities that fall into the formative assessment realm could also be categorized as *assessment for learning*. Proponents of the assessment-for-learning movement encourage the use of ongoing tasks intended to provide feedback to the learner and/or to the instructor, to identify misconceptions held by the learner, to enhance motivation, and to signal to the learner which concepts are especially important (Stobart, 2008; Wiliam & Thompson, 2008). This initiative focuses on the active engagement of learners, including the extensive use of self-assessments designed to build a sense of ownership and responsibility within students regarding their learning, This awareness and control of one's own thinking, typically referred to as *metacognition,* enables learners to evolve into autonomous learners and develop skills of self-regulation. This subset of formative evaluation is learner-focused, whereas the revision-centric definition offered above is primarily concerned with the instruction itself. Finally, formative assessments may be intended to develop skills in the learner not directly related to the content area, such as collaboration, critical thinking, writing, or problem solving.

Summative assessments are outcomes focused and emphasize the final results of a course or module. Standardized, non–course-related exams such as the ACT, GRE, or GMAT, fall into this category as well because they provide a snapshot of knowledge and skills from which the only feedback is a numeric score and possibly percentile rank. Summative assessments are typically intended for administrative purposes such as assigning grades, reporting the success or failure of specific programs, awarding a certificate or license, or compiling evidence of program quality for accreditation purposes. By definition, summative assessments are almost always comprehensive, measuring the mastery of a specified body of knowledge or completed curricular unit.

Although summative assessments can be beneficial when used appropriately, the misuse of standardized tests (especially in the K–12 arena) has contributed to an overall distrust of how test scores are used, a lack of confidence in their objectivity, and doubt that such exams can actually measure anything of importance. Research suggests that these high-stakes assessments can be demotivating for many learners (Harlen & Deakin Crick, 2003), leading to an increasingly large gap between high and low achievers, increased focus on extrinsic versus intrinsic rewards, and decreasing levels of persistence when tasks were perceived as difficult. Obviously, not all summative assessments result in such dire outcomes but the importance of administering and interpreting such tests carefully cannot be overemphasized.

A possible third category—diagnostic assessments—is sometimes considered its own type of assessment. In this text, however, it has been subsumed into the other two. Diagnostic tests or other tasks may be used in a formative manner to adapt instruction based on learner needs or as a summative measurement to determine readiness for more advanced levels of learning, as in the case of the GRE test, for example. Because diagnostic assessments can be used in both ways, they have not been singled out as a separate category for the purposes of this text.

When designing assessment measures, their usefulness will depend primarily on a clear understanding of whether the resulting information is intended for formative or summative purposes. The assessment techniques used for each type may be quite similar; the distinction lies in how the resulting data are used.

ASSESSMENT STRATEGIES

Much of this chapter's content could be applied to any instructional setting, whether online, face-to-face, or something in between. As mentioned previously, explaining good assessment, like defining good teaching, requires an understanding and explication of core concepts—validity, reliability, and so on—that remain constant across learning environments. Likewise, this section will describe several types of assessment activities and their use in distance learning environments, but any of them could be used for face-to-face instruction, as well.

Online Quizzes and Tests

Online quizzes, using either a course management system (CMS) or a dedicated testing package (such as Respondus or Questionmark), offer numerous advantages over their pencil-and-paper cousins. Quizzes can be set up to select questions randomly from a pool, display graphics or video with the question text, provide immediate feedback based on the learner's response, offer spell-checking, allow multiple retakes, and enter the quiz scores directly into an online gradebook, as just a few examples of available features. A variety of question formats are available, including multiple-choice, short answer, numeric, and many others. Online quizzes are best used as formative, self-study activities that provide feedback to learners, motivate them to keep up with course readings, and provide reinforcement of important ideas.

Online testing tools may also be utilized for high-stakes assessments (final exams or licensure tests, for example), but are best administered in a proctored setting. For many distance education programs, hiring test proctors to monitor student exams provides a reasonable element of accountability to offset the unsecure nature of the online environment. Proctored testing centers typically require students to present identification prior to taking an exam, and may also elect to install browser lock-down software to prevent printing or copying of the test questions, surfing the Web, or interacting with others via e-mail or instant messaging. (One such product, Securexam, even includes features such as fingerprint analysis, voice recognition, and video surveillance.) An additional advantage of integrating proctored assessments into instruction is that student performance levels in a proctored setting that are consistent with scores earned for work completed at a distance will help validate the assessment regimen and enhance credibility.

Asynchronous Communication

One of the most frequently used features in any CMS is the asynchronous *discussion forum*. These flexible online utilities can be used to implement a wide variety of assessment activities. The most obvious approach is to have students respond to questions or discuss course material within the forum environment. Some instructors have been distressed to discover that if student participation is not required, few will actually join in the conversation, but those same instructors, ultimately, are often pleased at the quality of the messages posted. Not surprisingly, when learners are given time to think about their responses, the contributions are apt to be more meaningful, on topic, and well organized than those offered in a traditional classroom environment. Of course, as in all discussions, good questions are more likely to produce good answers.

One useful strategy is to post a thought-provoking question that encourages higher-order thinking; after students respond to the prompt, have them to return to the forum and reply to one or several of their peers' messages. In many cases, students will read all of the messages posted to determine which ones they'll respond to, with the result being a discussion in which everyone gets to talk and everyone listens. Additionally, students will often return yet again to the discussion area to read the comments offered on their initial messages, and respond to those posts. These communication threads more closely resemble true discussion, as opposed to the post-and-go nature of interactions that result when students merely respond once to whatever question the instructor poses.

Other ways of using the discussion forum include student debates, student-moderated discussions with questions generated from readings, or the use of the forum as a repository for student assignments (sans the instructor's evaluative marks or scores, obviously). The latter method has been used successfully by many faculty who have found that requiring students to post their papers or projects in a common location often results in excellent work and offers the added benefit of providing students with benchmarks for their own performance.

Blogs are sometimes used instead of, or in conjunction with, discussion boards in an online class. The advantage of a blog over a discussion is the ability to customize who "owns" the page, who can read it or comment on it, and when. For example, an instructor may choose to establish a blog that a small group can post messages in, but other students are able to read those messages and comment on them if they choose. There is also an affective component to the use of a blog that may provide additional motivation for students to share their ideas. As one instructor explained, "When students use the discussion board they see it as belonging to the entire class, and they're allowed to use it. But a blog seems more like it's *theirs*." This sense of ownership brings with it the responsibility to post meaningful commentary and to engage with other participants who may elect to comment on the blogger's postings.

As an assessment tool, a blog can be used much like a discussion board, with students responding to prompts, posing their own questions, summarizing reading assignments, and so on. Blogs may be part of an integrated course management system or they may be established as free-standing utilities. If an open-access blog tool is used (i.e., one freely available through providers such as Blogger.com), instructors should understand the risks of sites being hacked or the chance that the provider may cease operations without warning.

Another asynchronous communication tool especially useful for distant students is a *wiki,* which (like a blog) may be part of a course management system or function as a stand-alone utility. These online environments allow groups of students to collaborate online, incorporating text, graphics, and other digital materials into a cohesive final result. The wiki site (depending on the software used) can be visible to only a few group members, to anyone in the course, or only to members initially, then later made available to others. Permissions for editing and commenting can also be assigned to specific individuals or left open to anyone who's interested. Every version of the site is retained, so if a student inadvertently deletes something important it can be retrieved or if a user determines that an earlier incarnation of the work is preferred, that version can easily be restored.

Using a wiki as an assessment tool has distinct advantages over traditional group work. Typically, the instructor will be able to see which group member made which contributions or edits to the most recent version of the site, thus alleviating one of the major headaches related to student collaboration. Additionally, because all group members can edit the site, students get practice with important teamwork skills such as negotiation and consensus building.

Instructors working with students engaged in field work such as clinicals, student teaching, or internships find *online journals* useful for keeping track of student progress. Journals typically allow only the teacher or tutor to read the postings and are especially appropriate for assignments or tasks requiring student reflection or activities that occur over an extended period. As with a discussion forum, the instructor will probably need to require students to make regular posts to their journals but it will quickly become a habit. Assigning journal writing provides the distance education teacher an opportunity to model an honest and direct communication style, offer meaningful guidance, and provide sincere and constructive feedback when working with students. Care must be taken, however to ensure that journal topics and assignments are clearly course related and that interactions are never allowed to stray into the realm of confession or counseling.

Synchronous Communication

Communication tools such as desktop videoconferencing, audioconferencing, chat, or instant messaging provide a real-time dynamic for assessment that can offer instructors an immediate sense of how well students grasp the course content. This is especially helpful when specific course objectives require students to apply newly learned skills and content extemporaneously. For example, the ability to speak a foreign language fluently is most appropriately assessed in a real-time, audio- or video-based interaction. Similarly, learners hoping to become successful customer service representatives may be expected to reply immediately (orally or with text-based messaging) to various "angry client" scenarios, without the luxury of time to sift through the many possible responses.

Synchronous tools can be used for groups or one-to-one sessions between the instructor and a student, with students calling or logging in individually to a conference site or chat room. Instant messaging also works well for individual interactions and has the added advantage of allowing several simultaneous conversations to occur, each a private exchange between the teacher and one student. Such one-to-one sessions might be used for "oral exam" types of assessments, or to mimic a private appointment during office hours. Synchronous communication tools also facilitate the use of student presentations as an assessment option, during which a group of individuals need only to log in to view and comment on their peers' speech or other real-time presentation.

One disadvantage to real-time assessments is that only a small group of learners can be actively involved simultaneously. Attempting to conduct synchronous activities with a large group of students (more than a dozen, for example) typically results either in chaos or a substantial percentage of the students lurking passively in the background. One method for avoiding a string of disordered exchanges (or, even worse, none at all) is for the instructor to guide the conversation around a series of discussion questions, with ample opportunity for everyone to respond. Some professors handle this by posing a question in the chat and then "calling on" two or three students to respond. Once these individuals have presented their responses, other students are given the chance to join in and add their ideas or ask follow-up questions, if they choose to. Students have the option to waive a particular question and be called on again, but by keeping track of who has participated throughout, the professor ensures that everyone has a chance to contribute.

Finally, synchronous assessment activities offer two related and especially important capabilities to distance education programs: building a sense of immediacy between students and instructor, and facilitating the formation of the learning group. *Immediacy* refers to the perception of social presence, or that sense of "being with" someone else, and is based on Mehrabian's work (see, for example, Mehrabian, 1969) on communication and social dynamics. For students working at a distance, possibly in geographic isolation, membership in the learning group offers a sense of belonging and adds relevance to the instructional experience. Synchronous interactions, such as online chats or audioconferences, enhance those perceptions and students often remark that it makes a difference to know that the teacher is "really there, right then" during these sessions. Another possible benefit is that when students feel closer to the instructor or other students, undesirable behaviors, such as flaming others in online discussions or cheating on an assignment, may be less likely to occur.

Portfolios

Portfolios have a long history as summative assessment tools in fields such as graphic design, architecture, and marketing, but are gaining acceptance quickly for their value as formative compilations of work in a much broader range of disciplines. A portfolio might consist of a variety of materials (papers, video clips, photographs, etc.) reflecting generalized learning across disciplines, or it might be a more specific gathering of content-based materials, such as tests, reports, or art projects. One of the key elements of portfolio creation is that the student decides (typically with an instructor's guidance) what materials to include in the collection. Self-reflection leading to the development of standards and the determination of criteria to use in selecting these materials are integral components of this process. Identifying what constitutes one's own "best work" represents a level of self-assessment requiring thoughtful consideration of learning goals and progress toward significant milestones.

For students working at a distance, the development of a portfolio can provide a meaningful connection with the instructor as criteria are established, materials exchanged, and time lines for completion negotiated. Some digital portfolio software packages, such as Digication, enable the instructor to integrate rubrics or licensure standards within the site, allowing the student to then link items to each criterion measure to demonstrate mastery. These types of software systems allow portfolio owners to establish permissions for others (potential employers, for example) to view some or all of the portfolio, and to download the materials for storage on a variety of media.

Papers and Multimedia Products

The ubiquitous "term paper" assignment is still a valuable assessment tool for distant students and those in traditional settings. However, technology has made it a less labor-intensive process both for students and teachers, and opened up possibilities for multimedia products as well. The obvious advantages of composing papers electronically combined with the use of more recently introduced options (online drop boxes, wikis, and enhanced presentation software) make hardcopy paper assignments seem old-fashioned by comparison.

Most CMSs have some form of drop box where students can submit assignments electronically. This feature is typically set up so that a student's work goes directly into a folder that is accessible only to the instructor and contains all submissions of the same assignment. This keeps student files collected in one place, provides time/date stamping to verify when files were submitted, enables batch downloading of files, and allows the instructor to return materials easily to the student's drop box.

Wikis provide the ideal environment for collaborative writing and editing, enabling multiple users to contribute, edit, or comment on the work in progress. For papers or other projects created by more than one person, a wiki offers a flexible and robust feature set, with the added advantage of making the final product viewable by other students in the course with a button click.

Multimedia products, such as videos, websites, or presentations can be incorporated into one's assessment plan with the use of inexpensive, easy-to-use software and the CMS. Basic slide presentations (such as those using the seemingly ubiquitous PowerPoint software) can be enhanced with audio narration, video clips, graphics, and links to external websites and may be viewable to an entire class or simply submitted to the instructor for review and feedback. Student-produced materials in digital formats can be embedded in blogs, wikis, discussion forums, or simply posted within an area inside the CMS or on a standalone website.

Problem-Based Activities, Games, and Simulations

Problem-based instruction approach has been used successfully in medical education for decades and has been adopted recently by many other disciplines. Learners are presented with a case or scenario and are expected to analyze the situation and recommend a course of action. This strategy has the advantage of built-in authenticity because this is how challenges occur in real life. (Few of us are suddenly faced with dilemmas or untoward circumstances that—coincidentally—we have just spent three weeks studying.) As in real life, students must learn about the problem itself, analyze its components, gather resources, and synthesize this information to prepare recommendations. Problem-based learning is most successful when scenarios reflect real-world professional challenges, and when they provide opportunities for students to work collaboratively with peers toward resolution.

Simple, instructor-developed games may lack the impressive effects of their digital counterparts, but can be created to match the specific learning objectives of a lesson or module. Some examples include quiz-type games, group problem-solving exercises, or strategic planning activities. For students who may be geographically removed from the learning group, games can assist in building a sense of belonging and can be helpful for promoting collaboration and teamwork.

Simulations, especially those incorporating a variety of multimedia elements, provide learners with a rich environment in which to make decisions and see the consequences of those decisions, thus prompting another round of problem solving. Simulation or game activities may involve role playing, group or individual decision making, extensive branching to accommodate multiple scenarios, and a critical balance between an easy-to-learn game and an intellectual challenge (Gee, 2003). The motivating aspects of these activities are obvious, but how they fit into an assessment plan is a bit more subtle. The simulation itself must be carefully designed to reinforce concepts, provide opportunities to practice new skills, and offer feedback based on performance. Ideally, a repository of student performance data is also made available for instructor review. Unfortunately, although simulations and complex game activities show great promise for assessment, they aren't quickly or easily developed and require extensive programming and graphics design expertise to build. Therefore, most instructors or trainers must look for already-created packages until a greater selection of educational simulations becomes available.

Graphic Organizers

The use of concept maps, flowcharts, Venn diagrams, and other graphical representations of concepts and how they're related to one another to assess student learning is a relatively recent phenomenon. This technique originated in the 1960s (see, for example, Ausubel, Novak, & Hanesian, 1978) but it wasn't until the diagrams could be created, stored, modified, and shared easily (i.e., using a computer) that their use in education flourished. These models, which may resemble extensive webs or simple line drawings, allow learners to organize their thoughts visually and incorporate lines, arrows, grids, circles, boxes, or other visual elements. For many learners, using a visual model to illustrate their understanding will be a freeing experience and lead to more robust and creative thinking; for many topics, creating a graphic image with concepts linked together with lines or arrows denoting the types of relationships among the ideas will be the optimal assessment of understanding. Students can create their own graphics as a pretest activity to identify gaps in understanding, and gradually add nodes and links to them as they build a more comprehensive understanding of the course content. Or, the instructor might give students a template for a graphic model that has some of the concepts already included to serve as an advance organizer as well as an assessment tool when students finish filling in the model.

These graphics can be created with simple computer-based drawing tools, or built using software especially developed for this purpose. Inspiration is probably the most popular commercially produced package for creating graphic organizers, but a variety of freeware and shareware can be obtained online, as well (for example, Freemind, Cmap Tools, or Gliffy). Because graphic organizers can be created electronically and are easily distributed, such tools can be indispensable for engaging in collaborative group work, diagnosing learner misconceptions, or modeling the synthesis of ideas whether students are at a distance or face-to-face.

IMPLEMENTATION STRATEGIES

The assessment strategies described in the previous section are not unique to the distance education environment, although their implementation may vary based on how geographically dispersed students are, what delivery systems are being used, the personal characteristics of students, or other factors. This section will offer additional suggestions for implementing various assessment activities, along with practical strategies to improve the effectiveness of those measures.

Ongoing and Nongraded Assessment Measures

Distance education students who are returning to formal education, in particular, derive great benefit from the use of ongoing assessment. *Ongoing* (sometimes called *embedded*) assessment activities are woven into the fabric of the instructional process so that determining student progress does not necessarily represent to students a threat, a disciplinary function, or a necessary evil, but simply occurs as another thread within the seamless pattern of day-to-day classroom or training events. One advantage of this approach is that any misconceptions held by learners that might interfere with later progress are identified and addressed before they become obstacles to further learning. The American Association for Higher Education encourages this in its "9 Principles of Good Practice for Assessing Student Learning" (2000) and goes on to state, "The point is to monitor progress toward intended goals in a spirit of continuous improvement." A natural advantage for the instructor is that the dreaded "crunch" of grading that presents itself when assessments occur in large blocks is avoided; ongoing assessment provides information on student progress in smaller increments over the course of a unit, training module, or academic semester (Stiggins, 2007).

Using *nongraded* assessment measures for part of the course alleviates much of the strain of assigning scores to massive amounts of student work, while still providing several of the benefits of traditional assessments. Spontaneous question-and-answer activities (either verbal or written, similar to pop quizzes) can be integrated easily into synchronous group activities where they act to reinforce content, supply feedback on student progress to students and teacher, and provide motivational support. Likewise, instructors can use the discussion board as a kind of ongoing assessment that doesn't require an excessive time commitment; occasional participation provides students with the reassurance that the instructor is present without being intrusive.

Balancing Flexibility and Structure

Course structure, including the timing of assessment deadlines, can often be flexed without negative consequences. Most learners (traditional and nontraditional) function most effectively with moderate amounts of structure, including deadlines for assignments or activities. This needn't mean, however, that the course schedule isn't negotiable. By alleviating the pressure of time constraints, adult learners (who may have less-than-flexible family or work schedules) have the opportunity to prepare papers, projects, or other evidence of learning while not tying them to a rigid and potentially unworkable timetable. Obviously, the degree of flexibility should be determined based on the maturity of the student, but unless course objectives require learners to create products within a specific time frame, it makes little sense to demand adherence to an inflexible calendar. An example of this type of flexible pacing might be the assignment of a research paper with a series of milestone deadlines (topic and rough outline, first rough draft, second edited draft, etc.) jointly determined by the student and teacher.

Using Scoring Rubrics

One of the major disadvantages of subjective assessment measures is the difficulty of assigning scores or ratings to learner performance. To facilitate this process, and improve the consistency and fairness of scoring, many instructors use scoring rubrics. A *rubric* is a descriptive framework to guide the evaluation of complex assignments or those requiring individual judgment. Sometimes a rubric consists of a simple list of characteristics or descriptions, aligned with levels of quality, such as *outstanding, good, fair,* and *unacceptable,* or point values given for each level. For example, the criteria for an "outstanding" rating on a set of arithmetic problems could include that the work was submitted on time, completed with at least 90% accuracy, and was written neatly; a rating of "good" might require at least 80% accuracy, submission on time, and written legibly; and so on. Other rubrics may be significantly more comprehensive, developed using a matrix format that includes categories of activities within the task (e.g., spelling, vocabulary, organization, etc., for a book report) down one side, and quality levels across the top. The criteria are then included for each cell in the matrix.

Scoring rubrics can be used for almost any type of subjective assessment activity. One clever professor distributed the rubric and sample papers to her students early in the semester; their assignment was to grade one of the papers using the rubric. This not only helped students understand how their papers would be assessed, but also gave them practice with critical thinking. Many instructors hesitate to require student participation in Web-based discussions or synchronous chat sessions, because of the difficulties inherent in scoring such activities. Simply requiring a minimum number of postings from each student doesn't usually work and may instead result in a few students monopolizing the forum or chat, much like poorly run discussions in a face-to-face classroom. Instead, the instructor can provide students with a rubric for discussions or chats, or better yet, enlist the students to help create one (Bauer, 2002). Criteria included in a rubric for participating in discussions might refer to elements such as posting messages by the due date or logging in to the chat on time, or have a more qualitative emphasis with points given for adhering to the topic at hand, supporting opinions with evidence, or demonstrating a grasp of key concepts. (See Figure 9–1 for an example of a scoring matrix created specifically to assess asynchronous discussion contributions.) After the rubric is developed, the instructor may wish to provide example responses that demonstrate the various criterion levels, to model exemplary answers, and to clarify specifically why points would be deducted from the average or poor responses.

FIGURE 9–1 Example rubric for asynchronous discussion contributions.

	Unacceptable Response—0 points	Marginal Response—1 point	Good Response—2 points	Outstanding Response—3 points
Mechanics	Many errors in spelling, grammar, or vocabulary; message posted after due date	Some errors in spelling, grammar, or vocabulary; message posted after due date	Few errors in spelling, grammar, or vocabulary; message posted on time	No errors in spelling, grammar, or vocabulary; message posted on time
Clarity	Message is not organized; does not address the original question; includes irrelevant information or rambles on	Message is not well organized; contains some irrelevant information; may have neglected to answer a part of the question	Message is clear and well organized but may include irrelevant information; answers all parts of the question	Message is written clearly and concisely; well organized and complete
Comprehension	Little, if any, understanding demonstrated; evidence to support statements missing	Some understanding of concepts demonstrated; supporting evidence for statements shaky or missing	Demonstrates a basic understanding of key concepts; refers to evidence to support statements	Demonstrates a keen grasp of key concepts; provides evidence to support statements
Original Thinking	Original thinking not demonstrated; no synthesis or evaluation of others' ideas; does not draw conclusions from material	Displays few original ideas; does not synthesize ideas well; conclusions are not supportable; interprets others' ideas minimally	Demonstrates some original thought through synthesis, evaluation, or interpretation of others' ideas; draws conclusions that may be supportable	Displays original thought in synthesizing concepts, interpreting or critically evaluating the ideas of others, or drawing reasonable conclusions

As helpful as they are, creating meaningful rubrics can be daunting, not to mention time consuming. Fortunately, "rubric generators" have begun to appear on the Web for teachers to use as templates that can then be customized to their instructional needs. For example, RubiStar is a template that guides the instructor through the rubric creation process and provides example criteria for use in developing a scoring matrix for assignments ranging from oral presentations to science fair experiments. (RubiStar is provided freely for educational use through the High Plains Regional Technology in Education Consortium, 1 of 10 federally funded R-TEC centers nationwide. See RubiStar at http://rubistar.4teachers.org.)

Facilitating Student Collaboration

Collaborative work is the norm in many professions, and it's the rare individual who works entirely alone without relying on others for input or assistance. Unfortunately, many students are more familiar with schools in which competitive models of education reign and collaborative learning looks to them like a risky venture. Therefore, collaborative activities are best designed with these students in mind. The ideal collaborative project requires interdependent work by students, during which reciprocal, social interactions result in positive outcomes for the entire group. Projects that are not easily broken into discrete tasks work well, to prevent students from simply completing each portion individually and assembling the pieces like a jigsaw puzzle. Although a significant body of research supports the use of collaborative learning and its benefits, many instructors and an even greater number of students prefer not to engage in such activities. Two reasons typically emerge when one asks students why they avoid collaborative group work: logistical difficulties and, as one student rather bluntly exclaimed, "Slackers!" Logistical issues are significantly alleviated with the use of online tools such as wikis, discussion boards, chat utilities, and file sharing repositories, but teachers share their students' concerns about scoring, and worry that they'll never be able to assign grades fairly when an individual student's efforts may be masked by the good, or not-so-good, work of his or her teammates.

Strategies to mitigate these concerns with scoring group work include defining the grading criteria at the outset, monitoring student progress throughout the process, and not relying on the collaborative work for the majority of a course or unit grade. Defining the criteria will reinforce exactly what the expectations are and how performance will be rated. Monitoring student progress by using a CMS provides instructors with the opportunity to see at a glance who's contributing to wikis or discussions, who's asking important questions during group chats, or who's producing work to be shared among the group for feedback.

Some instructors also invite students to assess the contributions of their teammates, by assigning percentages or point values to each group member. Another method is to ask students, midway through the project, to report on how well their group is working, in terms of task sharing, negotiating consensus, communication, and related criteria. Although the initial resistance to collaboration may prove daunting, ultimately these valuable work skills will be a practical addition to any student's abilities.

Technical Difficulties

"The network was down so I couldn't turn in my paper on time." Is this the new version of "The dog ate my homework"? Regardless of the specific details, there will be times when students will claim that technical problems interfered with their ability to complete an assessment activity, and sometimes they'll be right. There are several things an instructor can do to prepare for this eventuality.

First, establish a close working relationship with the tech support staff and keep lines of communication open. If there are technical problems, whoever hears about it first can inform the others. Tech support will be able to address glitches more quickly and instructors will be able to alert students. Second, let students know what their responsibilities are regarding technical difficulties. Should they identify a backup work-station (a computer at the local library, for example) in case they're unable to work from home? Are they expected to call a help desk to report technical problems? Finally, allow enough flexibility in the assessment process that technical problems don't overshadow the value of the course itself. If a student makes a good faith attempt to do the assignment and runs into problems, that experience can strengthen the bond between teacher and learner as they negotiate a resolution satisfactory to both.

SELECTING APPROPRIATE ASSESSMENT MEASURES

Figure 9–2 suggests a way to determine which assessment measures might be most appropriate for a given purpose. Several types of assessment activities are listed, with their possible uses noted. This is not intended as a comprehensive model, but rather a way to explore and appraise the usefulness of various assessments, and should be modified based on learning goals, student characteristics, delivery media, and instructor preference.

ACADEMIC MISCONDUCT

While there appears to be no single, agreed-upon definition of academic misconduct, it may be that, like art, "you know it when you see it." Most institutions have policies stating what constitutes academic misconduct—misrepresentation, plagiarism, disruption of classes, and so on—and how infractions will be handled. Unfortunately, such policies seem to have little effect as deterrents to unethical behavior. Speculation about why students cheat typically includes such reasons as "pressure to succeed" (and its twin, "fear of failure") and the sense that "everyone" is doing it coupled with the perception that if other students are cheating, those who don't will be at a competitive disadvantage.

Although cheating and plagiarism are not problems exclusive to the distance education domain, the use of advanced communications technologies, coupled with the perceived absence (at least geographically) of an authority figure, has led to what many teachers and trainers consider a growing problem on campus and off. Although public awareness of academic misconduct has grown, arguments are inconclusive concerning whether the number of occurrences has actually increased, or if an increase in *reported* occurrences is responsible for the perception of rampant dishonesty. What everyone can agree on is that cheating and plagiarism are serious problems, and that they have never been easier to commit, thanks to the increased technological literacy of our students and the wide availability of term papers (among other things) for sale online.

Plagiarism

Clarifying precisely what constitutes plagiarism and having clear policies for dealing with it are two strategies suggested by the Council of Writing Program Administrators for alleviating this problem (2003). Instructors should also attempt to distinguish

FIGURE 9–2 Selecting appropriate assessment measures.

	Provide immediate feedback	Encourage reflection	Facilitate efficient scoring	Facilitate high-stakes scoring	Encourage synthesis	Enhance motivation	Encourage collaboration	Facilitate self-assessment	Demonstrate skill mastery (psychomotor)
Online Quizzing	X		X			X		X	
Proctored Examination	X		X	X		X			X
Discussion (Asynchronous)		X					X	X	
Chat/Audioconference (Synchronous)	X				X	X			
Developmental Portfolio		X		X	X	X		X	
Concept Map Creation		X			X	X		X	
Papers/Essays		X			X				
Design/Creation of Product		X			X	X	X		
Journal		X			X	X		X	
Simulation/Role Play	X					X	X	X	X
Presentation (audio or video)						X	X		X
Case-based/Problem-based activities		X			X	X	X	X	

284

between plagiarism (i.e., the intent to claim as one's own someone else's words or ideas), and the simple misuse of sources, resulting from ignorance or carelessness. Dee and Jacob (2010) conducted a field study to determine the utility of an anti-plagiarism tutorial in reducing such infractions, and discovered that students who completed the tutorial were less likely to plagiarize. McKenzie (1998) suggested requiring that students differentiate between their own words and ideas and those of others with different colored text for each, a strategy that not only reinforces the ethics of proper citation, but also highlights the value of the student's work as it extends beyond cut-and-paste accumulations of data.

Of the technologies that have influenced cheating and plagiarism, the most frequently cited as troublesome are the online entrepreneurs who sell papers already formatted for easy submission. Although purchasing prewritten essays or term papers is hardly a recent phenomenon, the relative anonymity of the marketplace, coupled with the ease of "customizing" the purchased papers, has contributed to the boom of companies offering these products. In the past, the danger of being caught buying a term paper might deter the faint of heart, but now a credit card and an e-mail address are all that are required to connect buyer and seller. In addition, yesteryear's purchased paper often had to be completely retyped, in order to present an "original" to the instructor. Now that most instructors prefer papers submitted via e-mail or online, even this minor inconvenience has vanished.

Kerlin (2000) found that term paper mills are considered both a cause and by-product of the perceived growth of student cheating in recent years, and that this has, in turn, fueled interest in plagiarism detection services, such as TurnItIn.com or SafeAssign, built directly into the Blackboard system. These tools compare papers turned in by students to those already included in databases of previously submitted papers, as well as thousands found publicly online or in digital library collections. There's no denying that this helps to detect plagiarism, but such methods may set students and teachers in adversarial roles—not the ideal learning relationship. Additionally, because these services often retain student papers to add to their databases (with which to compare papers submitted in the future), many educators have concerns about the intellectual property rights of students. Ideally, if an instructor anticipates using a plagiarism detection service, he or she should notify students of this in writing.

Unfortunately, students who are determined to misrepresent themselves in this way are finding routes around these electronic dragnets. For example, one Internet-based firm promises, "Your project isn't added to a database, sent to TurnItIn.com or put on the internet for others to use" (Paper Masters.com, 2010). Of course, this completely ignores the fact that as soon as the student (the customer) claims the paper as his or her own work he or she has committed academic fraud.

Cheating

To a great extent, teachers assume that students are honest individuals. For example, few instructors in a face-to-face classroom environment would consider checking identification to verify that each person sitting in that room is, in fact, who she or he claims to be. And so it is with distance education programs—when students submit assignments, participate in discussions, or request instructor assistance, they are rarely questioned as to their identity. However, as discussed earlier, proctored exams provide a checkpoint to balance the perceived anonymity of learning at a distance, ensuring that the student upon whose transcript the course credit and grade will reside, or whose license validates his or her abilities, is actually the student doing the work.

Technological measures to combat cheating on tests include randomizing the order of test items, randomly selecting a percentage of items from a test pool, and utilizing browser lock-down software. Instructional or logistical means to alleviate these problems might involve requiring students to take exams in a proctored setting, expecting or allowing students to work collaboratively on a test (thereby turning a problem into a learning strategy), or simply abandoning the use of objective tests for other assessment methods. Heightened awareness of unethical behavior may be a signal for course designers and instructors to rethink what types of tests are most useful, what sorts of feedback tests might provide, and how those tests might be deployed most appropriately.

Deterring Academic Misconduct

Distance education programs walk a fine line between creating a climate of suspicion and mistrust, and condoning a completely laissez-faire attitude toward serious transgressions, particularly when students feel removed both geographically and psychologically from the educational process. Notwithstanding the popular media attention given to academic misconduct (see, for example, Trex, 2010), evidence remains questionable as to whether instances of cheating, plagiarism, and other forms of dishonesty among students are skyrocketing. As media reports of unethical behavior in politics, business, journalism, and other professions escalate, the perception that "it's no big deal" may, in fact, lead to greater honesty in self-reported academic misconduct, and may also unwittingly encourage such activities.

An analogy of how instructional design might deter academic dishonesty is that of the person who decides to learn a foreign language before moving to another country. Would she cheat on assignments, avoid studying, or duck out of tutoring sessions? Not likely! When the assessment activity is relevant to a student's need (practice with new vocabulary) and the end result is tied directly to a desirable outcome (fluency in the new language), cheating is, at best, a self-defeating activity. Or maybe a neighbor decides to learn how to build a deck on his house. Would he have someone else attend the workshop to learn how to do it? Would he avoid opportunities to practice using the appropriate tools and get helpful advice? Here again, this sounds almost ridiculous, but the need to design relevant assessment activities that result in meaningful outcomes is not exaggerated.

Another instructional strategy that may circumvent dishonesty is to incorporate many small assessments throughout the unit, course, or module. These ongoing activities or embedded assessments can reduce student anxiety and alleviate the one-chance-to-prove-myself pressure that may nudge students over a line they shouldn't cross. These might include short exercises over course readings, requiring students to participate in a weekly poll about topics relevant to the course content, or a version of the "one-minute paper," during which students write a summary of what they considered the most important concepts of that unit (Angelo & Cross, 1993). These motivational activities also encourage students to not fall behind, and they provide valuable feedback with minimal effort for teachers or students.

Many schools have adopted honor codes as a way to reinforce the concepts of academic integrity. These codes typically require students to sign a pledge (once or each time they submit a major assignment or test) and involve a peer judiciary to deal with infractions. Research conducted under the auspices of the Center for Academic Integrity at Duke University suggests that these codes do, in fact, deter academic misconduct (McCabe, Trevino, & Butterfield, 1999). At a time when society seems to present dishonesty as the norm, an honor code may, at the very least, reinforce the notion that cheating is considered aberrant behavior and will not be tolerated.

Utilizing tools such as browser lock-downs during online tests or secure logins can help, but the real issues related to cheating and plagiarism may be cultural. Many teachers are now questioning the increased emphasis on cheating because of the adversarial feeling it can generate, and are advocating a more moderate approach that promotes trust and balances the seriousness of the offense with only as much attention as it deserves. Spending large quantities of valuable time chasing after a small percentage of cheaters can quickly lead to diminishing returns. In the end, as ingenuous as it may seem, it really is the student who loses out by avoiding opportunities for scholarly growth.

WHAT'S AHEAD FOR ASSESSMENT?

A promising array of technological, pedagogical, and theoretical advances forecasts enhanced flexibility for assessing learning and greater credibility for assessment results, whether at a distance or in traditional environments. Two in particular, automated essay scoring and the use of mobile devices, are worth watching.

Automated (and External) Essay Scoring

Automated scoring of essays or other written work shows significant potential for reducing the workload of teachers who have long bemoaned the labor-intensity of reading successive drafts of papers. Although few instructors would feel comfortable delegating the review of all student writing, automated scoring can be used to provide feedback on early drafts by checking mechanical features, such as sentence length and complexity, vocabulary, spelling and grammar, as well as content-related elements. Complex formulas, many of which were initially developed in the 1960s to assist with document indexing systems, have incorporated artificial intelligence operations using natural language processing technology and evolved into powerful writing analysis systems. There are currently four systems being widely used: Project Essay Grade, e-rater, IntelliMetric, and Intelligent Essay Assessor (Wang & Brown, 2007).

Researchers comparing automated scoring systems with human raters report high correlations, and several of these tools are already being used for scoring the writing portions of standardized tests.

Although the potential benefits and pitfalls of automated scoring of student writing aren't exclusive to distance learning, there are interesting corollaries seen in reactions to both of these innovative ideas. Distance learning advocates continue to struggle with the assumption held by many educators that the traditional, face-to-face classroom model is an ideal to be emulated whenever possible. Likewise, many critics of automated essay scoring systems lament the absence of a discerning human in the process, forgetting that many (if not most) teachers have limited expertise in assessing writing, may grade inconsistently or unfairly, or simply put, can make mistakes. In spite of the controversy over its implementation, automated scoring may offer an option to teachers who otherwise wouldn't assign writing projects at all, and deserves careful consideration as the software becomes more widely available.

A related (and no less controversial) trend is the outsourcing of grading. SmarThinking, a company that provides a variety of online tutoring services and remedial assistance, began grading papers on a contract basis in 2005 (Jaschik, 2005). Another company, Edumetry, offers "Virtual TA," a grading service that contracts with individuals in Malaysia, India, Singapore, the United States, and elsewhere to review student papers and provide detailed feedback. In a 2010 *Chronicle of Higher Education* article, several instructors discussed their use of the Virtual TA service, their initial misgivings, and some of the positive outcomes they've witnessed—from fewer students dropping out of online courses to freeing up time for one-to-one instruction with students (Williams June, 2010). Not surprisingly, however, the response to the news about SmarThinking and Virtual TA was nearly unanimously against the practice of outsourcing grading. As with automated essay scoring, outsourced grading may require a cultural sea change in traditional educational environments before it's considered acceptable.

Mobile Devices

Although not an advance related only to distance education or assessment, mobile learning technologies have the potential to influence both significantly. The use of small, portable computing devices (for example, netbooks or feature-rich cellular telephones) is seen by many faculty as a way to get students' attention or to put materials in front of them when they have a few minutes to kill. There seems to be general agreement that these devices aren't intended to replace full-size computers, but their ubiquity lends itself to just-in-time access to coursework and anyplace/anytime interaction. Designing instruction specifically with mobile devices in mind has been adopted more rapidly in Japan and several European countries than in the United States, possibly due to greater adoption of cell phones per capita. However, considering that one estimate put cell phone usage at 98% among U.S. college students as recently as 2008 (Smith, Salaway, & Caruso, 2009), instructors will soon realize the potential these portable technologies hold.

Uses of mobile technology for instruction (sometimes abbreviated to "M-learning") include the distribution of audio and video files, messaging, gathering field data for research activities, and polling (McConatha, Praul, & Lynch, 2008). Assessment activities could easily be integrated into any of those capabilities. And, even though the Horizon Report for 2010 considers mobile computing to be only one year from mainstream use (Johnson, Levine, & Stone, 2010), effective integration with instruction is likely to take much longer.

SUMMARY

Assessment is the means of measuring learning gains and can be used to improve the teaching–learning process in distance education settings as well as more traditional environments. Determining content mastery and transferability of skills helps teachers and students identify gaps in learning; it gives feedback to the teacher about the instruction and feedback to the student on strengths and weaknesses in performance. It can also reinforce content and identify misconceptions, and act as a motivating force that prods learners toward content mastery.

Some final conclusions and recommendations remain. First, assessment must be an integrated and transparent component of the instructional process. Aligning the desired learner outcomes, instructional activities, and assessment tools provides clear expectations and a sense of relevance for student participation. In any instructional environment, assessments should reinforce course content, provide opportunities to practice newly acquired skills, result in meaningful feedback, and motivate learners to succeed. Second, instructional designers, teachers, and program planners need to pay attention when news reports suggest that academic misconduct, in the form of cheating and plagiarism, is being reported at record levels. Students are more likely to cheat when assessment activities are considered irrelevant, trivial, or unfair, and although a few individuals will behave unethically no matter what, there is reason to think that the majority of such behavior can be deterred with a combination of approaches. Finally, good quality assessment practices require attention to possible confounding effects of the learning environment, mediating technologies, and instructional strategies, as well as interactions among these factors and student characteristics. Designing with an awareness of the constraints and opportunities faced by learners at a distance ensures that each student's progress will be recorded accurately and fulfill the purposes of diagnosis, reinforcement of concepts, feedback, and motivation.

Distance education can serve as a catalyst for change and growth in the education arena. By rethinking our ideas about what a classroom is, what teaching and learning are, where learning can occur, and how to measure it most effectively, we can use the best of what we know that works and discover new ways to facilitate this change. Distance education can be more than doing the same old things in many places instead of just one, and we need not feel bound to emulate worn-out models. Assessment, as a component of the instructional design process, can explore new ideas and refine the old as we reflect on our best practices for teaching and learning in whatever environmental configurations may confront us in the future.

DISCUSSION QUESTIONS

1. Although instructional design models prescribe the development of assessment instruments or activities prior to instruction, in reality, many (if not most) teachers wait until after instruction to do this. What are some reasons this occurs, and how might this affect the assessment results?

2. What are the advantages of using asynchronous assessment measures instead of synchronous, and how might you decide which are most appropriate for a given course, unit, or module?

3. Although scoring rubrics are generally considered useful for grading subjective assessments, they are not used as frequently as they might be because of the difficulty of creating instruments that are reliable and fair. Why is this so difficult? Are there ways that the process could be streamlined?

4. Academic misconduct is considered a critical problem in education today. What measures might you undertake to deter cheating, plagiarism, or other unethical practices in a distance learning program?

REFERENCES

American Association for Higher Education. (2000). *9 Principles of good practice for assessing student learning.* Available: www.aahe.org/assessment/principl.htm.

Angelo, T. A., & Cross, K. P. (1993). *Classroom assessment techniques: A handbook for college teachers* (2nd ed.). San Francisco: Jossey-Bass.

Ausubel, D., Novak, J., & Hanesian, H. (1978). *Educational psychology: A cognitive view* (2nd ed.). New York: Holt, Rinehart and Winston.

Bauer, J. (2002). Assessing student work from chatrooms and bulletin boards. *New Directions for Teaching and Learning, No. 91.* San Francisco:Jossey-Bass.

Council of Writing Program Administrators. (2003). *Defining and avoiding plagiarism: The WPA statement on best practices.* Available: www.wpacouncil.org.

Dee, T., & Jacob, B. (2010). *Rational ignorance in education: A field experiment in student plagiarism.* National Bureau of Economic Research Working Paper No. 15672. January 2010. JEL No. 12, K4. Retrieved May 21, 2010 from www.swarthmore.edu/Documents/academics/economics/Dee/w15672.pdf.

Gee, J. (2003). *What video games have to teach us about learning and literacy.* New York: Palgrave Macmillan.

Hare, M., & Graber, K. (2007). Investigating knowledge acquisition and developing misconceptions of high school students enrolled in an invasion games unit. *The High School Journal, 90*(4), 1–14.

Harlen, W., & Deakin Crick, R. (2003). Testing and motivation for learning. *Assessment in Education, 10* (2), 169–207.

Higher Education Opportunity Act. (2008). Retrieved March 1, 2009, from http://frwebgate.access.gpo.gov/cgi-bin/getdoc.cgi?dbname=110_cong_public_laws&docid=f:publ315.110.

Higher Learning Commission. (2009). *Summary of policies related to the Higher Education Opportunity Act.* Retrieved March 11, 2009 from www.ncahlc.org/download/Policies%20Adopted%20Final%202-2009.pdf.

Jaschik, S. (2005, September 22). Outsourced grading. *Inside Higher Ed.* Archived at www.insidehighered.com/news/2005/09/22/outsource/. Retrieved May 11, 2010.

Johnson, L., Levine, A., Smith, R., & Stone, S. (2010). *The 2010 horizon report.* Austin, TX: The New Media Consortium.

Keller, J., & Suzuki, K. (2004). Learner motivation and e-learning design: A mutinationally validated process. *Journal of Educational Media, 29*(3), 229–239.

Kerlin, S. (2000). *Query on student plagiarism: Problems and remedies.* Contribution to discussion list TL@LISTSERV.EDUCAUSE.EDU. Posted 12-6-00.

McCabe, D., Trevino, L., & Butterfield, D. (1999). Academic integrity in honor code and non-honor code environments: A qualitative investigation. *Journal of Higher Education, 70*(2), 211–234.

McConatha, D., Praul, M., & Lynch, M. (2008). Mobile learning in higher education: An empirical assessment of a new educational tool. The Turkish Online Journal of Educational Technology, *7*(3),

McKenzie, J. (1998). The new plagiarism: Seven antidotes to prevent highway robbery in an electronic age. *From Now On: The Educational Technology Journal, 7*(8). Available: www.fno.org/may98/cov98may.html.

Mehrabian, A. (1969). Some referents and measures of nonverbal behavior. *Behavior Research Methods and Instrumentation, 1*(6), 205–207.

Mueller, J. (2010). *Authentic assessment toolbox.* Available at http://jonathan.mueller.faculty.noctrl.edu/toolbox. Retrieved May 16, 2010.

Paper Masters.com. (2010). Paper Masters: A division of E World Publishing, Inc. Retrieved May 16, 2010 from http://papermasters.com/.

Rust, C., O'Donovan, B., & Price, M. (2005). A social constructivist assessment process model: How the research literature shows us this could be best practice. *Assessment and Evaluation in Higher Education, 30*(3), 231–240.

Smith, S., Salaway, G., & Caruso, J. (2009, October). *The ECAR study of undergraduate students and information technology, 2009.* Educause Center for Applied Research, Key Findings. Boulden, Co.

Stiggins, R. (2007). Assessment through the student's eyes. *Educational Leadership, 64*(8), 22–26.

Stobart, G. (2008). *Testing times: The uses and abuses of assessment.* London: Routledge.

Trex, E. (2010). 7 college cheating scandals. *Mental_floss.* Archived at http://blogs.static.mentalfloss.com/blogs/archives/25259.html. Retrieved March 4, 2010.

Wang, J., & Brown, M. S. (2007). Automated essay scoring versus human scoring: A comparative study. *Journal of Technology, Learning, and Assessment, 6*(2). Retrieved April 26, 2010 from www.jtla.org.

Wiliam, D. & Thompson, M. (2008). Integrating assessment with learning: What will it take to make it work? In D. Dwyer (Ed.), *The future of assessment: Shaping teaching and learning* (pp. 53–82). New York: Erlbaum.

Williams-June, A. (2010). Some papers are uploaded to Bangalore to be graded. In *Chronicle of Higher Education*, April 4, 2010. Archived at http://chronicle.com/article/Outsourced-Grading-With/64954/ . Retrieved May 11, 2010.

Managing and Evaluating Distance Education

CHAPTER 10

Copyright and Distance Education

CHAPTER GOAL

The purpose of this chapter is to discuss the implications of U.S. copyright law for teaching in distance education environments.

CHAPTER OBJECTIVES

After reading and reviewing this chapter, you should be able to

1. Differentiate between myth and fact related to copyright applications in distance education.
2. Recognize the exclusive rights granted to copyright holders by the U.S. copyright law.
3. Determine when copyrighted material enters the public domain.
4. Apply the four essential fair use criteria and published guidelines to determine whether use of copyrighted materials requires permission from rights holders.
5. Identify and track the status of current copyright legislation in Congress, and be aware of the implications of new legislation.
6. Recognize what materials may be placed on the Internet without permission.
7. Recognize the circumstances under which Internet materials copyrighted by others may be utilized in a distance education course.
8. Follow appropriate procedures for obtaining permission from rights holders to use copyrighted materials in a distance education course.
9. Recognize the potential consequences of copyright infringement.

COPYRIGHT MYTHS

Not long ago, an instructional developer at a large state university was helping a faculty member create a website for his course on ancient Greece that he was going to teach totally online the following semester. One day, the professor strolled into the instructional developer's office carrying a stack of books, each with dozens of tabs of paper marking pages of interest. He explained that in the face-to-face version of the course, he used a document camera and multimedia projector to display these photographs and illustrations to his students. "The Internet is great!" he exclaimed. "We can digitize these images and put them on the website, and students can look at them and study them anytime they want!" He broke into a big grin, excited about how he could use this new technology to help his students learn. The instructional developer was stunned. "But what about copyright?" she asked. "Did you get permission from the publishers to digitize all these images for the Web?" The professor's grin broke into a sneer. "Get permission? Of course not. This is for educational purposes, and besides, we'll have password protection, so the publishers will never know. . . . "

This example represents the kind of mythology that has evolved as educators try to determine what is copyrighted and what is not, and what can be used in an online course and what cannot, at least without permission, and how it can be used. Misinterpretations of copyright are commonplace:

Myth 1. A work has to be published and registered with the United States Copyright Office to receive copyright protection. Any work, published or unpublished, meeting the criteria specified in the copyright law receives protection as soon as it is fixed in a tangible medium of expression. For example, an original manuscript prepared on a word processor is protected as soon as the file is saved to a disk or printed. Copyright covers a slide or digital image as soon as the image is recorded on the film or saved onto a storage device. Registration with the Copyright Office is optional, not a requirement. However, a work must be registered before a plaintiff can collect statutory damages in the event of an infringement.

Myth 2. If it does not have a copyright notice, it is public domain. As of March 1, 1989, when the United States adopted the Berne Convention international copyright treaty, a work is not required to include a copyright notice in order to receive protection. If a notice does appear, it may include either the familiar © symbol or the word *copyright*.

Myth 3. Anything on the Internet is public domain. Nothing could be further from the truth. Original works of authorship placed on the Internet are entitled to protection just like any other works meeting the law's criteria. However, the Internet has made possible copyright infringements on a global scale.

Myth 4. A work copyrighted in another country is public domain in the United States. This myth seems to arise when instructors want to use video recordings or publications from another nation in a U.S. distance education course. The Berne Convention treaty specifies that the copyright laws of any signatory country apply within that country to a work copyrighted in another signatory country. In other words, within the United States, any work copyrighted in any other Berne Convention nation (i.e., most nations) receives the same protection as a work copyrighted in the United States.

Myth 5. The doctrine of "fair use" means that copyrighted materials can be used in an educational setting without permission. As a blanket statement, this is perhaps the biggest myth of all. Education is one of the purposes for which fair use *may* apply, but fair use can be determined only after careful consideration of four rather complex criteria. Many educational applications are completely beyond fair use and require permission—for example, the development of most coursepacks.

Myth 6. Any copyrighted materials can be digitized and placed on a course website without permission, as long as the site is password protected. Recent legislation has expanded the scope of materials that may be digitized and placed on a password-protected course website, but fair use criteria still apply. In the previous example, although a fair use case may be made for a limited number of images from each book to be incorporated into the course (depending on whether each image was individually copyrighted, which often is the case), the sheer numbers involved likely extend well beyond fair use. (As a sidebar, the professor does not realize how easily a publisher can be made aware of a copyright infringement by a disgruntled student unhappy with a course grade.)

COPYRIGHT ESSENTIALS

Copyright is hardly a new concept. The first forms of legal copyright protection appeared in fifteenth-century Venice shortly after Gutenberg invented the printing press (Zobel, 1997). In 1557, Queen Mary chartered the Stationer's Company to "enlist the covetous self-interests of the very printers and booksellers," as a means of imposing censorship during a time of political and religious turmoil in England (Kaplan, cited in Miller, 1975). Registration of a book with the Stationer's Company provided the printer exclusive rights to print copies of the book and sell them.

The Statute of Anne, passed by Parliament in 1714, contained features similar to some of those found in U.S. copyright law today. Existing books were entitled to 21 years of copyright protection. Books published subsequent to the statute were copyrighted for 14 years, with the copyright assigned to the author. If the author were still living at the end of this period, the copyright could be renewed for another 14 years. The law provided for the payment of fines for copyright infringements (one penny per page—a substantial amount in the early eighteenth century), with the penalties split evenly between the copyright holder and the Crown. Such protection was not extended to books that had not been registered with the Stationer's Company (Miller, 1975).

The first copyright legislation in the United States was enacted by Congress in 1790, a bill modeled after the Statute of Anne. The law, Title 17 of the U.S. Code, has undergone several major revisions, the latest in 1976 as Public Law 94-553. Section 102 specifies that copyright protection subsists *in original works of authorship fixed in a tangible medium of expression, now known or later developed, from which they can be perceived, reproduced, or otherwise communicated, either directly or with the aid of a machine or device.*

Two critical conditions thus exist before a work is eligible for copyright protection. First, copyright applies to *works of authorship* representing the *tangible expression of ideas*, requiring originality and some degree of creativity. Copyrighted works of authorship in a distance education course may include the instructor's lecture notes, e-mail messages, comments made in online discussions and chats, graphic and photographic images, digital audio and video files and animations, presentation graphics such as PowerPoint files, printed materials reproduced for student study, and works created by the students themselves, either individually or collaboratively. In Web 2.0 terms, copyright protection extends to original content and comments posted on blogs, the content of wikis, podcast files, video files posted on YouTube, Twitter "tweets," and any other original content posted on the Web by anyone, as long as it meets the fundamental criteria for copyright protection. Copyright protection does not extend to facts, titles, names, familiar symbols, standard forms, procedures, and works consisting of common property, although some items in these categories may be eligible for patent or trademark protection.

Second, the *work must be fixed in a tangible medium of expression*. The previous examples are self-evident because they can be *perceived, reproduced, or otherwise communicated* (the actual terminology used in the law). Copyright would not apply to comments made in a live, face-to-face classroom discussion unless the interaction were recorded or otherwise transcribed. However, the situation is different in an online course, because online discussions are "fixed" in digital form. Even oral communications in real-time, audio- and video-based classes are fixed in a tangible medium of expression if they are recorded and archived for on-demand access at a later time, and therefore fall under copyright protection. Courses themselves are eligible for copyright protection if they are recorded digitally or offered online via an Internet server, and consist of original content, including content licensed for this purpose if applicable.

Exclusive Rights of Copyright Holders

The law grants to copyright owners exclusive rights to do, or to authorize others to do, any of the following:

■ Reproduce the copyrighted work
■ Prepare derivative works based on the copyrighted original
■ Distribute copies of the copyrighted work
■ Perform the copyrighted work
■ Display the copyrighted work publicly

Fortunately, Congress recognized that, under certain circumstances, the use of protected materials could be acceptable without permission from the copyright holder. In fact, limitations on exclusive rights consume the majority of Chapter 1 of Title 17. Two sections are of particular importance to distance educators: Section 107, which provides the criteria for "fair use" and Section 110, which addresses public performance and display.

Fair Use

According to Section 107, "the fair use of a copyrighted work . . . for purposes such as criticism, comment, news reporting, teaching (including multiple copies for classroom use), scholarship, or research, is not an infringement." The legislative history of the law (House of Representatives Report No. 94-1476) noted that no adequate definition of the concept of fair use had emerged, and that no generally applicable definition was possible. Rather, the doctrine should be viewed as "an equitable rule of reason," with each case to be decided on its own merits against the criteria provided in the law.

The phrasing here is critically important. Section 107 does not grant educators wholesale permission to use copyrighted materials simply because they work in nonprofit educational organizations. Only a *fair use* is legal, and fair use cannot be determined until four essential criteria have been considered. Congress deliberately wrote the criteria in broad, general terms to provide a flexible structure that could be applied across a multitude of potential fair use scenarios without the need for constant revisions to the law. No single criterion is enough to deny fair use. Even if one criterion weighs against, the use may still be legal if the other three criteria weigh in favor. The criteria include the following:

- **"The purpose and character of the use, including whether such use is of a commercial nature or is for nonprofit educational purposes. . . . "** Uses in a nonprofit, educational setting are more likely to be fair use than those in a corporate training or proprietary college setting. Reproduction for purposes of criticism or commentary may be considered more favorably, even if for commercial purposes.
- **"The nature of the copyrighted work. . . . "** Nonfiction works are more likely to be considered fair use than fictional or artistic works containing a higher degree of creative expression. Published works are generally favored by courts more than unpublished materials, and printed works more than audiovisual materials. Publications designed to be consumable, such as workbook pages or standardized test forms, should never be reproduced without permission.
- **"The amount and substantiality of the portion used in relation to the copyrighted work as a whole. . . . "** The law itself does not provide specific limits or percentages, although criteria have been set in negotiated guidelines that will be discussed later in this chapter. In many cases with printed materials, the entire copyrighted work is desired, such as a journal article, illustration, or photograph. The case for fair use can be enhanced if no more of the published original is taken than is necessary to meet the user's needs. This criterion also has a qualitative component in that reproduction of even a small proportion of a work may exceed fair use if that portion contains the heart or essence of the original.
- **"The effect of the use upon the potential market for or value of the copyrighted work. . . . "** In infringement suits, the courts consider whether it is reasonable to expect the ultimate recipient of a reproduction to have purchased that copy or paid a licensing fee. Courts also consider effect in the context of the potential financial harm to the copyright holder if the act in question is a widespread practice.

Public Performance and Display

Section 110 of the copyright law permits the performance or display of a work during the face-to-face teaching activities of a nonprofit educational institution, in a classroom or similar place devoted to instruction, with a lawfully made or acquired copy (if applicable). This has become known as the "face-to-face teaching exemption." Section 110 covers activities such as the reading aloud of literature, performance of dramatic works by class members (but not by actors from outside the class), performance of compositions in music classes, and display of video recordings and other audiovisual materials that take place in the face-to-face classroom.

The House of Representatives Report 94-1476 noted specifically that the face-to-face teaching exemption did not extend to the transmission of audiovisual materials into the classroom from a location outside the building. For many years, this restriction was quite problematic for libraries and media centers that transmitted videotapes from centralized collections into classrooms via school networks, if transmission and reception occurred in separate buildings. The distribution of materials in this manner required specific licensing agreements with the rights holders.

Of greater concern for distance educators for a quarter century after enactment of the 1976 revision was the problem of incorporating video recordings and other audiovisual media (defined in the law as works that consist of a series of related images which are intrinsically intended to be shown by the use of machines or devices such as projectors, viewers, or electronic equipment) into courses transmitted to remote sites via distance education delivery systems, including both video- and Internet-based distribution. Such use clearly was outside the limits specified in Section 110. Passage of the Technology, Education, and Copyright Harmonization (TEACH) Act by Congress in 2002, which will be discussed in detail later in this chapter, greatly alleviated this situation.

Section 110 cannot be applied to training events that take place in for-profit settings, for example, in proprietary institutions and industry. Classroom display of materials such as video recordings in for-profit locations should be covered by licensing agreements when the materials are purchased.

Duration of Copyright

Several formulas have been devised to help determine when works pass into the public domain. Terms of protection vary according to the date of creation, whether the work was published, whether ownership resides with an individual or an employer or other legal entity, and whether the original copyright on an older work was renewed. Table 10–1, which was adapted from a website maintained by Lolly Gasaway (2003), provides a general guide. In granting permission to reproduce the guide in this publication, Gasaway urged readers to check her site for possible updated information. In summary:

- A work published before 1923 is now in the public domain.
- A work created on or after January 1, 1978, is protected for the lifetime of the author plus 70 years, or if of corporate authorship, 95 years from publication. In other words, the earliest such a work could fall into the public domain is January 2048.
- A work published between 1964 and 1977 cannot fall into the public domain until at least 2059.
- A work created before January 1, 1978, but not published is protected for the lifetime of the author plus 70 years, or until December 31, 2002, whichever is later.

These dates reflect the term limits as revised in 1998 by the Sonny Bono Copyright Term Extension Act, named after the late entertainer and congressional representative who served as a member of the House Judiciary Committee until his premature death in a skiing accident earlier that year.

The task of determining the actual term of copyright is compounded by the layers of protection that may exist for a given work. For example, Mozart's symphonies are long since in the public domain, but a 1998 recording of the Symphony No. 41 will receive protection until long after the original playback device has become hopelessly obsolete. A textbook photo of an artwork may be copyrighted at several levels: by the publisher, the photographer, the owner of the original work, and perhaps even the owner of another intermediate stage, such as a digitized image taken from the photographer's slide.

TABLE 10–1 ■ Duration of Copyright Under U.S. Law: When U.S. Works Pass into the Public Domain

By Lolly Gasaway, University of North Carolina

Definition: A public domain work is a creative work that is not protected by copyright and that may be freely used by everyone. The reasons that the work is not protected include (1) the term of copyright for the work has expired, (2) the author failed to satisfy statutory formalities to perfect the copyright, or (3) the work is a work of the U.S. government.

Date of Work	Protected From	Term
Created 1-1-78 or after	When work is fixed in tangible medium of expression	Life + 70 years[1] (or if work of corporate authorship, the shorter of 95 years from publication, or 120 years from creation)[2]
Published before 1923	In public domain	None
Published from 1923–1963	When published with notice[3]	28 years + could be renewed for 47 years, now extended by 20 years, for a total renewal of 67 years. If not so renewed, now in public domain
Published from 1964–1977	When published with notice	28 years for first term; now automatic extension of 67 years for second term
Created before 1-1-78 but not published	1-1-78, the effective date of the 1976 Act that eliminated common law copyright	Life + 70 years or 12-31-2002, whichever is greater
Created before 1-1-78 but published between then and 12-31-2002	1-1-78, the effective date of the 1976 Act that eliminated common law copyright	Life + 70 years or 12-31-2047, whichever is greater

[1] Term of joint works is measured by life of the longest-lived author.
[2] Works for hire, anonymous, and pseudonymous works also have this term. 17 U.S.C. § 302(c).
[3] Under the 1909 Act, works published without notice went into the public domain upon publication. Works published without notice between 1-1-78 and 3-1-89, effective date of the Berne Convention Implementation Act, retained copyright only if efforts to correct the accidental omission of notice was made within 5 years, such as by placing notice on unsold copies. 17 U.S.C. § 405. (Notes courtesy of Professor Tom Field, Franklin Pierce Law Center, and Lolly Gasaway.)
Source: http://www.unc.edu/~unclng/public-d.htm.

Public Domain

Any work in the public domain may be used freely in a distance education course. Works may enter the public domain several ways, most often simply through expiration of copyright protection. Most materials published by the U.S. government are specifically excluded from copyright protection by Section 105 and are in the public domain from the date of creation. However, audiovisual works produced for federal agencies by independent contractors are eligible for copyright protection and must be treated in distance education courses like any other audiovisual work. Also, freedom to use materials published by the federal government may not apply to states. Works developed by or for state agencies, including video recordings and other audiovisual materials, may be declared public domain according to the state's policies but are more likely to be copyrighted.

Another means by which works enter the public domain is for owners to abandon their copyrights. For example, as Myth 3 previously illustrated, a popular and widespread misconception holds that materials posted to the Internet become public domain because the Internet is such a public and uncontrolled medium. Abandonment of copyright actually requires an explicit and overt statement from the copyright holder—and rarely occurs.

Creative Commons

The Creative Commons (see URL at the end of this chapter) is a nonprofit corporation established in 2001 to give intellectual property creators alternatives in the ways they allow others to use their works without the need to apply fair use criteria or obtain permission. Authors who license their works through the Creative Commons do not give up their copyright ownership. They simply specify, according to the type of license selected, the rights they are willing to share with users of the works. The concept of "All Rights Reserved" is modified to "Some Rights Reserved."

The Creative Commons offers six licensing formats ranging from "Attribution Non-commercial No Derivatives," which is the most restrictive and permits sharing but no modifications or commercial use, to "Attribution," which is the least restrictive and permits unlimited distribution and modification, even if for commercial purposes. All Creative Commons licenses require that the author/copyright owner receive full attribution.

Mention of the Creative Commons is important in this chapter because a growing inventory of intellectual property is now covered by its licenses. It is entirely possible that faculty in distance education settings might wish to use Creative Commons–licensed works in course activities. The type of license must be clearly indicated on the work.

GUIDELINES

As the 1909 copyright law was undergoing revision in the mid-1970s, Congress recognized that the nonprofit educational community could benefit from guidelines that help define acceptable practices under fair use. The House report contained guidelines for classroom copying and educational uses of music that had been negotiated by educator and publisher groups. A third set of guidelines was approved in 1979 to cover off-air recording of broadcast programming for educational purposes.

Although the authors of the law tried to accommodate future technological developments with vague terminology such as "fixed in a tangible medium of expression, now known or later developed" and "with the aid of a machine or device," they had no way of anticipating the phenomenal growth of digital media authoring, storage, and distribution systems, or the incredible range of technology now easily available to both educators and consumers. As a result, application of a 1976 statute in the early twenty-first century is often the source of considerable frustration and confusion. The problem has long been evident.

In September 1994, the U.S. Department of Commerce convened the Conference on Fair Use (CONFU), bringing together information proprietors and user groups in an attempt to develop fair use guidelines addressing new technologies. Over a 2.5-year period, representatives of more than 100 organizations met as a whole and in smaller work groups to draft guidelines for distance learning, image collections, multimedia, electronic reserves, and interlibrary loan. By May 1997, only the first three work groups had developed formal proposals, and none of the three garnered widespread support in the education community. Ultimately, CONFU elected neither to endorse nor to reject any of the proposals but to continue the negotiation processes. Table 10–2 summarizes the seven sets of fair use guidelines that were accepted by the U.S. Congress or have appeared in draft form under CONFU. Even though the CONFU drafts were never operationalized, they are useful because they may represent the limits to which the rights-holder community considers fair use. On the other hand, education and library organizations are quick to point out that the limits of fair use may in fact extend beyond the guidelines and can only be determined by the courts.

The draft Educational Fair Use Guidelines for Distance Learning and the other guidelines may be found on the Web. (See the list of websites at the end of the chapter.) The Distance Learning work group agreed not to address online learning technologies in their draft. At that time in the mid-1990s, the work group members felt the technologies were evolving too quickly and that the delivery of courses by educational

TABLE 10–2 ■ Status of Fair Use Guidelines of Interest to Distance Educators

Guidelines	Applies to	Status
Guidelines for Classroom Copying in Not-for-Profit Educational Institutions	Text and other resources (e.g., photographs, illustrations) in printed publications	Accepted by Congress
Guidelines for Educational Uses of Music	Published music and sound recordings used in music classes	Accepted by Congress
Guidelines for Off-Air Recording of Broadcast Programming for Educational Purposes	Broadcast programming recorded off-air (excludes cable channel programs)	Accepted by Congress
Fair Use Guidelines for Educational Multimedia	Copyrighted materials incorporated into multimedia works (includes use in distance education)	Accepted by Congress
Guidelines for the Educational Use of Digital Images	Digitized versions of visual images such as photographs, illustrations, and works of art	Conference on Fair Use (CONFU) draft; not widely endorsed
Educational Fair Use Guidelines for Distance Learning	Audiovisual works used in video-based distance education (excludes asynchronous delivery)	CONFU draft; not widely endorsed
Fair Use Guidelines for Electronic Reserve Systems	Digitized publications maintained online as counterpart to library reserve system for printed materials	Draft prepared as part of CONFU process but not submitted for consideration

institutions via the Internet was still in the experimental stage. The guidelines thus focused almost exclusively on video-based delivery systems. The greatest resistance to the guidelines came from K–12, higher education, and library groups, who felt the criteria were too restrictive. The lack of attention to online courses was also seen as a major shortcoming. Ultimately, some of the draft guidelines were addressed in the TEACH Act of 2002, which we will discuss in the next section.

RECENT COPYRIGHT-RELATED LEGISLATION

The copyright law itself is a document in a perpetual state of change. The law was amended by Congress a total of 63 times between its enactment in 1976 and the end of 2009. Typically, about two dozen copyright-related acts are introduced in each two-year congressional session. (Educators can track the status of proposed legislation at the U.S. Copyright Office website.) Most of these never become law, and of those that have survived the process and been enacted, few have been significant for the education community. One of these was the aforementioned Sonny Bono Copyright Term Extension Act of 1998, which delayed the transition of many classic publications and audiovisual media, such as early Disney productions, into the public domain. Another was the Digital Millennium Copyright Act (DMCA), also of 1998, and the subsequent legislation it spawned, the TEACH Act.

Digital Millennium Copyright Act

The DMCA, 59 pages long in its PDF version, has been the most comprehensive revision of the 1976 copyright law of interest to educators to date, with far-reaching implications for distance education. The act was intended to bring the United States into compliance with two treaties agreed on by the World Intellectual Property Organization (WIPO) in 1996. Three components of the DMCA are particularly relevant to this chapter.

Infringement Liability Protections. The DMCA specifies that if a copyright infringement is found on a website maintained by a service provider, the rights holder may request that the service provider "take down" or block access to the infringing material and escape organizational liability for the infringement. Many school districts and most higher education campuses provide Internet access for their faculty, staff, and students, and thus fall into the category of "service provider." (For the remainder of this section, *service provider* will refer to the school, district, or higher education institution providing Internet services for its internal constituencies. This responsibility is normally placed within an instructional or information technology department.)

If, for example, a faculty member has placed copyrighted material on a course website without the appropriate clearance or legitimate fair use claim, the copyright owner can request that the service provider remove it, or at least block access to it. If the service provider does not, it may be liable for the infringement along with the teacher. The service provider must also give notification of the takedown to the person who placed the infringing material on the website. In order to be eligible for liability protection, the service provider must formerly be unaware of the infringing activity, meaning that course development staff employed by the service provider and working with the faculty member cannot have placed the infringing material on the website, and the service provider cannot receive any financial gain from the infringement.

The DMCA lists several protective measures that schools and colleges must take to limit their liability as service providers:

- An "agent" must be registered with the Copyright Office to receive copyright infringement complaints and respond appropriately. Instructions for registration of an agent and a list of agents may be found at the Copyright Office website. Procedures for contacting the agent must also be posted on the service provider's website.
- A current copyright policy for the service provider's Internet users must be in place and posted on the organizational website. The policy must contain provisions stating that access privileges will be terminated for repeat offenders.
- The service provider must maintain an ongoing program for educating its Internet users about copyright and requirements for obtaining appropriate permissions before placing protected material on institutional web pages, including course websites.

Education and library groups have pointed out that takedown of course materials that are the target of infringement complaints may have serious implications for fair use and academic freedom, not to mention a potentially deleterious impact on student learning. The DMCA permits the faculty member to serve a counter-notification that she or he believes the initial complaint was filed erroneously, for example, in a claim of fair use. Unless the copyright owner files legal action as the result of the counter-notification, the service provider must restore access to the materials in question within 10–14 working days, or essentially within 2–3 weeks. However, filing the counter-notification could place the faculty member at risk of litigation, and the period of time during which the materials are offline may jeopardize the lesson plan.

Circumvention of Technological Protection Measures.   The DMCA addresses measures taken by copyright owners to control both access to and reproduction of their protected materials. For example, the act contained a provision requiring the manufacturers of videocassette recorders (VCRs) to incorporate technology preventing unauthorized copying of videotapes while permitting the recording of programs from off-air and basic and extended-tier (excluding premium) cable television channels. Related to websites, the DMCA not only prohibits the sale and use of devices that circumvent access restriction methods such as password protection, but it also makes illegal the simple act of informing others how to circumvent these measures and even linking to sites that provide this information. Among other purposes, these provisions are intended to protect the encryption schemes used in online banking and credit card transactions connected with Web-based commerce, which readers may find comforting.

However, as with the infringement liability issues described above, the education and library communities have vociferously protested the circumvention limitations of the DMCA as threats to fair use and academic freedom. Specifically, these organizations hoped for broader access to such materials as literary works and audio and video materials that exist online but require fee payment before access is granted.

Distance Education Study. Section 403 of the DMCA required the Copyright Office to collect information from all stakeholders and make recommendations to Congress on how to promote the use of digital technologies in distance education. The Office's *Report on Digital Distance Education* was released in May 1999 (U.S. Copyright Office, 1999). Most of its recommendations focused on amending Section 110 of the copyright law to extend the exemptions granted in face-to-face instructional situations to distance learning environments.

The *Report on Digital Distance Education* led to the introduction of several related acts in both the House and Senate. Another major impetus leading to this legislation was the highly acclaimed report of the Web-Based Education Commission compiled for the president and Congress, entitled *The Power of the Internet for Learning: Moving from Promise to Practice* (Web-Based Education Commission, 2000), which considered the challenge of providing twenty-first-century distance education with obsolete copyright laws as analogous to trying "to manage the interstate highway system with the rules of the horse and buggy era" (p. 97).

Technology, Education, and Copyright Harmonization (TEACH) Act

This is the legislation in response to the DMCA that ultimately emerged to address distance learning issues. The TEACH Act was enacted by Congress and signed into law by President George W. Bush in November 2002. The Act was a long-anticipated blessing for distance educators, because it amended Section 110 and loosened the restrictions. However, strings were attached. The changes provided by the TEACH Act do not apply unless two critical institutional requirements are met. First, the provisions only apply to *accredited* nonprofit educational institutions, at both the K–12 and higher education levels. Accreditation is an important qualification. Second, the educational organization must have a published policy regarding teacher use of copyrighted materials and an ongoing copyright training program for faculty, staff, and students in place. In other words, the organization must be in compliance with the DMCA.

Other requirements of the Act relate to teacher use of the materials and the materials themselves.

■ Access to the digitized materials must be restricted to students enrolled in the course.
■ The digitized materials must be used in the same manner in an online course as they would be in a face-to-face (f2f) course. For example, if a video segment would have been displayed by the teacher in the face-to-face setting, it may be digitized for the online course. If students would have viewed the video independently in a learning resources center instead of the f2f classroom, the TEACH Act would not apply. Moreover, the digital materials must only be available to the students during approximately the same time period in which they would be available to an f2f class.
■ In the case of a video recording, only the essential portions that the teacher would display in the f2f classroom may be incorporated into the online course. In many cases, that would not be the entire production.

- The materials must have been *lawfully acquired.*
- The students must be notified of the relevant copyright information for the materials and that the materials are protected by copyright law.
- The materials may be digitized for online use only if digital versions are not already available.

If these provisions are met, the TEACH Act has opened the door to a much wider range of instructional technologies in distance education than were permitted by the old Section 110. Online courses may now permit performances of nondramatic literary and musical works and "reasonable and limited portions" of dramatic and audiovisual works, including video. The Act also eliminated the requirement that students receiving the instruction be located in a classroom or other site devoted to instruction. In other words, students at home or in the workplace now are eligible.

User Training

The DMCA requires educational institutions to engage in an ongoing program for educating its Internet users about copyright issues. How should that training be conducted? Is it sufficient to post the copyright policy on the organization's website? That alone is required by the DMCA, but more should be done. Optional workshops about copyright are likely to set new institutional standards for nonattendance. One approach might be to incorporate copyright topics into other regularly scheduled venues, such as faculty meetings, or communication media, such as campus or school newsletters. Discussing copyright matters within the context of other institutional issues can attach context and encourage faculty attention. Frequently asked questions (FAQs), even if they are asked only by the author of the FAQ column, can also be helpful if applied to situations faculty face, but they should be incorporated into media the faculty normally read, such as newsletters. FAQs posted on obscure pages on the campus website will hardly ever be seen by anyone other than the site manager.

Providing copyright training to students may be an even greater challenge. Ongoing skirmishes between rights-holder organizations and students related to online file sharing, predominantly music and movies, indicate not only lack of knowledge of the copyright law among students but an overtly cavalier attitude toward it. This issue is also well illustrated by the massive scale of uploading video files to websites such as YouTube, in many cases by students and others who are not the legal owners of that intellectual property. Students do not attend workshops on this topic and are unlikely to read and respect printed guides to "safe copyright." Some higher education institutions have had success by limiting access, but this issue remains largely unresolved.

COPYRIGHT APPLICATIONS IN DISTANCE EDUCATION

What are the major implications of U.S. copyright law for distance education? The information presented here applies to either video- or Internet-based distance education, except as noted. We must provide the disclaimer that the authors of this book are not attorneys, and this chapter does not constitute legal advice.

Printed Materials

Regardless of the delivery vehicle, teachers of distance education courses may want their students to have copyrighted articles and other printed materials in hand for study purposes. In most cases, these materials would be digitized and posted on the course website or incorporated into coursepacks. The Guidelines for Classroom Copying in Not-for-Profit Educational Institutions permit limited reproduction and distribution of copyrighted materials (no more than one copy per student in the course) as long as the tests of brevity, spontaneity, and cumulative effects are met. A discussion of numerical limitations is beyond the scope of this chapter. Readers are referred to the guidelines for limits from a single author or publication. The test of spontaneity requires that the inspiration to use the work and the moment in time of actual use in the course do not allow for a reasonable attempt to obtain permission. This test effectively prohibits use of the same materials in subsequent academic terms without the copyright holder's approval. "Spontaneity" is rarely measured in terms of semesters. The cumulative effects test caps the number of items copied for a single course at nine per academic term.

The criteria specified in the guidelines help determine what can be reproduced *without the need to seek permission.* The development of coursepacks, particularly those including the same materials term after term, normally requires licensing and the payment of fees. The licensing of printed materials is not an overwhelming task. The Copyright Clearance Center (CCC) (see URL at the end of this chapter) has been established as the reproduction rights organization (RRO) for the United States and serves this clearinghouse function. Since its founding in 1978 to provide book and periodical clearance services in response to the then newly revised copyright act, the CCC has evolved into a comprehensive organization that has managed over 300 million clearances, including permissions for a wide variety of publications in traditional printed formats as well as products such as digital media, books in electronic form (e-books), blogs, and websites, and collected and distributed royalties (Rosen, 2009). To expedite the process, products in the CCC's inventory have been preauthorized for licensing by the rights holders.

As a frame of reference, the Copyright Clearance Center distributed over $144 million in royalties in 2009, income that likely would have been lost to rights owners without a convenient means for users of those works to obtain and pay for permissions. Many copy centers and bookstores serving academic institutions maintain accounts with the CCC, provide liaison on the teacher's behalf, and then duplicate and sell the coursepacks. More than 50 RROs exist worldwide, providing similar services to faculty in other countries.

In addition to licensing conventional paper coursepacks, the Copyright Clearance Center will also develop, license, and distribute electronic coursepacks and work with academic libraries to develop electronic reserve collections for student use. Electronic coursepacks may be of particular interest to distance educators who do not wish to distribute paper coursepacks to remote-site students. The concept of the electronic coursepack is not exclusive to the CCC. For-profit companies such as XanEdu and University Readers also have emerged to help distance educators incorporate electronic coursepacks into their courses.

With services such as XanEdu, for example, faculty create accounts and identify the publications they wish to include. The service provider then obtains the appropriate permissions, compiles the coursepacks, sets prices, and sends access information to the faculty member, who forwards it to the students. Students set up their own accounts with the service provider, pay the fee, normally by credit card, and then receive immediate electronic access to the coursepacks, which can then be downloaded in PDF format, saved, and printed. Electronic coursepacks can include not only journal articles, but also individual book chapters or sections of chapters such as isolated tables or figures, workbook sections, conference papers, reports, and virtually any other document that has educational value and for which appropriate permission can be obtained.

Electronic coursepacks and the payment of fees by students should always be the last legal option. Many periodical publications freely offer their contents in full text online and can be linked to from within course websites without permission. Some require no-cost site registration. Academic libraries typically subscribe to online databases containing full-text publications that can be freely accessed by users from within the organization's Internet domain or by login from off-campus sites. A wide variety of reports and other documents published by government and nonprofit agencies, as well as by many commercial organizations, are also freely available on the Internet in HTML and/or PDF format, as are many conference papers posted on the Web by their authors or the conference organizers. The reference lists in this book serve as good examples. Teachers of distance education courses should check these resources before going through the process of licensing coursepacks.

Video

Many faculty use video in their conventional, face-to-face classes and want to use the same resources in their courses delivered online or via a video network. The TEACH Act sets specific guidelines for the use of video in a distance education environment, but what does "lawfully acquired" mean? The most obvious response is that the original videotape or DVD has been purchased or rented by the educational organization for the specific purpose of supporting instruction. Does this apply to the use of entertainment films in tape or DVD format that are marked "For Home Use Only" and purchased over the counter or rented from the neighborhood Blockbuster? The Motion Picture Licensing Corporation (undated) acknowledges that such videos may be used by nonprofit educational institutions under the provisions of Section 110, but in distance learning settings it is imperative that the school or college be in compliance with the TEACH Act.

Most instructors will likely wish to use commercially available video materials produced for education or training purposes rather than entertainment films. Distributors of these products typically do not include online use in their license agreements without a separate, specific permission. Please refer to the TEACH Act discussion a few pages back. Note that virtually all of the bullets in that section apply to the distribution of digitized video materials, so those criteria apply here. DVDs, of course, are already in digital form, and conventional VHS videotapes can easily be digitized by most school district and college instructional technology or information technology centers. These files will likely need to be edited and digitally compressed before placement on a course website or incorporation into a lecture during a real-time, video-based lecture, to conform to TEACH Act specifications.

However, a caveat is in order here. Legal proceedings involving applications of the TEACH Act are just beginning to work their way through the courts. The Library

Copyright Alliance, a consortium of the three major library organizations in higher education, recently released an "Issue Brief" citing several appellate court decisions that found video streaming of entire works without permission to be fair use. In general, the paper argued for a very liberal approach to application of the TEACH Act in distance education courses (Library Copyright Alliance, 2010). To be sure, the final chapter of this saga has not yet been written. Ultimately, it will be the courts that define what is fair use and what is not, and under what conditions.

Perhaps the simplest solution to copyright limitations is to use video produced at your own school or college. Unless unusual circumstances exist, your institution holds the copyright to these video files, and you should be able to use them without restrictions.

Photographs and Digital Images

The reproduction of photographs, illustrations, graphic designs, and other still images for use in a distance education course presents a perplexing copyright dilemma because, as we noted earlier in this chapter, intellectual property may be involved at several levels. For example, a teacher may wish to make a slide from or digitize a textbook photograph. The book and the photograph may be copyrighted separately, and depending on the subject matter, the original object may also be protected. Moreover, the chain from the original to the photo in the book may involve intermediate steps, each entitled to copyright protection. Even if the original object is in the public domain, the photograph and book may not be.

Section 110 permits the classroom display of photographic material that has been lawfully acquired. In other words, slide or digital image sets purchased for educational use from someone authorized by the rights holders are the safest alternative. The "lawfully acquired" condition may apply to slide sets compiled locally from books and magazines using a copy stand. The *Guidelines for Classroom Copying* indicate that one picture per book or periodical issue is permissible. Fair use guidelines published by the Consortium for Educational Technology in University Systems (CETUS, 1995) suggest that "a small number of images from any one textbook" (p. 26) may fall under fair use, particularly if slides are not available from the publisher. Any slidemaking or imaging beyond these guides requires a very careful consideration of the four criteria for determining fair use.

Guidelines for the educational use of digital images were drafted by a CONFU working group but were quite restrictive and failed to garner much support in the educational community. The draft does provide some insight into the limits to which some copyright holders perceive fair use. The guidelines include the following selected provisions:

- Only lawfully acquired analog images may be digitized.
- Educational institutions may not digitize images that are already available in usable digital form for purchase or license at a fair price.
- Educational institutions may display and provide access to images digitized under these guidelines through a secure electronic network, provided that access is controlled via a password or PIN and restricted to students enrolled in the course.
- Use of images digitized from a known source may only be used for one academic term; subsequent use requires permission. If permission is not received, subsequent use is subject to the four-factor fair use analysis.

- If the rights holder is unknown, the image may be used for three years from first use, provided that the institution conducts a reasonable effort to identify the rights holder and seek permission.
- Images digitized under these guidelines may be used in face-to-face teaching, independent study by students, and research and scholarly activities at the institution.
- The images may not be used in publications without permission.

Electronic Mail, Course Websites, and Other Internet Resources

Materials placed on the Internet, whether e-mail messages, postings to mailing lists (often inappropriately referred to as "listservs"), websites, blogs, wikis, podcasts, and other digital resources, represent intellectual property fixed in a tangible medium of expression and are entitled to copyright protection just like any other work of authorship. From a legal perspective, placement of the material on the Internet is no different from any other form of distribution, except that access and the potential for abuse are both greatly expanded. Although some persons contend that such action implies an abandonment of copyright, clearly this is not the case without an explicit statement to that effect on the part of the copyright holder (which often is someone other than the individual who posted the material).

The presence of Print and Save buttons on browser toolbars may imply that documents on the Web are fair game. On the contrary, unless they are specifically dedicated to the public domain or grant downloading privileges, or are licensed for such use through the Creative Commons, Web documents are entitled to full copyright protection. The CETUS fair use handbook suggests that copying a short Internet document for personal study or research likely falls within fair use but recommends that the four-factor fair use analysis be applied (CETUS, 1995). Saving or printing from sites that have restricted access or contain documents that are commercially available may be more difficult to justify as fair use. Many websites include copyright policies that provide the site sponsor's positions on downloading. Care must be taken to confirm that the site sponsor actually is the rights holder of the desired document.

Is it necessary to obtain permission before linking to someone else's website? Although some purists insist that the answer is yes, most authorities feel that freely linking to the websites of others not only is legal but is encouraged, and that those who object to setting up hyperlinks are essentially missing the point of the Web. Generally speaking, it is not necessary to obtain permission prior to installing links to external resources within a course web site. Indeed, faculty who fail to do so may be missing some excellent opportunities to expand student access to valuable online resources and promote learning in the course content areas.

As discussed throughout this book, many courses, particularly in higher education and corporate training settings, are now offered via some form of Internet conferencing or course management system such as Blackboard or Desire2Learn. The copyright implications just described are equally applicable in these settings, even though most of these systems require special client software and/or passwords that restrict access to the participants. Placing full text of copyrighted documents, such as journal articles, behind password protection strengthens the case for fair use, but until the courts rule otherwise, this practice is risky without the proper permissions or licensing. Publishers and copyright management organizations are acutely aware of the potential for copyright infringement within course management systems, and some provide copyright guidance for faculty teaching within that context (e.g., Copyright Clearance Center, 2009).

 ## OBTAINING PERMISSION

If guidelines are not applicable, fair use cannot be determined, and the TEACH Act does not apply, distance educators should obtain permission from rights holders before using copyrighted materials in their courses, as challenging as that task may seem. Begin by contacting the publisher or distributor. If no address or telephone number is provided, check catalogs or ask a reference librarian for assistance. As a last resort, a plea for help sent to appropriate Internet mailing lists often delivers the desired contact information.

The first contact with the rights holder should be made by telephone to confirm precisely to whom the request should be addressed. A phone call also provides an opportunity to discuss the circumstances of the request and negotiate fees, if any. Ultimately, the rights holder will likely ask for a written copy of the request, by either mail or fax, for record purposes and to avoid misunderstandings. See Figure 10–1 for a sample letter. At a minimum, the rights holder will need the following information:

- Name, position, institution, mailing address, and phone and fax numbers for the person making the request
- Identification of the item to be used, including title, author or producer, publication title and date in the case of periodicals, and quantity desired
- Complete description of the intended use, including purpose, course name, number of copies, means of distribution, intended dates of use, description of recipients, and precautions anticipated to prevent further reproductions (if applicable)
- Date by which permission is requested (allow at least six weeks)

Although approval can be granted over the telephone, for record purposes written permission is strongly recommended, preferably on the copyright holder's letterhead. This provides tangible evidence confirming exactly who provided permission for what, and when.

 ## INTELLECTUAL PROPERTY RIGHTS

The matter of intellectual property (IP) rights is currently one of the hot buttons in distance education, particularly among faculty unions. Who owns an online course? The school/university? The faculty member providing the content? Should the ownership be shared between the two, and if so, under what conditions? Is it even *possible* to "own" an entire online course, given the various levels of IP that likely went into its development and delivery? Intellectual property rights related to multimedia and online course materials have long been an issue in higher education and are becoming an increasingly prominent concern at the K–12 level.

FIGURE 10–1 Sample permission letter.

Department of English
328 Loess Hall
University of Western Iowa
Council Bluffs, Iowa 51508

July 16, 20XX

Mrs. Caroline B. Day
Manager of Permissions
American Heritage Productions
2877 Revere Highway
Boston, MA 02226

Dear Mrs. Day:

As a follow-up to our telephone conversation this morning, I am hereby requesting permission to digitize six illustrations from your book, *Early Art of New England,* by F. N. Peterson, for use in my online class entitled Art 244, Nineteenth Century American Art, here at the University of Western Iowa. Many of our students are from low-income families, and I cannot in good conscience ask them to purchase the book at its $105 price, when we cover only six paintings illustrated in the book. Yet, these six are critical of their understanding of how painting was evolving in America during this period.

The six paintings to be digitized are:

Calm Before the Storm, by Shelton (p. 26)
Lilacs, by Jones (p. 32)
A Cambridge Garden, also by Jones (p. 33)
Portrait of Farragut, by Weldon (p. 41)
Serenity, by Adamson (p. 46)
The Haunted Manor, by MacTavish (p. 60)

The course uses the Blackboard course management system. These digitized images will be password-protected and only accessible to enrolled students and myself. Students will be asked to view the images online and not to save or print them. Because the course is taught annually, I am requesting permission to continue using these images in this manner for a period of five years, through Fall 20XX, at which time I will send another request for subsequent use.

Since the Fall semester begins on September 12, I would appreciate hearing from you by August 23, so I will have time to digitize the images and place them online, or revise my course content if permission is denied. Thank you for your consideration. Please contact me directly if I can provide further information.

Sincerely,

Michael T. James

Associate Professor English

Phone: (712) 555-2838
Fax: (712) 555-2840
E-Mail: mtjames@westiowa.edu

LOOKING FORWARD

Somewhere in the not-too-distant future, our homes, workplaces, and schools will be equipped with advanced telecommunications systems such as modern personal smart phones integrating what are known today as telephone services, Internet access, online financial and news services, and cable or satellite television, probably with many other features not yet conceived. Distance education will play a central role in that future, as technology-delivered curricula will be offered by educational institutions and private corporations on a global basis to anyone, anywhere, at any time. The current copyright law, even with all its revisions, will likely be unable to deal with the enormous complexity of protecting intellectual property rights while providing legal access in this international information marketplace and will require a major overhaul. The Web-Based Education Commission (2000) called for "a radical rethinking of the relevant body of regulation and law" (p. 97). Certainly, the basic concepts of copyright and fair use may need to be reconsidered. However, a more probable intermediate solution is the development of technologies that prevent reproduction of copyrighted materials from networked sources. The DMCA took the first significant steps down that path.

Meanwhile, the present law may be inadequate, but educators must abide by its provisions or face the consequences. For the most part, the copyright statute is civil law, not criminal law. Unless violators have made a business out of infringements, they are likely to be sued, not sent to jail. The penalties can be severe—statutory damages of up to $150,000 per instance, plus payment of the plaintiff's legal fees, which can be substantial. Distance educators have not only a legal and ethical obligation to "practice safe copyright" but monetary incentives as well.

DISCUSSION QUESTIONS

1. What did you read in this chapter that alerted you to copyright infringements you have witnessed, either in the workplace or at your own educational setting? What was the most blatant copyright violation you've ever seen, and what was done about it?

2. What did you read in this chapter that will change the way in which you use the intellectual property of others?

3. You have been appointed chair of a committee to develop a copyright policy for your organization. This policy will cover employee and student use of intellectual property for which ownership rests outside the organization (i.e., your organization does not own the copyright). What would you argue are the most important points to make in the policy?

4. Who (position, not name) in your organization should have accountability for addressing and resolving issues involving internal copyright violations? Should "copyright police" be part of that person's job description? What are the ethical and personal dilemmas involved?

5. In order to comply with the requirements of the Digital Millennium Copyright Act, an educational organization must provide copyright training to its membership on a regular basis. What do you think would be the most effective means of providing that training, so that the participants "get it" and follow the organization's copyright policy?
6. You are the instructional developer to whom the professor in the first paragraph of this chapter brings the stack of bookmarked Greek civilization books. How do you handle this? He is a senior full professor and is very influential on campus. What do you say to him about fair use, and what do you do?
7. What are the unique copyright issues present in the corporate, for-profit training sector?

REFERENCES

Consortium for Educational Technology in University Systems. (1995). *Fair use of copyrighted works.* Seal Beach, CA: California State University Chancellor's Office. Available online at http://hall-davidson.net/FAIRUSE.pdf.

Copyright Clearance Center. (2009). *Using course management systems: Guidelines and best practices for copyright compliance.* Danvers, MA: Author. Available online at http://copyright.com/media/pdfs/Using-Course-Management-Systems.pdf.

Gasaway, L. (2003). *When works pass into the public domain.* Available online at www.unc.edu/~unclng/public-d.htm.

Library Copyright Alliance. (2010). *Issue Brief: Streaming of films for educational purposes.* Available online at www.librarycopyrightalliance.org/bm~doc/ibstreamingfilms_021810.pdf.

Miller, J. K. (1975). A brief history of copyright. *Audiovisual Instruction, 20*(10), 44.

Motion Picture Licensing Corporation. (Undated). *About U.S. copyright law.* Available online at www.mplc.com/aboutLaw.php.

Rosen, J. (2009). Copyright Clearance Center piles up the numbers. *Publishers Weekly,* May 18, 2009. Available online at www.publishersweekly.com/pw/by-topic/book-news/deals/article/15852-copyright-clearance-center-piles-up-the-numbers-.html.

U.S. Copyright Office. (1999). *Report on copyright and digital distance education.* Washington, DC: Author. Available online at www.copyright.gov/reports/de_rprt.pdf.

Web-Based Education Commission. (2000). *The power of the Internet for learning: Moving from promise to practice.* Washington, DC: Author. Available online at www.ed.gov/offices/AC/WBEC/FinalReport/WBECReport.pdf.

Zobel, S. M. (1997). Legal implications of intellectual property and the World Wide Web. In B. H. Khan (Ed.), *Web-based instruction* (pp. 337–340). Englewood Cliffs, NJ: Educational Technology Publications.

WEBSITES REFERENCED IN THIS CHAPTER

Copyright Clearance Center
http://www.copyright.com

Website for the reproduction rights organization serving the United States.

Creative Commons
http://creativecommons.org

Nonprofit organization providing a variety of licensing options to allow creators of intellectual property to share their works with others.

U.S. Copyright Office
http://www.copyright.gov/

Online source of Copyright Office publications, forms, and other information, including status of pending copyright legislation and full text of the copyright law.

UT System Crash Course on Copyright
www.utsystem.edu/ogc/intellectualproperty/cprtindx.htm

Georgia Harper's widely acclaimed guide to copyright, including applications in distance learning, maintained by the University of Texas System Office of General Counsel.

University Readers
www.universityreaders.com

XanEdu
www.xanedu.com

Two for-profit companies that assist faculty in compiling, licensing, and distributing electronic coursepacks.

The Fair Use guidelines listed in Table 10.2, in either their published or final draft form, may be found at these locations:

Guidelines for Classroom Copying in Not-for-Profit Educational Institutions
(University Libraries, University of Connecticut)
www.lib.uconn.edu/services/reserve/housereport941476.html

Guidelines for Educational Uses of Music
(University of Texas System Office of General Counsel)
www.utsystem.edu/ogc/intellectualproperty/musguid.htm

Guidelines for Off-Air Recording of Broadcast Programming for Educational Purposes
(Educational Communications Center, Binghamton University)
www.ecc.binghamton.edu/offair.html

Fair Use Guidelines for Educational Multimedia
(University of Texas System Office of General Counsel)
http://www.utsystem.edu/ogc/intellectualproperty/ccmcguid.htm

Guidelines for the Educational Use of Digital Images
(University of Texas System Office of General Counsel)
www.utsystem.edu/ogc/intellectualproperty/imagguid.htm

Educational Fair Use Guidelines for Distance Learning
(University of Texas System Office of General Counsel)
www.utsystem.edu/ogc/intellectualproperty/distguid.htm

Fair Use Guidelines for Electronic Reserve Systems
(University of Texas System Office of General Counsel)
www.utsystem.edu/ogc/intellectualproperty/rsrvguid.htm

ADDITIONAL HELPFUL WEBSITES ON COPYRIGHT ISSUES

Copyright and Fair Use
http://fairuse.stanford.edu/

Stanford University Libraries' extensive online listing of copyright resources, with a special emphasis on fair use.

Cornell University Legal Information Institute
http://topics.law.cornell.edu/wex/copyright

Cornell LII's collection of extremely useful resources on copyright, including court cases.

Educause Archive of Copyright/Intellectual Property Policies and Resources
www.educause.edu/Browse/645?PARENT_ID=112

Links to a wide variety of institutional policies and other documents related to copyright and intellectual property policies in higher education.

CHAPTER 11

Managing and Leading a Distance Education Organization

CHAPTER GOAL

The purpose of this chapter is to describe the functions and professional concerns of an administrator of distance education programs.

CHAPTER OBJECTIVES

After reading and reviewing this chapter, you should be able to

1. Describe the typical job functions of a distance education administrator.
2. Discuss the major areas of interest during the planning stage for distance education programs.
3. Identify the major distance education readiness issues related to an educational organization itself, and discuss how they should be addressed.
4. Identify the major distance education readiness issues related to faculty teaching distance education courses, and discuss how they should be addressed.
5. Discuss the most important areas of concern related to the assessment of an organization's technological readiness for distance education.
6. Describe the most important policy issues related to distance education, both internally within the educational organization and externally.
7. Discuss the procedures that can help ensure quality control of a distance education program.
8. Identify and discuss the regulatory issues that can affect a distance education program.
9. Discuss the issues related to the development and use of intellectual property in a distance education program.
10. Describe the most critical issues related to the support of students enrolled in a distance education program.

THE DISTANCE LEARNING LEADER

It is one thing to participate in distance education as a student or teacher. It is quite another to manage and provide leadership for a distance education program. Management of distance education requires a rather different perspective of the topic. This chapter will describe the functions of a distance education manager and explore the current issues that an administrator will need to address. The terms *distance education administrator* and *distance education manager* will be used interchangeably.

While the concept of leading a distance education organization is implied in the role of administrator or manager, there is a growing body of literature that differentiates the leader from the manager. This chapter will focus on managing, but

317

FIGURE 11–1   The distance learning leader pyramid of competencies.

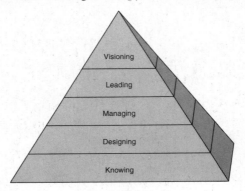

the role of leader should not be ignored. Figure 11–1 shows the pyramid of competencies needed by the distance learning leader. The pyramid has the broad base of knowledge about distance education at the bottom and is topped by a clear vision for distance education within the organization. Simonson (2004) defined the *distance learning leader* as

> a visionary capable of action who guides an organization's future, its vision, mission, goals, and objectives. The leader guides the organization and its people who have faith in the leader, and have a clear understanding and acceptance of the organization's worthwhile and shared vision and goals. A distance learning leader has competence in knowing, designing, managing, leading, and visioning distance education. (p. 48)

MANAGEMENT WITHIN THE CONTEXT OF READINESS

At the very heart of the distance education administrator's responsibility is the matter of readiness—institutional readiness, faculty readiness, and student readiness. Abedor and Sachs (1978) felt that organizational development activities (that address institutional readiness issues) and faculty development activities (that address faculty readiness concerns) *should precede* instructional development, in this case the development and delivery of courses and programs at a distance, to help maximize the chances for an instructional innovation to be successful. While distance education is hardly an "innovation" as we progress into the twenty-first century, it remains an alternative to conventional classroom instruction that still has many skeptics among mainstream faculty and academic administrators. Therefore, it is imperative that distance education activities take place in an environment most conducive to achieving success. Leading the initiatives to attain organizational and individual faculty readiness should be central to a distance education administrator's duties.

ORGANIZATIONAL READINESS

Abedor and Sachs (1978) identified organizational structure, a receptive reward system for faculty, the availability of resources, and institutional policies that encourage instructional innovation among the most potent factors in achieving organizational readiness. You will see these themes recurring throughout this chapter. We will also discuss other readiness issues directly applicable to distance education, such as planning, quality control, accessibility and other legal matters, regulatory concerns, and costing.

Leadership and Direction for the Distance Education Program

If an educational organization offers or plans to engage in distance education activities, a qualified individual at an appropriate administrative echelon should be designated with responsibility for providing leadership, direction, oversight, quality control, and accountability for those courses and programs. Figure 11–2 lists common functions of a distance education administrator and illustrates the scope of responsibilities that may come with the position. Achieving success with distance learning initiatives will be difficult unless these duties are focused in one office, with one individual tasked with overall accountability for carrying them out successfully.

Planning for Distance Education

No organization should enter into the distance education marketplace without a clearly thought through plan that has gained the consensus approval of all key players. In addition to the general plan, each individual academic program to be delivered at a distance should have a realistic business plan that justifies the existence of the program, clearly identifies the target student population and describes how it will be recruited, describes its means of delivery, and projects the anticipated cash flow at a level acceptable to the organization. The absence of a realistic business plan is a foremost reason why online learning ventures fail. Some very prominent universities in the United States have wandered into this tar pit.

Analysis of potential markets. Distance education has become a saturated marketplace. A study of the 2006–07 academic year conducted for the National Center for Education Statistics (Parsad & Lewis, 2008) found that 65% of all higher education institutions offered distance education courses for college credit and 23% offered noncredit courses at a distance. The study also showed that 29% offered degree programs and 17% offered certificate programs that could be completed entirely via distance education. At the K–12 level, statewide virtual schools were maintained in 27 U.S. states in 2009, and 18 additional states operated full-time online schools not available statewide (Watson, Gemin, Ryan, & Wicks, 2009). The abundance of players in this field mandates that needs assessments be conducted to determine what market niches might be available to an educational organization and what students in those

FIGURE 11–2   Typical position responsibilities for a distance education administrator.

Administrative Functions

■ Provides strategic leadership and direction for all organizational distance education programs.

■ Provides leadership in operational and strategic planning and policy related to distance education initiatives; ensures that organizational policies accommodate distance education programs.

■ Conducts market analysis and works with faculty and academic units to develop business plans for proposed distance learning programs.

■ Actively promotes distance education programs to target student populations.

■ Maintains the organization's website for distance education activities.

■ Serves as a source of information and referrals to appropriate academic programs for new students who are interested in the organization's distance education programs.

■ Ensures availability and responsiveness for all student support requirements.

■ Ensures that students enrolled in the organization's distance education programs are given appropriate, timely training in use of the course delivery technologies and are provided effective guidance regarding navigation of the institution's administrative procedures and requirements.

■ Ensures fiscal responsibility for online courses and programs.

■ Seeks out and applies for external funding to support the organization's distance education initiatives, as appropriate.

■ Provides overall leadership and direction for distance education support staff, ensuring the most efficient and effective utilization of human resources with a strong emphasis on quality service.

Academic Functions

■ Coordinates program and individual course development for delivery via distance education.

■ Hires or consults with academic units in the employment of instructors for distance education courses.

■ Ensures that all distance education coursework and support services meet appropriate accessibility standards.

■ Provides appropriate training/professional development activities for faculty teaching the organization's distance education courses; certifies instructors as "ready" to teach these courses.

■ Ensures that faculty teaching distance education courses receive the necessary level of technical and pedagogical support on an ongoing basis.

■ Ensures quality control of distance education courses and programs and conducts appropriate activities to assess course/program effectiveness and facilitate necessary improvements; facilitates a comprehensive evaluation of every distance education program on a periodic basis.

■ Ensures organizational compliance with appropriate standards, guidelines, and regulations, including those required by the institution's accreditation agencies.

niches need and expect. It is far better to spend $100,000 on a market analysis to learn that a market is not there than to assume it is, discover the hard way that it isn't, and waste a potentially million-dollar investment.

Why do educational institutions engage in distance education activities? The 2006–07 NCES study found that the most common reasons were to meet student demand for flexible scheduling (68%), provide access to students who would otherwise not have access (67%), make more courses available (46%), and increase overall enrollment (45%) (Parsad & Lewis, 2008). Coupled with figures cited in the previous paragraph showing that 65% of colleges and universities offer courses at a distance but just 29% offer complete degree programs, these data strongly suggest that an important market for online courses is an institution's own residential students. Other potential markets for distance education were discussed in earlier chapters of this book.

It is important to determine whether the potential market exists in an academic content area that is consistent with the core mission and values of the host organization. Online programs should never be developed just to jump onto the online learning bandwagon or make a few dollars. The absence of such compatibility is a red flag for regional accreditation agencies.

Other planning concerns.　　Once the presence of an appropriate, receptive market has been confirmed, planning should then turn to institutional and faculty readiness issues. Is the organization collectively ready to offer and support distance education programs? Specifically, is the technology infrastructure sufficiently robust to support distance education at the desired level? Is the organization ready to support faculty teaching in the distance education program? Is the organization ready to support off-campus students? Are institutional policies ready to accommodate distance education courses and programs?

Procedural questions need to be addressed. How will quality control be assured? What procedures will be implemented to make sure the courses are effectively taught and maintained at least the same level of academic rigor as classroom versions of the same courses? How will tuition and fees, if applicable, be determined? A thorough analysis of the up-front and ongoing costs of the program and the strategies for recovering those costs, and perhaps generating additional revenue if that is a goal of the program, is imperative as part of the planning process.

Scope of Task in Developing Distance Courses and Programs

Another important readiness issue that must be addressed in the planning stage is whether the organization has the resources, or can obtain the resources, to accommodate the scope of the task in developing and supporting courses and programs to be delivered at a distance. If the scope is relatively small, for example just a few courses, an assessment should be done to see if the course development and ongoing support can be accomplished with existing resources. However, the development of a large-scale program will likely require more resources than currently available. The additional funding needs will have a significant effect on the cost analysis.

For example, let us consider the scale of a project that would put an associate's degree fully online at a community college, or a two-year degree completion program at a baccalaureate institution targeted toward students who have associates degrees. These are fairly common scenarios. Two-year online degree programs typically require roughly 60 semester hours' worth of courses. *That is the equivalent of 20 three-credit hour courses that must be developed and supported*, not counting optional elective courses across the variety of academic departments that service the major. The actual hours and resources required to develop each course could vary significantly according to the amount of research time involved, how much course activity and learning object development is involved (particularly important in courses with lab activities in the conventional classroom setting), how extensively instructional development staff are involved in addition to the instructor's own time, whether licensing of learning materials or additional technology is necessary, how much training time for the instructor, if any, is required, and so forth.

Suffice it to say that the development of a single course can be an extraordinarily time-consuming venture. Then multiply that times the number of courses required to deliver the program and provide ongoing support to the instructor and students. Then double that total if the institution wishes to mount a four-year online program. If the organization does not have the current resources to mount such an effort, and cannot or will not make the commitment to dedicate additional resources to achieve the required level, it has no business even considering offering online programs. The absence of readiness is clearly demonstrated.

Student Support

The quality of student support services available and easily accessible to a distant learner will play a major role in determining whether that student learns about the program, enrolls, and remains through to completion. This is an essential organizational readiness concern. Students enrolled in online courses and programs have certain expectations of their institutions:

- That they will receive the same access to support services as on-campus students, and that those services will be integrated with those available to residential students rather than through separate offices that only serve distant students
- That as much information as possible will be provided online
- That contact information related to student services will be easily accessible, as well as the contact people themselves
- That services will be self-service to the greatest degree possible, with transactions conducted online
- That services will be personalized, rather than generic (e.g., personal responses rather than computer-generated responses or form letters)
- That responses to requests for information or assistance will be provided accurately and in a timely manner

A project entitled *Beyond the Administrative Core: Creating Web-Based Student Services for Online Learners*, developed by the Western Cooperative for Educational Telecommunications (WCET), provides excellent guidance for identifying service areas and facilitating student support in an online environment. The essential model is depicted in the form of a "Web of Student Services for Online Learners" included in the project report (WCET, 2010a). See Figure 11–3. This model organizes student services into five general areas—Administrative Core, Academic Services, Communications, Personal Services, and Student Communities—and identifies examples of student support that should be provided under each. Although WCET's focus in this project was on online learning, for all practical purposes the model applies to all forms of distance education.

Student training and ongoing guidance is another critical student support issue that could fall under "technical support" in the WCET model but merits special attention here. Students need clear instructions regarding all technologies they will use while enrolled in the program, from the course management system to online library services to all Web and other software applications that faculty might employ, such as a blogging site or plagiarism detection service. Even though most students today are technology-fluent, it cannot be assumed that they will easily learn these applications

FIGURE 11–3   WCET's "Web of Student Services for Online Learners." Reprinted with permission.

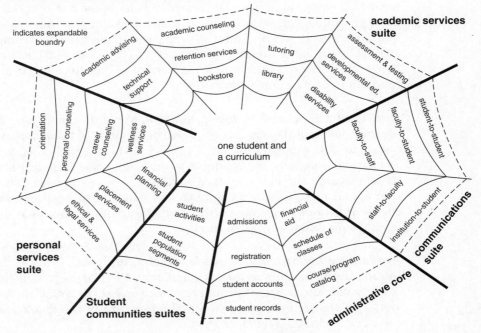

on their own, particularly those who do find technology confusing and intimidating. Moreover, students also need to have clear instructions for institutional procedures, such as for admission, advising and course registration, paying their bills, and obtaining transcripts. These should be easily available on the organization's website, preferably in the section addressing distance education.

Readiness of the Technology Infrastructure

The institution must ensure that the technology infrastructure is sufficiently robust, reliable, and well supported, or it must make a firm commitment, backed up with the necessary funding, to bring campus technology to the necessary level. Inadequate and/or unreliable technology is one of the quickest ways to kill a distance education program. Is the technology ready? If not, what has to happen to make it ready? Instructional/information technology staff must be party to the discussions regarding readiness that follow.

Capacity and quality of network infrastructure.   In planning for a Web-based distance education program, including programs delivered via video-over-IP (VOIP) systems, the entire network infrastructure should be reviewed. Does the network have sufficient bandwidth to accommodate not only on-campus users effectively but also to allow off-campus students to connect with campus servers to access course materials without service slowdowns? This is a particularly important concern if courses utilize streaming audio or video or other bandwidth-intensive learning objects or applications. Does the organization have reliable Internet access of its own, sufficient server capacity, adequate routers, servers for redundancy in the case of server failure, emergency generators during power failure, and a file backup system and off-site storage? The same network security issues that apply in intraorganizational computing also are applicable to distance education programs. Off-campus students have an even greater need than residential students, for example, to be able to conduct campus business transactions over a secure network.

Quality of the administrative computing system.   As we have noted, remote-site students enrolled in distance education programs need to conduct as much institutional business as possible online. This begins with the admission and financial aid application procedures and continues through advising, course registration, access to student records, and business office services. These systems need to be user friendly, secure, and maintained expeditiously. An educational organization that fails to effectively provide these core electronic administrative services to its distant students sends them a distinctly negative message.

Availability and quality of academic technologies.   Most educational institutions today use course management systems (CMSs) to deliver their online courses and supplement and support video-based courses. Course management systems have been discussed at length elsewhere in this book and will not be explored in detail here. Suffice it to say that the robustness and reliability of the course management system is an essential organizational readiness concern, as is, of course, the skills with which course instructors utilize the CMS tools to promote student learning. Web 2.0 functions, such as blogging, wiki development, and the posting of student-developed learning media, have become integrated into more advanced CMS versions or may be licensed through independent vendors and linked to directly from course websites. In addition, the organization may provide or license other technology applications, such as for streaming audio and/or video, audio recording and archiving support for speech and language courses, electronic coursepacks, and a plagiarism detection service. A tool for electronic portfolios may also be licensed. This agenda of available academic technologies and their integration within the overall institutional technology infrastructure to promote access and user-friendliness, as well as provisions for instructor and student training and ongoing support, should be central to the technology readiness assessment for distance education.

Overall staffing support.   Does the organization maintain the technology staffing level that will be required to effectively support the distance education program? If not, what additional staffing will be needed, and how will it be funded?

A vitally important consideration is Help Desk support. The availability of timely technical assistance for distant learners is another hot button for accreditors. Students frequently need assistance with matters beyond interrupted access and forgotten passwords. Many requests for help will involve some aspect of the course management system or other relevant delivery system (for example, if the courses are delivered in real time in video-over-IP format and then archived for later student access). For this reason, Help Desk staff should be well versed in navigating and troubleshooting these applications and, in general, every technology application supported by the institution for instructional purposes. Detailed user guides for all campus technologies used by students should be posted on all relevant websites and also made available to the Help Desk staff for convenient reference. These guides and searchable online databases called knowledge bases can also be extremely helpful to students and faculty, especially when the Help Desk is closed.

Working relationship between distance education and information technology.   In many cases, information technology support for distance education programs will be provided by a department administratively independent from the office managing distance education programs. Does an effective working relationship exist between the administrative office for distance education and the IT unit? Students who cannot connect because of server or network failure are likely to contact the instructor first, who then would contact the distance education office for resolution of a problem that may fall under the responsibility of the IT office. Not only must communication channels constantly be open, but monitoring and problem resolution systems must be in place to address issues as soon as they occur and minimize down time. The lack thereof is another serious red flag for accreditors.

Repair and replacement funding. An organization that does not annually budget for repair and replacement of its technology will have grave difficulty in sustaining a successful technology-based distance education program. This is another important readiness issue. At some institutions, equipment replacement is accommodated through fiscal year-end "budget dust" and is not planned, hardly a reliable approach. Much information technology equipment, such as servers and routers, should be replaced every four to five years at a maximum. The organization's technology plan should provide annual schedules for equipment replacement, so that the "refresh" is systematic and institutionalized, and so that funding needs can be anticipated in the planning process for upcoming budget cycles.

Institutional Policies

A review of existing institutional policies that have implications for distance education is imperative when assessing an organization's readiness. Some current policies may require revision. The review may disclose that new policies must be developed.

Distance Education Policy

Policy development and implementation, as well as revision of existing institutional policies when appropriate, is an important topic to be addressed when an organization considers offering distance courses and programs. Gellman-Danley and Fetzner (1998) identified seven critical areas of policy development for distance education: academic, fiscal, geographic, governance, labor-management, legal, and student support services. See Table 11–1 for a listing of key issues to be addressed under each of these areas. Note that these are internal policies within the organization.

A specific institutional policy on distance education or online learning may be highly appropriate and could address most or all of these issues. Such a policy should be drafted by those administering the distance education program, in collaboration with appropriate administrative offices and relevant governance bodies, and be vetted and approved through the organization's normal policy development process.

Distance education (or online learning) policy. It may be most appropriate for the organization to develop an omnibus distance education or online learning policy, if one does not already exist. The policy can consolidate or reference relevant sections of other existing institutional policies and incorporate new policy areas as appropriate. Such a policy should be drafted by those administering the distance education program, in collaboration with appropriate administrative offices, governance bodies, and faculty representatives, and be vetted and approved through the organization's normal policy development procedures. A distance education/online learning policy could cover the following areas of concern:

***Governance and administration of the distance education/online learning
     program.*** Overall responsibility and accountability for the organization's distance
     learning programs should be clearly identified in the policy (by title, not name), and

TABLE 11–1 ■ Policy Development Areas for Distance Learning

Policy Development Area	Key Issues
Academic	Academic calendar, course integrity, transferability, transcripts, evaluation process, admission standards, curriculum approval process, accreditation, quality standards and assurance, course and program assessment, student academic dishonesty, course dates and deadlines (e.g., last dates for drop/add, withdrawal, makeup of incomplete grades), enrollment caps
Fiscal	Tuition rate, technology fee, FTEs (Full-Time Equivalents), consortia contacts, state fiscal regulations
Geographic	Service area regional limitations, local versus out-of-state tuition, consortia agreements
Governance	Single versus multiple board oversight, staffing, existing structure versus shadow colleges or enclaves, institutional accountability
Labor-Management	Compensation and workload, development incentives, intellectual property, faculty training, congruence with existing union contracts, promotion and tenure
Legal	Use of copyrighted materials, intellectual property of students, DMCA and TEACH Act implications, accessibility, liability
Student Support	Student services (e.g., admissions, advising, tutoring, financial aid), computing system accounts, library access for off-site students, materials delivery, student training, test proctoring, handling of student complaints

Source: Adapted from Gellman-Danley & Fetzner (1998).

that person's administrative reporting relationship should also be identified. The policy might also list the distance education administrator's position functions.

Academic policies.   The distance education/online learning policy will likely refer to existing institutional academic policies but may emphasize how some are specifically applied in distance/online course situations. For example, the policy might:

■ Require that the academic rigor of all courses delivered by distance education must be maintained at least at the level expected for traditional-classroom-based courses.

■ Specify that distance education courses normally will conform to the same academic calendar as traditional classroom courses and follow the institution's standard schedule for drops, adds, last day for credit/no-credit grading, course withdrawals, and resolution of incomplete grades; state that flexible course scheduling is possible and encouraged when justified.

■ Establish enrollment caps for distance education courses, typically 20 in online courses.

■ Set a limit on the number of credit hours that can be completed by a nonmatriculated student, typically 12 semester hours, before formal application and admission to the institution is required.

This section of the policy should also specify the requirements and timeline for pre-approval of distance education courses and programs. The timeline for course approval is very important. Courses to be offered at a distance must be indicated in the official course schedule, which is compiled and distributed well before the registration period for that academic term, normally during the previous term. Distance education marketing staff need early identification of distance education courses so they can be effectively promoted to target off-campus student populations. Identification in the course schedule also benefits residential students who may wish to take online courses because of scheduling conflicts or other reasons such as instructor preference.

Quality control.   The organization's overall commitment to quality control should be emphasized in the distance education/online learning policy. This topic is sufficiently important that it rates its own section in this chapter and will be explored in more detail later.

Faculty-related issues.   A variety of faculty-related issues may be addressed in a distance education/online learning policy. Referrals to other official institutional policies (such as those related to faculty contracts, workload, faculty evaluation, promotion and tenure, ranks and titles, and intellectual property, which will be discussed later in this chapter) will be common in this section, but matters such as the following may receive special attention in this policy. *These are examples only and may not reflect the official position of every institution.*

- It is the organization's first priority to assign core faculty to teach distance education courses; if core faculty are unable or unwilling to teach these courses, the teaching assignments will be given to adjunct faculty. ("Core faculty" would refer to full-time, tenured or tenure-track faculty.)
- An instructor may not be required to teach a distance education course against his or her wishes.
- The development and utilization of distance education courses shall never be used to reduce or eliminate core faculty positions.
- The teaching of distance education courses will be considered part of an instructor's normal workload and will not merit additional compensation unless assigned as an overload. If at all possible, the institution will avoid assigning overloads if one or more courses is/are taught online.
- No overload should be assigned to a faculty member teaching a distance education course for the first time.
- The teaching of distance education courses shall be considered during the promotion and tenure approval process according to the same standards as for conventional classroom teaching. No faculty member shall ever be penalized during the promotion and tenure process for teaching distance education courses.
- Instructors teaching distance education courses shall maintain "virtual" office hours for students completing these courses at a distance. This includes physical office hours for student phone calls, as well as timely response to electronic mail messages. The use of other electronic communication tools, such as chats, texting, and instant messaging, in communicating with students is strongly encouraged.

Student-related policies.   This section of the distance education/online learning policy should refer to appropriate policies for campus-based students but may also do the following:

■ Require that accounts and passwords for e-mail, course management systems, administrative databases for student use, and any other technologies utilized by students at a distance be established as soon as new students are admitted into these programs, or when new nonmatriculated students are enrolled in individual courses, as appropriate. The policy may also specify the procedure for new students to be informed of their account access and given guidance for using these systems.

■ Specify the information to be collected from a new student at the time of application or registration as a nonmatriculated student, such as complete name, primary contact e-mail address, complete home address, and home and/or cell phone numbers, and designate responsibility for collecting this information. This is particularly important for making initial contact with these students and providing essential information for course access, well before courses begin, such as via welcome letters.

■ Limit the number of distance education courses that may be taken simultaneously during academic terms by students who are employed full time.

■ Establish procedures for submission of student concerns or complaints regarding distance education courses and programs.

Fiscal issues. The fiscal issues section of the policy will typically specify how the organization approaches the matter of tuition and fees paid by students at a distance, if applicable. For example, should students enrolled in distance education programs pay the same tuition and fees as residential students? Should they pay a surcharge to help cover the cost of the delivery technologies, or should they pay less, because remote-site students may not need the same level of support services as on-site students? For example, activity fees are often waived for students not in residence and unlikely to participate. Does a higher education institution set a different tuition schedule for high school students enrolled in dual credit courses? Because the tuition rates and fees typically change annually, they should not be listed in the policy itself. The policy should refer to the appropriate website where the current charges are maintained. The policy normally requires that distance education courses and programs be offered on a financially sound basis. Procedures should be identified for cancelling courses that do not meet minimum enrollments prior to the first day of class, or merging sections if more than one are offered.

Legal issues. Legal issues are commonly addressed in other organizational policies that apply to all programs and courses, faculty and students, not just to those at a distance. However, those policies themselves should be identified and referenced in the distance education/online learning policy. For example:

■ "Ownership" matters related to distance education courses and course materials should be addressed in the institutional intellectual property (IP) policy. IP policies will be discussed briefly in the Faculty Readiness section, later in this chapter.

■ The intellectual property policy should also address ownership and rights related to works created by students for a course, such as assignments. This includes all student comments made in an online discussion forum.

■ The use of materials copyrighted by others in distance education courses should be addressed in the organization's copyright policy. Copyright was discussed at length in Chapter 10 of this book. It is particularly important that the copyright policy establishes institutional requirements regarding compliance with the Digital Millennium Copyright Act (DMCA) and the TEACH Act.

■ The distance education/online learning policy should also require that all distance education courses offered by the organization be in compliance with the accessibility standards specified by the Americans with Disabilities Act and the Rehabilitation Act. This legislation will be discussed more extensively later in this chapter.

Library policy.   Two other institutional policies may or may not be referenced by the distance education/online learning policy but need to be discussed briefly here. Every academic library maintains its own policies regarding its services. Related to distance education, the library policy must address how these services will be provided to off-campus students. Specifically:

■ How will remote-site students access the catalog, and by what processes will they obtain and return the library resources they require? Who pays for what shipping costs?

■ How will off-campus students obtain Interlibrary Loan services? Ditto for shipping or reproduction costs, as necessary.

■ By what means will the library provide access to online databases (which often are licensed for access from within the institution's Internet domain) to remote students?

■ How will off-campus students obtain reference services?

Policy on acceptable use of IT resources.   Most educational organizations maintain one of these policies. The "acceptable use policy" describes how the information technology (IT) resources of the organization may and may not be utilized by its user base, including instructors and students. Of primary interest is the prohibition of institutional accounts for commercial and illegal purposes. File sharing immediately comes to mind here. All students, including those at a distance, need to be made aware of the acceptable use policy and where to find it, with an emphasis on the implications if the policy is violated.

Accessibility

According to the National Center for Educational Statistics (2010), approximately 6% of all undergraduate students have some kind of disability requiring support services and/or accommodation. Of these, about 29% have learning disabilities, 23% orthopedic impairments, 16% hearing impairments, 16% vision impairments, and 21% other health-related disabilities or limitations. (These percentages exceed 100 because of students with multiple disabilities.)

The Americans with Disabilities Act (ADA), passed in 1990, and Section 504 of the Rehabilitation Act, enacted in 1973, require that "standard assistive technologies" be made available to persons with disabilities. Congress expanded the Rehabilitation Act in 1998 to add Section 508, requiring that all federal government websites be fully accessible by June 21, 2001. Section 508 also applies to educational organizations that receive federal funding, including most school districts and both private and public colleges and universities. The bottom line is that any organization receiving federal funding must make its web pages accessible. Even for those organizations that don't receive federal funds, ethical considerations should apply. Course management system vendors claim that their products are compliant with Section 508. However, organizations that provide distance education courses must be aware of possible limitations of CMS products as well as of other technologies that may be employed, when attracting some disabled student populations, and be ready to accommodate as necessary.

The Web can be an important tool for disabled students. Students at a distance, however, can be at a greater disadvantage if they are without easy access to campus-based disability resources and advocacy for accessible Web resources. Beyond the accessibility of these resources and availability of consultation, however, distance education providers have limited obligations regarding a disabled student's home or off-campus workplace situations. For example, school counselors can assist disabled students in identifying and obtaining required adaptive software so they can take on-line courses, but the school is not required to purchase the software and install it on the student's personally owned computer.

Quality Control

Quality control of distance education programs is an area of specific interest for accreditation agencies. In March 2006, the Office of Postsecondary Education (OPE) of the U.S. Department of Education released a report entitled *Evidence of Quality in Distance Education Programs Drawn from Interviews with the Accreditation Community* (OPE, 2006). The report was derived from a series of meetings with eight regional and five national accrediting associations and described what these agencies considered "best practices" related to distance education.

The document also identified characteristics of distance education programs that are viewed as "red flags" by accreditors. These include the inability of senior administrators to articulate the role of distance education within the overall mission of the institution, curriculum design that does not appear to consider the needs of the intended student group, absence of specified learning outcomes, underutilization of online discussions, rapid turnover of faculty who teach online courses, inattention to the unique characteristics of distance education pedagogy, insufficient technical support, distance education courses taught by faculty as an overload, requirements for distant students to come to the main campus to receive support services, and new programs launched without adequate evidence of need. Many of the indicators of quality identified by OPE are discussed elsewhere in this chapter. The *Evidence of Quality* report should be considered "must reading" for distance education program administrators.

Minimum course expectations. While respecting academic freedom, an institution may set minimum expectations for courses offered a distance, such as requiring course learning outcomes that emphasize higher cognitive levels, and application of course content to real-world needs, problems, and issues; use of a course's discussion forums and other online resources to facilitate critical thinking and student engagement in the learning process; standards for course organization and structure; standards for student assessment; and a requirement for instructor commitment to monitor student participation and follow up with students who do not participate on a regular basis. These may be published in the distance education/online learning policy.

Instructor training and certification requirement. Another widely implemented quality control measure is a requirement for all instructors of distance education courses to receive appropriate training and be "certified" before being allowed to teach these courses. Appropriate faculty training is an absolutely imperative readiness concern. The distance education/online learning policy will likely vest in the distance education program administrator the authority to determine what this training will include and the procedure for instructors to be certified. For example, the training may be provided via intense workshops that often are online themselves, putting the instructors in the role of online learners while the workshop leader models effective online teaching methods and course structure. We will discuss faculty training later in the chapter.

Mandatory course evaluations. Every course offered at a distance should be evaluated by students at the end of every term. Program administrators should use student responses to provide constructive feedback to the instructors and set goals for course and/or teaching performance improvement. Faculty with consistently poor evaluations should not be permitted to teach subsequent courses at a distance.

Periodic program evaluations. The distance education administrator should work with individual program administrators to evaluate the programs themselves on a periodic basis. The distance education/online learning policy should specify the frequency for these reviews, typically every five to seven years, although the policy may require new programs to be evaluated more frequently, perhaps every three years. Program evaluation is discussed at length in Chapter XX of this book but needs a brief mention here as a readiness concern. See Figure 11–4 for examples of questions that may be asked. This certainly is not an all-inclusive list.

Compliance with applicable laws, standards, and guidelines. We have already mentioned legally mandated accessibility requirements. The distance education administrator can also help ensure quality control by keeping the organization in compliance with applicable standards and guidelines published by regulatory entities such as accreditation agencies, to be discussed in the next section below, and professional associations interested in distance education quality. Examples include

FIGURE 11–4 Examples of distance education program review questions.

Institutional Context/Overall Effectiveness

- Is the program in alignment with the institution's mission and strategic objectives?
- Is the program sufficiently accessible to the target student population?
- Is the intended student population responding with applications and enrollments?
- How do the program costs compare with program revenues?
- What are the measurable results of the program thus far?
- How does the academic department itself feel that the program is going? Is the department satisfied with the students and their achievement? Is it satisfied with the ability of other campus units to support the program?

Overall Program Quality

- Is the program content meeting the needs and expectations of the students? Are students satisfied with the overall quality of instruction they are receiving?
- How are program graduates perceived by employers? Are employers satisfied with program graduates' degree of preparation? In what areas must graduates receive further training from employers?
- What is the percentage of students who continue in the program through to the degree (if applicable)? Is there an unacceptable attrition rate?
- Are the students who leave the program, including graduates, given exit interviews? What do they say in these interviews? How are we responding to problem areas identified?

Student Support

- Are students satisfied with support services (e.g., library, help desk, student support services) available to them? Do they need services they are not getting?
- Are the off-campus students effectively using electronic resources available to them, such as through the library?
- Are the students able to use course technologies effectively?
- Are online students satisfied with advising and course registration procedures?
- Are the students satisfied with the level of communications from the institution, the academic department, and the faculty?
- Do the students feel that they are part of the institutional community?

Best Practices for Electronically Offered Degree and Certificate Programs (WCET, 2001), developed by the eight regional accrediting commissions in cooperation with the Western Cooperative for Educational Telecommunications, and *Quality on the Line: Benchmarks for Success in Internet-Based Distance Education* (IHEP, 2000), published by the Institute for Higher Education Policy.

Regulatory Issues

Regulatory matters may affect an organization's readiness for distance education in any number of ways. We have already addressed policy at the local level. Policy in a much broader perspective is also determined by those who regulate distance education. Regulation occurs at several levels—by the federal government, state governments, and by regional and professional accreditation agencies.

Federal government.   The U.S. Constitution delegates the primary responsibility for public education to the individual states. However, the federal government has considerable influence on distance education policy and practice. Here are a few examples.

Student Financial Aid.   Historically, it has been difficult for students enrolled in distance education programs at the postsecondary level to obtain federal financial aid, a situation dating from abuses in the correspondence course era that continued into the age of instructional television in the 1960s and 1970s. Enactment of amendments to the Higher Education Act in 1996 began to ease the restrictions, and most remaining rules were eliminated by congressional action in 2006, largely as a result of intense lobbying by for-profit and predominantly online educational institutions. The easing of these restrictions also greatly assisted conventional nonprofit colleges and universities with large online programs, although critics of distance education warned that the doors could be opened for abuse by diploma mills. In addition, a fraud conviction in Arizona in early 2010 illustrated the potential for identity theft artists to tap into federal financial aid following the eased restrictions (Parry, 2010). The U.S. Department of Education was refining detection procedures as this chapter was updated for the current edition.

Copyright.   Make no mistake about the impact that the TEACH Act will have on distance education. Through such legislation, the federal government has influenced how distance education courses can be taught. Specifics will need to be determined in upcoming years.

School and Public Access.   The federal government has significantly increased access to Internet-based instruction, including distance education opportunities, at the K–12 level through enactment of the Telecommunications Act of 1996 and its resulting Universal Service Fund, distributed through the e-Rate. Created by the Telecommunications Act of 1996, the Universal Service Fund has provided more than $26 billion dollars on a competitive basis to schools and libraries for improvements in their telecommunications infrastructure. The E-Rate has enabled almost every school and library in the United States to connect to the Internet, greatly increasing student access to online distance learning opportunities. This fund is supported by the charges for "universal service" on consumer telephone bills.

Data gathering.   The federal government maintains a massive data collection capability. For example, the National Center for Educational Statistics (2003) tracks trends in distance education in postsecondary institutions (see Parsad & Lewis, 2008.) The Department of Education's Office of Inspector General also compiles information on state and accreditation agency controls over distance education programs. These are just two of many examples.

State governments. Individual states maintain the right to establish their own rules regarding education, and this extends to the delivery of distance education programs into those states by educational organizations based in other states. Historically, states have used the yardstick of "physical presence" to determine whether education programs offered by out-of-state entities come under their jurisdiction. These situations were obvious when colleges and universities established physical locations for such purposes as instruction, laboratory activities, student assessment, tutoring, recruiting, and admissions. The ubiquitous directional signs to University of Phoenix facilities in most U.S. states serve as an example. Phoenix is licensed in those states.

How, though, do physical presence standards apply in the cases of distance education programs that cross state lines? This question has been an issue since the early 1960s, when educational programming was distributed to multiple states via broadcast television, and it became even muddier during the 1970s and 80s, when courses delivered by communications satellites could be viewed virtually everywhere in the country, including Alaska and Hawaii. Attempts to standardize or at least coordinate state regulations related to telecommunications-based learning at that time were fruitless (Goldstein, Lacey, & Janiga, 2006).

The Internet extended the marketplace to worldwide proportions and brought the cost of delivering distance learning programs down to affordable levels for almost any educational entrepreneur with a server. According to Michael Goldstein, in his introduction to the report *The State of State Regulation of Cross-Border Postsecondary Education*, published by the Washington, DC, law firm of Dow Lohnes (Goldstein, Lacey, & Janiga, 2006), "The advent of the Internet and the exponential growth of e-learning has not been accompanied by a rationalizing of the regulatory environment. . . . If anything, the cross-border barriers have become more significant as more state regulators (and legislatures) have come to realize the potential audience for and impact of technology-mediated learning" (p. ii).

The Dow Lohnes report illustrated the wide variations in the ways in which states determined whether online programs originating out-of-state would fall under their jurisdiction, and therefore would require some level of state licensure. For example, states consider factors such as whether:

- Courses are completely online with no in-state support whatsoever.
- Local community colleges provide library, information technology, or other support services.
- An in-state address, phone, and/or fax number is provided.
- In-state tutors or advisors are provided.
- Students must take examinations or other forms of assessment at local sites.
- Students participate in lab or clinical activities at an in-state site.
- The organization maintains an in-state administrative office, even if no instructional activities occur there.
- In-state students are targeted for direct mail or Internet advertising.
- The institution participates in in-state college fairs.

The bottom line is that states vary significantly in their criteria for determining whether licensure is required for delivery of online courses and programs into those jurisdictions. The Dow Lohnes report is an excellent starting point for distance education administrators whose institutions are considering programs that potentially cross state lines. Contacting the individual regulatory agencies in those states is an essential next step. Contact information for each is provided in the report.

Accreditation agencies.   The United States has 6 regional accreditation agencies (e.g., the North Central Association of Colleges and Schools), 2 of which have separate agencies for K–12 and higher education, for an actual total of 8. In addition, the Council for Higher Education Accreditation (CHEA, 2010) identifies 55 national accreditation organizations, divided into the categories of Faith-Related, Career-Related, and Programmatic (or discipline-specific).

Depending on their respective missions, these commissions accredit entire institutions and schools, and/or individual degree and diploma programs. Their primary emphasis is on program quality, to protect the public from diploma mills. The regional accreditation agencies in particular are rapidly becoming distance education administrators' best friends in promoting distance education and upholding quality standards. All are making every attempt to understand distance education and put themselves in a position to evaluate it effectively.

The regional accrediting associations have issued a *Statement of Commitment* (Regional Accrediting Commissions, 2002), in which they recognized the values of conventional educational programs and acknowledged that "these values may be expressed in valid new ways as inventive institutions seek to utilize technology to achieve their goals" (p. 3). The association continued, "Moreover, the commissions are seeking to assure that technologically mediated instruction offered at a distance by whatever institution in whatever region meets the same high standards for quality through the application of an evaluative framework utilizing peer review common to all the regions. . . . " (p. 4). In other words, programs delivered via distance education will receive the same rigid reviews and be held to the same high standards as on-campus programs. This is a good thing, for credibility purposes.

Individual degree programs in postsecondary education are typically accredited by professional associations (included in the 55 national organizations identified by CHEA). These organizations can be more conservative and protective of the status quo. They are more likely to offer resistance to distance education programs. Those associations that have reservations about distance education have at their disposal an extremely effective tool for controlling academic programs—the power to deny accreditation, although in reality this rarely happens on the basis of distance education programs alone.

Cost Issues

The costs of delivering distance education and ensuring return on investment are foremost concerns of many distance education administrators. Few organizations can afford to hemorrhage large amounts of money to support distance education programs that do not have the desired results. Skeptics of distance education are quick to point out the failures in recent years of distance education ventures by high-profile universities and consortia, likely the result of unrealistic expectations, the lack of sound business plans, and/or erosion of enthusiasm for the programs among senior administrators.

Distance education is expensive. Look back several pages to the resources that must be brought to bear to plan, deliver, and evaluate distance education programs. The costs range from basic operation of the administrative office for distance education to faculty salaries to instructional design and technical support personnel to student support personnel to the delivery technology infrastructure, and to course and program promotion, including advertising. Personnel costs typically are the majority of the total budgets for distance education programs. Even if these costs are prorated portions of the overall organizational budget, they can be extraordinary, depending upon the size of the program. The distance education business plan must account for all these expenses, and then balance them against revenues and other benefits of the program. Money-losing distance education programs may be acceptable if other benefits are significant, such as providing education to homebound or incarcerated students or advanced courses to remote regions that would otherwise be deprived.

A detailed discussion of costing distance education is far too broad a topic for this chapter. The Western Cooperative for Educational Telecommunications maintains an ongoing Technology Costing Methodology (TCM) project (WCET, 2010b) that offers a handbook, case studies, and a set of tools for calculating the costs of distance education programs. In addition, extensive discussions of calculating the costs of distance education programs may be found in Bates (2000).

FACULTY READINESS

Depending on the scope of the distance education programs offered by an organization, the administrator may be in a position to hire instructors, or at the very least should work with the academic program directors to select the faculty who will teach courses at a distance. It is very important that the instructors hired or designated to teach these courses exhibit characteristics that will facilitate effective teaching at a distance. Brown (1998) described successful distance education faculty members as:

- Serious, lifelong learners
- Teachers favoring experimental and collaborative styles
- Those who enjoy up-front conceptual work
- Skilled group-process facilitators
- Teachers who make expectations explicit
- Those who construct evaluation/assessment schemes
- Providers of detailed, developmental feedback
- People willing to give feedback at frequent intervals

This is not to suggest that instructors who do not exhibit these attributes cannot be successful in teaching courses at a distance, only that they are likely to find the endeavor more challenging. If the selected faculty are making the transition from conventional classroom teaching for the first time, it is imperative that they understand that the distance education environment is likely to be rather different from the one with which they are familiar. For example, the demands on their workload will likely increase, probably significantly. A distance education course, particularly an online course, will need much more organization, structure, and detail than typical classroom courses. Students, especially those new to distance education and new to the institution, will need precise, detailed instructions to help guide their activities throughout the course and keep them on task, and this structure and detail needs to be in place from the first day of the class.

Constant communication with students will be an imperative throughout the course. This is particularly important in an online course in which the instructor and students may never see each other face-to-face, compared with a conventional classroom course in which the students typically see the instructor's smiling face two or three times a week. Course communication has been covered at length in other chapters in this book. Perhaps above all, new distance education instructors must understand that quality control is essential in their courses. If students have bad experiences, they will likely not be back, and the word will get around. Conversely, if students have positive, educationally and personally rewarding experiences, they will return and bring friends. Either way, their experiences will be persuasive. Instructors who cannot make these commitments should not attempt to teach courses at a distance.

Faculty Support

Faculty support in a distance education environment is a particular concern of accreditors. The readiness of the institution regarding the impact of online courses and programs on faculty workload, compensation, and the institutional reward system must be addressed. Other faculty issues such as training, course development support, course evaluation support, and technology support must be evaluated and addressed.

Training.   Faculty training programs often begin and end with workshops on using the delivery technologies, such as teleclassrooms or course management systems, but many instructors need additional assistance in reconceptualizing their face-to-face courses to be effective in a distance education environment and in adjusting to what is likely to be significantly different teaching demands. The training curriculum should include, at a minimum:

- The unique attributes and needs of distance learners
- Course instructional design for distance delivery with an emphasis on pedagogies that promote higher-order learning and critical thinking
- Online discussion facilitation, management and assessment
- Effective use of embedded technologies such as learning objects and Web 2.0 technologies
- Assessment of students at a distance
- Course evaluation
- Course management factors such as office hours, assignment collection and return, copyright compliance, and student support concerns and resources

Assistance with course development and delivery. Effective training can provide instructors with the essential foundations for course development, delivery, and assessment, but many can also benefit from access to a professional instructional developer who can provide consultation and guidance throughout the entire process. Instructional developer input can play a significant role in course quality control and assist the instructor in thinking through creative ways to promote higher order learning. Regretfully, positions such as these are rare in educational organizations and are often among the first to be jettisoned when budgets get cut.

Help Desk support. A competent, well-informed, dedicated Help Desk staff provides essential technical support to both faculty and students. Help Desk support was discussed earlier in this chapter but must be reemphasized here.

Intellectual Property

Intellectual property (IP) rights related to online courses and the media embedded within are a significant issue in distance education. Use of the intellectual property of others within an online course was addressed in Chapter 6. Here, the essential concerns are ownership of components of online courses and rights pertaining thereto. In other words, who actually owns an online course, or who owns the individual parts of an online course, and who has what rights to use what under what conditions?

The matter is compounded by the different layers of ownership that may exist within a single online course—*especially* an online course. For example, content that is the original creation of the instructor (e.g., the syllabus, lecture notes, assignment instructions, discussion questions, case studies) normally remains the intellectual property of that person. (An exception may occur if the instructor was hired specifically to develop the course but not teach it, in which case the IP may become the property of the institution.) The course may link to readings in the library's electronic reserve section that were licensed specifically for this use. The course could also link to digitized images or video clips that also were licensed for this use in the absence of a fair use claim, or in fact *were* used under the assumption of fair use. The overall instructional design and additional digital media could have been created by the academic technology support staff (work for hire, or owned by the institution). Some materials in the course may legitimately be in the public domain. Comments made by students in the course's discussion forums certainly belong to them. Other student intellectual property may be displayed within the course. And, the entire course could be delivered to students via a proprietary course management system, such as Blackboard, Desire2Learn, or eCollege, licensed by the institution.

Now, who "owns" that course? The instructor? The district or university? Blackboard? The state? What if the instructor (or the district) wanted to sell it to an online course vendor? What if the instructor decides to move to another state and wants to take the course with her so she can use it there? What if the department decides that another instructor should teach the course next semester and use those same course materials? What if 80% of the course is discovered to be one massive copyright infringement, and the legal rights holders decide to sue? Whom do they sue?

The best thing to do, well in advance, before these questions become issues, is to develop an organizational intellectual property policy to which all parties agree. The policy should address who owns what, who has the right to use what and under what conditions, and who should be compensated and how much (usually stated in terms of percentages or flat rates) and under what conditions.

The rights of students are another important concern of distance education managers. If an instructor gives a student an assignment that is completed and turned in to the instructor, who owns the intellectual property the student's work contains? The student? The instructor? The school, district, or college? Some universities (primarily outside the United States) state in their intellectual property policies that all student work submitted for course assignments becomes the property of the university. At most educational institutions, particularly in North America, students retain the rights to their own school assignment-related creations.

Intellectual property policies are comparatively rare at the K–12 level. In the absence of an intellectual property policy, the ownership of online courses or course materials developed by a teacher should be specified in the employment contract or collective bargaining agreement. The default position taken by most districts seems to be that such intellectual property is created under "work for hire" conditions, and therefore is the property of the district.

Other Faculty-related Issues

Intellectual property is just one of a number of distance education–related issues that trouble faculty and their unions. Teaching at a distance also presents sensitive questions related to faculty workload, compensation, and, especially in post-secondary education, promotion and tenure. Faculty are very concerned about the amount of time required to develop an online course, as well as the additional time required to teach it.

Compensation is a related issue. Because of the extra workload, many faculty feel that teaching distance education courses should rate additional compensation. Or, as an alternative, they may seek "released time" that they can dedicate to course development and delivery. Released time essentially means that a percentage of the faculty member's time is "bought out" for this purpose, such as a one-course reduction in the professor's teaching load. This results in a financial strain for someone in the budget chain, because another faculty member must be hired to teach that course.

The institution's reward system is another important faculty concern. Colleges and universities, as well as school districts, have policies related to retention, tenure, and promotion (RTP), most of which were written long before distance education became a gleam in the dean's eye. For the most part, these policies do not accommodate instructional innovation in general, and do not forgive faculty for spending a disproportionate amount of their time teaching online. Distance education managers must work with faculty unions, academic senates, and administrators to revise their respective reward systems to provide faculty incentives for teaching in a distance education environment.

STUDENT READINESS

According to a 2009 survey by the Pew Internet & American Life Project (Lenhart, Purcell, Smith, & Zickuhr, 2010), 93% of teenagers between the ages of 12 and 17 used the Internet. As one might expect, 73% of teens in this age group used social networking sites such as Facebook, but, surprisingly, just 8% used Twitter, and only 14% engaged in blogging, down from 28% in 2006 Internet use is even higher among college-age students. A 2009 survey of more than 30,000 college and university students from 103 higher education institutions, conducted by the EDUCAUSE Center for Applied Research (Smith, Salaway, & Caruso, 2009) found that 98% brought personal computers to campus, 90% did text messaging daily, 90% had accounts on social networking sites and 76% accessed them daily, 84% downloaded music at least weekly, 45% contributed to video websites, 42% contributed to wikis, 37% contributed to blogs, and 38% made their phone calls over the Internet.

Numerous other studies have explored characteristics of the "Millennials," "Digital Natives," or "Net Generation" (essentially those born in or after 1982; Simonson, 2010). In general, contemporary students embrace technology, multitask fluently, and easily integrate into groups that often are found online. The use of online communication tools has become second nature to them and in many cases consumes a significant portion of their days. A friend of EDUCAUSE Vice President Richard Katz once observed that asking teenagers about technology "is like asking a fish about water" (Kvavik & Caruso, 2005, p. 8.) The vast majority of high school and college-age students are *technologically* ready for distance education, although we cannot forget that some are technophobes and are not ready.

Student readiness for distance education itself, and particularly online learning, is another matter entirely. Many providers of online courses and programs provide "readiness checks" on their websites, designed to assist potential students in deciding whether online learning is right for them. Martinez, Torres, and Geisel (2006) examined a variety of these self-assessment sites and found that, although the readiness areas of emphasis varied from one site to another, most self-assessments focused on technical skill, study skills and motivation, and learning styles. For example, the University of Georgia's Student Online Readiness Tool (SORT) includes modules on technology experience, access to hardware and software tools, study habits, lifestyle compatibility with online learning, motivation for learning, and learning style preferences, whereas the Wisconsin Virtual School (WVS) self-assessment tool emphasized the attributes of self-motivation, independent learning, computer literacy, time management skills, written communication skills, and personal commitment. Martinez, Torres, and Geisel felt that the WVS model followed an emerging trend with its emphasis on students' responsibility for their own learning.

The distance learning administrator should help ensure, either through self-assessment tools or personal interviews, that incoming students have the appropriate level of readiness, including commitment, self-discipline, and time management skills to be successful in an online environment. Then, as we have stressed, it is imperative that students be supported throughout the program with guidance regarding navigation of the institution's administrative systems and technologies, and that individual courses have a high level of structure, detail, and communication.

LOOKING FORWARD

Since its first annual Sloan Survey of Online Learning in 2003, the Sloan Consortium has documented a steady growth in online course enrollments in American colleges and universities. The 2009 survey (Allen & Seaman, 2010) found that more than 4.6 million students took at least one online course in fall 2008, up from 1.6 million in fall 2002 and 3.1 million in fall 2005. Moreover, online enrollments as a percent of total enrollment soared from 9.6 percent in fall 2002 to a stunning 25.3 percent of all enrollments in fall 2008. Likewise, online learning at the K–12 level continues to grow. The Evergreen Education Group study found that for-credit online course enrollment in state virtual schools exceeded 320,000 in 2008–09 (Watson, Gemin, Ryan, & Wicks, 2009), up from an estimated 40,000 to 50,000 in fall 2001 (Clark, 2001).

Although college enrollment normally increases during times of economic stress and high unemployment, and whereas some of the reported enrollment increase was attributed to the threat of an H1N1 flu epidemic, it is clear that distance education, and especially online learning, is here to stay, and is likely to continue to expand in the foreseeable future. In addition, advances in high-speed delivery technologies will facilitate the distribution of distance education courses, and evolution of tools for learning will continue to enhance the learning experience. The challenges and rewards of distance education administration have made this an exciting career track for many individuals at all levels of education. The overall worldwide growth of distance education programs promises many opportunities for others who wish to follow this path.

A LOOK AT BEST PRACTICE ISSUES

Distance Education: Eight Steps for Transforming an Organization

One question distance learning leaders ask is "How do I transform my organization so it successfully adopts appropriate distance education applications?" John Kotter (1999) wrote clearly and forcefully about organizational transformation. By considering his ideas and relating them to distance education, a strategic distance education transformation can be implemented. By carefully managing the process, an organization can reduce mistakes and multiply successes. Here are the steps in the process.

First, establish a sense of urgency. Most likely this will be by identifying the major opportunities offered by adopting distance education strategies. Outcomes should be identified, such as more diverse students, cost savings, more compelling instruction, and even more satisfying interaction with learners.

Second, form a powerful planning group. The team that develops the plan for an organization must have enough power to lead the effort, and have the correct opinion leaders so the members of the organization will be changed. Change comes because of a manager's directions, and because of the opinion leader's influence.

Third, create a vision. Visioning is one of the most important but most poorly understood aspects of the change process. The vision directs the transformation effort and is a "rallying cry" for the organization.

Fourth, communicate the vision. The planning group is the key here. Opinion leaders and powerful managers can present the vision, but they must also "live" the vision. Changes should be observable. Trainers and teachers should see changes in their leaders.

Fifth, give power to those who act on the vision. Risk taking should be encouraged and the activities and actions of those who adopt distance education should be supported.

Sixth, plan for and create short-term wins. Visible, early, and impressive distance education events and activities should be orchestrated by the planning group. If trainers and teachers can see the relative advantages of adopting distance education strategies, they will be more willing and more ready to try on their own.

Seventh, combine and collect successful distance education activities to produce more change. Hire, promote, and encourage those who practice distance education, and continue to support ongoing activities.

Eighth, incorporate distance education successes. Clearly show how distance education events are connected to the organization's mission, and to other educational and training activities. Continue to develop new leaders to ensure a succession of support.

A leader can control change, an inevitable process. The eight steps just described will help start the distance education transformation—if it is not already too late!

DISCUSSION QUESTIONS

The following seven questions all are based on the same scenario. Assume that the administration/management of your organization has made a commitment to a major new distance education program, and you have been appointed its director. (For the purpose of these questions, you select the specific program and target student population.)

1. What would be your highest priorities in getting the program off the ground, and where would you start? Why are these issues the highest priorities for you?
2. Specifically, how would you approach the planning issues related to faculty? Assume that instructors for the program would be drawn from existing faculty in the organization. What issues do you need to address, and how would you address them?
3. Assume that you would be the person responsible for selecting and training the program's faculty. What specific characteristics would you look for in these individuals, and why?

4. What procedures will you follow to effectively train the program faculty? What topics would you include? How would you structure the training, and why would you do it this way?

5. How would you approach the planning issues related to student support services for the new program? In other words, how would you determine if the existing student support infrastructure is sufficient for the program? If it isn't, what would you do? Assume that the organization has funding limits.

6. Select any state in the United States (or your own country if you live outside the United States). Using the Dow Lohnes report, online resources, and personal contacts if appropriate, determine the requirements of that state for your organization to be legally able to deliver this new distance education program to residents of that state. Share them with the class in the online discussions and compare what you found. (Each student should select a different state.)

7. What steps would you take to ensure quality control of the new program?

REFERENCES

Abedor, A. J., & Sachs, S. G. (1978). The relationship between faculty development (FD), organizational development (OD), and Instructional Development (ID): Readiness for instructional innovation in higher education. In R. K. Bass & D. B. Lumsden (Eds.), *Instructional development: The state of the art* (pp. 2–19). Columbus, OH: Collegiate Publishers.

Allen, I. E., & Seaman, J. (2010). *Learning on demand: Online education in the United States, 2009.* Wellesley, MA: Babson College. Available online at www.sloanconsortium.org/publications/survey/pdf/learningondemand.pdf.

Bates, A. W. (2000). *Managing technological change.* San Francisco: Jossey-Bass.

Brown, B. M. (1998). Digital classrooms: Some myths about developing new educational programs using the Internet. *Syllabus, 26*(5), 56–59.

Clark, T. (2001). Virtual schools: Trends and issues. Phoenix, AZ: Distance Learning Resource Network. Available online at www.wested.org/online_pubs/virtualschools.pdf.

Council for Higher Education Accreditation. (2010). *2009–2010 Directory of CHEA recognized organizations.* Available online at www.chea.org/pdf/2009_2010_Directory_of_CHEA_Recognized_Organizations.pdf.

Gellman-Danley, B., & Fetzner, M. J. (1998). Asking the really tough questions: Policy issues for distance learning. *Online Journal of Distance Learning Administration, 1*(1), available online at www.westga.edu/~distance/danley11.html.

Goldstein, M. B., Lacey, A. D., & Janiga, N. S. (2006). *The state of state regulation of cross-border postsecondary education: A survey and report on the basis for assertion of state authority to regulate distance learning.* Washington, DC: Dow Lohnes. Available online at www.dowlohnes.com/files/upload/survey.pdf.

Institute for Higher Education Policy. (2000). *Quality on the line: Benchmarks for success in Internet-based distance education.* Washington, DC: Author. Available online at www.ihep.org/assets/files/publications/m-r/QualityOnTheLine.pdf.

Kotter, J. (1999). Making change happen. In F. Hesselbein & P. Cohen (Eds.), *Leader to leader.* New York: Drucker Foundation.

Kvavik, R. B., & Caruso, J. B. (2005). *ECAR study of students and information technology, 2005: Convenience, connection, control, and learning.* Boulder, CO: EDUCAUSE. Available online at http://net.educause.edu/ir/library/pdf/ers0506/rs/ERS0506w.pdf.

Lenhart, A., Purcell, K., Smith, A., & Zickuhr, K. (2010). *Social media & mobile Internet use among teens and young adults.* Washington, DC: Pew Internet & American Life Project. Available online at http://pewinternet.org/~/media//Files/Reports/2010/PIP_Social_Media_and_Young_Adults_Report.pdf.

Martinez, S., Torres, H., & Geisel, V. (2006). *Determining student readiness for online instruction.* Available online at www.onlinestudentsupport.org/Monograph/readiness.php.

National Center for Educational Statistics. (2010). *Postsecondary students with disabilities: Enrollment, services, and persistence.* Available online at http://nces.ed.gov/pubs2010/

National Center for Educational Statistics. (2003). *Distance education at degree-granting postsecondary institutions, 2000–2001.* Available online at http://nces.ed.gov/surveys/peqis/publications/2003017/.

Office of Postsecondary Education, U.S. Department of Education. (2006). *Evidence of quality in distance education programs drawn from interviews with the accreditation community.* Available online at http://www.ysu.edu/accreditation/Resources/Accreditation-Evidence-of-Quality-in-DE-Programs.pdf.

Parry, M. (2010). *Online scheme triggers new fears about distance education fraud.* Chronicle of Higher Education, January 17, 2010. Available online at http://chronicle.com/article/Online-Scheme-Triggers-New/63532/.

Parsad, B., & Lewis, L. (2008). *Distance education at degree-granting postsecondary institutions: 2006–07.* Washington, DC: National Center for Education Statistics. Available online at http://nces.ed.gov/pubs2009/2009044.pdf.

Regional Accrediting Commissions for the Evaluation of Electronically Offered Degree and Certificate Programs. (2002). *Statement of commitment.* Available online at http://wiche.edu/attachment_library/Accrediting_Commitment.pdf.

Simonson, M. (2004). Distance learning leaders. Who are they? *Distance Learning, 1*(3), 47, 48.

Simonson, M. (2010). Millennials. *Distance Learning: For Educators, Trainers, and Leaders, 7*(2), 80–79.

Smith, S., Salaway, G., & Caruso, J.B. (2009). *The ECAR study of undergraduate students and information technology, 2009.* Boulder, CO: EDUCAUSE. Available online at http://net.educause.edu/ir/library/pdf/ers0906/rs/ERS0906w.pdf.

Watson, J., Gemin, B., Ryan, J., & Wicks, M. (2009). *Keeping pace with K–12 online learning: An annual review of state-level policy and practice.* Evergreen, CO: Evergreen Education Group. Available online at www.kpk12.com/downloads/KeepingPace09-fullreport.pdf .

Western Cooperative for Educational Telecommunications. (2001). *Best practices for electronically offered degree and certificate programs.* Boulder, CO: Author. Available online at http://wiche.edu/attachment_library/Accrediting_BestPractices.pdf.

Western Cooperative for Educational Telecommunications (2010a). *Beyond the administrative core: Creating web-based student services for online learners.* Boulder, CO: Author. Available online at http://www.wcet.info/2.0/index.php?q=node/1322.

Western Cooperative for Educational Telecommunications (2010b). *Technology Costing Methodology Project.* Boulder, CO: Author. Available online at www.wcet.info/2.0/index.php?q=TCM_Home_Page.

A LOOK AT BEST PRACTICE ISSUES

U.S. Department of Education Technology Plan

The U.S. Department of Education has developed the National Educational Technology Plan, titled "Toward a New Golden Age in America Education" (www.ed.gov/about/offices/list/os/technology/plan/2004/plan.pdf). One recurring theme of this plan is the importance today and in the future of distance education/e-learning/virtual schools. According to the report, "About 25 percent of all K–12 public schools now offer some form of e-learning or virtual school instruction. Within the next decade every state and most schools will be doing so . . . traditional schools are turning to distance education to expand offerings for students and increase professional development opportunities for teachers" (34–35).

The report goes on to list and explain major recommendations. These recommendations are:

1. Strengthen leadership
2. Consider innovative budgeting
3. Improve teacher training
4. Support e-learning and virtual schools
5. Encourage broadband access
6. Move toward digital content
7. Integrate data systems

The plan's 46 pages are supplemented by lists of federal activities that support the use of technology in education. It is interesting that this plan often identifies some aspect of distance education as critical to the future of education. Virtual schools are given special attention as important to the future of American education. It is also significant that the importance of leadership is stressed in the plan and is the first of the 7 recommendations. It is implied that without enlightened leaders, effective technology implementation will not occur, and without technology schools will continue to fail.

CHAPTER 12

Evaluating Teaching and Learning at a Distance

CHAPTER GOAL

The purpose of this chapter is to present approaches for evaluation of distance education courses, programs, and systems.

CHAPTER OBJECTIVES

After reading and reviewing this chapter, you should be able to

1. Differentiate between research and evaluation.
2. Define *evaluation.*
3. Explain the six categories of evaluation information: in measures of activity, efficiency, outcomes, program aims, policy, and organizations.
4. Describe the AEIOU approach to evaluation and its five levels—accountability, effectiveness, impact, organizational context, and unanticipated consequences.

 ## RESEARCH AND EVALUATION

> The best way to find things out is not to ask questions at all. If you fire off a question, it is like firing off a gun—bang it goes, and everything takes flight and runs for shelter. But if you sit quite still and pretend not to be looking, all the little facts will come and peck around your feet, situations will venture forth from thickets, and intentions will creep out and sun themselves on a stone; and if you are very patient, you will see and understand a great deal more than a person with a gun does. (Huxley, 1982, p. 20)

This marvelous quote from Huxley's *The Flame Trees of Thika* illustrates a metaphorical rationale for a major refocusing of procedures for evaluation of distance education systems. Traditional evaluation models have concentrated on the empirical and quantitative procedures that have been practiced for decades (Fitzpatrick, Sanders, & Worthen, 2004; Stufflebeam & Shinkfield, 2007). More recently, evaluators of distance education programs have begun to propose more qualitative models that include the collection of many nonnumerical types of information (Rovai, 2003; Sherry, 2003).

Because it is easy to think of them as being the same thing, it is important to differentiate between theory-based research and evaluation. Hanson, et al. (1996) and Simonson (2002) have provided reviews of distance education literature including research on and about distance education. Hanson et al. summarized distance education research as follows:

- Distance education is just as effective as traditional education in regard to learner outcomes.
- Distance education learners generally have more favorable attitudes toward distance education than traditional learners, and distance learners feel they learn as well as nondistant students.
- The research clearly shows that distance education is an effective method for teaching and learning (p.1).

Evaluation, as contrasted to research, is the systematic investigation of the worth or merit of an object. Program evaluation is the systematic investigation of the worth of an ongoing or continuing distance education activity (Joint Committee on Standards for Educational Evaluation, 1994). Martinez, Liu, Watson, and Bichelmeyer (2006) discuss the importance of evaluating distance education programs. Evaluation of programs is used to identify strengths and weaknesses as well as the benefits and drawbacks of teaching and learning online. They asked students, administrators, and instructors to evaluate course management categories, such as registration, support services, advising, and sense of community. One important finding of this study was the equivalence of the distance education program to the traditional program (Martinez et al., 2006).

This chapter focuses on approaches to evaluation for the purpose of improving distance education and determining the worth of distance education activities. Rose (2000) identified a number of databases related to evaluation of distance education courses that are available on the Internet. These online databases provide a repository of up-to-date information about online courses. Additional information related to evaluation and distance education is available in Cyrs and Smith (1990), Fitz-Gibbon and Morris (1987), Fitzpatrick et al. (2004), Rossi, Lipsey, and Freeman (2003), Ruhe and Zumbo (2009), Thompson and Irele (2007), and Willis (1994).

EVALUATION AND DISTANCE EDUCATION—FIVE STEPS

Evaluation procedures are becoming of critical interest to trainers and teachers who are adopting e-learning or distance education (Peak & Berge, 2006; Strother, 2002). As new distance education systems are being planned and implemented there is considerable concern that the time and effort required to move to distance delivery of instruction produced a valuable educational experience, thus, evaluation is regularly a part of plans to move from traditional face-to-face instruction to distance education.

Kirkpatrick's (2006) evaluation approach with its four levels of evaluation as shown below, supplemented by Phillips's (2003) fifth evaluation level—return on investment (ROI)—seems to be the preferred approach of many trainers, and some educators.

Kirkpatrick's evaluation approach has been traditionally used to evaluate classroom training and teaching, especially in the private, government, and military sectors. It is a straightforward approach that produces usable information for the trainer. The four levels of the approach are designed to obtain answers to commonly asked questions about training: Did they like it? Did they learn it? Will they use it? Will it matter? (Simonson, 2007).

Level 1—Reactions (Did they like it?)

As the word *reactions* implies, evaluation at this level measures how participants in the training program feel about the educational activity. Students are asked what they liked and did not like about training, sometimes several times during a course or program. Students are required to use checklists, Likert responses (selecting from one of several options, such as highly agree, agree, disagree and strongly disagree) to statements, and open-ended comments, all to determine if the training was perceived positively by participants.

Level 2—Learning (Did they learn it?)

At this level, evaluation strategies attempt to determine more than learner satisfaction. Rather, evaluators assess the extent to which learners have advanced in skills, knowledge, or attitude. What and how much did participants learn? What new skills do they possess? And, what new and appropriate attitudinal positions have been produced?

Methods include objective testing, team assessment, and self-assessment. Often pretest– posttest change is used as a measure at level 2.

Level 3—Transfer (Will they use it?)

At this level, evaluators attempt to determine if the skills, knowledge, and attitudes learned as a result of training are being transferred to the workplace or to actual learner activities. Evaluation questions deal with the use of new skills or the application of new knowledge to events. Timing of the evaluation at this level is critical and problematic since it is difficult to know when transfer actually occurs.

Level 4—Results (Will it matter?)

Evaluation activities at this level attempt to measure the success of the training or teaching program in terms of increased productivity, improved quality, lower costs, and, for businesses, even higher profits. Trainers are increasingly being asked to demonstrate the direct and indirect impact of training on the success of the organization and to relate training to mission accomplishment. In schools, level 4 evaluations often look at enrollments in additional courses, learning motivation, and educational achievement.

Level 5—Return on Investment

Increasingly, many training and educational organizations that are adopting e-learning and distance education are interested in the concept of *return on investment (ROI)*—converting training results from e-learning activities into monetary values and comparing these costs to the cost of the training program to determine a return on investment. Phillips (1996), Graber, Post, and Erwin(n.d), and J. Phillips, P. Phillips, Duresky and Gaudet (2002) describes a five-step process to determine return on investment.

1. First, it is necessary to collect level-4 data to determine if there is a change in job or educational performance that is positive and also measurable. This assumes that there were evaluation data collected concerning the first four levels of the Kirkpatrick model.
2. Second, evaluators need to identify the training that contributed to the change in performance. Testing can be used, as can control groups that receive different training or no training at all.
3. Third, it is necessary to convert the results of training or education into monetary values. This often means a relatively subjective process must be undertaken to quantify outcomes related to the training.
4. Next, the evaluation process requires the determination of the total cost of training. This includes trainer costs, facilities expenses, materials purchased, and other expenses.
5. Fifth, return on investment is determined by comparing the monetary benefits to the costs. In this manner, it is possible to quantify the impact of training, the effectiveness of education and the value of the instruction.

The ROI process is time consuming, requires a skilled evaluation team, and is sometimes criticized because it produces evaluation results that look at what has happened rather than what will happen. Peak and Berge (2006) also recommend that not everything needs to be measured. Rather, leaders should determine what they think is important and then trainers can evaluate those areas.

Although evaluation has always been somewhat important in corporate and military training and of interest to a lesser extent in education, the recent phenomenal growth of e-learning and distance education has made many leaders want to know what the implications are of moving to training and teaching that is not face-to-face. Thus, Kirkpatrick's and Phillips's evaluation approaches have received increased attention, especially since most evidence clearly demonstrates distance education works academically to produce required achievement gains. The evidence is clear that students learn just as effectively when they are taught at a distance as compared to when they learn in a traditional classroom (Simonson, 2002). Thus, it can be generalized that traditional training and e-learning work equally well. The question for evaluators then becomes the determination of the advantages, if any, of moving to an e-learning environment. Evaluators are looking at cost savings, time savings, increased motivation and satisfaction, economies of scale, and other nonachievement outcome metrics. Evaluation of e-learning should provide leaders evidence they need to support or to refute training decisions.

EVALUATION AND THE OPEN UNIVERSITY

Program evaluation at the Open University of Great Britain is the systematic investigation of the merit of a particular distance education program, curriculum, or teaching method, and how it might be improved compared with alternatives. As part of the evaluation procedures for distance education by the Open University (Woodley & Kirkwood, 1986), two alternative strategies have been merged. The first is the traditional, positivist–empiricist approach to evaluation. This represents an attempt to apply the rules and procedures of the physical sciences to evaluation. The second is a more eclectic view of evaluation that incorporates qualitative and naturalistic techniques for the evaluation of distance education.

The traditional strategy normally includes an experiment that determines the effectiveness of a distance education strategy. The distance education project is structured from its beginning with the requirements of the evaluator in mind. Carefully matched samples are picked, controls are established, and variables are selected for which comparison data will be collected. Next, objective tests of variables are selected or constructed. Data are collected before, during, and always after the instructional event or procedures. Then the evaluator takes the data and prepares the evaluation report, which is submitted weeks or months later.

The primary outcome of this type of evaluation is the comparison of the data collected from the two or more categories of learners. For example, the distant learners are compared with those taught locally, and conclusions about the effectiveness of the distance education activity are made.

This approach represents the traditional process for the evaluation of distance education. Recently at the Open University and elsewhere, a countermovement has emerged (House, 2010). Advocates of this counterapproach are united in one primary way: They are opposed to the traditional, quantitative procedures for evaluation. Increasingly, evaluation activities are incorporating more naturalistic methodologies with holistic perspectives. This second perspective for evaluation uses focus groups, interviews, observations, and journals to collect evaluation information in order to obtain a rich and colorful understanding of events related to the distance education activity.

From a practical standpoint, most evaluators now use a combination of quantitative and qualitative measures. Certainly, there is a need to quantify and count. Just as certainly, there is a need to understand opinions and hear perspectives.

According to Woodley and Kirkwood (1986), six categories of evaluation information can be collected about distance education activities:

1. **Measures of activity.** These measures are counts of the numbers of events, people, and objects. Administrative records often provide data for activity questions. Activity questions are ones such as:
   - How many courses were produced?
   - How many students were served?
   - How many potential students were turned away?
2. **Measures of efficiency.** Measures of efficiency are closely related to measures of activity, and often administrative records can be the source of efficiency information. Efficiency questions often asked are ones such as:
   - How many students successfully completed the course?
   - What was the average student's workload?

- How many students enrolled in additional courses?
- How much did the course cost?
- How much tuition was generated?

3. **Measures of outcomes.**   Measures of adequate learning are usually considered the most important measures of outcomes of distance education activities. Often, interviews with learners are used to supplement course grades in order to find students' perceptions about a distance education activity. Mail surveys are also efficient ways to collect outcome information from distant learners. Other outcome measures include documenting the borrowing and use of courses and course materials by other institutions as an indicator of effectiveness, and the enrollment by students in additional, similar courses as indicators of a preliminary course's success.

4. **Measures of program aims.**   Some distance teaching programs specify their aims in terms of what and whom they intend to teach, and evaluation information is collected to establish the extent to which these aims were met. One common aim of distance education programs is to reach learners who otherwise would not be students. Surveys of learners can be used to collect this type of information.

5. **Measures of policy.**   Evaluation in the policy area often takes the form of market research. Surveys of prospective students and employers can be used to determine the demand for distance education activities.

   Policy evaluation can also include monitoring. Students can be surveyed to determine if tuition is too high, if appropriate courses are being offered, and if there are impediments to course success, such as the lack of access to computers or the library.

   Sometimes policy evaluation can be used to determine the success of experimental programs, such as those for low achievers or for students who normally are not qualified for a program. The purpose of policy evaluation is to identify procedures that are needed or that need to be changed, and to develop new policies.

6. **Measures of organizations.**   Sometimes it is important to evaluate a distance education institution in terms of its internal organization and procedures. Evaluators sometimes are asked to monitor the process of course development or program delivery to help an organization be more efficient. This category of evaluation requires on-site visits, interviews, and sometimes the use of journals by key organization leaders.

These six categories of evaluation are not used for every distance education activity. Certainly, some modest evaluation activity is almost always necessary. It is important that the activities of evaluators be matched to programmatic needs. Woodley and Kirkwood (1986) have summarized evaluation in distance education as being a fairly eclectic process that utilizes procedures that should match program needs to evaluation activities.

THE AEIOU APPROACH

Fortune and Keith (1992) proposed the AEIOU approach for program evaluation, especially the evaluation of distance education projects. The effectiveness of this approach has been demonstrated through evaluating the activities of the Iowa Distance Education Alliance Star Schools Project (Simonson & Schlosser, 1995a;

Sorensen, 1996; Sorensen & Sweeney, 1995, 1996, 1997; Sweeney, 1995), a multiyear, statewide distance education activity. Additionally, the model has been used to evaluate a number of other innovative projects, such as the Iowa Chemistry Education Alliance in 1995, the Iowa General Chemistry Network in 1994, and the DaVinci Project: Interactive Multimedia for Art and Chemistry (Simonson & Schlosser, 1995b). More recently, a major distance education initiative in South Dakota used a modified version of the AEIOU approach (Simonson, 2005).

The AEIOU approach is similar to Woodley and Kirkwood's in that it is an eclectic one that uses quantitative and qualitative methodologies. It has two primary purposes as an evaluation strategy. First, the model provides formative information to the staff about the implementation of their project. Second, it provides summative information about the value of the project and its activities. The AEIOU evaluation process provides a framework for identifying key questions necessary for effective evaluation. Some evaluation plans use only parts of the framework, whereas other, more comprehensive plans use all components. Some examples of evaluation questions asked in comprehensive distance education projects are presented next.

Component 1—*Accountability (A)*

Did the project planners do what they said they were going to do?   This is the first step in determining the effectiveness of the project or course and is targeted at determining if the project's objectives and activities were completed. Evaluation questions typically center on the completion of a specific activity and often are answered "yes" or "no." Additionally, counts of numbers of people, things, and activities are often collected.

Questions such as the following are often asked to determine project accountability:

- Were the appropriate number of class sessions held?
- How many students were enrolled?
- How many copies of program materials were produced, and how many were distributed?

Methods Used: Accountability information is often collected from project administrative records. Project leaders are often asked to provide documentation of the level of completion of each of the project's goals, objectives, and activities. Sometimes evaluators interview project staff to collect accountability data.

Component 2—*Effectiveness (E)*

How well done was the project?   This component of the evaluation process attempts to place some value on the project's activities. Effectiveness questions often focus on participant attitudes and knowledge. Obviously, grades, achievement tests, and attitude inventories are measures of effectiveness. Less obvious are other ways to determine quality. Often, raters are asked to review course materials and course presentations to determine their effectiveness, and student course evaluations can be used to collect reactions from distance education participants.

Examples of questions to determine effectiveness include:

■ Were the in-service participants satisfied with their distance education instruction?
■ Did the students learn what they were supposed to learn?
■ Did the teachers feel adequately prepared to teach distant learners?

Methods Used: Standardized measures of achievement and attitude are traditionally used to determine program effectiveness. Surveys of students and faculty can be used to ask questions related to perceptions about the appropriateness of a project or program. Focus groups (Morgan, 1996) also provide valuable information. Participants are systematically asked to respond to questions about the program. Finally, journals are sometimes kept by project participants and then analyzed to determine the day-to-day effectiveness of an ongoing program.

Component 3— *Impact (I)*

Did the project, course, or program make a difference?   During this phase of the evaluation, questions focus on identifying the changes that resulted from the project's activities, and are tied to the stated outcomes of the project or course. In other words, if the project had not happened, what incident of importance would not have occurred? A key element of measurement of impact is the collection of longitudinal data. The impact of distance education courses is often determined by following learners' progress in subsequent courses or in the workplace to determine if what was learned in the distance education course was useful.

Determinants of impact are difficult to identify. Often, evaluators use follow-up studies to determine the impressions made on project participants; and sometimes in distance education programs, learners are followed and questioned by evaluators in subsequent courses and activities.

Questions might include:

■ Did students register for additional distance education courses?
■ Has the use of the distance education system increased?
■ Have policies and procedures related to the use of the distance education system been developed or changed?

Methods Used: Qualitative measures provide the most information to the evaluator interested in program impact. Standardized tests, record data, and surveys are sometimes used. Also, interviews, focus groups, and direct observations are used to identify a program's impact.

Component 4— *Organizational Context (O)*

What structures, policies, or events in the organization or environment helped or hindered the project in accomplishing its goals?   This component of evaluation has traditionally not been important even though evaluators have often hinted in their reports about organizational policies that either hindered or helped a program. Recently, however, distance educators have become very interested in organizational policy analysis in order to determine barriers to the successful implementation of distance education systems, especially when those systems are new activities of traditional educational organizations such as large public universities.

The focus of this component of the evaluation is on identifying those contextual or environmental factors that contributed to, or detracted from, the project or course's ability to conduct activities. Usually, these factors are beyond the control of the project's participants. Effective evaluation of organizational context requires the evaluator to be intimately involved with the project or course in order to have a good understanding of the environment in which the project or course operates.

Questions typically addressed in evaluating organizational context include:

- What factors made it difficult to implement the project or to successfully complete the course?
- What contributed most to the success or failure of the project or the students in the course?
- What should be done differently to improve things and make the course more effective?

Methods Used: Organizational context evaluation uses interviews of key personnel such as faculty or students, focus groups made up of those impacted by a program, and document analysis that identifies policies and procedures that influence a program or course. Direct participation in program activities by the evaluator is also important. Sometimes evaluators enroll in distance education courses. More often, a student is asked to complete a journal while enrolled in a course. By participating, the evaluator is confronted directly with the organizational context in which a program exists, and can comment on this context firsthand.

Component 5—*Unanticipated Consequences (U)*

What changes or consequences of importance happened as a result of the project that were not expected? This component of the AEIOU approach is to identify unexpected changes of either a positive or negative nature that occurred as a direct or indirect result of the project or course. Effective evaluators have long been interested in reporting anecdotal information about the project or program that they were evaluating. It is only recently that this category of information has become recognized as important, largely because of the positive influence on evaluation of qualitative procedures. Often, evaluators, especially internal evaluators who are actively involved in the project or course's implementation, have many opportunities to observe successes and failures during the trial-and-error process of beginning a new program. Unanticipated consequences of developing new or modified programs, especially in the dynamic field of distance education, are a rich source of information about why some projects are successful and others are not. Central to the measurement of unanticipated outcomes is the collection of ex post facto data.

Examples of questions asked include:

■ Have relationships between collaborators or students changed in ways not expected?
■ Have related, complementary projects been developed?
■ Were unexpected linkages developed between groups or participants?
■ Was the distance education system used in unanticipated ways?
■ Did the distance education system have an impact on student learning other than that expected?

Methods Used: Interviews, focus groups, journals, and surveys that ask for narrative information can be used to identify interesting and potentially important consequences of implementing a new program. Often, evaluators must interact with project participants or course students on a regular basis to learn about the little successes and failures that less sensitive procedures overlook. Active and continuous involvement by evaluators permits them to learn about the project as it occurs.

Sweeney (1995) advocates an eclectic approach to evaluation, an approach also supported by Fitzpatrick et al. (2004). The AEIOU model is a dynamic one that permits the evaluator to tailor the process of program evaluation to the specific situation being studied.

PROGRAM EVALUATION: EXAMPLES

South Dakota

South Dakota has a network for distance education that connects every school in the state. Currently, hundreds of classrooms are connected to the Digital Dakota Network (DDN). The DDN was funded using state monies and grants from telecommunications providers, such as QWEST Communications.

Implementation of the DDN was called the Connecting the Schools project. As the network came online and began to be used, it was decided that a comprehensive evaluation effort was needed. Evaluators used the AEIOU approach and collected both quantitative and qualitative information (Simonson, 2005; Simonson & Bauck, 2001).

Quantitative information was collected using a locally developed survey called the Connecting the Schools Questionnaire (CSQ). The CSQ asked respondents to provide four categories of information: demographics, information about personal innovativeness, questions about organizational innovativeness, and questions about distance education.

Demographic information was collected in order to obtain a profile of the teachers in the state, and included questions about age, years of experience, gender, academic background, and professional involvement. The second part of the CSQ was a modified version of Hurt, Joseph, and Cook's (1977) innovativeness scale (IS). The IS is a standardized measure of how innovative a person thinks he or she is. Part three of the CSQ was a modified version of Hurt and Tiegen's (1977) Perceived Organizational Innovativeness Scale (PORGI). The PORGI is a standardized measure of a person's perception of his or her employer's organizational innovativeness. The final section of the CSQ asked questions about distance education. These questions were to find out how much South Dakota teachers knew about distance education and to determine their general feelings about the impact of distance education on teaching and learning.

The qualitative portion of the CSQ evaluation in South Dakota used focus groups, participant observations, interviews, and site visits. Three questions were at the heart of the quantitative evaluation. First, evaluators tried to determine what educators thought would be the greatest benefits provided by implementing distance education. Second, attempts were made to determine what was preventing individuals from becoming involved in distance education. Next, school superintendents were selected randomly and interviewed to determine their perceptions of the impact of distance education and the Digital Dakota Network on education in their school districts (Calderone, 2003). Finally, questions were asked about the impediments to distance education.

When quantitative data were combined with qualitative information, a rich understanding was provided to education leaders about South Dakota's ability to adopt distance education (Learning at a Distance: South Dakota, www.tresystems.com/projects/). Complete results of the evaluation were reported in Simonson (2005). In general, the evaluation of the South Dakota project verified that Rogers's (2003) theory concerning the diffusion of innovations was directly applicable to distance education efforts in South Dakota and that this theory could effectively serve as a model for promoting the adoption of innovations, such as the DDN specifically, and distance education in public schools, more generally.

Iowa

Several years ago, it was decided that a three-phase plan should be implemented to establish distance education classrooms throughout the state of Iowa. For the first phase, 15 area community colleges, 3 public universities, and Iowa Public Television had classrooms built and connected with fiber-optic cables capable of carrying 48 full-motion video signals in addition to virtually unlimited voice and data information. The second phase of the plan connected a classroom site in any of Iowa's 99 counties that was not already served by a community college site. These classrooms were connected with 12 fiber-optic cables. A total of 103 sites were built and connected as part of phases 1 and 2. During phase 3, additional sites were connected throughout the state. Recently, over 750 sites were connected to this distance education infrastructure, which was named the Iowa Communications Network (ICN).

As part of the implementation plan for the ICN, a comprehensive evaluation program was put into action. This program utilized the AEIOU approach and collected data from thousands of sources and individuals. The evaluation approach went through several stages during the five years it was used. First, evaluators concentrated on evaluating the construction, connection, and implementation of the ICN's physical infrastructure. Records related to classroom design, construction schedules, and dollars spent were collected and reviewed, and summary results were reported. This related to the accountability component of the AEIOU approach.

Next, those involved in the decision-making process for establishing the network were interviewed and completed surveys. Evaluators used the results to develop reports on the effectiveness of the processes used to construct the ICN. To determine impact, evaluators conducted follow-up investigations of classroom utilization and examined records of how the system was used.

The program evaluators examined many interesting organizational issues, such as who made decisions about where classrooms were located, how funds were obtained and spent, and who controlled access to the system. Finally, program evaluators identified unanticipated outcomes. One of the most significant was the infusion of several millions of dollars from federal, state, and local sources to support the development of the network. How these funds were obtained and used added to the importance of the evaluation report.

Once the network was built and a plan for its continued growth was put into place, evaluators shifted their primary focus to the human side of the growth of distance education in the state. Staff development, technical training, curriculum revisions, and school restructuring became the focus of network planners and funding agencies, so program evaluators used the AEIOU model to obtain information about these activities. The approach was used to provide formative information about the development of programs and their impact on teachers and learners, and also to provide information on outcomes, or summative information, to document the successes and failures of various program activities.

A true understanding of activities of evaluators of this statewide, multiyear project can only be gained by reviewing the yearly reports they submitted. However, it is important to note that the evaluation plan provided the following information:

Accountability. Evaluators checked records, interviewed staff, and visited classrooms to determine the status of the development of the ICN, both as a physical system and as a tool used by teachers to deliver courses to distant learners. The accountability focus shifted during the project as its activities shifted from construction to implementation and finally to maintenance.

Effectiveness. Evaluators conducted interviews and questioned focus groups to determine what impact the availability of the ICN had on classroom education. Surveys were sent and reports were generated that helped education leaders to better understand what role distance education was playing.

Impact. As the network became widely available and the number of courses and activities increased, it became possible to determine the impact of the ICN and distance education events on education in the state. Students were tested and grades reported. Most of the achievement data showed that learning occurred and good grades were obtained. More importantly, the availability of new learning experiences grew considerably.

Organizational Context. From the beginning of the ICN project, the role of the state as compared with local educational organizations was a focus of evaluation activities. One outcome was to identify where cooperation between agencies was necessary (e.g., as in scheduling) and where local control (e.g., as in course selection) should be maintained. Project evaluators identified and reported on what the data seemed to indicate were the barriers and the contributors to the effective growth and utilization of the ICN.

Unanticipated Outcomes. During the project, scores of unanticipated outcomes were identified and reported. Among the most interesting were:

■ The movement of the ICN into the role of Internet service provider
■ The role of the ICN in attracting external grants

- The role of distance education and the ICN in the movement to restructure schools
- The impact of the ICN on positive attitudes toward technology in education
- The emerging role of the public television station in Iowa education

There were also many other unanticipated outcomes. The AEIOU approach was useful in helping the state's educators evaluate the role of distance education as an approach and the ICN as an infrastructure. Evaluation played a significant part in the positive implementation and use of this new technology in the state of Iowa.

STUDENT EVALUATION OF DISTANCE EDUCATION COURSES

The purpose of a course evaluation is to fulfill accreditation requirements and to provide a means for reporting course and instructor effectiveness. Standardized course evaluation forms are available that have already been developed and have gone through rigorous psychometric analyses. The literature suggests course and instructor evaluation models that focus on six constructs:

- Teaching and learning
- Developing a community of learners
- The instructor
- The student
- Implementation of the course
- Technology use

Evaluation instruments should possess the psychometric characteristics of standardized measures, meaning they should be valid, reliable, administered in a consistent manner, and have normative tables so scores can be compared.

Valid instruments measure what they are supposed to measure, in this case the effectiveness of online courses and online teaching. Reliable measures are consistent—in other words, if the measure were administered a second time the scores should be very similar. Consistent administration of course evaluations ensures that more or less favorable conditions of testing do not influence the results. Finally, scores for any course evaluation are difficult to decipher if there is no comparison data. Often, scores from evaluations for many courses are collected so that the scores for any individual course and instructor can be compared with others. Usually, any identifiers for comparison courses are removed. It is important to remember that course and instructor evaluations are to be used for continuous improvement, and to provide input for course revisions.

A sample evaluation instrument to collect students' perceptions about the six constructs, the Online Course Evaluation Instrument (OCEI, pronounced ooh-see), is shown in Figure 12–1.

FIGURE 12–1   An evaluation instrument.

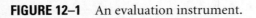

ONLINE COURSE EVALUATION INSTRUMENT (OCIE)

Course Name:

Gender: _____ Male	**Class Size:** _____ Class size 1 to 10
_____ Female	_____ Class size 11 to 20
	_____ Class size 21 to 30
Age: _____ Years	_____ Class size 31 to 40
Class Level: _____ Undergraduate	_____ Class size 41 and above
_____ Master	
_____ Doctorate	**First Experience in an Online Course:** _____ Yes _____ No

Class Term: _____ Summer

_____ Fall

_____ Winter

Please rate each item using the following scale:

5 – Strongly agree
4 – Agree
3 – Neither agree nor disagree
2 – Disagree
1 – Strongly disagree

Teaching and Learning

1. The course has clearly stated objectives _____
2. The course activities are consistent with course objectives _____
3. The course syllabus is an accurate guide to course requirements _____
4. The course materials are a helpful guide to key concepts covered in the class _____
5. The course projects and assignments build understanding of concepts and principles _____
6. The course presents appropriate skills and techniques _____
7. The course is current with developments in the field _____

Developing a Community of Learners

1. Collaborative work is a valuable part of this course _____
2. There is opportunity to learn from other students _____
3. Differing viewpoints and discussions are encouraged in this class _____
4. Mutual respect is a concept practiced in this course _____
5. Each student has an opportunity to contribute to class learning _____

The Instructor

1. The instructor clearly states the methods of evaluation that will be used to assess student work _____
2. The instructor uses a variety of methods to evaluate student progress on class objectives _____

FIGURE 12–1 *(continued)*

3. The instructor shows respect for the various points of view represented in this class _____
4. The instructor makes learning interesting and motivates students to learn _____
5. The instructor uses technology in ways that help learning of concepts and principles _____
6. The instructor responds to questions with consideration _____
7. The instructor displays a clear understanding of course topics _____

SUMMARY

As distance education in the United States increases in importance, evaluation will continue to be a critical component of the process of improvement. Certainly, the literature is clear. Eclectic models of evaluation such as the ones advocated by Woodley and Kirkwood (1986) and Sweeney (1995) are most applicable to distance education program evaluation. Evaluators should use quantitative and qualitative procedures. Distance education programs and even single courses should be accountable to their goals, should be at least as effective as alternative approaches, and should have a positive impact. Evaluators should attempt, when possible, to identify what organizational contexts support effective distance education systems, and unanticipated events should be shared with interested readers and should be used to improve courses.

If you are very patient, you will see and understand. (Huxley, 1982, p. 20)

REFERENCES

Calderone, T. (2003). Superintendents' perception of their role in the diffusion of distance education. Unpublished doctoral dissertation. Nova Southeastern University, Fort Lauderdale, FL.

Cyrs, T., & Smith, F. (1990). *Teleclass teaching: A resource guide* (2nd ed.). Las Cruces, NM: Center for Educational Development.

Fitz-Gibbon, C., & Morris, L. (1987). *How to design a program evaluation.* Newbury Park, CA: Sage.

Fitzpatrick, J., Sanders, J., & Worthen, B. (2004). *Program evaluation: Alternative approaches and practical guidelines* (3rd ed.). Upper Saddle River, NJ: Pearson/Allyn and Bacon.

Fortune, J., & Keith, P. (1992). *Program evaluation for Buchanan County Even Start.* Blacksburg, VA: College of Education, Virginia Polytechnic Institute and State University.

Graber, J., Post, G., & Erwin R. (n.d.) *Using ROI forecasting to develop a high-impact, high-volume training curriculum.* Retrieved August 20, 2007 from www.businessdecisions.com/docs/ASTDROIChapter.doc.

Hanson, D., Maushak, N, Schlosser, C., Anderson, M, & Sorensen, M (1997). Distance education: Review of the Literature, 2nd ed. Washington, DC: Assn for Educational Communities and Technology.

House, E. (Ed) (2010), New directions in educational evaluation, Lewes, England: Falmer, Press.

Hurt, H., Joseph, K., & Cook, C. (1977). Scales for the measurement of innovativeness. *Human Communications Research, 4*(1), 58–65.

Hurt, H., & Teigen, C. (1977). The development of a measure of perceived organizational innovativeness. *Communication Yearbook I* (pp. 377–385). New Brunswick, NJ: International Communications Association.

Huxley, E. (1982). *The flame trees of Thika: Memories of an African childhood.* London: Chatto and Windus.

Joint Committee on Standards for Educational Evaluation. (1994). *The program evaluation standards* (2nd ed.). Thousand Oaks, CA: Sage.

Kirkpatrick, D., & Kirkpatrick, J. (2006). *Evaluating training programs: The four levels* (3rd ed.). San Francisco, CA: Berrett-Koehler.

Martinez, R., Liu, S., Watson, W., & Bichelmeyer, B. (2006). Evaluation of a web-based master's degree program: Lessons learned from an online instructional design and technology program. *Quarterly Review of Distance Education, 7*(3), 267–283.

Morgan, D. (1996). *Focus groups as qualitative research.* Newbury Park, CA: Sage.

Phillips, J. (2003). Return on investment, 2nd ed. Burlington, MA: Butterworth-Heinmann.

Peak, D. & Berge, Z (2006). Evaluation and eLearning, *Turkish Online Journal of Distance Education, 7*(1), Article 11.

Phillips, J., Phillips, P., Duresky, L. & Gaudet, C. (2002). Evaluating the return on investment of elearning. In Alison Rossett (Ed.). *The ASTD Elearning Handbook* (pp. 387–397). Madison, WI: McGraw-Hill.

Rogers, E. (2003). *Diffusion of innovations* (5th ed.). New York: Free Press.

Rose, E. (2000). An evaluation of online distance education course databases. *DEOSNEWS, 10*(11), 1–6. Available online at www.ed.psu.edu/acsde/deos/deosnews.deosarchives.asp.

Rossi, P., Lipsey, M., & Freeman, H. (2003). *Evaluation: A systematic approach* (7th ed.). Newbury Park, CA: Sage.

Rovai, A. (2003). A practical framework for evaluting online distance education programs. *Internet and Higher Education, 6*(2), 109–124.

Ruhe, V., & Zumbo, B. (2009) *Evaluation in distance education and e'learning.* New York: Guilford.

Sherry, A. (2003). Quality and its measurement in distance educaton. In M. Moore & W. Anderson (Eds.), *Handbook of distance education* (pp. 435–459). Mahwah, NJ: Erlbaum.

Simonson, M. (2002). In case you are asked: The effectiveness of distance education. *Quarterly Review of Distance Education, 3*(4), vii.

Simonson, M. (2005). South Dakota's statewide distance education project. In Z. Berge & T. Clark (Eds.), *Virtual schools: Planning for success* (pp. 183–197). New York: Teachers College Press.

Simonson, M. (2007). Evaluation and distance Education. *Quarterly Review of Distance Education, 8*(3), vii–ix.

Simonson, M., & Bauck, T. (2001). Learning at a distance in South Dakota: Description and evaluation of the diffusion of an innovation. Proceedings of Research and Development Papers presented at the Annual Convention of the Association for Educational Communications and Technology, Atlanta, GA. (ERIC Document Reproduction Service No. ED47103).

Simonson, M., & Schlosser, C. (1995a). More than fiber: Distance education in Iowa. *Tech Trends, 40*(3), 13–15.

Simonson, M., & Schlosser, C. (1995b). The DaVinci Project. Iowa Computer-Using Educators Conference, Des Moines.

Sorensen, C. (1996). *Final evaluation report: Iowa distance education alliance.* Ames, IA: Research Institute for Studies in Education.

Sorensen, C., & Sweeney, J. (1995). ICN Technology Demonstration Evaluation. *USDLA Education at a Distance, 9*(5), 11, 21.

Sorensen, C., & Sweeney, J. (1996, November). AEIOU: An approach to evaluating the statewide integration of distance education. Paper presented at the annual meeting of the American Evaluation Association, Atlanta, GA.

Sorensen, C., & Sweeney, J. (1997, November). A-E-I-O-U: An inclusive framework for evaluation. Paper presented at the annual meeting of the American Evaluation Association, San Diego, CA.

Strother, J. (2002). An assessment of the effectiveness of e-learning in corporate training programs. *International Review of Research in Open and Distance Learning, 3*(1), 1–17.

Stufflebeam, D., & Shinkfield, A. (2007). *Evaluation theory, models, and applications.* Hoboken, NJ: Jossey-Bass.

Sweeney, J. (1995). *Vision 2020: Evaluation report.* Ames, IA: Research Institute for Studies in Education.

Thompson, M., & Irele, M. (2007). Evaluating distance education programs. In M. Moore (Ed.), *Handbook of distance education* (2nd ed.). Mahwah, NJ: Erlbaum.

Willis, B. (Ed.). (1994). *Distance education: Strategies and tools.* Englewood Cliffs, NJ: Educational Technology Publications.

Woodley, A., & Kirkwood, A. (1986). *Evaluation in distance learning.* Paper 10. Resources in Education. (ERIC Document Reproduction Service No. ED304122).

SUGGESTED READING

Cronbach, L. (1982). *Designing evaluations of educational and social programs.* San Francisco: Jossey-Bass.

INDEX

Note: The letters 'f' and 't' following the locators refers to figures and tables cited in the text.